Photograph by Thomas Merton, taken at Gethsemani, Kentucky on 13 Oct 1966 during Maritain's last visit to America. Used by permission of Merton Legacy Trust.

Understanding Maritain:
Philosopher and Friend

edited by
DEAL W. HUDSON
and MATTHEW J. MANCINI

Understanding Maritain: Philosopher and Friend

MERCER UNIVERSITY PRESS

ISBN 0-86554-279-1

B 2430
M34
u53
1987

The paper used in this publication meets
the minimum requirements of American National Standard
for Information Sciences—Permanence of Paper
for Printed Library Materials, ANSI Z 39.48-1984.

Library of Congress Cataloging-in-Publication Data
Understanding Maritain : philosopher and friend
edited by Deal W. Hudson and Matthew J. Mancini.
   xviii + 334 pp.   16x23.5 cm.
   Includes bibliographies and index.
   ISBN 0-86554-279-1 (alk. paper) : $39.95
   1. Maritain, Jacques, 1882-1973.
I. Hudson, Deal W.   II. Mancini, Matthew J.
B2430.M34U53   1987   87-22446
194—dc19   CIP

Contents

JUN 8 1988

Foreword

There were giants in the earth in those days. Those days, for most of us—and I am invited to write in the first person—are times when we were shaped by people of heroic dimensions. We all know enough from reading biography to accept that our heroines and heroes had cosmic flaws; flaws tend to come with genius and sainthood. If you doubt that, read the autobiography of a reflective saint. Yet we live with those flaws in order to draw on the wells of courage and wisdom that great people represent.

There were giants in the earth for those who, when young, wanted to find ways to relate our Christian faith to the public order and to the higher humanisms that we saw mirrored in art and literature. Some of them, like poet and essayist T. S. Eliot, lured us with a poetic sensibility and an against-the-times pursuit of "a Christian culture." Few of us would have welcomed the culture he depicted, but that depiction was a marvelous alternative to the sterile secular cultures he had taken into himself and described in, for example, *The Waste Land*.

A counterpart in the description of society and culture in the realm of prose, magisterial prose, was Jacques Maritain, the subject of this book. A Protestant kid from the Great Plains was no more ready or willing to accept Maritain's Roman Catholic context than he was able or eager to side with Eliot's Anglo-Catholicism. While our masters effected syntheses, it was for us to pick and choose, to criticize and to adopt selectively.

What mattered in Maritain was the quality of mind, the seriousness of faith, the integrity of his "integral humanism," and the audacity of the syntheses he promoted. For me the encounters with both Eliot and Maritain (and others who were nearly their peers) began in the years of World War II—soon to be half a century ago—when as a prep school sophomore I began hitchhiking to Chicago with a more urbane roommate to hear the English poet or the French philosopher lecture.

We were nothing more than faces in the crowd to Maritain back then, or again in 1956, when he returned for more lectures. These were the years after Robert M. Hutchins and Mortimer J. Adler had inspired devotion to classics, great minds, Great Books. There was no doubt but that Maritain belonged on their list of Greats. He was securely fixed in the mental pantheon of his audiences and of others in that university at that time. Whether one agreed with or understood all that he said or not was beside the point: here was a presence that engaged all with its intellectual power, personal fervor, and grace, and one sensed that the speaker was somehow "transparent" to another order of being about which he spoke.

Occasional meetings with Chicago radical Saul Alinsky, in all of which he was likely to bring up his memories of Maritain, served as a thread through the subsequent years. Here is a challenge to the most hardhearted among readers: try to read the Alinsky letters after the death of his wife in chapter 3 in this book without coming to tears. Maritain had a way of bringing such emotions out of a person, gifted as he was with what Gabriel Marcel called *disponibilité*, the ability to make one's self philosophically and personally "available" to another.

Those years were marked as well by the kind of drift from Maritain, or rage against him, that many felt who saw him posed as *The Peasant of the Garonne* in a frustrated, angry, somehow crabby book that took post-Vatican II Catholicism to task (and, I must add, helped endear him to some who would repeal its efforts and effects). Whether or not he would have written that tract or taken quiet religious vows in his last days of widowerhood, he would have gone into eclipse for some time. Great thinkers do, as the subsequent generation reacts, is befuddled, or finds itself over against the previous generation's masters.

Then came a personal return, marked in the career of others by public events such as the publication of this book. The prep school and later college roommate who inspired the hitchhiking ventures to hear Maritain had gone on to study philosophy at Chicago but died tragically young. Twenty-five years later, I, now a widower, married his widow. To establish some bonds that would evoke her long-late husband, we read to each other some letters and other writings between Maritain and his beloved Raïssa, who merits and receives a chapter of her own in this book. Meanwhile, I had found occasion to use an epigraph by Maritain to name my history *Pilgrims in Their Own Land*. The shadow of Maritain was not able to be left behind.

Thus ends a personal accounting of the sort almost anyone who had wrestled with Maritain two generations ago would be able to parallel. It matches the structure of this book. While the chapters in part III are clear expositions, their subject matter—metaphysics, epistemology, science, aesthetics, philosophy of history, ethics, politics, integral humanism, mysticism, and contemplation—is so forbidding to the uninitiated and so overwhelming to those used to taking them one at a time that it is good that the editors eased in with the personal materials of part I and the broad thematic material of part II.

The authors deal with the issue of the Maritainian eclipse. Their subject's stock remains bearish at Princeton and Chicago, we read, though there is a society and there are meetings and there is a journal and there will be more books like these, we can be sure. The generation of eclipse is past. The obvious irrelevancies that connect with anyone who is as alert to his times as Maritain was get to be overlooked or walked past. Then a reader comes, one hopes, not to Maritain's "park bench," to use Marshall McLuhan's metaphor quoted in this book, but to his "signposts."

Catholic and other neoconservatives or others who would resurrect Maritain as part of the Golden Age will have to deal with the suggestions of numerous authors here that all was not golden back then. Those who live in such ages, we are reminded, thought of what was around them as yellow, instead. Maritain is too comprehensive to be yielded over to "conservative chic" or "more nostalgic than thou" camps. Yet they do a service if they keep his writings in print and up front. They can provoke what is becoming a necessary confrontation.

"Back to Maritain," for example, would not mean a simple "Back to Thomas Aquinas," we are informed below. Maritain plundered and reshaped Thomas to his and his age's needs and purposes. That is a radical and rewarding thing to do. Now is a moment when both Thomas and Maritain could be vital in any movement of *ressourcement*. One reached to them, not as "back" to a stagnant pond— the tradition of traditionalists—but forward to them, as flowing streams. They remain ahead of us in many ways.

What one may well take from the essays in part III is a sense of signposts to natural, rational, and Scholastic foundations on which one can build new if lighter edifices. (Let's not test the weight-bearing character of those foundations too vigorously!) Paul Tillich, for instance, liked to tell students that he could deal best with those Catholic, Reformed, or Lutheran types who had been well schooled in the structures and systems of thirteenth- or seventeenth-century school thought. He had more difficulty with moderns who had no acquaintance with, no empathy for, such systems. Of course, Tillich did very different things on their groundings, and they might have become unrecognizable to historians who seek purity in continuity. Yet he and his students got their freedom for their venturing from some measure of mastery of the systems.

Mention of Tillich calls to mind another aspect of approach to a thinker like Maritain. After the publication of Tillich's own *Systematic Theology*, he protested reviews by language analysts who stood outside it and saw nothing to it because it was built on and reflected a metaphysic they found no way to verify, falsify, or share. Tillich instead beckoned his actual and potential readers: think of a complex system of thought as a cathedral. One may criticize its windows, its carvings, its special arrangements—but only after having first come in.

So it should be with Maritain in these years in which a Maritain revival has begun, a revival that this book evidences. One must "come in" and let the architecture of this great man's thought do its work on one's sensibilities. After that there can come criticisms, but they will now be seen in perspective.

Maritain is both beckoning and forbidding. I find on rereading him that he is alluring as ever, for the clarity, compactness, forcefulness, and still grace of his argument. It is exciting to find a mind so firmly related to a philosophical system that it promotes consistency, yet located in a person so full of passion that he can interrupt the system for personal opinion and expression. After the bedazzlement there is time for mentioning some reservations. These may happen to match those of some other readers, while each is at liberty to come forth with others. Is that not what we mean by a creative process in reading?

To take one instance where I resist, and where I expect others to have to do some wrestling: some of us believe that a pluralist state that allows for great religious freedom, voluntary patterns of religious life, and the right to persuade others is more congenial for Christian and generally human development than is any society that seeks in its laws to give privilege to the Catholic synthesis. Maritain, it is true, did make some major efforts to help Catholics feel at home with and even take credit for religious liberty, but he often surrounded these with affirmations of a Catholic order that most Catholics and even more non-Catholics today would reject.

Why bother with him, then, if it takes some effort to go inside the cathedral and to let the light that falls through its windows shine on us readers? The answer to that question is clear when one simply follows Maritain's thought in this collection of essays: what a wide variety of thinkers and actors are drawn to him. It helps if the reader is a Christian or one who finds some congeniality in the biblical and Catholic traditions, but many—one thinks of Saul Alinsky—were not even put off by these commitments. It helps if one has become familiar with the language of Saint Thomas, but many who never bothered have had little difficulty with Maritain. Some may find his noble piety a bit credulous.

As I commend this book and this thinker to you, I have no doubt that your investment of time will be well worth it. Those familiar with Maritain can do some refreshing and comparing. Newcomers, I suspect, will enter the cathedral of his thought, follow the signposts, or stand on his foundations, to draw on just a few of the metaphors that he evokes.

Maritain is not likely to come back either to the solitary prominence he knew or to find the company of great minds of the sort described in these chapters. Instead he is to be seen as one of the latest of the "doctors of the church," of the bridges between Athens and Jerusalem. He takes his place among the many on whom one draws to do the philosophical and faith-full thinking a new time demands. This book will help him find that place by pointing to a figure and his thought, a combination that will not let one go.

Martin E. Marty

Preface

Jacques Maritain (1882-1973), widely and accurately regarded as the twentieth century's greatest Catholic philosopher, experienced during his lifetime a series of geologic shifts in his reputation: always eminent, he nevertheless appeared different from time to time as the underlying plates of twentieth-century history constantly dislocated the certainties of the immediately preceding years. The shifting fortunes of his reputation were connected intimately with that second adjective used above to describe him—Catholic. During his young manhood, the Catholic Church in his native, strife-torn France appeared to many intellectuals a Bastille of superstitious obscurantism, a haven from the truths gradually being revealed by positive science. Again, in his full maturity, during the twenties and thirties, it represented everything that opposed the advance of republican institutions; it seemed instead to stand for privilege, aristocracy, even monarchism. Still later, in Maritain's old age, the Church pried open its ancient windows to let in the sharp breezes of *aggiornamento*. In each of these phases of the Church's history, Maritain was a prominent lay actor: converting to Catholicism with his Jewish wife early in the century, to the horror of many intellectuals, including Jacques's formidable mother, Geneviève Favre—and then vowing to make a pilgrimage to the shrine of Notre Dame de La Salette, site of an apparition revealed to a poor shepherd girl; maintaining links with reactionary Catholics in Action Française during the twenties, at least until that nest of antidemocratic ranters had been denounced by Rome; and finally being embraced by Pope Paul VI at the time of the Second Vatican Council and honored as a major source and inspiration of the Council's teachings.

Yet it was completely characteristic of Maritain that on each of these occasions his position was far from univocal. He affirmed that faith, far from nurturing superstition, deepened and clarified the intelligence. He did more to reconcile Christianity with democracy than any of his contemporaries; he was indeed almost alone in doing so, and this project stands as one of his greatest monuments. And as for the Council, no sooner had it adjourned than Maritain sharply—some said irascibly—criticized what he perceived to be some of its unexpected negative consequences.

Maritain's thought, then, was always both timely and elusive. It does not settle contentedly in one popular compartment or another, in spite of the efforts of the simplifiers who tried to appropriate his prestigious name. Thus it would be shortsighted simply to file Maritain in the "Catholic" or "Thomist" compartment and pretend that he is by such a clerical tactic adequately understood, or even approached. His influence has extended beyond the earnest moral debates and philosophical discussions of his coreligionists to affect contemporary thought in a great many fields and embrace men and women of many religious and political persuasions. The present collection, with a foreword by a Lutheran, numbering among its contributors Eastern Orthodox Christians, Roman Catholic priests, converted Protestants, and persons with no denominational affiliation, and published by a press associated with a Southern Baptist university, is itself indicative of the expanding compass of contemporary Maritain studies.

The project of understanding Maritain requires that the subject of our understanding not be pulled in one direction at the expense of attention to his other desires and concerns. To look closely at any aspect of his life and work makes one aware of a subtle counterpoint between his traditional spirituality and philosophical realism, on the one hand, and his full engagement with the perplexities of modern life, on the other.

"On the one hand, on the other": what a typical Maritainian phrase that is. Always alive to complexity, always sensitive to the truth obscurely present in an adversary's position, Maritain was nevertheless, during his lifetime, damned or praised in sometimes extravagant fashion—damned by critics from right and left who often had to caricature his ideas in order to attack them; and praised by men and women moved perhaps as much by his transparent saintliness as by the power of his thought. But now the passage of time and the steady augmentation in Maritain's reputation have made possible a new project, that of understanding Maritain in a context of critical sympathy.

To accomplish this elusive, challenging, and fascinating task, we have here gathered fourteen original essays and one—Stanley L. Jaki's extraordinary meditation on Maritain and modern science—that has appeared, in a different version, elsewhere.[1] To these we have added Henry Bars's indispensable bio-bibliography, not previously available in English, now revised, enlarged, and translated for this volume by Anthony O. Simon, Véra Oumançoff's godson. Thus

---

[1] *The New Scholasticism* 48:3 (Summer 1984): 267-92.

the reader has in hand both a storehouse of information about Maritain's life and work and an introduction, in the form of these comprehensive and fervently argued essays, to his major contemporary themes, philosophical foundations, and friendships. We have placed this last section at the beginning of our volume because we agree with Julie Kernan that Maritain's "genius for friendship" had a decisive effect upon his life and the power of his thought.[2] Through this volume we hope that Maritain might be presented afresh to a new generation of students and scholars, and considered afresh by an older one.

The editors would like to thank some friends for their help and advice in the preparation of the manuscript—Sue Fisher, David Hesla, Myrtle Lamb, and Rae Lynn Mattis. We would also like to thank Dean James Yerkes and Mercer University Atlanta for their support for this project.

Deal W. Hudson and *Matthew J. Mancini*

---

[2]Julie Kernan, *Our Friend, Jacques Maritain: A Personal Memoir* (Garden City NY: Doubleday, 1975) foreword.

Abbreviations

(Bibliographical details of the works listed can be found in the footnotes to the individual chapters. Except where noted otherwise, all works are by Jacques Maritain.)

AE   *Approches sans entraves*

AF   *Art and Faith: Letters between Jacques Maritain and Jean Cocteau*

AS   *Art and Scholasticism* and *The Frontiers of Poetry*

BPT   *Bergsonian Philosophy and Thomism*

CD   *Christianity and Democracy*

CI   *Creative Intuition in Art and Poetry*

CN   *Carnet de notes*

DK   *Distinguish to Unite or The Degrees of Knowledge*

EC   *Education at the Crossroads*

ECP   *An Essay on Christian Philosophy*

EE   *Existence and the Existent*

EM   *The Education of Man*

GA   Raïssa Maritain, *Les grandes amitiés*

IH   *Integral Humanism:*
     Temporal and Spiritual Problems of a New Christendom

IP   *An Introduction to Philosophy*

JR   Raïssa Maritain, *Journal de Raïssa*

LB   Léon Bloy, *Oeuvres de Léon Bloy*

LPG *Le paysan de la Garonne*

MP *Moral Philosophy*

MS *Man and the State*

N *Notebooks*

OC *Oeuvres complètes*

PCG *The Person and the Common Good*

PG *The Peasant of the Garonne*

PH *On the Philosophy of History*

PM *A Preface to Metaphysics*

PT Etienne Gilson, *The Philosopher and Theology*

RA *Reflections on America*

RMNL *The Rights of Man and Natural Law*

RR *The Range of Reason*

RT *Ransoming the Time* (published in Great Britain as *Redeeming the Time*)

SP *Scholasticism and Politics*

SPP *The Social and Political Philosophy of Jacques Maritain*

STA *St. Thomas Aquinas: Angel of the Schools*

SW *Science and Wisdom*

T *The Twilight of Civilization*

TR *Three Reformers: Luther, Descartes, Rousseau*

TRA *The Responsibility of the Artist*

TSP *The Situation of Poetry*

UGA Julien Green and Jacques Maritain,
Une grande amitié: Correspondance 1926-1972

WHB Raïssa Maritain, *We Have Been Friends Together: Memoirs*

DEAL W. HUDSON
and MATTHEW J. MANCINI

Introduction:
Maritain and the Ambivalence
of the "Modern" World

I

STRAVINSKY, BRAQUE, AND PICASSO were his exact contemporaries. So were James Joyce, Virginia Woolf, and Franklin D. Roosevelt. In the year of his birth, 1882, Italy, Austria, and Germany forged the Triple Alliance, a link that, in retrospect, looms as a decisive step toward the great tragedy of 1914-18. Across the English Channel, as if in concert, an inventor named Hiram Maxim took out a patent on the machine gun.

That same year, in France, Léon Gambetta, the chief architect of the chronically unstable Third Republic, died tragically at the age of forty-four from the effects of an accident. On September 4, 1870, during the Franco-Prussian War, Gambetta and Jules Favre had proclaimed the Third Republic. In a dramatic eposide six weeks later, with Paris under siege by the Germans, Gambetta had been dispatched over German lines by balloon to Tours, there to raise fresh troops, while Favre, as Foreign Minister, was left to deal with the effects of the mighty German armies. The signatures on the momentous Treaty of Frankfurt, which ended the Franco-Prussian War, are those of Otto von Bismarck and Jules Favre.

These men and women, from Joyce to Favre, shaped the world in which Jacques Maritain lived, struggled, and wrote. Jules Favre, indeed, was Maritain's grandfather. The world Maritain inherited was a world of seemingly idiosyncratic new currents in literature, music, the visual arts, and philosophy; of the "second industrial revolution"; of the expansion of democracy; and of secularization and mass society; and it has come to be characterized by the expression "modern."

Maritain's thought unfolds most clearly before the observer who can grasp his *ambivalent* relation to these "modern" currents of thought and feeling. Although the most important influence on his thought was Thomas Aquinas, its basic directions were already set before he was pestered into reading the *Summa theologica* in September of 1910 by his wife, Raïssa, who already had been steadily reading it for more than a year and a half. Maritain wrote in his journal of that first reading of Thomas: "As it was for her, it is a deliverance, an inundation of light. The intellect finds its home."[1] But it is easy to overlook the fact that the discovery of Thomas comes relatively late among the dramatic changes that mark the young life of Jacques and Raïssa Maritain. Nearly ten years earlier they had been saved from carrying out a suicide pact by the teachings of Henri Bergson, which had restored their belief in the existence of an Absolute and freed Jacques's "metaphysical desire."[2]

Bergson was the guiding spirit behind the new century's intellectual mood and the primary shaper of the modernist context. For the modernist writers and painters, as for Bergson, time was of the essence, as Harry Levin shrewdly put it. These artists and thinkers drew strength from the paradoxical feeling of being simultaneously anachronistic and up to date; that tension is what gave rise to the modernist "will to change." Ezra Pound's injunction, "Make it new," became the modernist imperative.[3] Maritain's own sympathies with modernism are evident throughout his very large corpus of more than fifty books—one of which is entitled *Antimoderne*. This affinity has precisely the same roots as modernism itself, an early and decisive encounter with Bergson, and an ambivalence about time.

If Jacques and Raïssa had remained faithful disciples of Bergson, their fate might have been quite different. Perhaps they would have become purveyors of modernism. But they met Léon Bloy. Bloy gave a concrete spiritual and moral content to the vague Absolute of Bergson. Fourteen months after meeting Bloy, they were received into the Catholic church, she a Russian Jew, he in the liberal Protestant lineage of the Favres and his father, Paul Maritain.

---

[1]Jacques Maritain, *Notebooks*, trans. Joseph W. Evans (Albany: Magi Books, 1984) 65; cited hereafter as *N*.

[2]Jacques Maritain, *Bergsonian Philosophy and Thomism*, second ed., trans. Mabelle L. Andison in collaboration with J. Gordon Andison (New York: Philosophical Library, 1955) 345; hereafter cited as *BPT*.

[3]Harry Levin, *Refractions: Essays in Comparative Literature* (New York: Oxford, 1966) 271-95.

The next four years, before the reading of the *Summa*, were spent reading the lives of the saints and spiritual and mystical writings under the guidance of Bloy and Father Humbert Clérissac, their spiritual director. But for two of those years (crucial ones, as Stanley L. Jaki demonstrates in his contribution to this work) they lived in Heidelberg, where Jacques worked with Hans Driesch, the eminent biologist. It was here that he began the intellectual struggle of reconciling his faith with the Bergsonism he had learned at the Collège de France. For Maritain, God had revealed certain basic truths to the intellect by means of concepts and propositions. Bergson's critique of the concept contradicted this ability of God to communicate himself to his creatures and, even further, the possibility of the intellect to gain cognition of being in any respect. The conclusion he reached in 1908, two years before reading Thomas, that these two positions were irreconcilable, was to place Maritain in an ambivalent relation to modernism for the rest of his life. The confidence in human reason that he found in Aquinas powerfully reinforced the conclusion reached at Heidelberg; he had been, he discovered, "a Thomist without being aware of it" (*BPT* 17).

While some of Maritain's early works can justly be called reactionary rather than ambivalent in their stance toward modernism, it would be a mistake to make too much of this. Maritain himself apologized for the contentiousness and gruffness of his first book *Bergsonian Philosophy and Thomism* (1914) in his preface to the second edition (1930) but maintained nevertheless that such a tone was necessary to defy the anti-intellectualism he felt Bergson was encouraging. He sought in this later edition to differentiate the "Bergsonism of fact" from the "Bergsonism of intention," whose "invaluable presentiments," "fundamentally correct views," and "salutary metaphysical *directions*" Maritain could embrace. In fact, these "intentions" can be seen to animate Maritain's own thought in a way that keeps it in contact with modernism. Is this not the underlying explanation for Maritain's remark that he and Bergson

> met one another as it were halfway, each having journeyed unwittingly in such a manner as to approach the other: he, toward those who alone represent without betraying it the faith to which I belong, I toward a comprehension, a little less deficient, of the human task of those who seek without yet having found? (*BPT* 345)

Bergson's influence on Maritain rescued his Thomism from the rigidity frequently found among many Scholastics, including even some of Maritain's teachers and disciples. Some may object by saying that Maritain's fluidity and dynamism of thought were wholly to be found in Thomas, but this would be ignoring his own testimony and the traces of Bergson's thought throughout Maritain's writings, especially in his aesthetics of creative intuition.

Yet he did choose Aquinas over Bergson, and when he did he necessarily moved himself out of the mainstream of modernist thought and expression. For

Maritain, the issue at stake was the restoration of the intellect, which even Bergson, who had contended with the Sorbonne positivists, had not achieved. Aquinas first became Maritain's teacher not for exclusively spiritual reasons but because of his firm and persuasive confidence in the capacity of the intellect to *know*. It is this affirmation of *intellect*, which has resonances in Maritain's aesthetics, politics, ethics, metaphysics, and, as Donald A. Gallagher demonstrates, his philosophy of education, that places him a step removed from both modernism and Bergson.

Still, Maritain recognized in Bergson's *The Two Sources of Morality and Religion* (1932)

> a testimony born at the heart of modern thought, both against the pseudo-Christianity of Hegel and the anti-Christianity of Comte. . . . [H]e sets against them a singularly significant riposte, a moral philosophy where the impetus toward Christianity and the person of Jesus stand out in the place of the aversion which Comte nourished in regard to them.[4]

According to Maritain, Bergson, in this last book published nine years before his death, had freed himself from that devotion to pure change and immanence that had plagued the "Bergsonism of fact" by revealing the aspiration of human nature toward grace in the moral and political spheres. The "Bergsonism of intention" had risen to the top, and Bergson himself reflected the change. Maritain cannot justly be accused of a misreading here; Bergson's will written in 1937 expresses a clear desire for Catholic baptism, which because of his solidarity with persecuted Jews he felt he must deny himself. Bloy and Thomas were not the only teachers who taught the Maritains the importance of integrity.

II

Bergson was of course instrumental, perhaps more instrumental than any other single individual, in creating the "modernist" context. But before "modernism" there was the simply modern, whose roots are sunk four centuries deep in the soil of our history. In 1925 Maritain published *Three Reformers: Luther, Descartes, Rousseau*. It was an excavation of those roots, and its findings were both illuminating and depressing. For what Maritain found in these three pioneers of individualism was the abandonment of the intellect.

Three Reformers is triply important—as a central source of the themes in Maritain's body of works, as a turning point of sorts in his career, and as the clearest exposition of those dilemmas of the modern with which we are here concerned.

---

[4]Jacques Maritain, *Moral Philosophy: An Historical and Critical Survey of the Great Systems* (London: Geoffrey Bles, 1964) 427.

It is not by any measure his greatest early work, only his most representative one. The book is a polemical triptych whose panels form an integrated whole, and it should not come as a surprise that at the center of the triptych one encounters the complacent visage of Descartes.

Viewed from one side, Maritain's thought is Thomistic; from the other, perhaps the modern side, it is just as certainly anti-Cartesian. Descartes opened a chasm between intellect and being, thought and things. He correspondingly divided human nature itself, and in the process beggared human culture, as the chapters by Matthew J. Mancini and Richard Fafara make clear. Descartes accomplished this by what Maritain saw as a subtle act of plagiarism: he appropriated wholesale one of the doctrines of those very Scholastics whom he professed to despise and applied it to human consciousness. This was the doctrine concerning angels, whose attribute of intuitive intellection and immediate apprehension of pure ideas separated from things became for Descartes a human characteristic. Maritain called this transposition "angelism," a term, he said, that was not just "a more or less picturesque approximation, but [one that] designates the special character of the Cartesian reformation in the metaphysical order."[5]

But the structure of the modern world has other reformations at its foundation in addition to Descartes's, and responsibility for those rests on different shoulders. Luther and Rousseau accomplished in the fields of religion and morality what Descartes had done in philosophy: they made the isolated self the arbiter of the problematic world outside and cut off the intellect from its source of nourishment in things. But there is this difference: whereas Descartes separates the self by denying the body, Luther and Rousseau accomplish the same end by denying the primacy of reason.

Perhaps it would be helpful at this point for the reader to recall to his or her mind a familiar picture derived from Plato, that of the tripartite division of the soul into appetite, reason, and will. We may find Plato's trichotomy refracted in the modern soul, whose progenitors are the three subjects of Maritain's critique. In Luther the *appetite* takes over nearly the whole human substance; in Rousseau, the *will;* in Descartes, *reason.* What Luther and Rousseau possess in common, then, is their anti-intellectualism, their profound and polemical aversion to reason. Such a denigration of intelligence is the natural consequence of the imbalance, the disharmony, as Plato would have put it, induced by their exaltation of feeling and will. Rousseau, who founded his science of politics exclusively on the will, was the most important pioneer of modern feeling; and Luther,

---

[5]Jacques Maritain, *Three Reformers: Luther, Descartes, Rousseau* (London: Sheed and Ward, 1928) 81; cited hereafter as *TR.*

who surrendered to the demands of his appetite, likewise converted grace itself into a feeling, a sensation of spiritual bliss despite concupiscence.

In contrast to Luther and Rousseau, Descartes undertook a reformation in the opposite direction, one that was just as extreme in its own way; for Descartes elevated intellect to the level of the very angels. Where Luther and Rousseau frankly acknowledged the pull of things—Luther in resignation, Rousseau in ecstasy—Descartes tore the mind from the realm of being and enthroned it above things. Thought's main characteristic became "independence of things" (*TR* 55); the mind can know only its thoughts, he said. The soul's glance, as Maritain put it, stops at itself, "congeals in self-consciousness." The resulting "reification of ideas" constitutes "the original sin of modern philosophy" (*TR* 77).

Maritain believed, further, that the most destructive consequence of the idealism induced by the Cartesian system was its optimism:

> What is the cultural significance of idealism? It carries along with it a sort of anthropocentric optimism of thought. Optimism, because thought is a god who unfolds himself, and because things either conform to it, or do not even exist apart from it. What drama could possibly occur? Either there is no being to set off against thought, or there is only being completely docile to thought. An optimism which is anthropocentric, because the thought in question is the thought of man; it is around human thought that objects revolve. All is well for that thought; and all will be better and better.

"But," he continued in the passage just quoted, "this optimism is, if I may say so, committed to suicide; for it presupposes a rupture with being."[6] There can be no doubt that this passage has far more than a metaphorical significance for its author; that instead it expresses the deep, remembered anguish of the young students Jacques and Raïssa at the outset of their pilgrimage, near to despair at the apparent emptiness of life, at the stubborn intransigence of the universe in refusing to yield significance. It recalls their own suicide pact, which may appear now, to us, so earnestly foolish, even romantic, undertaken in the Jardin des Plantes in 1902. That particular "commitment to suicide" had indeed been precipitated by the "rupture with being" that all the positivism in the Sorbonne proclaimed. It was in seeking the roots of that rupture, after their encounter with Bergson, who, however imperfectly, had reyoked being and thought, that Maritain found, heavy-lidded and smiling an inward smile in the portrait by Hals, the figure of René Descartes. All expressions of thought in some sense limn their authors, all philosophy is autobiography. It is not necessary to take this truism

---

[6]Jacques Maritain, *The Dream of Descartes*, trans. Mabelle L. Andison (New York: Philosophical Library, 1944) 171.

to its reductionist conclusion to see that Maritain's writings are in many ways the concrete signs left behind by his own inward strife.

It was characteristic of Maritain, though, to fight fair. Credit was always proffered where credit was due, even if the creditor was Descartes. It was not so much Descartes as the spirit engendered by his philosophy from which Maritain, in seeking the source of the confusion of modern thought, so strongly dissented. Yet, defenders of Maritain's polemical targets—Bergson, Descartes, Teilhard— are quick to overlook this distinction, which Maritain takes pains to make in every case. His treatment of the great modernists in painting and poetry, such as Baudelaire and Picasso, reflects the same critical sympathy, rather than a reactionary dismissal.

Nowhere did Maritain's attitude toward modernism gain more attention than in his *The Peasant of the Garonne.* There he took on the evolutionary scheme of the then very popular Teilhard de Chardin and the growing influence of the phenomenologists Husserl and Heidegger in theology. Critical reaction to *The Peasant* was sharply negative. Maritain's reputation went into a decline, and to this day many of his admirers prefer the book not to be mentioned. Why? Have they forgotten the Maritain who wrote *Bergsonian Philosophy and Thomism, Antimoderne, Three Reformers,* and *The Dream of Descartes?* Or do they think that Maritain was merely going through a youthful phase in those earlier books? The chapters by Joseph Pappin III and Paul E. Sigmund show that such a conclusion would be mistaken: certainly Maritain himself was apologetic for the fury of his earliest polemics, but he never ceased attacking the enemies of the human person and the human intellect, as his later political writings attest.

III

Maritain's project of restoring the intellect, begun in epistemology, metaphysics, and aesthetics, quickly took on political ramifications as the pressure of world events intensified. Sometimes it is forgotten that his first passion was politics: in a letter written to the family gardener, young Jacques, age sixteen, wrote, "I will be a socialist and live for the revolution" (*N* 8). The scene was far more serious forty or so years later when on 8 February 1939 Maritain delivered a public lecture at the Marigny Theater in Paris entitled "The Twilight of Civilization." His starting point once again was the disfigurement of the intellect, which, he argued, had become insulated from both the supernatural lights above and the irrational forces below. Human nature and reason have been *"shut up* in themselves."[7] The ever-widening split between a pure rationalism and a pure irra-

---

[7]Jacques Maritain, *The Twilight of Civilization,* trans. Lionel Landry (New York: Sheed and Ward, 1943) 10; cited hereafter as *T.*

tionalism has had the disastrous social consequence of making the ground fertile for totalitarianism in either its fascist or communist forms. "The irrationalist tidal wave is in reality the tragic catastrophe of rationalist humanism," he told his audience (*T* 13). Fascism places historical events outside the domain of reason, leaving human beings helpless against them. Marxism, on the other hand, proposes a rational program, but one that, by being founded on atheism, denies the priority of the person, spiritually constituted, over the material individual. For Maritain, a truly humanist social order is impossible in either case.

For sixty years Jacques Maritain would argue that modernism was heading in the direction of the irrational, of the destruction of the intellect. Is it surprising that his writings express more of a call for the restoration and liberation of the intellect than a call to faith? Maritain's insight into the spiritual situation of this century was that no true faith could be exercised that did not reside in an intellect that was confident of its ability to know the truth. For Maritain, as for Thomas, the virtue of faith is primarily a *habitus* of the intellect. Maritain had learned this lesson early, and it had drawn him away from Bergson. In *The Peasant of the Garonne* he remembers the impact of his faith in Christian revelation on his philosophical development.

> That is what teaches a philosopher to respect human intelligence, the concepts and the other instruments it fashions in order to lay hold of things, and of which the prophets of Israel and He whom they were announcing have made use of to open doors against which philosophers bump their noses. It is in the course of meditating on this that, once upon a time, a fervent Bergsonian began to perceive the weakness of that critique of the concept upon which Bergson laid so must stress, and which, after all, he himself belied in writing his great books.[8]

Reading this book twenty years after it was published amid the euphoria that followed the Second Vatican Council helps us to see it not as an aberration in Maritain's thought (with the exception of some uncharacteristically bitter asides), but as another example of its remarkable unity. Doubtless this unity cannot be seen by those who are interested only in ideology. Maritain himself comments in *The Peasant* on the jumbled labeling of "right" and "left" in their various intellectual, political, and religious meanings. Resorting to humorous archetypes of his own invention—for the left, "the Sheep of Panurge," and for the right, "the Ruminators of the Holy Alliance"—Maritain confesses to a split in his own allegiance, which has often confused and divided his followers. Regarding the things that are Caesar's, Maritain says, he feels "less distant" from the left, and

---

[8]Jacques Maritain, *The Peasant of the Garonne: An Old Layman Questions Himself about the Present Time*, trans. Michael Cuddihy and Elizabeth Hughes (New York: Holt, Rinehart and Winston, 1968) 90; hereafter cited as *PG*.

regarding the things that are God's, "less distant" from the right (*PG* 26). The various uses of Maritain made by the members of the "Holy Alliance" in the United States clearly evince a failure to recognize Maritain's obvious social and economic sympathies, as Bernard Doering's chapter in this volume makes clear, whereas the Catholic "Sheep," of course, tend to shy away from the traditional metaphysics and the spirituality that underlie Maritain's political thought. The differences in attitude toward Léon Bloy and his influence on the young Maritains, evidenced in the chapters by John Hellman, William Bush, and Erasmo Leiva-Merikakis, provide a good example of this spectrum in Maritain interpretation.

The figure of Bloy can never be forgotten when one seeks to know Maritain. In embracing philosophy, Maritain had chosen to pursue a vocation that Bloy did not trust, but his project of restoring the intellect and, consequently, the human person, to its proper place would always rest on a kind of spiritual experience. Curtis L. Hancock, Erasmo Leiva-Merikakis, and others make clear that this early influence is clearly felt in everything Maritain wrote, from the pamphlets he coauthored with Raïssa on the importance of prayer and contemplation to his massive *The Degrees of Knowledge*. It would not be going too far to say that Maritain sought to restore the intellect by reminding us of the inherent *spirituality* of knowing, which is illustrated by the immaterial union of the knower and the known. That is to say, the intellect needs contact with an *other*, with both things and God. Faith and reason are joined at the hip; the one cannot flourish without the other.

Faith will help effect what Maritain calls the "inner renewal" of the intellect in our time and liberate the "philosophic eros." "Faith can enter the domain of reason, bringing along the help of a light and a truth which are superior, and which elevate reason in its own order—that is what happens with Christian philosophy" (*PG* 142). Christian philosophy, as proposed by Maritain—and criticized herein by Peter Redpath—addresses the character of the philosopher as well as the content of his philosophy. Faith can provide certain "signals," as Maritain calls them, but even more it can strengthen the power of the intellect from within to resist confusion and to rest its attention on being. As Simone Weil observes in *Waiting for God*, the forms of attention used in academic studies and in prayer are mutually strengthening, and the joy of learning is an inchoate awakening of the human desire for God. Like Maritain, Weil did not observe the neat boundaries that modernism had drawn for the exercise of reason. Instead they both took their lessons from the great contemplatives and artists. Perhaps this is a clue not only to the breadth of their spiritually inspired vision but also to the exemplary quality of their involvement in practical action to achieve concrete ends. For Maritain and Weil, the vocation of philosopher was not exempt from the demands of sanctity.

IV

Modernist philosophy and theology are not alone in divorcing the thinking mind from the desire of the heart for God. *The Peasant of the Garonne* contains an attack, often overlooked, on a school of Catholic thinkers who are contributing to the same error—Thomists. While excepting a few, Maritain characterizes contemporary Thomists as the "learned ossified," preening with an alienating self-importance. Thomism, he thought, was losing its openness to the mystery of Being by a process of unnecessary cataloging of Thomistic "abstract essences" in Scholastic manuals of instruction. The "ever-alert intuitivity" necessary to a genuine and vital Thomism is largely abandoned in this misguided effort to ape the precision of the sciences (*PG* 148-49).

Intuitivity—the capacity of being sensitive to intuitions—was a powerful catalyst for the development of Maritain's thought. One is even tempted, Marx-like, to "unmask" it as the secret force underlying and animating all its aspects. In his metaphysics, for example, Maritain explicitly invoked intuition; he affirmed that at the base of metaphysical thought lies the preconceptual intuition of being. (In the present work, Raymond Dennehy explains the precise role of this intuition.) Elsewhere in Maritain's philosophy intuition seems rather to hover behind the scene; but at bottom it seems clear that (although in an altogether non-Cartesian sense) to him the philosopher's task is *to see:* to see and then by means of concepts to distinguish, to distinguish and then to unite.

For Maritain, every great philosopher is the custodian of some deep intuitive truth grasped once and thereafter continually articulated. The implications of the intuition are further clarified over the course of time; and, as this necessary process unfolds, the errors surrounding the initial vision likewise intensify. The philosopher's task is to peer into the obscure deeps of the great doctrines, to extract the correct intuitions, and to purify them. Such a project justifies the claim that philosophy is useful, and it provides the basis for the human fellowship of philosophers.[9] In *On the Philosophy of History*, for example, Maritain credited Hegel—the man whom Thomas Flynn, in his chapter on Maritain's philosophy of history, quite rightly characterizes as "Maritain's bête noir in this domain"— with a fundamentally correct intuition. It was an intuition of the ferment of life, of "the mobility and disquiet which are essential to [it]."[10] Hegel's mistake came in trying to systematize his intuition in the dialectic, thus reifying logic. But it

---

[9]Jacques Maritain, *On The Use of Philosophy: Three Essays* (New York: Atheneum, 1965) 16-43.

[10]Jacques Maritain, *On the Philosophy of History*, ed. Joseph W. Evans (New York: Scribner, 1957) 20.

remains clear that, as Hegel believed, the great ideas in history reach fulfillment only as they finally engender their opposites.

Once more we are reminded of Henri Bergson, who not only unfolded the consequences of a profound intuition of his own, that of duration, but also—how often is this the case!—resembled Maritain in stressing the role of intuition itself. Bergson defined intuition as "the kind of *intellectual sympathy* by which one places oneself within an object in order to coincide with what is unique in it and consequently inexpressible."[11]

How dangerous such intuitions can be, how essential it is to subject them to the discipline of the concept, is illustrated by the case of Descartes. He too had an intuition of sorts, though in his case the word "vision" might be more appropriate. The vision he had was that of a single science that could account for everything, thus ignoring the specificity of the sciences. But of Descartes's vision enough has been said for the present.

Maritain's fundamental point about intuition is itself intuitive: he saw that all great philosophers, including, or even perhaps especially, his beloved Thomas Aquinas, must be constantly studied, their works sifted for the seeds of wisdom they contain. One never slavishly imposes the thought of Saint Thomas upon modern situations; instead one allows the spirit of that thought to distill itself through the best insights of the age in order to serve the progress of knowledge. Just how that process ought to take place has been shown by Thomas himself. It is called analogical reasoning, and it displays, in Maritain's works, his own amazingly intuitive sensibility.

For example, when Maritain writes of a just social order and calls it a "new Christendom," whose fundamental characteristics recall certain medieval tendencies, he is reasoning by analogy. He seeks from an epoch, as he does from a doctrine, the nugget of wisdom it contains about a more fully human social order. It would never have occurred to him to advocate any sort of sentimental "return" to a lost golden age, as did a number of the reactionary romantic medievalists of his day. Instead he perceived, in the society of the Middle Ages, certain healthful directions that have been derailed by those tendencies of modern thought begun by his trio of reformers. Maritain looked to the development of a social order that would be, as he put it, personalist, communal, pluralist, and "theist or Christian" (in the sense that it recognized God as the source of natural law).[12] These characteristics can be found in the Middle Ages, too, but embodied in institutional forms hardly recognizable to the modern world, forms

---

[11]Henri Bergson, *An Introduction to Metaphysics*, trans. T. E. Hulme (New York: Putnam, 1912) 7.

[12]Jacques Maritain, *The Rights of Man and Natural Law*, trans. Doris C. Anson (New York: Scribner's, 1943) 14-15.

appropriate to the level of intellectual and technological development that medieval society had achieved. To recognize the value of these characteristics, hidden as they were, so to speak, in their institutional structures, was an achievement analogous to capturing the central intuitions of great philosophers. For the modern world, such values are embodied in the institutions of representative democracy, which makes democracy both an advance over the Middle Ages and an analog to it.

Analogical reasoning informs other realms of Maritain's philosophy. Deal W. Hudson's account of Maritain's aesthetics explains how the artist's "creative intuition" is itself a dim analog to the creativity of God. And in moral philosophy, too, Maritain held that men and women enjoy a preconceptual, intuitive knowledge by "connaturality," which serves as the basis for good actions in the myriad of concrete situations in which they are called on to perform as moral agents.

And always, behind and, as it were, inside the philosophic discourse of Maritain's elegant sentences, animating them and imparting the author's sensibility to them, was Maritain's own "ever-alert intuitivity." His sensitiveness and keenness to manifestations of suffering and love as well as intelligence, bring us to a key of sorts to understanding Maritain. For the question naturally arises, what sparks this intuitiveness? What is its source? The answer is simply that it arises from love. Love activates latent moral and intellectual potentialities. "*The unity of mankind* is at the basis of Christianity," Maritain wrote. But he also knew a deeper truth about that unity. "As long as love does not call it forth, that unity slumbers. in a metaphysical retreat where we can perceive it only as an abstraction."[13]

In 1934 Maritain attended a performance in Paris of Shakespeare's *Coriolanus*. At the point in the play when one of the characters heaps scorn on the plebeians—the masses—members of the audience roared their approval. Maritain was shaken and upset by this display of contempt.[14] His own love for the masses, the working and peasant classes, was no posture. It stemmed from a deep intuition of the historical patrimony of these men and women, an intuition called forth by a Christian understanding of the unity of mankind.

It should come as no surprise that Maritain makes constant reference to a saying of Jesus recorded in the Book of Acts (20:35): "It is better to give than to receive." The life and work of Jacques Maritain is a gloss on that line of scripture.

For Maritain, love was the meaning of life; this he was not afraid to say explicitly. Yet, it is the way of suffering as well. In *Creative Intuition in Art and*

---

[13]Jacques Maritain, *Ransoming the Time*, trans. Harry Lorin Binsse (New York: Sribner, 1941) 15, 17.

[14]Wallace Fowlie, *Jacob's Night: The Religious Renascence in France* (New York: Sheed and Ward, 1947) 72.

Poetry he spoke about Dante's *wound,* the wound he received upon first seeing Beatrice and that set free his urge to create. All of Dante's poetry, Maritain believed, issued forth from that wound—Dante "knows his wound and believes in it; and cherishes it."[15] Like Dante, Maritain was wounded as well, wounded by God through his spiritual mentor Léon Bloy and, most of all, his wife Raïssa. Their vow made in 1912 to sacrifice carnal relations was a decision to keep the wound open, to suffer it, and to receive its blessing. Of course, such a choice is not for most of us to make but a special vocation given only to a few. Jacques never spoke about it until his final years, after Raïssa's death, when he confessed obliquely that he had struggled against God until he was "broken" (N 251). And this he admitted only between parentheses! Whatever difficulty we may have in understanding such a severe choice, the fact remains that many of us have received light through Maritain's wound and are wounded by it.

---

[15] Jacques Maritain, *Creative Intuition in Art and Poetry* (Princeton: Princeton University Press, 1977) 371.

HENRY BARS
Edited and translated by ANTHONY O. SIMON

A Maritain Bio-Bibliography*

18 November 1882	Birth of Jacques Maritain in Paris. He is the son of Paul Maritain (who died on 20 February 1904) and Geneviève Favre (who died in 1943). In 1882 Léon Bloy is thirty-six years old, Henri Bergson twenty-three, Humbert Clérissac eighteen, Charles Péguy almost ten.
12 September 1883	August 31 according to the Russian calendar: Birth of Raïssa Oumançoff in Rostoff on-the-Don.
27 September	Birth of Ernest Psichari.
2 July 1886	June 20 according to the Russian calendar: Birth of Véra Oumançoff in Mariopol.
1893	The Oumançoffs arrive in Paris.
1898-1899	Jacques Maritain, in "rhetoric" at Lycée Henri IV, becomes friends with Ernest Psichari.
Winter 1900	Jacques Maritain meets Raïssa Oumançoff, a student like himself at the Sorbonne.
1901	Jacques and Charles Péguy meet.
Winter 1901-1902	Péguy takes Jacques and Raïssa to attend Bergson's course at the Collège de France.
1902	Jacques and Raïssa are engaged.
26 November 1904	Jacques and Raïssa marry. They begin to read Léon Bloy.
25 June 1905	First visit to Léon Bloy. Maritain passes the *agrégation* exam in philosophy.

---

*This bio-bibliography is based upon an earlier version that appeared in *Jacques Maritain: Oeuvres 1912-1939*, ed. Henry Bars (Paris: Desclée de Brouwer, 1975).

11 June 1906	Baptism of Jacques, Raïssa, and Véra Oumançoff at Saint John the Evangelist Church. Two months later Jacques and Raïssa leave for Heidelberg, where they will spend two years. Véra joins them soon after and remains with them from then on.
8 September 1907	The *Pascendi dominici gregis* papal encyclical letter. Bergson publishes *L'évolution créatrice*.
Spring 1908	Jacques Maritain realizes he must abandon Bergsonism.
June 1908	They return to France.
September	Péguy announces to Joseph Lotte that he has regained his faith.
Autumn	The Maritains' first visit to Father Clérissac, who becomes their spiritual director.
	They take up lodgings on rue des Feuillantines in Paris. Jacques earns his living writing a spelling lexicon (later a dictionary of practical living) to protect his independence as a philosopher.
October 1909	They take up lodgings in Versailles, where they live until 1923.
June 1910	"La science moderne et la raison," Jacques Maritain's first article, appears in the *Revue de Philosophie*.
15 September	He begins to read the *Summa theologica* of Saint Thomas and "falls in love" with it.
21-24 February 1912	Baptism and death of Mr. Oumançoff.
October	Jacques Maritain becomes professor of philosophy at the Collège Stanislas in Paris.
13 February 1913	Ernest Psichari's conversion.
June 1914	Jacques Maritain is appointed Associate Professor at the Institut Catholique of Paris (Chair of Modern Philosophy).
2 August	World War I begins.
22 August	Psichari's death.
October	Publication of *La philosophie Bergsonienne*.
11-12 November	First meetings with Father Dehau, who becomes the spiritual director of Jacques, Raïssa, and Véra.
15-16 November	Father Clérissac's death.
Spring 1917	Temporary mobilization to Satory's camp.
16 April	Pierre Villard's first letter to Maritain.
3 November	Léon Bloy's death.
26 March-8 April 1918	Jacques and Raïssa's trip to Rome; visits to Pope Benedict XV and Cardinal Billot concerning La Salette.
June 30	Pierre Villard's death; he wills his estate to Jacques and to Charles Maurras equally.

1918-1919   A year of vacation spent at Vernie rectory in order to write the first volumes of the philosophy manual; an Episcopal commission asked Maritain to compile this work.

September 1919   Manifesto of the "Parti de l'intelligence," *Revue Universelle*, is founded. Maritain is the philosophy editor. He writes frequent articles at first; they become rarer and stop completely after July 1926. At the Maritain home, beginning of the meetings from which the Thomist Circles will eventuate.

1920   Publication of *Art et scholastique*.

1921   Publication of *Théonas*.

Spring 1922   Jacques and Raïssa write the spiritual directory for the Cercles Thomistes. It is published that autumn as *De la vie d'oraison*.
Yves R. Simon becomes a student of Maritain and begins a lifetime friendship and collaboration.

20 July   First meeting with Charles Journet in Switzerland.

30 September   First retreat of the Cercles Thomistes.

4 October   Father Reginald Garrigou-Lagrange, O.P., leads the retreat at Versailles.
Publication of *Antimoderne*.

5 June 1923   Jacques, Raïssa, and Véra move to 10 rue du Parc in Meudon near Versailles, where they will live until the outbreak of the war.

26-30 September   Second retreat of the Cercle Thomistes at Meudon. (40 regular participants). The retreats will be held annually (except for 1936); attendance grows to 300 in the final meetings.

13 October   Frédéric Lefèvre interviews Jacques Maritain and Henri Massis.

14 December   Jacques takes steps to persuade André Gide to stop publication of *Corydon*.

1924   Publication of *Réflections sur intelligence et sur sa vie propre*.

October   Maritain meets Father Lebbe.

March 1925   Maritain founds the Roseau d'or book series in Paris. Meets Nicholas Berdiaev.

1 June   "Intelligence and Mr. Maritain," article by Ramon Fernandez, in the *Nouvelle Revue Française*.

15 June   Jean Cocteau meets Father Charles at the Maritains' home in Meudon; Cocteau is overwhelmed and three days later confesses to him.

2 July   Erik Satie dies.
Publication of *Trois réformateurs*.

2 August   Madame Oumançoff is baptized.

29 August   Baptism of Maurice Sachs.

January 1926	Simultaneous publication of the *Lettre à Jacques Maritain* by Cocteau and *Réponse à Jean Cocteau* by Maritain. Maritain meets Olivier Lacombe and Julien Green.
27 August	Cardinal Andrieu publishes a declaration to the French youth concerning the Action Française, followed by Pope Pius XI's answer to Cardinal Andrieu on 5 September.
25 September	Charles Maurras, accompanied by Henri Massis, interviews Father Reginald Garrigou-Lagrange and Maritain in Meudon.
20 December	Pope Pius XI's condemnation of the Action Française, followed by the "Non possumus" of Charles Maurras and Léon Daudet on the 24th.
11 January 1927	Jacques Maritain's letter to Charles Maurras.
July	Publication of *Primauté du spirituel*.
30 July	Conversion of Charles du Bos, who has just become intimate with the Maritains. Jacques Maritain is called to Rome by Pope Pius XI; as a result Maritain publishes *Pourquoi Rome a parlé*, a work written by Maritain in collaboration with others. It is published in December. "Relationships become very tense with some of our friends," Raïssa writes in her journal.
May 1928	Peter Wust visits in Meudon. Jean Cocteau writes the preface for *J'adore* by Jean Desbordes. Emmanuel Mounier begins to attend the meetings at Meudon. Jacques Maritain exchanges the Chair of History of Modern Philosophy for that of Logic and Cosmology at the Institut Catholique of Paris.
23 March 1929	Gabriel Marcel is baptized. Roman Catholics, Greek Orthodox, and Protestants meet at Meudon and in Clamart at the Berdiaev home.
1929-1930	A year off, during which Maritain writes his massive work on the degrees of knowledge.
4 January 1930	Pierre Lasserre publishes "Le néo-thomisme et l'esprit primaire" in *Nouvelle Littéraires*. Publication of *Le docteur angélique* and *Religion et culture*.
21 March 1931	The Société Française de Philosophie sponsors a conference concerning the notion of Christian philosophy. Contributions by Gilson, Bréhier, Maritain, and others.
1932	Bergson publishes *Les deux sources de la morale et la religion*. Jacques Maritain publishes *La songe de Descartes, Distinguer pour unir; ou, les degrés du savior*, and *De la philosophie chrétienne*.
1 October	First issue of the review *Esprit*, edited by Mounier with advice and support of Maritain.
End of 1932	"Les Illes" collection follows Roseau d'or book series.

January-March 1933   Jacques Maritain makes first trip to Toronto, then visits the University of Notre Dame and the University of Chicago, where he delivers a manuscript to be published as *Religion and Culture*.
Publication of *Du régime temporel et de la liberté*.

1934   Publication of *Sept leçons sur l'être*.
Manifestos "For the Common Good" and "Concerning Repression of Troubles in Vienna."

25 January 1935   The play *Procès*, by André Gide, at the Union for Truth. Publication of *Frontéres de la poese et autres essais Science et sagesse*, and *La philosophie de la nature*, and poems by Raïssa: *La vie donnée*. Two contradictory manifestos provoked by the Ethiopian War. Maritain proposes a third, "Pour la justice et pour la paix," which attracts many signatures.

1 November   Publication of *Lettre sur l'indépendance*.

26 May 1936   Raïssa visits Bergson.

15 June, 1 July   "Primauté de l'être; religion et politique," pamphlet by Joseph Desclausais against Maritain in the *Revue Universelle*.

18 June   "Letter by Maritain to the Director of the *Revue Universelle*" (Henri Massis).

July   Publication of *Humanisme intégral*.

26 July-7 November   Jacques, Raïssa, and Véra travel to Argentina.

22 August   "Mr. Jacques Maritain, Christian Marxist?" article by Louis Salleron in the *Revue Hebdomadaire*.

1937   Maritain takes a stand concerning the Spanish Civil War. He generates the "Manifesto of Catholic Writers against the Bombardment of Guernica."
On the radio, Serrano Suner declares that Maritain is "Spain's number 1 enemy."
Sept is suppressed by intervention of ecclesiastical authority. The weekly *Temps présent* is founded by Stanislas Fumet, Yves R. Simon, Maritain, Pierre Henri-Simon, and others.

5 February 1938   Turbulent lecture by Maritain in the Ambassador Theater and the publication of the text *Les juifs parmi les nations*.

End of September   At Meudon, days of Thomist studies with small attendance replacing the annual retreat.

1 October   Jacques, Raïssa, and Véra leave for the United States. Visits with Yves R. Simon and Charles Du Bos at the University of Notre Dame and St. Mary's College, Indiana.

Middle November   Raïssa and Véra return.

Christmas   Jacques returns.
Publication of *Questions de conscience*, and *Situation de la poésie* in collaboration with Raïssa.

8 February 1939	Lecture at the Ambassador Theater: "La crépuscule de la civilisation."
10 February	Death of Pope Pius XI.
	Publication of *Quatre essais sur l'esprit dans sa condition charnelle.*
	Attacks by Marcel de Corte, Paul Claudel; replies by Maritain.
16 April	At mass in Ernolsheim, Raïssa offers her life for peace.
July-December	Jacques, Raïssa, and Véra stay in Fontgombaud, then in Avoise.
5 August	Death of Charles Du Bos.
3 September	Declaration of war.
4 January 1940	Commissioned by the French Department of Cultural Relations, Jacques Maritain leaves Marseilles for America on the *Exachorda;* Raïssa and Véra accompany him.
January-February	They stay in Toronto.
1 March	Departure for New York.
April	Maritain's influence spreads in the United States. He is asked to remain or at least to prolong his stay. He decides to do so after the occupation of France and the creation of the Vichy government.
September	The Maritains move to 30 Fifth Avenue, New York.
4 January 1941	Death of Henri Bergson.
6 March	First radio message from Maritain to France.
	Publication of *A travers le désastre* (a clandestine edition is circulated in France), *Confession de foi, La pensée de Saint Paul,* and the first volume of *Les grandes amitiés,* by Raïssa.
February 1942	French professors and scholars, Maritain included, found the École Libre des Hautes Études in New York. Publication of *Les droits de l'homme et la loi naturelle.*
9 January 1943	*The Maritain Volume of the Thomist* is dedicated to Maritain for his sixtieth birthday. It contains articles by Mortimer Adler, Yves R. Simon, John U. Nef, and others.
	Geneviève Favre dies in Paris.
	Publication of *Christianisme et démocratie,* "in homage to the French people," and publication of *Education at the Crossroads.*
1944	Publication of *Les principes d'une politique humaniste* and of *De Bergson à Thomas d'Aquin.*
6 June	D-Day: the Allies invade Normandy.
September	"Through Victory," message from Maritain in *Lettres françaises.*
10 November -end of December	Jacques Maritain travels to Paris. He tries in vain to escape his nomination as ambassador to the Vatican.
	Publication of the second volume of *Les grandes amitiés.*
1 April 1945	Jacques Maritain leaves for Rome.

10 May   Maritain presents his diplomatic credentials to the pope.

Spring   Suzanne Marx, Raïssa's godchild, is baptized.

9 August   Disparagement campaign against Maritain, especially by Julio Meinville in Buenos Aires. Raïssa and Véra arrive in Rome.

1947   Maritain publishes *Court traité de l'existence et de l'existant* and *La personne et le bien commun;* Raïssa publishes *L'historie d'Abraham; ou, Les premiers ages de la conscience morale.*

6 November-3 December   UNESCO conference in Mexico. Maritain is president of the French delegation, and he gives the opening speech. He decides to resign his functions as ambassador and accepts a chair at Princeton.

January 1948   Publication of *Raison et raisons.*

14 June   Jacques, Raïssa, and Véra leave Italy by ship from Naples.

27 June   Arrival in New York.

19 August   Arrival in Princeton.

Spring 1949   Trip to France.

8 May   Maritain opens the Week of Catholic Intellectuals and gives a lecture at the Institut Catholique; the lecture is quickly published as *La signification de l'athéisme contemporain.*
The *Revue Thomiste* dedicates a special issue to Maritain: *Jacques Maritain, His Philosophical Work.*

4 June   Maurice Blondel dies.

September   The Maritains return to Princeton and move to 26 Linden Lane, where they live until 1960.

22 March 1950   Emmanuel Mounier dies.

1951   Publication of *Man and the State* and in France of *Neuf leçons sur les notions premières de la philosophie morale.*

28 March   Jacques Maritain is awarded the Spellman-Aquinas Medal by the American Catholic Philosophical Association. Subsequent recipients are friends Etienne Gilson, Yves R. Simon, and G. B. Phelan.

June 1952   Maritain retires from Princeton University as emeritus professor.

1953   Publication of *Creative Intuition in Art and Poetry* and, in France, publication of *Approches de Dieu;* also, poems by Raïssa are published: *Au creux du rocher.*

March 1954   Jacques Maritain suffers a coronary attack. He conceives the idea of a *Carnet de notes* and begins writing it the following summer.

February 1955   Death of Paul Claudel.

Summer   Vacation in France; Raïssa's accident.

October   Jacques's sister, Jeanne Maritain, dies.

1 September 1956 "L'umanesimo integrale," article by Father Messineo, S. J., against Maritain in the *Civiltà Cattolica.*

30 September Charles Journet's reply to the preceding article in *Nova et Vetera.*

10 December Public meeting in homage to Jacques Maritain organized in Paris by the Catholic Center of French Intellectuals.

Beginning of Véra's last illness.

End of 1957 Publication in New York of *On the Philosophy of History.*

1958 Publication of *Reflections on America.*

September The Jacques Maritain Center is founded at the University of Notre Dame.

1959 Publication in France of *Liturgie et contemplation*, coauthored with Raïssa.

13 November Yves R. Simon delivers his last and famous lecture, "Jacques Maritain," at the University of Notre Dame.

31 December Véra dies.

January 1960 Publication in France of *Le philosophie dans le cité.*

30 June Jacques and Raïssa leave for France.

7 July Arrival in Paris. Beginning of Raïssa's last illness.

4 November Death of Raïssa Maritain.

9 November Raïssa is buried at Kolbsheim, Alsace.

December Publication of *La philosophie morale.*

January 1961 Maritain returns briefly to the United States.

March Jacques Maritain takes up residence in Toulouse with the Little Brothers of Jesus.

11 May Death of Yves R. Simon.

June L'Academie Française awards Maritain its Grand Prix de Littérature.

Autumn Trip to the United States.

January 1962 First edition of Raïssa's *Notes sur le Pater.*

April Private edition of *Journal de Raïssa.*

11 October Opening of Second Vatican Council.

Louis Massignon dies.

June 1963 Pope John XXIII dies.
Election of Pope Paul VI (who calls Maritain his teacher).

November Jacques Maritain receives the Grand Prix National des Lettres.

January 1965 Monsignor Charles Journet is elevated to cardinal.

February Publication of *Carnet de notes.*

September Jacques Maritain is received by Pope Paul VI at Castel Gandolfo.

8 December Meeting in seclusion of the Council. Pope Paul VI gives Jacques Maritain the message directed to the world's intellectual community.

Autumn 1966 Jacques Maritain's last trip to the United States. He is interviewed by John Howard Griffin for *The National Catholic Reporter* concerning his forthcoming book.
Visits with Thomas Merton.

3 November Publishes *Le paysan de la Garonne.*

15 December Beginning of the intense controversy over "Le paysan," which lasts for months.

May 1967 Publishes *De la grâce et de l'humanité de Jesus.*

Autumn 1968 Publication in one volume of the *Poèmes et essais* by Raïssa.

Autumn 1970 Publishes *De l'eglise du Christ.*

15 October Jacques Maritain takes the habit of the Little Brothers in Toulouse.

Autumn 1971 He professes his religious vows.
Private publication of *Cantique des cantiques.*

28 April 1973 Jacques Maritain dies in Toulouse.

2 May Maritain is buried at Kolbsheim, Alsace, in the same tomb with Raïssa. The inscription on the tombstone reads—

RAÏSSA MARITAIN

et Jacques

PART I

Friendships

BERNARD DOERING

Maritain
and America—Friendships

IN 1956, AFTER SIXTEEN YEARS of permanent residence in the United
States, interrupted only by the three years he spent as French ambassador to the
Vatican, Jacques Maritain was invited to give a series of three lectures at the University
of Chicago entitled "Random Reflections on the American Scene" under
the auspices of the Committee for Social Thought, whose director was his long-time
friend John U. Nef. These three conferences were revised and published two
years later by Scribner under the title *Reflections in America*. The book was so widely
read that it was republished in paperback form in 1964 by Doubleday under the
Image Books imprint.

This little volume was a kind of love letter from Maritain to the country he
had come to love in a very special way, in his "inmost affections." He insisted
that it was "not meant to be read in a hurry," but meditated upon "at leisure."
He had written it at the urging and with the collaboration of his beloved Raïssa,
who shared his experiences and his convictions and whose "admiration and love
for this country," he said, "are as deep as mine."

This love letter to America is indeed a rarity because, as one reviewer remarked,
it is "a book about Americans which is full of praise and optimism,"
of "high hopes," of "confidence and esteem." Yet Maritain's love for America
was not blind. In his foreword to *Reflections on America*, he stated specifically that
he would make no allusion to politics, for "if I were ever to write on these matters,
especially international politics, I would have many things to say, and not
always flattering, even for the countries I love most." As a true lover Maritain
loved America in spite of its faults, indeed sometimes even because of its faults,
which he realized are so often no more than virtues turned inside out. The depths
of his love did not eliminate his critical distance, and though he wrote with com-

passion and understanding of "A Few Vulnerable Points" in section one and of "Some American Illusions" at the beginning of section three, he did so with perfect candor.

Elsewhere in the foreword Maritain remarked that a philosopher's attention is captivated, not by governments, but by peoples. Maritain loved America first and foremost because of its people. As much as he recognized the vital importance of political activity produced in America, he was only too aware of how deeply both depend "on the most disappointing contingencies." Maritain fell in love with the people, and he did so because as much as, perhaps more than, any other foreigner he was privileged to become most intimately "part and parcel," as he put it, "of today's American cultural life." Americans reciprocated and took Jacques Maritain to their hearts—Americans from all walks of life: philosophers, artists, politicians, clergymen, religious, social activists, poets, novelists, journalists, and academicians from the most varied disciplines.

This love affair is the subject of the following pages, in which I would like to give some idea of the surrounding breadth and variety of Maritain's friendship with Americans, of the various levels that these different friendships attained, with a few specific examples, and then treat at length his friendship with one particular individual, Saul Alinsky, in whom probably more than in any other Maritain found the embodiment of those national character traits he admired and loved so deeply in the American people.

Writing today of Jacques Maritain's presence and of his friendships in the United States may very well seem a futile and irrelevant undertaking. Such a discussion might appear no more than an exercise in historical curiosity about a figure of the past, whom the changes of time have left a stranger at the side of the road, recognized only by the dwindling number of friends and disciples who have survived him.

Though in recent years there is evidence of a renewal of interest in him and his works, for a long time Maritain seemed to have gone into eclipse. Time has passed, profound changes have come about, and one has the impression that he is no longer considered relevant to the present situation in America. Maritain himself seems to have sensed this approaching oblivion. In 1965 he wrote to Julien Green: "At my age one has strange impressions. A stranger to everything, one is not in eternity, yet everything seems to chase you out of time, to deny you that poor little place, that poor little moment, in which you existed in the past, while this present moment means nothing at all."[1]

---

[1]Julien Green and Jacques Maritain, *Une grande amitié: Correspondance 1926-1972,* second ed., ed. J. P. Piriou (Paris: Gallimard, 1982) 248; hereafter cited as *UGA.* English edition forthcoming from Fordham University Press, trans. Bernard Doering. All translations from the French in this chapter are mine.

Yet for those university-educated Catholic Americans who came of intellectual age in the 1940s and the 1950s, Jacques Maritain was an unmistakable presence. Hardly a man or woman of these several generations, which include my own, passed through a program of university studies without having come into contact with the writings of Jacques Maritain, whether those studies were directed toward philosophical or theological inquiry, the understanding and appreciation of the fine arts, or the political and social problems of the contemporary world. The years Maritain spent in America were some of the busiest of his life, and it was during these years that he reached the apogee of his renown, surpassing perhaps even the prestige he had enjoyed in his own native land during the 1930s.

And his prestige in the United States was not confined to Catholic circles. He was sought after everywhere and was invited to lecture or to teach at prestigious non-Catholic universities like Columbia, Yale, Princeton, the University of Pennsylvania, and Hunter College, as well as at innumerable Catholic colleges and universities. On 24 September 1950, when Maritain was invited to give a lecture at Brooklyn College entitled "Problem of World Government," Professor Florence Roll wrote to Maritain that the event of his coming was "without exception, the most important, significant event in the history of the college." When he accepted the invitation, she wrote on 2 October: "at the committee meeting today at Brooklyn College there was a feeling not only of jubilation, but, indeed, of exaltation, as your name was spoken and plans got under way for the event of your lecture."[2] Because of the huge crowd expected, a larger auditorium than that of Brooklyn College, which held an audience of well over a thousand, had to be found.

From every side Maritain received solicitations to participate in round tables, to contribute to collections of essays, to sit on editorial boards, to give advice about the founding and directing of periodicals, to participate in prestigious lecture series like the Terry lectures at Yale, which produced the book *Education at the Crossroads*, or the Mellon Lectures in the Fine Arts at the National Gallery, which were published later as *Creative Intuition in Art and Poetry*, or the Charles R. Walgreen Foundation Lectures at the University of Chicago, which later appeared as *Man and the State*. Many such invitations had to be turned down.

Maritain's friendships extended far outside the academic community. Many Catholics and non-Catholics as well, working for the establishment of political and social justice, for the rescue of European Jews from Nazi persecution, for racial equality, for the dignity and rights of labor, and for the alleviation of the

---

[2]Unpublished letters in the Archives of the Centre d'Études Jacques et Raïssa Maritain, Kolbsheim, France. Unless otherwise indicated, all letters quoted in the rest of this chapter are from the Kolbsheim archives and are published with its kind permission.

sufferings of the poor, looked to Maritain for inspiration and support, and he gave generously of his time and effort. For twenty years he was an unmistakable presence in America, a pervading influence that extended in many directions.

Friendship with Jacques Maritain invariably began with some kind of intellectual encounter. For example, Maritain might send a copy of one of his books to another intellectual who was interested in the same problem to let him know what was being published on the subject or perhaps to elicit comments on his treatment of the subject. Or some author would send a book to Maritain for the same reason. Maritain might read a book or an article that held a particular interest for him and he would seek out an occasion to meet the author personally, or someone might ask for an interview with Maritain for the same reason. Sometimes a mutual acquaintance would decide that Maritain and another friend should meet. Often it was a question of someone's being designated to invite Maritain to give a conference or sit on a panel or chosen just to take care of the logistical organization of such an event. Frequently a simple request for help would result in a friendship. On occasion it would be Maritain who took the initiative in continuing the encounters and developing the friendship; in most cases it was the other who sought to continue and deepen the relationship. The depths to which such friendships developed varied immensely, of course, but Maritain seems never to have refused an overture of friendship. One has the impression that he never cut anyone off, even those who became a source of personal discomfort and embarrassment for him because of their excessive adulation. His charm seemed irresistible, and he had that quality of making the one to whom he was speaking feel that he or she was the most important person in all the world.

In her book *Our Friend, Jacques Maritain*, Julie Kernan gives a good idea of the surprising number of friends Maritain had in the United States. In the Maritain archives at the Centre d'Études Jacques et Raïssa Maritain in Kolbsheim, where the correspondence of Jacques Maritain is being classified, there is an astoundingly long list of Maritain's correspondents, with the number of letters received behind each name. The number of names is in the hundreds. In some cases the number of letters exchanged is in the hundreds. For example, there are 250 letters in the second edition of the Jacques Maritain-Julien Green correspondence. There are just as many, if not more, in his correspondence with Cardinal Journet or John U. Nef. There are certainly many more in his correspondence with Yves Simon. The number of letters Maritain wrote is baffling, and how he found time to write them defies explanation.

The number of letters alone in any particular correspondence is not necessarily an indication of the depth and intimacy of that friendship. For example, the first edition of the Maritain-Green correspondence was published in the same year (1979) as the rather extensive correspondence between Maritain and Emmanuel Mounier. In his letters to Mounier there is a certain fatherly care on the part of Maritain for his promising young disciple. They are full of advice, encouragement, and exhortation, even of firm reproach when Mounier seems not to have understood or to have heeded a fatherly admonition. Mounier shows a certain respect and deference, sometimes a bit restive. But there is no real intimacy between them. We learn nothing of Maritain's inner life in these letters. He is deeply, even passionately interested in Mounier and his work; he never opens to Mounier the secret door of his heart. The subject matter of the letters is almost exclusively the political and social turmoil of the thirties, the founding and funding of *Esprit* and its editorial policy.

On the other hand, in the correspondence between Maritain and Julien Green, who was his first "American" friend, the events of this world hardly enter into consideration. These letters are rather a conversation that lasted more than fifty years between two souls about the soul. In a series of letters where one would expect to find a chronicle of an epoch particularly fertile in catastrophies, one finds a conversation about a vision of God and his relation to the soul, about the presence of evil in the world and the soul's struggle against it, about the mystery of suffering, death, and the afterlife. The philosopher calmed the metaphysical terrors of the young novelist, communicated to him a sense of serenity and peace, and provided him with answers that the priests he consulted either refused to give or were incapable of giving. Julien Green, in fact, chose Jacques Maritain as his spiritual director.

Green came face to face with serenity at a moment when he was experiencing, perhaps more intensely than at any other period of his life, that "sourde inquietude" [muted disquiet] from whose spiritual and carnal discomfort he suffered almost all his life. He wrote "right now I am working in a disquietude that sometimes approaches despair, but letters like the ones you have been good enough to write me restore my confidence" (*UGA* 57). Maritain, for his part, recognizing how much the young novelist depended on him, tried to respond as best he could to the call for help that is present in so many of Green's letters.

This correspondence between souls about the soul took little time to rise above the practical questions of the publication of Green's novels. After a short early exchange of letters, Green began to bare his soul to Maritain, and the subsequent letters, all the way to Maritain's death, illuminate for us in a very personal way the interior, spiritual journey of their author. Until the last years, especially the years after the death of Raïssa in 1960, Maritain replied to Green with a lofty but humble serenity and with an assurance that reveals little about his personal interior life. After the death of Raïssa, however, the roles seem to be reversed. It was Maritain who sought comfort and reassurance from Green. When Green tried to comfort his friend by writing to him that from her place in heaven Raïssa wanted him to be happy, Maritain replied with a letter that unlocks for us the enclosed garden of his heart. "I firmly believe, as you do, that Raïssa is happy, and that she wants me to be brave. But happy, Julien, how could I be happy? I have lost the physical presence of her whom I loved more than myself. I have witnessed the slow and implacable destruction of her poor body" (*UGA* 186).

In another letter he describes to Green the state of "bewildered aberration" in which he lived without his beloved Raïssa. For all the lofty self-assurance of his speculations on *God and the Permission of Evil*, on learning of the sufferings of Green's sister Anne, he wrote: "The suffering of the innocent is unbearable for the heart" (*UGA* 280). In his last years Maritain repeatedly sought from Green the reassurance that he was not sinking into a state of senility and that what he wrote still made sense. After one such reassurance, of which he said he had a terrible need, he confided to Green the disquieting sense of strangeness and solitude described in the 1965 letter quoted earlier.

The limited number of letters in some exchanges of correspondence does not necessarily indicate a lack of intimacy. While he was living in America, Maritain stayed in very close contact with many friends who lived near enough to New York or, later, Princeton to see him regularly on a very personal basis. There was no need for an exchange of letters except when Maritain was away in Europe for summer visits or during his stay in Rome as French ambassador to the Vatican. Often in such limited exchanges of correspondence there are only hints and indirect signs of real intimacy, and the reader must guess at the depth of the friendship from the letters Maritain received, his letters being as yet unavailable or lost.

One such series of letters in the Maritain archives in Kolbsheim gives us hints about the friendship between Jacques Maritain and the famous American journalist and political analyst Walter Lippmann. The first indication we have of this friendship is a letter of 6 May 1939, while Maritain was still living in Meudon. Lippmann expressed his thanks for the copy of *Le crépuscule de la civilisation* that Maritain had sent him. "I read it," he wrote, "as I read everything you write, with profound interest and with a sense of progressive enlightenment." He then announced that he and his wife would be in Europe in June and would like very much to meet Maritain in person. Maritain, of course, received him most graciously. This visit was the beginning of a warm and fruitful friendship. A few months after his return to the United States, Walter Lippmann wrote to Maritain to thank him for the gift of another book, "which Mrs. Lippmann and I greatly appreciate and which I shall be reading now that Congress has adjourned and we have a little freedom from domestic political excitement." He also thanked Maritain for the article he had furnished for *Commonweal* at the beginning of the war ("To My American Friends: Views of the Importance of the Present Conflict," 13 October 1939) and discussed Maritain's position. He concluded with the hope that Maritain would be coming to the United States that winter. "There are things that you can say over here that no one else could say, and of course it would give us the greatest pleasure to see you again. Mrs. Lippmann asks me to send her best greetings to Mme. Maritain and yourself."

Maritain did come to the United States on a lecture tour, and while he was in America, France fell to the Nazis. He did not return to his native land until after its liberation. Lippmann worked for the *New York Herald Tribune,* and during the time that both Maritain and Lippmann lived in New York and saw each other regularly, there was no need for letters. When Lippmann's work required his move to Washington, personal contact was more limited. They regularly sent each other copies of the books and articles they published. Lippmann wrote of his enthusiastic admiration and regard for Maritain's books, which he would read "almost immediately," and on one occasion expressed his gratitude for the "generous inscription" Maritain's book contained. Maritain read Lippmann's books with very special care and several times seems to have written him long letters that must have contained detailed and incisive criticism, for which Lippmann expressed his sincere gratitude, but which consisted mainly of enthusiastic approval and repeated exhortations to Lippmann to propound at much greater length his ideas about the establishment of security forces in Europe after the war, about the feasibility or the possibility of proposing as "an ultimate end" the "federation of peoples inspired by an heroic ideal" (which Maritain seems to have urged upon him), about the relations between the "security forces" and whatever "juridical and institutional order of nations" might be set up, about the grave danger of regarding any member of the security forces "as a potential priest, teacher and constructor of the good life" instead of limiting his powers and activity strictly to those of an officer of security, and about the importance of France in the construction of a new Europe. They must have spoken together about these matters when Lippmann came to New York, for in one letter (1 July 1943) referring to a point made about one of the questions mentioned above, Lippmann wrote "It goes without saying, for you know where I stand." Mrs. Lippmann too shared in this dialogue and frequently took the side of Maritain. "My wife has read your letter, I know that it expresses doubts which she has shared."

Two other friends whose closeness to Maritain can be judged by the intimacy of the letters they wrote to him are the literary figures Allen Tate and Francis Fergusson. Both were professors at Princeton during the time that Maritain taught there, and they saw him regularly both professionally and socially. Both were of enormous help to Maritain in the preparation of his lectures at the National Gallery in Washington and of his book *Creative Intuition in Art and Poetry*, especially those parts that concerned poetry and literary criticism. Francis Fergusson was director of the seminars in literary criticism at Princeton University at the time, and he provided Maritain with "an opportunity for an indispensable preparatory phase of research." Maritain acknowledges that it was by their firm, "friendly insistence" (especially Fergusson's) that he wrote his essay on Dante for the *Kenyon Review*.[3] This article was later included as the central part of his final lecture

---

[3]"Dante's Innocence and Luck," *Kenyon Review* 14:3 (Spring 1952): 301-23.

at the National Gallery and of the last chapter of *Creative Intuition*. It was Jacques and Raïssa who together prepared a French translation of Allen Tate's poem "Ode to the Confederate Dead" for *Le Figaro Litteraire* (24 May 1952), which later appeared in the *Sewanee Review*.[4] Both Tate and Fergusson spent long periods away from Princeton, and it was during these separations from Maritain that they wrote to him.

In 1952 Allen Tate was away from Princeton teaching in Minneapolis, and from there he wrote to Maritain concerning problems involved in the founding of a Catholic literary academy. A Committee of Catholics for Cultural Action had been formed for this purpose, but Tate, who had recently become a Catholic himself, was deeply disturbed, along with other prominent Catholic literary figures like Frederick Morgan, Robert Fitzgerald, and Father William F. Lynch, S.J., by the efforts of certain members of the committee to orient such an academy toward partisan political and religious propaganda. He wrote a long letter on 1 March 1952 to Robert Fitzgerald explaining his views on the subject, which, he said, were "partly the result of . . . talks with Father Lynch, and partly the results of talks last year with Jacques Maritain and Frank Sheed."

He insisted that the academy be given a name that would clearly indicate its adherence to the long tradition of Catholic humanism, that it draw up and publish a "far-reaching philosophy for a Catholic humanism, and that the association feel no commitment to take any direct action in public affairs."

> Our program [he insisted] should thus be cultural enrichment from *within* the Church. A too self-conscious desire to convince the general public that we are enlightened Catholics should be no part of our fundamental purpose, though the existence of such an association may well redound incidentally to the credit of the Church. Our aim should be the advancement of humanistic culture within the Church herself for the greater glory of God. For the glory of God will be advanced by the deepest culture of the social order of which the Members of the Mystical Body are capable. As such a program develops, its influence would inevitably extend beyond the Catholic community. But this extrinsic result cannot be achieved as a conscious aim. A great Catholic culture as an end in itself—that should be, as I see it, the aim, simple and ambitious, of an association of Catholic men of letters. The chief end must be pursued through the practice of the arts of letters, not through propaganda.

The conclusion of his letter shows Maritain's direct influence on Tate, even if he had not mentioned their conversations of the previous year while they were together at Princeton. Tate insisted that he had never favored the existence of a

---

[4]*Sewanee Review* 61: Supplement I-II (January-March 1953). This is a reprint with corrections of a version appearing in the Summer 1952 issue.

group for political action, "such as the sensational French group which formerly published *L'Action Française*." Maritain must have spoken to him specifically and at length of the difficulties he had experienced after his conversion, because he had failed to make clear and necessary distinctions in his anomalous association with the right-wing poltical movement Action Française.

No sooner had Tate finished his letter to Fitzgerald than he received one from Maritain that contained a copy of a letter that Maritain had sent to Frederick Morgan on the very same subject. Father Lynch, who had come to Minneapolis for the express purpose of discussing this problem with Tate, remarked that the "timing" was nothing less than providential, "for had I received your letter first," wrote Tate, "I should not have been able to deny an imputation of influence. In entirely different language we had arrived at the same position." In his reply to Maritain, Tate included a copy of his letter to Fitzgerald of 2 March 1952.

> My opinion from the beginning . . . [he wrote to Maritain] was that we should form a Catholic literary academy, not a group for political action. . . . I agree with you that the only way to make works of imagination and sensibility a part of Catholic life is to produce enough of them, of sufficient power and distinction, to affect the education of the Catholic community as a whole, clergy as well as laity. This is a platitude in the history of literature which we should be very imprudent to neglect.

Business having been taken care of, Tate turned to more personal matters. "In this difficult period how I have longed to walk down Nassau Street to Linden Lane! But I must be content with the letters you can find time to write." He expressed his delight that Raïssa and Jacques were pleased with the prospect of their translation of his "Ode to the Confederate Dead" appearing in the *Sewanee Review*. He wrote that "if Francis [Fergusson] and I led you to write your Dante chaper, we may thank God that he made us His instruments," and he mentioned how complimented he felt that Maritain should wish to quote from his "Poe and the Power of Words." The conclusion to the letter shows how close Maritain was to the whole Tate family, including the children who had remained in Princeton for their schooling. "The very presence of the Maritain family in Princeton is a source of strength to our children, and we thank God for you. And we pray that He will so dispose all our affairs as to bring us together soon. We send our love to you all."

Since Maritain was still in Europe when Tate returned to Princeton near the end of the summer, he wrote to him on 4 August 1952:

> We have missed you here this summer. We arrived after many complicated trips, on July 5, and in spite of the brutal heat we have greatly enjoyed the children and the few old friends who are sticking it out through the summer.

I am sending you tear sheets from the *Sewanee Review* of your magnificent translation of my Ode. Nothing could diminish my pleasure in it.

He wrote of a forthcoming trip to Venice that would take him through Paris at a time when Maritain would be there, and he arranged for their meeting. He gave news of his wife, Caroline, and then concluded: "We send you both our fondest love, and much affection to Vera who we are glad to know can be in France without anxiety. I shall hope to hear from you before I leave or find a message from you when I arrive in Paris."

The last letter from Tate to Maritain in the Kolbsheim archives is dated 28 November 1960, not long after the tragic death of Raïssa. When Tate learned that Maritain would come back briefly to the United States to settle his affairs before returning permanently to France, he wrote:

My dear Jacques,

Cornelia Borgerhoff[5] writes me that you are flying back on 30th to stay a month or perhaps five weeks, but that you expect to live in France in the future. I have been anxious about your worldly arrangements: who will look after you? I know that you have family and old friends in France; so I am sure your decision is the right one. But what a loss your absence will be for us—for *me* even though miles have separated us for years. Your wisdom and grace nevertheless have sustained me, and of course will continue to do so even though the distance will be greater.

I wish there were a prospect of my being in Princeton before you leave. I can scarcely believe that, after your ordeal, you will be equal to coming to Chicago and South Bend for your annual lectures. But if you do come, I shall fly to Chicago to see you.

I pray for Raïssa and for you, my dear friend, morning and night, and you are in my heart all day.

My love to you,
Allen

In 1953 Francis Fergusson was absent from Princeton because he was teaching for the year at Indiana University. From there he wrote on 6 April to thank Maritain for the copy of "your handsome book" *Creative Intuition in Art and Poetry.*

As you know, I always derive new hope and courage from your work, and it is a great satisfaction to me to have this book especially, which I am sure is the best treatment of the subject which we will see in our time. You are very generous to me in your acknowledgements. I am afraid I burdened you with my insistence,

---

[5]Cornelia Borgerhoff, the wife of a Princeton professor, was Maritain's secretary during his stay at Princeton.

when you were already over-worked; but when I see the result I cannot regret my persecutions.

He then told Maritain of his new appointment as visiting professor of comparative literature at Rutgers University.

> Marion and I, and all our children [he continued] are happy to be going east again. Rutgers is only about fifteen miles from Princeton, and I am hoping that I may call on you when we are settled. That would be a great joy.
>
> My book on Dante is supposed to be published this month, and I have asked the Princeton Press to send you a copy. I offer it to you and Raïssa with my hommages, gratitude and affection.
>
> As ever, your friend
> Francis

Maritain, as was his wont, read the book on Dante with great care and was so impressed by it that he suggested Fergusson have a copy sent to *Nova et Vetera*, a prestigious Swiss theological and philosophical journal whose editor was one of Maritain's closest friends, the Abbé Charles Journet, with the object of having it translated and published in French. Fergusson, of course was delighted at the prospect and wrote back immediately, on 25 May 1953.

> Your letter about my Dante book has touched me more deeply than I can say. You have seen exactly what I was trying to do; it is as though you had been watching all my inner efforts with perfect sympathy. It is for this that one works! I have almost memorized your words, and repeat them to myself for encouragement. But I hope you will not have made me too proud. . . . .
>
> We are now packing up, and we shall start our drive back to the East in a week. We are going first to Hopewell, New Jersey, where we have rented Helen Blackmur's apartment for the summer. That will be "headquarters" for us while we look for a place to live near Rutgers; but we shall not be there very much. First we go to Cambridge to see Harvey graduate from Harvard, then I must teach in Vermont. But we expect to be settled in September, and then it will be our great pleasure to get in touch with you. . . . .
>
> All my gratitude to you and to Raïssa, and warmest affection to you from all of us.

As soon as the Fergussons were settled in at Kingston, New Jersey, and the Maritains had returned from their annual summer visit to France, Jacques sent a letter commenting on Fergusson's work and told the news of Raïssa's accident: she had been knocked down by a motorcycle while crossing a street in Paris. On 1 October Fergusson replied:

Dear Jacques,

It was a very deep joy for me to read your letter, which Borge[6] gave me the other day. You always understand my work better than I do myself; you are a source of both clairvoyance and sympathy. Now I find myself encouraged to go on, and to try to write more verse when I can summon up the time and energy. For all of this I am profoundly grateful to you and to Raïssa.

I was very much distressed to hear of Raïssa's accident with the motorcycle. What bad luck for that to happen at the very moment when you were enjoying a glimpse of Paris! I trust she is completely recovered now, and that you will have a good year in Princeton.

He then gave news of his two children, of their travels, and of their departure for college and graduate school and added:

so Marion and I are alone once more. We should love to see you soon. Perhaps we can bring you all out for tea when Raïssa is quite well—I want you to admire our funny little house and our amateurish attempts to paint and fix it up. I'll telephone soon to see when you can come. Meanwhile love to you from us both.

As was the case with Allen Tate, Francis Fergusson's last letter to Maritain was occasioned by the sad death of Raïssa. He wrote on 7 November 1960:

Dearest Jacques,

The terrible ordeal which you and Raïssa suffered together is over, and now that she is at peace your lonely ordeal begins. When Marion died, your words gave me great strength, and now, I hope, the love and gratitude which I, and so many others, feel for you, and for Raïssa, may help to sustain you. My love is always with you.

Francis

During his stay in America Maritain developed an astounding number of such friendships with people who lived near enough to him to be in regular personal contact and at whose depth and intimacy we can only guess because most of those involved, like Maritain, are now dead, and we must be content with secondhand accounts and with the few letters exchanged during periods of separation. There are other friendships, far more limited in number, about which there need be no guesswork. Because of continuous geographical separation, such friendships could be fostered only by regular, sustained correspondence. Fortunately Maritain kept almost all the letters he received and copies of many of those he sent to his friends or of the notes from which he composed final drafts of his letters. Unfortunately his system of filing was not the most orthodox and consisted often of using the newly received letters as markers in the books he was reading or consulting at the

---

[6]Professor Borgerhoff.

moment, where they remain until they are discovered by those who are organizing and cataloging his library and papers.

Another way of judging the closeness of Maritain to his American friends is the care with which they organized reunions, particularly during his last visits to the United States when his health was failing and he had to limit drastically the number and duration of his contacts. Among the American friends who fit into these last two categories are Dorothy Day,[7] John Howard Griffin,[8] Thomas Merton,[9] and Saul Alinsky.

I have chosen to consider in detail Maritain's friendship with Saul Alinsky because I believe that, more than any other American of Maritain's acquaintance, Saul Alinsky was for him the most complete embodiment of those peculiar characteristics he loved so much in the American people.

In *Le paysan de la Garonne* Maritain insisted that, among his contemporaries who were still alive at the time he was writing the book, he recognized in the Western world only three revolutionaries worthy of the name. With tongue in cheek he identified himself as one of them, "qui compte pour du beurre," as he remarked (a French expression that means that he was rather like a little child whom the big boys let play along without strictly observing the rules of the game), for "my vocation as a philosopher has completely overshadowed my possibilities as an agitator." The two other authentic revolutionaries were "Eduardo Frei in Chile and Saul Alinsky in America." In a footnote Maritain identified Saul Alinsky as "one of my very closest friends [who] is an indomitable and dreaded organizer of 'People's Organizations' and an anti-racist leader whose methods are as efficacious as they are unorthodox."[10]

At first glance, a friendship between Jacques Maritain and Saul Alinsky seems totally anomalous. Maritain, known to many as "gentle Jacques," was the soul of discretion, politeness, and deference. He disliked noisy crowds, argumentative confrontations and violent disputation. He lived a life of retirement and quiet contemplation, preferring peaceful, reflective conversations with a few intimate, chosen friends to the pressing, admiring crowds that filled the halls for his lectures. He was a fervent convert to a Catholicism that provided a basis for all his thought: philosophical, political, aesthetic, or social. Perhaps their friendship

---

[7]See my article "Jacques Maritain's Friendship with Dorothy Day," *New Oxford Review* 52:10 (December 1985): 16-23.

[8]See John Howard Griffin and Yves R. Simon, *Jacques Maritain: Homage in Words and Pictures* (Albany: Magi Books, 1974).

[9]Ibid.

[10]*Le paysan de la Garonne: Un vieux laïc s'interroge à propos du temps présent* (Paris: Desclée de Brouwer, 1966) 41.

can be explained by the clichéd "attraction of opposites," for Alinsky, from many points of view, was certainly the opposite of Maritain.

Saul Alinsky was an agnostic Jew for whom religion of any kind held very little importance and just as little relation to the focus of his life's work: the struggle for economic and social justice, for human dignity and human rights, and for the alleviation of the sufferings of the poor and downtrodden. He loved crowds, the more unruly the better. His gestures and language were muscular, and he used the vernacular of a tough street fighter. Alinsky's primary tactic was to stir up nonviolent conflict, "to rub raw the resentment of the people of the community; fan the latent hostilities . . . to the point of overt expression,"[11] to set cities and neighborhoods on edge, to incite municipal jitters; and the soul of this tactic was a healthy, vocal, and aggressive irreverence. He loved to tweak the noses and pluck the beards of the establishment, of those who pretended to power. One commentator called him "part stuntman," whose "method depends to a great degree on the element of surprise, calculated to outrage."[12]

This aggressive and imaginative irreverence was so much a part of his makeup that sometimes the threat of it alone was enough to bring about capitulation. Father Charles Curran tells us that when Alinsky organized the black ghetto community in Rochester, New York, and targeted the Eastman Kodak Company and the local power establishment,

> one suggested tactic was to buy one hundred tickets to the opening performance of the Rochester Symphony Orchestra, a cultural jewel highly prized in the city. The tickets would be given to one hundred ghetto blacks, who would first be entertained at a dinner party lasting three hours, served in the ghetto and consisting solely of baked beans. In the end Alinsky never carried through on the tactic, but the threat alone accomplished much.[13]

When the San Francisco Presbytery was debating whether or not to hire Alinsky to organize the black community of Oakland, California, in order to avoid the violence that had recently erupted in Watts, the very specter of his presence was enough to induce changes, for when Alinsky was consulted about the situation, he insisted that

> the "problem in Oakland is that the power structure doesn't know there are any Negroes. We'd show them some Negroes." He would stage a "Watermelon

---

[11]Saul Alinsky, *Rules for Radicals: A Practical Primer for Realistic Radicals* (New York: Vintage Books, 1972) 116-17.

[12]Charles E. Curran, *Directions in Catholic Social Ethics* (Notre Dame IN: University of Notre Dame Press, 1985) 155.

[13]Ibid.

March," and a "Sunday Walk." Several hundred of the blackest Negroes would be dressed in coveralls, handed watermelons and marched from City Hall to the Oakland *Tribune* . . . . Equally dark-skinned Negroes, elegantly attired, would take a Sunday stroll through the best white neighborhoods. He would move Negroes into places where the "white establishment has built its finest amenities," with the anticipated result that the "white people will move out and you've got their goodies."[14]

One can imagine the delicate and dignified aging Maritain, whose vocation as a philosopher completely overshadowed his possibilities as an agitator, gleefully reading or listening to the accounts of such tactics and nostalgically harkening back to his youthful days as a student agitator.

Maritain was born into the comfort and refinement of the French "grande bourgeoisie," grew up in the enlightened atmosphere of liberal Protestantism and humanitarian rationalism, and received the classical education traditionally associated with his social rank at the Lycée Henri IV. He entered the Sorbonne as a student of natural science but after his conversion to Catholicism turned to the study of speculative philosophy. Maritain's Catholicism inclined him toward a very literal kind of evangelism, and from his student days he had manifested a passionate love for the poor and the humble who thirst after justice. During the thirties he continued his career as a speculative philosopher, but with the rise of totalitarianism and the worsening condition of the poor, he felt himself more and more obliged to turn his pen to the economic and social problems posed by the world and the church.

Alinsky, the gruff and rough-hewn son of impoverished Russian Orthodox Jewish immigrants, grew up in one of the poorest slums of Chicago. During his childhood, like Maritain, he suffered the traumatic experience of his parents' divorce. After alternating between high schools in Chicago and on the West Coast, he entered the University of Chicago and graduated with a degree in archaeology. Finding no market for his archaeological skills, he applied for a graduate social science fellowship in criminology, a subject in which he had only a superficial interest. Appalled by the rise of Fascist groups in America and abroad, he turned to the work of organizing the impoverished and exploited immigrants who lived in the notorious slum behind the gigantic Chicago Stockyards, which was known as the Back of the Yards and which inspired the title of Upton Sinclair's novel *The Jungle*.

Under the tutelage of Saul Alinsky, and following the rules for grass-roots community organization that he laid down later in his books *Reveille for Radicals* and *Rules for Radicals*, the poor, exploited immigrants who lived in the night-

---

[14]"Alinsky and Oakland," *The New Republic*, 12 May 1966, 8.

mare of this ghetto, by themselves, made their neighborhood a national model of efficacious local organization of the people against all forms of discrimination and exploitation, whether religious, social, or economic, and established local services of public health, housing, and social welfare that enhanced the spiritual and temporal happiness of the local community. Because of the success of the Back of the Yards Council, Saul Alinsky rose to national prominence and attracted the attention of Maritain.

During his wartime exile in America, Maritain met Alinsky some time after the founding of the Back of the Yards Council through George N. Schuster, former president of Hunter College, editor of *Commonweal*, and chairman of the Board of Trustees of Alinsky's Industrial Areas Foundation. In spite of the radical differences in their personalities and educational backgrounds, Maritain was immediately attracted to this truculent genius of social reform, and the two men recognized their very profound intellectual affinities. Whenever they met they spent long hours exploring the democratic dream of people working out their own destiny. Both accepted democracy as the best form of government. As Alinsky tried to share with Maritain his ideas about what it is to be a free citizen in a democratic society, about the right of free association of citizens to undertake action and organize institutions to determine their own destiny, about the necessity of community organizations as mediating structures between the individual and the state, structures that help the government do what it is supposed to do, and as Maritain explained painstakingly to Alinsky his ideas about the distinction between the individual and the person, the primacy of the individual conscience in a religiously and politically pluralist democracy, about the primacy of the common good, about the source of authority residing in the people, who accord that authority to the government that acts in their name, each recognized in the other a truly kindred soul.

Alinsky and Maritain shared a profound confidence and trust in the common man, expressed so well by Maritain in his article "Exister avec le peuple"[15] and in his address to "le petit peuple de France" during the Occupation, and shown by Alinsky in his firm belief that, though common men might be mistaken in this or that electoral choice, in this or that choice of political or social action, in the long haul they could be trusted, more than any other group, to make the right and just choice, because they had the least to lose. Once, when asked by his friend Msgr. John Egan why he gave himself so unstintingly to the ungrateful work of social reform, Alinsky replied: "I hate to see people pushed around."

In an interview for *Harper's Magazine*, Alinsky once said:

---

[15]"To Exist with the People," *The Range of Reason* (New York: Scribner, 1952) 121-28.

I've never treated anyone with reverence. And that goes for top business magnates and top figures in the church. Some people call my irreverence rudeness and they think it's a deliberate technique. That isn't so. I believe irreverence should be a part of the democratic faith because in a free society everyone should be questioning and challenging.[16]

What Alinsky says of himself is not entirely true; his statement is subject to at least one notable exception: Jacques Maritain. From their very first meeting Alinsky treated Maritain with an extraordinarily profound and enduring reverence. Though in later years he showed a kind of gruff and ready familiarity, which Maritain seems to have appreciated and enjoyed, this familiarity never turned to irreverence. Indeed Alinsky often showed for Maritain a very touching delicacy and even tenderness, all the more touching in one known for his rude and aggressive truculence. This surprising reverence and delicacy is nowhere more evident than in the letters Alinsky wrote to his friend.

It was Alinsky, it seems, who initiated the correspondence. In an undated letter that appears to be the first letter he sent to Maritain after their meeting, he included for Maritain's perusal a copy of a speech he had given and that had "secured a most unpopular reaction" in many "so-called Catholic quarters." "Christianity," wrote Alinsky, "is certainly an unpopular subject in many parts of the Church." He then spoke of their meeting and asked of Maritain a favor that certainly does not betoken irreverence.

Mr. Shaw[17] and I talked a great deal about you the evening of the day you and I met. . . . Both you and Mr. Shaw represent those rare persons—actual real Christians. If there is a heaven, and only *real* Christians, Jews, etc. are admitted to it, I am absolutely convinced that there are very few people there—I am just as sure that an Archbishop who gets in must be regarded by the heavenly residents as a great curiosity.

There is one great favor I would like to ask of you—I must do it in writing as I would have great difficulty in asking you face to face. It is this—in my work it has always been more helpful to come out of weeks of organizational work, weeks of coping with straight cynicism and materialism and sit down at my study desk with Howland Shaw's picture looking at me. This is most difficult to write because I have an aversion towards sentimentality and a horror of idols, hero worshipers, etc. But what I am trying to say is that a picture of you with some per-

---

[16]"The Professional Radical: Conversations with Saul Alinsky," *Harper's Magazine*, July 1965, 58.

[17]Howland Shaw was a close friend of both Maritain and Alinsky. He worked in the diplomatic service in Washington.

sonal statement on it would be one of my most cherished possessions. There I have said it.

With affectionate regards to you and your wife,
Saul

P.S. It will also serve as a constant reminder to finish the book—Trust me to find some logical basis for a sentimental request.

Maritain, of course, sent him an inscribed photograph. His letters to Alinsky from these early days have not been found, but it is apparent from Alinsky's reply that Maritan had suggested that his friend address him by his first name, "Jacques," instead of by the pretentious title "Professor Maritain." One would think that for the "irreverent" Alinsky this would be an easy request to fulfill. It was not. He wrote:

Dear Professor Maritain,

I don't dare address you otherwise because if I did I would most certainly begin with "Dear Saint Jacques Maritain" which would be anticipating the certain action of the Church in the future. If the Church does not—then I will definitely never feel friendly towards the hierarchy, in neither this life nor any future one.

Your addressing me by my first name is one of the nicest things that has happened to me. Always look upon me as a devoted friend. Through all that may come, *always* I will be that. One of the greatest experiences of my life was to get to know you and greater still to be regarded by you as a friend.

After I finished reading your letter I left my office and walked for some time thinking—I suppose you would call it meditating. Jacques Maritain, you are so filled with love, humility and compassion for your fellowmen that you annihilate my defences of skepticism and cynicism of you know what. Your letter almost restored the feeling that swept me as a 13 year old boy standing before the congregation in an orthodox synagogue and celebrating my Bar Mitzvah.

Life is odd—that I should feel twice that there is a good and great spirit close to me—once in a Jewish synagogue and once from one of the greatest Catholic philosophers—who will in time be ranked with Thomas Aquinas. I can never be anywhere near the person you are because you really love all people, and understand with a great wisdom. There are some people I not only do not love but hate with a cold fury that would stop at nothing. I hate people who act unjustly and cause many to suffer. I become violently angry when I see misery and am filled with a bitter vindictiveness towards those responsible. That is not good and I know it. I know just as well that I will continue to feel and act as I have.

The picture is wonderful—it is you. I can't tell you how deeply appreciative I am of the inscription. It is only natural that many of my actions of the future will be dictated by my conscience plus that inner voice that will say: "Would Jacques Maritain think this right or would he think it wrong?" . . .

As you know I do not pray in the conventional sense but I will frequently, most frequently, think of you and my thoughts will be in their own fashion heartfelt prayers. To know and have friends as yourself and Howland Shaw and Bishop Sheil is to know that life is good. My most affectionate regards to your wife and God bless you, keep you safely and return you speedily back to us here who love and need you.

This last letter, which is undated, was written in the fall of 1944. The trip in question is the one Maritain made to France after its liberation at the invitation of General de Gaulle who wanted Maritain to serve in the new government. Maritain refused a position offered him but, after much urging, did accept the post of French ambassador to the Vatican. He returned to the States for the first three months of the new year to set his American affairs in order before leaving for Rome. In his next letter, written during this period (dated 26 March 1945), Alinsky finally addressed Maritain by his first name.

My very dear Jacques,

You see I have finally capitulated and am using your given name. I have deliberately delayed answering your last letter because I wanted time to think over your discussion of the separation between hating evil and hating the one who does evil. You feel it can be understood only through the mystery of the Cross and that the search for the solution of this problem will "lead me where I do not want to go."

I have pondered over this thought and have reached two, not conclusions, but trends. The first is I know definitely I do *not* want to go where you feel the only solution lies. Secondly, and again being a most doubting Thomas, I believe the mystery of all religions or systems of morality are basically the same regardless of their symbols which in this case would be the Cross and the Star of David.

Alinsky then expressed his hatred for the confusion and misunderstanding that result from the application of sectarian labels and told of his discomfort and anger at being introduced at a mass meeting by a rabbi, who "with a troubled voice" presented him to the crowd as "a Catholic Jew." "Apparently my belief in God or morality is secondary to a label. I hate such muddles. You affect and disturb my inner tranquility not by Catholicism but by your personal example of everything good." Apparently Maritain had in turn asked Alinsky for a picture of himself. He had one taken, but, disappointed with the results, promised to have another taken and to send it on to Maritain in Rome.

During his three years as French ambassador to the Vatican, Maritain, as he had always done, sent Alinsky copies of books and articles he had written, and Alinsky in turn always sent Maritain copies of his new speeches and kept his friend informed of all activities. Msgr. John Egan said in an interview that Maritain was always pushing and encouraging Alinsky in his work with the downtrodden, always asking him what he was doing, what he was undertaking, what he was planning. He added that Alinsky was always sure to have something to tell Maritain, even if the project were only vaguely planned for the future, so as not to disappoint the friend he loved so much and for whose feelings he had a most delicate sensitivity.

From their first meeting Maritain had been urging, indeed relentlessly prodding, Alinsky to publish an explanation of his methods of community organization, a kind of handbook for authentic revolution. On 20 July 1945 Alinsky was able to write to Maritain in Rome that the book was finished. Even before *Reveille for Radicals* was bound, he arranged for two sewn but unbound copies of the book to be sent to Maritain and promised that the very first bound copy produced would be for his friend. Maritain's copy was inscribed:

To Jacques Maritain

That rare person who not only professes Christianity but whose heart is filled with it and who *lives* a Christian way of life. To Jacques Maritain who when he is made a Saint it will not be just for wisdom but for compassion and real love for his fellow-men.

To know Jacques Maritain is to know a richness and spiritual experience that makes life even more glorious.

To Jacques and Raïssa

With all my love

Saul Alinsky

The book was reviewed so enthusiastically in America that it was immediately predicted to be a nonfiction bestseller. Even before it was published, when arrangements were made to have it translated into foreign languages, Alinsky insisted on putting the editing of the French translation into Maritain's hands and signing over to him the complete rights of the French copyright, including royalties. "I informed the University [of Chicago] Press in no uncertain terms that I began to write this book at your personal request," he wrote on 20 July 1945. Since Alinsky knew Maritain would never accept the royalties from the French edition for his personal use, and since he did not want Maritain to incur any personal expenses in the preparation of the edition, he made "three specific requests" in case "by any strange chance" that edition "should secure a wide circulation with a consequent return of royalties." The three requests, presented in a letter of 21 August 1945, were as follows:

1. That you reimburse yourself from these royalties for all expenses you have been put to.
2. Above and beyond your expenses I would like to have what is left distributed through you according to your own judgment to the Spanish refugees from Franco Fascism and to those French movements which are dedicated to the principles in which we believe.

Knowing Maritain as well as he did, he added a third request, most likely to ensure Maritain's acceptance of the first two. At any rate, it is proof of his delicate sensitivity.

3. You keep aside a sufficient sum to provide fresh flowers every week for Mrs. Maritain.

In the course of their friendship each tried to make the other known to the broadest possible public. For example, it was Alinsky who invited the young Father John Egan to accompany him to Maritain's lectures at the University of Chicago. When Maritain found out that his friend and former student, Yves R. Simon, had been appointed to the Committee on Social Thought at the University of Chicago, he told him to be sure to get in touch with Alinsky (letter in possession of Anthony O. Simon dated 20 July 1946).

> I recommend to you with the warmest enthusiasm Alinsky's book *Reveille for Radicals*. I feel the deepest affection for this author, whom I regard as a truly great man, a real son of the pioneers. He has discovered in his people's organizations the creative sap of American life, and I believe that in them can be found the germ of an authentic renewal of democracy.

Two years later, when Simon was preparing a book on *La civilisation americaine* and sent a copy of the manuscript to his friend for advice, Maritain urged him to include several pages on Saul Alinsky and his work.

In 1958, when Maritain's friend Cardinal Montini, archbishop of Milan and later Pope Paul VI, became painfully aware that the church was losing the workers of Milan to the Communist labor unions, Maritain advised him to consult Saul Alinsky on methods of community organization and the training of leaders, and Montini brought Alinsky to Milan to do so.

Nothing is more indicative of the depth of friendship between Alinsky and Maritain than in the letters they exchanged over the tragic death of Alinsky's first wife, Helene. On a picnic at a Lake Michigan beach, an adopted daughter, Kathryn, and a playmate, both eight years old, were playing in the shallow water on a sand bar. Neither could swim. An undertow suddenly carried them both into deep water. Mrs. Alinsky swam out to them and held their heads above the surface until a rubber raft arrived to rescue them, but the weight of the two children held her own head under water and she drowned in her heroic effort. The two children were saved, but Mrs. Alinsky could not be revived. On 15 September 1947 Alinsky wrote to Maritain of the tragedy:

> Dear Jacques,
>
> It is unbearable for me to discuss what has happened. The attached editorial from the Chicago Daily News gives the facts of the horrible tragedy.
>
> As for myself there have been moments when I have felt that it was utterly impossible to go on—even for another instant. If it hadn't been for the children

I doubt if I would have survived or cared to survive that first monstrous week.
. . .

Helene and I were madly in love with each other for every minute of our eighteen years together. We were both very young and at the University of Chicago when we met. She had a serenity about her and a compassion for people that made everyone (even those she fought) love her.

As for me I have never envisaged the agony that now possesses my every hour. I suffer too because so many of our friends all over the world are suffering because of their inability to help. And there is nothing that can be done. The finality of this horrible thing is too much for me to grasp in its full totality. At this time life seems completely empty and all the fires within me are dead and cold.

I have had long talks with Bishop Shiel and Howland Shaw and they are convinced the fires will burn again. I do not know. It is one of those things that time will tell, and right now time is a terrible thing. There is nothing more to say.

Maritain must have written an extraordinarily beautiful and personal letter of condolence to Alinsky. As Alinsky notes in his answer, he was so moved by this letter that he decided to keep it, not with the rest of his correspondence, but in a special folder to have it readily accessible. Unfortunately for us it has been lost. Alinsky's reply gives us an idea of what it must have meant to him.

Jacques dear,

I wept over your letter. It has been placed in a special folder where I can always look at it. I want my children to have it so that in later years they will understand how their parents lived and died.

I am in Omaha, Nebraska tonight carrying on my work. Everyone comments: "We knew how strong you were and we are so happy at the way you have come back." Then they point out their misery to me more than they ever did before. Why I do not know. I do know where previously my only reaction was one of cold anger against the circumstances that are responsible for their plight—now there is something entirely new inside of me. I feel an all consuming pity for my people. Their pain—pains me too.

They think that I am "doing well." What they do not know is that my heart is completely broken and life seems utterly empty and horrible. The agony of the loneliness becomes at times unbearable. Every morning my pillow is wet from my tears and I can't tell you how many times I have prayed for death. The sight of my children forlornly inquiring for their Mommy and wondering why their father (whom they have worshiped as invincible) can do nothing—this smashes those pieces of my heart that still remain.

Oh Jacques, we loved each other so—sometimes I feel I cannot go on for another moment—yet I do—and sometimes wonder why.

Helene and I lived and worked together the kind of life, and those ideals of which you know. We made so many sacrifices (only we never thought of them as sacrifices) of careers, money and other materialistic things that many people thought there was something wrong with us. All we knew was that we were liv-

ing with our conscience and we were so terribly happy just having each other—
and now—was it asking too much to have her?

If I only knew, if I could only believe that there was more behind this life—
that sometime we could be together again. Oh God, I wish I could believe that.

Sometime ago you wrote an article for the *New Republic* or *The Nation* called,
I believe, "The Faith Men Live By." Jacques, you mentioned my name with the
names of really great men and she was so proud and so happy—and know, Jacques,
I am so tearfully grateful that you did it and made her feel as she did. I am grateful for everything that brought a smile to her lips or a feeling of joy.

I saw Bishop Shiel the other day for lunch and he wants to know when you
are coming here for the award. Could you let me know. I do so want to see you
and yet wonder whether I should. It would be such festiveness which should
characterize the affair.

I send you and Raïssa my embraces and my love.

> Your
>
> Saul

As soon as he learned, a month before the actual ceremony, that Maritain
would come to Chicago for the Bishop Shiel Award, he wrote:

My dear Jacques,

I am depressed to know that while I will see you both on the afternoon and
evening of Sunday, November 28, it will be with so many people about us that
we will not be able to talk and really be together. . . .

As for myself, the work goes extraordinarily well and I am also writing again.
Most important to me is that I have found relative peace by my complete acceptance of my mortality. You, above all, will grasp the terrible meaning of those
few words, I said "complete acceptance." Before Helene's death the very word
"acceptance" was anathema to me; it was a synonym for cowardly, abject surrender. Only persons devoid of courage and conviction "accepted." If a thing
was unpleasant, unjust, made people unhappy—one never accepted it, one fought
it. There might have to be a strategic retreat, a going "underground," but acceptance, never! I reveled in the battle and the greater the odds, the more eager
I was to cross swords.

This is one of the reasons why I nearly went out of my mind. Accustomed to
conflict, I was plunged into the depths beyond my wildest imagination. When
the one I loved more than anything on earth was so suddenly taken from me that
I was not even given the chance to fight for her. It was all over when I first learned
of it. She was gone and there was nothing, but nothing I could do. I had to learn
that some things cannot be fought, that one is utterly powerless, and death is
one of those issues that cannot be joined but must be accepted. I said earlier
"complete acceptance" and by that I mean not intellectual or verbal, but with
everything within me.

Also I now know that part of the horrible shock of Helene's death was my
realization that I too not only could, but would die. . . . I say this now in spite

of the character of my past life, its attendant risks and some of the weakness that is part of it. *But* I know that I never really believed that I was going to be killed when I took the risk of death.

We all live, or with few exceptions, as though we were immortal on earth. True we take out life insurance and verbalize our acceptance of death, but all of our plans, worries, ambitions, frustrations, hatreds, values and so-called life is based on the illusion of our immorality here—as though we never die. Death is like an automobile accident; it never happens to us, always to someone else. Once you *really, really* accept your own mortality, there is a certain peace.

I say a "certain" peace because the acceptance of your mortality carries within it the awesome question "What then is the meaning of life?" "What is the purpose of all this, or is there any purpose?" These questions had come up before during my university days but as I look back I realize it was a purely philosophical, intellectual exercise, not only for me, but for the faculty.

Here I stop. Having the question squarely before me, I do not inquire further. Sooner or later I probably will.

Forgive me Jacques for such detail on my learning one of the most elementary lessons in life—that death is part of life.

There is so much I would like to talk over with you. I would love to take you and Raïssa in my car into the country to some quiet inn where about a fire we can be together.

Years later in 1963, when the condition of his second wife, Jean, who was a victim of multiple sclerosis, was deteriorating so sharply that nothing could be foreseen for her but a few short years as an invalid in a wheelchair, Alinsky revealed how important Maritain's letters from this period, and his regularly re-reading them, were in bringing him to the acceptance of his mortality and to the inner peace he spoke of:

As you know, trouble has been no stranger but I have no complaints. Through the years I have finally realized what has happened and what I found as a result of Helene's death, and where the words of your letter at that time were incomprehensible to me, they have since become very clear and I understand. When I see you I will tell you that. . . . I will be in New York the second week of November and if you are in Princeton . . . I should love to come down and visit with you. . .

It is very important to me personally to be able to spend a few hours with you.

During the annual summer visit to France in 1960, when Raïssa was felled in a Paris hotel by an attack of cerebral thrombosis and death was imminent, it was Alinsky's turn to console his friend.

Jacques my beloved friend,

I am heartsick with what is happening with you and only wish I could be with you to be able to do something, anything which might make it more consolable.

If it must happen then I am glad you survive our dearest Raïssa as it is better that way—and in your heart I know you agree.

I suppose it is comforting to feel grateful for the many, many years you have both had together, but I know full well that such thoughts are swept aside in the enormity of the devastation when such a loss takes place.

You will have heard from our mutual friends Monsignors Egan and Burke and they will reach out their hand of common faith to you. I, as a congenital heretic, can only reach out with my heart and hands of love and devotion and abject misery because of your suffering.

Give Raïssa my love not only for herself but for her love for you.

I love you Jacques,
Saul

Of the letters Maritain wrote to Alinsky only three have been found. [18] In the Maritain archives in Kolbsheim there is a rough draft of a fourth letter that Maritain wrote from Rome after reading the manuscript of *Reveille for Radicals*, which Alinsky had sent with Raïssa when she joined her husband there. Like the three letters from the Alinsky papers, this rough draft shows the depth of Maritain's feeling for Alinsky. The main body of this letter concerns Maritain's enthusiasm for *Reveille for Radicals* and his eagerness to have a French translation made as soon as possible, but the introduction and the ending show that Alinsky was one of the rare friends to whom he confided his most intimate feelings.

Do you realize at what point I miss you and Howland and the Bishop? I pray every day for all three of you together. I have in my office the picture of the Bishop and Howland Shaw, and I feel sorry not to have yours. Please send it to me. I would like to have the three pictures together; it's full of meaning for me.

The sudden passage from New York to Rome is an extraordinary experience. There freedom from history: here the burden of history. . . .

Dear Saul, I have not the time of writing to you as I wish. You know what is already in my heart; in moments of sadness, which are not rare, I remember this dinner in New York with you and the dear Bishop and H.S., and my hope in men is burning anew. I believe that my present mission, which I do not choose, answers some definite purpose of God, but I don't know this purpose, and I advance in the full night of faith. Doubtless I needed this experience. At least Raïssa is at my side. She is brave and undertakes peacefully the official business which

---

[18]These letters are in the Alinsky papers at the Library of the University of Illinois, Chicago campus.

is so much against the grain of our nature. She gives you her affectionate regards. Pray for us. God bless you, dear Saul.

The three letters found among the Alinsky papers all date from the period of Maritain's retirement after the death of Raïssa to the community of the Little Brothers of Jesus in Toulouse. Maritain wrote very few letters during this period and only to his most intimate friends. As a matter of fact, Alinsky did not know Maritain's retirement address. He had to ask others for it and finally got it from George N. Schuster. During the early years of his retirement, Maritain spent most of the time in Toulouse and the summers at Kolbsheim and made occasional trips to the United States. The fact that the only Maritain letters kept by Alinsky are ones he received during this period shows, perhaps, how much he missed his old friend.

The first of these letters is dated 5 November 1962 and was written from Princeton during one of the rare trips Maritain made back to the United States after the death of Raïssa. He began by thanking Alinsky for coming all the way from Chicago to see his "poor old friend Jacques." "It was good and grand to have you here yesterday. I love you, Saul. All a living past, full of memories, sufferings and hopes, was burning in my heart. Please to God I can see you again."

Apparently Maritain's "congenital heretic" friend had some trouble understanding why he would want to abandon the "world" and bury himself in some obscure contemplative religious community. Maritain took pains to explain to Alinsky that he was not giving up the struggle for justice and for human dignity. He explained at length the difference between the active life and the contemplative life and the relative effectiveness of each in the struggle for justice and for human dignity, one operating in the temporal order, the other in the order of redemption. In both realms, the true love of one's neighbor demands the gift of oneself, but "the human condition obliges each of us to give priority to the one or to the other."

> You—being a Jew (whom I consider a Christian at heart, a better Christian perhaps than I am) committed to the quest of justice on the earth—are giving priority to the first kind of love's requirement and offering your life for the temporal salvation and emancipation of mankind. (And in the second place, you act and fight also, according to your possibilities, for the recovery by man of his inner moral dignity,—that is to say, finally, even if you don't have such purpose in your mind, for his spiritual redemption).

It was because of the depth of their friendship that Maritain felt he owed a lengthy explanation of his retirement from the world to Alinsky. "I think you have a right," he wrote, "to a complete knowledge of my views on the matter." Alinsky was not the only friend who found it difficult to understand Maritain's decision. He asked Alinsky to explain it to a mutual friend and "make him realize that my retirement from the world is not a fake. I have passed through death. A life-long task has been put to an end, in an unmistakable manner. And another job has been given me, for a while, by my Boss."

The second of these three letters is also about the distinction between the temporal and spiritual realms. Alinsky wrote many more letters than he received during this period and usually included whatever he thought would be of interest to his friend. One particular letter from Alinsky, which seems to have been lost, had many enclosures, among which was a book, inspired by the ideas and the work of Alinsky, concerning the use of power in the struggle for social reform.[19] Maritain excused his delay in answering the letter. "Illness, overwork and insuperable fatigue prevented me from writing you—much to my regret! For I was craving to do so. A million thanks for all that you sent me, and which interested me passionately."

Maritain greatly admired the book in spite of what he considered a serious lack: a disregard for moral power and the power of love. In his concern that Alinsky come to realize that his program for social reform was based on moral or spiritual power as well as secular power, he had "planned to write an immense letter to you on this matter. I could not." He did, however, take the time to write two pages, filled with tiny, compact script, explaining the difference between the "temporal realm (civilisation): in which it is normal to aim primarily at power in the ordinary sense (implying coercion, pressure)" and the spiritual order, in which "the only power to be *essentially and primarily* aimed at is the power of love," which can have a very real effect in the temporal order, "but only [in] a secondary way." But power in the ordinary sense, he added,

> will inevitably become corrupted if the only incorruptible power, the power of love, is not quickening the whole business. (Your own case, my dearest Saul. Remember your conversation with the guardian of the cemetery: all your fighting effort as an organizer is quickened *in reality* by *love for the human being and for God*, though you refuse to admit it, by virtue of a kind of inner *pudeur* [modesty or reserve]).

After stating his conviction that "there is no opposition, but only complementarity between your (and Silberman's) method and Martin Luther King's (Gandhi's) method," he insisted that Alinsky's method "implied in actual fact the exercise of moral power," and that "there will be no solution to the racial crisis in the United States if people like you and Silberman and people like Luther King do not meet together and recognize the essential unity of their effort, and the essential complementarity of their methods and inspiration, different as they

---

[19]Charles E. Silberman, *Crisis in Black and White* (New York: Random House, 1964). See especially chapter 7, "Power, Personality, and Protest."

may be and appear." He then announced his forthcoming visit to America and urged Alinsky to visit him in Princeton if he could possibly do so.

The last of these three letters was occasioned by the arrival of *Rules for Radicals*, which Alinsky had inscribed: "To my spiritual father and the man I love, from his prodigal and wayward son, Saul Alinsky." After claiming that he was unworthy of the dedication, which, nevertheless, "is a blessing for me," Maritain filled two pages with the praises of this "great book, admirably free, absolutely fearless, *radically* revolutionary," which "brings to us the fruit of your experience as an incomparable creative organizer—an experience which is both indomitable generosity and magnanimous sadness with regard to human nature, and which proceeds from the life-long dedication of the greatest man of action in our modern age." He then asked leave "to point out a few philosophical views with which your book had not been explicitly concerned, and give rein to my own inveterate habits, as an old grumbler."

Maritain was somewhat disturbed by Alinsky's praise of self-contradiction: "Seeking one's own intellectual liberation in an infinite proliferation of antinomies is madness on the level of philosophical thought. But on the level of pure action a kind of boldness in practical self-contradiction is probably, as you suggest it, the sign of a healthy and fecund mind. Yet it makes me jumpy." Maritain cited a number of passages from the book to bolster the contention that Alinsky was, in reality, an incurable idealist, a living, indeed a heroic, witness of Judeo-Christian tradition and true democracy: "in other words, and to tell the truth you are an admirable witness of Gospel love for human beings—who, at the same time, desperately busies himself in playing the part of a cynic." He then cited several contradictory statements, one of which he found particularly unsettling: "In war the end justifies almost any means." He wanted to know if by that Alinsky meant "torture? indiscriminate bombing? annihilation of cities? OK for Hitler and his like?" He then carefully explained the moral doctrine of "means" and the morality of human actions, a doctrine central to his thought on social action from the thirties on.

> It seems to me [he gently chided his friend] that in your book the philosophical truth in question, essential as it may be, is hardly emphasized or taken into consideration. . . .
>
> Dear Saul, [he concluded] forgive me those clumsy remarks of a pig-headed philosopher; and pardon, also, my bad English.
>
> I have been for many months, and still am, awfully tired; and I have much ado to find my words.
>
> You know that I am with you with all my heart and soul.
>
> Pray for me, Saul.
>
> And God bless you!
>
> To you the fervent admiration and the abiding love of your
>
> > old Jacques.

Since Alinsky was to be in New York at the time of Maritain's arrival he volunteered to accompany his frail old friend from there to Mansfield, Texas, where a visit had been arranged with John Howard Griffin. When he found out at the last minute that he was unable to accompany Maritain, he sent the following note to Cornelia Borgerhoff, who was arranging the details of Maritain's visit: "Will you please tell him to conserve his energies as much as possible and to remember that there are many of us who love him dearly and feel that he is the most priceless person in our lives." During this visit they saw each other for the last time. Alinsky died in 1972 and Maritain in the following year.

Maritain had many more friends in the United States, some very casual ones, many who confided in him and sought his help, and a very few to whom he in turn opened his heart completely. From all of them he learned a great deal, as they had learned so much from him. It was his living experience of friendship in America that changed radically his conception of democracy and the political enterprise. It was through his American friends that he came to understand the true nature of democracy even more profoundly than the very Americans who had taught it to him, as he once indicated to Saul Alinsky (20 August 1945): "Physical separation from our friends makes us realize how deeply we love America and have been intoxicated by her soul and her hopes, that great human dream which is permeated with the Gospel infinitely more than the Americans themselves believe."

WILLIAM BUSH

"RAÏSSA MARITAIN . . . et Jacques"

EVEN THE MOST CASUAL VISITOR to Jacques Maritain's Alsatian grave in Kolbsheim cannot but be struck by the singular form given the inscription on the gravestone. As I stood there for the first time in the spring of 1982 beside my hostess, the Baroness Grunelius, I even found myself on the verge of asking, "But where is *he* buried?" since, indeed, all one sees at first glance are the big letters in the center of the stone spelling out "RAÏSSA MARITAIN." Only after a second do the first-time visitor's eyes shift to take in the small letters inscribed in the lower righthand corner, where one reads two words only: "et Jacques." "That was the way he wanted it," Madame Grunelius said to me with a certain resignation.

Would one be justified at this point in proposing those lines of T. S. Eliot's *Four Quartets* that say that the communication of the dead is tongued with fire beyond the language of the living? I would reply no, for Jacques Maritain did, in fact, and particularly in his later years after Raïssa's death, say quite clearly just what he tells us once and for all on the tombstone: he owed everything to Raïssa and regarded himself as but an appendage, an afterthought, a name tacked on in small print to her life, just as the tombstone indicates.

But *why* is this so? Is there indeed some tangible, solid basis for it? Or would we be justified in dismissing it as just an eccentric whim expressing the grief of a bereaved husband who had lost his wife after more than fifty years of marriage?

In approaching this challenging question of Jacques Maritain's obsession with his wife's superiority to himself, I shall examine only three aspects in this relationship. Though somewhat limiting, these three aspects may perhaps open some new perspectives on it and, I should like to think, might even stimulate some Maritain specialists to go further still in probing Jacques's debt to Raïssa—or, at least, his obsession with his debt to Raïssa. I should propose therefore a few reflections, first on Raïssa, Jacques and the world of women; second on Raïssa, Jacques, and Saint Thomas Aquinas; and finally on Raïssa, Jacques, and Christian spirituality.

Raïssa, Jacques, and the World of Women

Is is important to recall Jacques Maritain's home background. He was the only male in a household where his divorced mother had given up Jacques's father's name to revert to her maiden name of Geneviève Favre. Moreover, Jacques had a sister but no brother. Thus the most dominant male influence within the household could only be that of his glorious dead maternal grandfather, Jules Favre, member of the French Academy, an outstanding lawyer and politician, fashioner of the Third Republic and negotiator with Bismarck at the end of the Franco-Prussian War. Even Maritain's absent father, the lawyer Paul Maritain, existed under Jules Favre's shadow, whether as his secretary or as the author of a volume on him published the year of Jacques's birth.[1] In any case, Paul Maritain died only months before Jacques's wedding with Raïssa, which definitively removed him from the picture formed by the new couple. What is far more significant for our consideration is the fact that the pattern already established in Geneviève Favre's house, where Jacques found himself between two females—his mother and his sister, Jeanne—would be, within less than three years, recreated in his marriage and maintained for the next half century.

It was in 1904 after a four-year friendship that included a two-year engagement that Jacques Maritain, twenty-two, married twenty-one-year-old Raïssa Oumançoff in a civil ceremony. We know that Geneviève Favre was not in favor of so early a marriage for her son and was gravely disappointed that he did not seem inclined to follow in his famous grandfather's footsteps.[2] In the light of what was about to happen in less than a year, however, that was to become the least of his mother's worries.

It would be difficult to imagine anyone more opposed in principle to everything Catholic than was Geneviève Favre. So far as she was concerned, the priests—the best of them highly suspect, to say nothing of the depths to which the worst of them might sink—had clearly stolen both Jacques and her daughter away from her as well as getting their clutches on two of her most cherished young male friends: Ernest Psichari and the great Charles Péguy, both brilliant writers killed in the first weeks of the First World War. It is in fact ironic that both Raïssa's parents, unbaptized Jews and not Christians at all, actually embraced Catholicism at the end of their respective lives with tears of joy while Geneviève Favre clung proudly, and perhaps even somewhat rather aggressively, to her old

---

[1]Paul Maritain, *Jules Favre: Mélanges politiques judiciaires et littéraires* (Paris: Arthur Rousseau, 1882).

[2]Geneviève Favre, "Souvenirs sur Péguy," in *Europe* 46 (Février 1938): 149. See also Jacques Maritain, *Carnet de notes* (Paris: Desclée de Brouwer, 1965) 58; cited hereafter as *CN*. Translations from this and all other volumes cited in this essay are mine.

humanitarian, romantic republicanism, calling herself a Protestant and undoubtedly regarding Ernest Renan's portrait of Jesus as the only true one. The fact that Ernest Renan's grandson and namesake, Ernest Psichari, had gone over to the priests in no way shook her anti-Catholic convictions.

Henri Massis reminds us that the attitudes of Geneviève Favre were still faithfully held by the young Jacques, whom Massis recalls at about age eighteen—and thus, we assume, just prior to his meeting Raïssa—joining with Ernest Psichari to stage theatricals for the working classes on Sundays, demonstrating in Socialist rallies, and firmly entrenched in the opinion of his mother that the Church was nothing but "a fortress of the rich and powerful."[3] It was Jacques's militant socialism moreover that brought him and his sister, Jeanne, into the orbit of Péguy. Ironically they both refused to take Péguy home to meet their mother, since they feared her too bourgeois—she who was, as it turned out, actually destined shortly thereafter to become Péguy's closest friend.

Jacques's political activities also brought him and Raïssa together in the winter of 1900,[4] when he was trying to form a committee to support Russian students in tsarist prisons, thinking, no doubt, that this Russian Jewish classmate at the Sorbonne would be of very practical use to him in contacting Russian residents in Paris. This meeting and Raïssa's acceptance were, of course, to be decisive for both of them. In Jacques, Raïssa found a real soulmate as well as an entry into a whole new world. It was, she tells us, through Jacques's enthusiastic and inimitable introduction to French art, including her very first trip to the Louvre—she who had already lived in Paris the better part of a decade—that Christian culture first entered her life (*GA* 57). Yet what Raïssa, even at this point, brought Jacques was also great. With her native intelligence, her finesse, and her great poetic sensitivity, Jacques met in her a feminine personality worthy of himself, a worth to be proven shortly by what soon became for them a mutual obsession: the search for truth.

We can pass quickly over the familiar story of their pact in the Jardin des Plantes whereby they agreed to commit suicide at the end of a year if they had not found some meaning to life before then (*GA* 90-91). Their discovery of Bergson shortly thereafter happily saved them for marriage in November of 1904 and for their first encounter with Léon Bloy just seven months later, on 25 June 1905. Almost a year later, on 11 June 1906, Léon Bloy would stand as godfather not only for Jacques and Raïssa but also for Raïssa's younger sister, Véra. The newly converted couple left in August following their June baptism for Heidelberg, where Jacques was to pursue his studies. On neither side were parents advised of

---

[3]Henri Massis, *Notre ami Psichari* (Paris: Flammarion, 1936) 65.

[4]*CN* 106; Raïsa Maritain, *Les grandes amitiés* (Paris: Desclée de Brouwer, 1949) 54; cited hereafter as *GA*.

the conversions. Perhaps this explains why, when Véra arrived in Heidelberg the following December with her mother for a visit (*CN* 52), she decided to stay on with her fellow converts rather than return to Paris with her mother. Thus began Véra's Christian vocation: that of assuring the well-being of Raïssa and Jacques. Only death, half a century later, would end it.

The following early spring outsiders apprised both Raïssa's parents and Jacques's mother of their children's infidelities to the respective faiths of their parents. On a rush trip to Paris in March of 1907, made expressly for that purpose, Jacques seems to have fared somewhat better in soothing his in-laws than his own mother (*CN* 57-58). In any case, the little trio of Jacques, Raïssa, and Véra had already set out on its almost five decades of existence as a highly unusual little community of three Christian converts living together in the twentieth century.

Within this tiny community, in spite of each taking a turn as superior in ordered fashion, there is, almost immediately, strong evidence that both Jacques and Véra deferred to Raïssa on spiritual matters. Although messages from heaven were by no means limited to Raïssa alone (*CN* 107, 284-92),[5] her special penchant for a life given to prayer was recognized by the other two members of the community as a very basic fact of their existence. Also, for Véra, Raïssa was of course her big sister who, unlike herself, had succeeded in French schools and who, being sickly by nature, brought out all Véra's motherly instincts, as did Jacques also, apparently. In popular parlance one would say that Véra was to play the role of Martha to Raïssa's Mary, though such a statement is surely open to qualifications, as we shall see shortly. Jacques, in any case, states categorically that "The first task of Véra was to watch over us" (*CN* 258), and from personal testimony of people who had reason to call, hoping to speak to Jacques, I am categorically assured that Véra could be extraordinarily efficient in protecting her charges.

The formation of this little community in late 1906 was to lead only five years later to their unanimous desire to become officially consecrated as semireligious, living in the world. Thus in 1911 they undertook a year's trial period as oblates of Saint Paul's Benedictine Abbey of Oosterhout, at the end of which, on 29 September 1912, all three made their vows as Benedictine oblates (*CN* 101-09). Three days later, on 2 October (*JR* 21), back in Versailles, Raïssa and Jacques pronounced their vows, consecrating a celibacy that, quite obviously, had already become a very familiar and preferred state for them. Thus was officially reestablished the pattern known to Jacques Maritain prior to his marriage. He was again between two women and, because of their vows, Raïssa had now become as inaccessible as ever had been his mother or sister.

---

[5]See also Raïssa Maritain, *Journal de Raïssa*, presented by Jacques Maritain (Paris: Desclée de Brouwer, 1963) 72, 93; cited hereafter as *JR*.

Certainly I do not in any way wish to cast aspersions upon these vows of celibacy that Jacques undertook in his twenty-ninth year, less than seven years after his marriage. If marriage be an honorable estate, equally honorable in unbroken Christian tradition is chastity. Yet I do not think that it would be unfair or untrue to speak in this case of a certain "etherealization" of Raïssa's influence on Jacques that was allowed for by this strictly celibate relationship. From all we read, we can only conclude that far from making Jacques more practical and ploddingly realistic in regard to certain human problems concerning the spiritual life, Raïssa's life as a contemplative tended to excite him toward rather exalted views as to what reality in the life of prayer is, and how it might be lived by Christians. Nor did their renunciation of conjugal ties in any way lessen Jacques's devotion to or idealization of his wife. He seems indeed to have lavished upon Raïssa's spiritual explorations and adventures (which, it must be admitted, sometimes were a bit overly naive and enthusiastic) those human energies normally sapped in a husband who must support and sustain his wife as they struggle with their offspring.

But then might it perhaps be shown that Raïssa's influence really justified this substitution in the long run? It is not, I think, to be neglected or passed over in silence that at the moment they were entering upon their novitiate as oblates, Dom Jean de Puniet, abbot of Oosterhout, said something to them that I think should be kept firmly before us in all our considerations of Raïssa and Jacques. After first of all telling them that as a little religious community of three they were a little branch of Saint Paul's Abbey of Oosterhout and that Saint Benedict loved everything that was little, he added these words, which were duly recorded by Jacques and which I see as the key to our subject: "You must desire to do nothing outside your life; it is your life which is your work" (CN 101).

Thus, though Jacques Maritain had at this point established himself in the familiar pattern of existing between two women, there was now a radical difference: all three were, through their lives, and not through what they wrote or said, to become living oblations to God. That Jacques would continue to set great store by a written "work," other than his life, made no difference to the fact that the oblation had been made and that it would be in fulfillment of that oblation and not in his writings on philosophy that Jacques Maritain had made himself, by his own act of consecration, responsible to God.

Raïssa, Jacques, and Saint Thomas Aquinas

In regard to this matter the facts are blatantly clear, as Jacques himself points out to us. It was in the early months of 1909—thus two years before they undertook their novitiate as oblates—that Raïssa began reading Thomas Aquinas (CN 74, 108). On 20 April the following year she was still advancing with joy in her reading of the Angelic Doctor at a moment when Jacques's need to improve his knowledge of Scholasticism was being pointed out to him by Father Clérissac, who had, Jacques reports, "pulverized" his article on "Modern Science and Reason" (*CN* 89). It was not, however, until 15 September of that year of 1910 that Jacques himself finally started his own reading of the *Summa theologica*, again, he notes, "Thanks to Raïssa" (*CN* 92).

What seems of more pertinence at this point than the mere incontrovertible fact that it was Raïssa who introduced Jacques to Saint Thomas Aquinas would be to ask why, in the midst of the twentieth century, Raïssa and Jacques latched on to this exponent of thirteenth-century Scholasticism whose one goal would appear to have been to prove that a Christian could handle Aristotle as well as any Arab in Spain's Muslim universities. Indeed, Raïssa and Jacques did cling to Saint Thomas Aquinas with such ardor that one can but wonder if there might not be other factors at work here beyond Pope Leo XIII's espousal of Thomism as the more or less official Catholic philosophy.

The *Statutes for Circles of Thomist Studies* that the Maritains drew up with episcopal blessing in 1922 opens with a categorical declaration: "God, in making Saint Thomas Aquinas the common Doctor of the Church, has given him to us as head and guide in the knowledge of truth" (*CN* 396). In those same *Statutes* we learn that the means par excellence to "*save*" the intellect is "an active, progressive and conquering fidelity to the principles, doctrine and spirit of Saint Thomas" (*CN* 397). The fact that Christianity did not have to wait for Saint Thomas Aquinas to come along in the thirteenth century to reveal the truth that is Christ (or that he is not considered a Doctor of the Orthodox) seems not to have crossed the Maritains' minds. The intellect must be saved and this could best be done by applying the teachings of Saint Thomas to all situations, as demonstrated in a great number of Maritain's books.

When one recalls that the Maritains were the godchildren of Léon Bloy, their adherence to such a systematic approach to the affairs of God as Thomism is certainly rather startling, indicating, I would suggest, a considerable distance between their Christianity and his. Always fiercely independent, Léon Bloy's Christianity was never to be determined, he would remind us, by some frightened Peter in Rome who, fulfilling the scriptures, was probably busy denying Christ by his pronouncements. Who can forget Bloy's ingenious exegesis in *La femme pauvre* of the phrase from the Gospels, "the cock crowed," announcing Peter's denial. Equating the cock to France, in accord with the old Celtic symbol for her, Bloy explains that that passage of the Gospels teaches us that the role of France (that is, the cock) is to crow, announcing the denial, whenever Peter in Rome denies the Lord.[6]

---

[6]Léon Bloy, *La femme pauvre* (Paris: Mercure de France, 1937) 211-12.

One would be hard put though, I fear, to find the Maritains ever mentioning such a reference, in spite of their genuine affection and love for Léon Bloy; for a Christian such as Bloy, unlike the Maritains, was not to be submitted either to Thomism or to any other systematic approach to God. Though he may never actually have come out and said, as did Dostoyevsky, that the Jesuits were demonic, for example, he did not hide that he held them responsible for inventing the new science of psychology, which is demonic. Nor would Léon Bloy's sense of what the mystery of the church is ever have allowed him to make such a simplistic error as that made by Leo XIII in trying to funnel the Gospel through the writings of one single man, an error repeated by the Maritains.

But what was it that prompted the Maritains, quite independently from their godfather's orientation, to cling so tenaciously to Thomism? I would suggest that they both discovered that through Thomism they could at last reconcile their artistic interests with their religious activities, something surely borne out in Jacques's *Art and Scholasticism.* Intellectually as Christians they could thereby be devotees of the latest poetry, the latest music, and the latest literature and even justify this activity by speaking of habits and virtues, of accidents and essence, of final causes, and of saving the intellect. Such an approach, however, totally neglected the whole of Orthodox Christian witness in which a Saint Basil in the fourth century spoke on the use of the classics by Christians, for example, but where God is known to exist beyond the human intellect, saved or not. In any case, Thomism did allow the Maritains to take the artistic world terribly seriously with all its styles, fads, and ever-shifting illusions.

Certainly old Léon Bloy was horrified whenever he looked upon the artistic world of Paris, which at best he would have viewed as a sort of freewheeling zoo, but at worst as nothing but a cesspool of abominations. Was it not there, he would remind us, that one would encounter the shimmering ploy of the opulent demonic that, like the serpent's scales, fascinates by its ever-changing irridescent light? Bloy's life of poverty, suffering, and prayer he set in opposition to that world, while constructing alongside it rare works of beauty that will remain a monument to Christian art of that time. Jacques and Raïssa on the other hand, very much caught up in the artistic world, needed the quasi-official spiritual justification they found in Saint Thomas to pursue this activity. Moreover the fact that Raïssa wrote poetry, inspired by the example of Saint John of the Cross, was not, I believe, a negligible factor in this preoccupation of theirs. On the positive side, however, one should not neglect to mention the launching by Jacques of collections such as the Roseau d'or in the 1920s and Les Isles at Desclée de Brouwer in the 1930s, whereby a whole generation of readers was much enriched. Nonetheless books such as *The Frontiers of Poetry, Creative Intuition in Art and Poetry*—to say nothing of *Art and Scholasticism*—certainly do bear witness to the sincere determination of the Maritains, if not to reconcile artistic creativity with sanctity, at least to compare them as related activities.

Very interesting, if perhaps a bit severe, are the numerous comments found on the Maritains in the recently published *Journal de l'abbé Mugnier, 1879-1939*. Jean Cocteau, briefly but noisily brought back to the sacraments in 1925 by the Maritains and one of Jacques's collaborators for the Roseau d'or series, is reported by his mother in 1929 as not liking the Maritains' mixing literature with their religion. Besides being afraid of Raïssa, he found that having the Blessed Sacrament in their home while never wanting to miss a concert made them seem as if they always wanted to be in on everything.[7]

Whatever one may think of the Maritains' attempt to mix religion and literature and to be in on everything artistic, it was primarily Saint Thomas Aquinas's philosophy that allowed them to do this and to carry their speculations about beauty to the infinite. That Jacques Maritain would, in cases such as his ridiculous and, I would say, almost heretical criticism of Bernanos's Orthodox Christianity in *Sous le soleil de Satan*, take his task far too seriously does not, however, concern us here.[8] We must recall the words of Dom Jean de Puniet, who told them that nothing counted but their lives—that their lives must be their work. And it is here that we shall see, at last, Raïssa's role in shaping Jacques's spirituality rising to the highest degree and, in the end, proving far more important to him than her introduction to Saint Thomas Aquinas.

Raïssa, Jacques, and Christian Spirituality

As early as 21 September 1909, two years before the little trio embarked upon their novitiate as Benedictine oblates, their then common spiritual director, Father Clérissac, was already encouraging them to follow what he called "the contemplative way in the world" (*CN* 82). With her usual thoroughness, plus, I believe, the thirst of her Jewish soul for dynamic intimacy with the God of Abraham, Isaac, and Jacob and not of the philosophers, as Pascal put it, Raïssa decided that such a life, whatever it might be, or wherever it might lead her, was for her.

At the root of this decision to opt for the pursuit of what they called the "contemplative life," however, is found that troubling dichotomy between the contemplative and the active made so much of in the Western church since the twelfth century, but a never-ending source of puzzlement for Orthodox Christians who can envisage no separation possible in the spiritual life of prayer before

---

[7] *Journal de l'abbé Mugnier, 1879-1939. Texte établi par Marcel Billot* (Paris: Mercure de France, 1985) 506.

[8] See my "Avant-Propos" in Georges Bernanos, *Sous le soleil de Satan: Première édition conform au manuscrit original* (Paris: Plon, 1982) 9-23; see also on the same question my article "Jacques Maritain and Georges Bernanos on the Problem of Evil in *Sous le soleil de Satan*," in *Notes et Documents* 4 (octobre-décembre 1983): 91-105.

God. Nor are the Orthodox alone. The Maritains' great friend, Charles Péguy, was, I believe, trying to say just that in his *Mystery of the Charity of Joan of Arc*, where he explores many facets of the nature of prayer and the Christian vocation. This work, incidentally, was one that prompted a very disapproving letter from Jacques Maritain concerning the authenticity of Péguy's devotion to the Virgin—a fact that today can only cause all of us to blush for the letter's author.

Be that as it may, Jacques certainly maintained the image of Raïssa's being apart from Véra and himself because of her taste for what they called "contemplation," and at Meudon her room was the one adjacent to the chapel. From what we read her existence for the most part was frequently spared the give and take of many daily chores. Yet, strangely enough, and seemingly representing a diametrically opposite point of view, we find Jacques at the end of his life strongly defending the contemplative life of the third member of their community, that Martha of the household, Véra, whose more active life he quite adamantly maintains did not prevent her too from living a life equally full of contemplation. "Véra lived by prayer as did Raïssa," he concludes (*CN* 260). Finally, in his ever-challenging volume, *The Peasant of the Garonne,* Jacques forcefully suggests that the idea of contemplation should be considered as a more normal activity for Christians in general.

Certainly it is to Raïssa's credit that as a fresh convert she did, early on, and with considerable energy, pursue what she considered to be "contemplative prayer," though she seemed to have problems with coming back to reality afterward, as she notes in her *Journal* (*JR* 27-103, passim). For this she was reproached by Father Clérissac, and though one may criticize Father Clérissac's direction of Raïssa,[9] I would humbly suggest that he was vainly attempting to accomplish from the beginning something that, I fear, no spiritual director of Raïssa Maritain was ever able to accomplish and that she would have to learn for herself—that is, to root her prayer in reality or, as that great master of Orthodox asceticism, Saint John of the Ladder, says, keep her soul *within* her body when she prayed. Indeed, a sort of escapism is only too evident in reading the early part of *Journal de Raïssa*, where not only her prayer life shows marks of a certain basic exaltation but also the things to which she was attracted when she was not praying or prostrate with her various chronic ailments seem exalted.[10]

---

[9]See Jacques's comments in *CN* 92-93, and Raïssa's in *GA* 237-38.

[10]Raïssa reports that Père Clérissac liked the idea of their becoming oblates of Saint Benedict in that it represented a sixth-century spirituality, far removed from the Counter-Reformation spirituality of sixteenth-century Spain, though the Maritains were not too sure that their love of Saint Benedict either affected or altered their esteem of Saints Teresa of Avila and John of the Cross as the "doctors *par exellence* of the spiritual life" (*GA* 239).

Undoubtedly Raïssa Maritain, in pursuing what she called, according to the Catholicism of her time, the "contemplative" way, was really seeking greater intimacy with God. And, as an Orthodox Christian, I would most surely agree that no other goal really should exist for any Christian. But there is a certain danger in categorizing and labeling this pursuit of intimacy with God "contemplation" and expecting special considerations and exemptions from the normal rules of daily life in order to pursue it. That, during the early decades of her life as a contemplative, Raïssa took for granted such considerations and exemptions, and that Jacques actually thought they were necessary if his wife were to pursue her life of intimacy with God, is obvious from the texts we have before us.

As I followed Raïssa Maritain's pursuit of her contemplative life as she portrays it in her *Journal*, I found it rather salutary, if not actually therapeutic, to recall that less than ten years before the Maritains' conversion in 1906 there had died in the Carmel of Lisieux a little French bourgeois girl who had also kept a journal but whose life has never been held up as that of a "contemplative" spelled out in big letters as has Raïssa Maritain's. Yet the brief witness of Thérèse of Lisieux, completely fulfilled by the time of her death at age twenty-four, helped me considerably to keep Raïssa Maritain's life as a contemplative in perspective. But then this has nothing to do with Raïssa's influence on Jacques, which for this essay is the important issue. And, regarding that, I would even propose that Raïssa's witness, within the economy of God, was probably of far greater importance to Jacques than was that of Thérèse of Lisieux. There seems in fact little evidence that Thérèse's canonization in 1925 had the same impact upon Jacques Maritain that it did on Georges Bernanos, whose spirituality is rooted in that of the young Carmelite. No, in Jacques's case it would seem that only his great devotion to his wife would be able to open for him certain Christian mysteries.

As one surveys Raïssa's life it is unbelievably refreshing to discover that when she was past sixty and into her fortieth year as a Christian, she seems at last to have gone beyond manuals of perfection and official teachings on the spiritual life to come to a less exalted approach to man's relationship with God. We thus find her writing on 1 April 1946: "There is a sanctity for each of us which is in accord with our destiny and which God proposes to bring about by ways not catalogued in any manual of perfection" (*JR* 281). It is also refreshing to discover that Jacques, having lived through the great sorrow of both Véra's and Raïssa's deaths, also came around to a more commonsense point of view about contemplation, as is evidenced in his quite remarkable pages on Véra as a contemplative, saying she equaled Raïssa. Thus, though I would never venture to say that Jacques Maritain would, as a philosopher who prided himself on "distinguishing in order to unite," ever have agreed to dropping the dichotomy entrenched in Western Christian vocabulary since the twelfth century that distinguished the contemplative from the active, he did, in fact, gravitate toward a much more orthodox position in regard to the fusion of the two, having learned from Véra's example.

In regard to this rather important point, let us recall that the timeless tradition of the desert fathers that prevailed in the Western church certainly through the sixth century and in many ways right up to the twelfth century, and that still thrives in Orthodoxy, shuns any distinguishing between active and contemplative lives, urging one to get on with the business of loving God by the ways God presents us to love Him. That is the basic spirituality of Thérèse of Lisieux, who after all sought to offer everything to God, regardless of what it was. That is also the spirituality announced by Pascal when he observes that events and circumstances are the surest of our spiritual masters. And where indeed does one find any idea of separating the active from the contemplative in the West's most venerable monastic rule—that of Saint Benedict? Indeed, the early Church shows us people given to prayer, yet Saint Paul would never have seen his prayer and his extraordinarily active Christian witness as being anything but one and the same.

The danger of distinguishing between the active and contemplative stems from the fact that it becomes entirely possible for clergy and even religious within the Western church to take a position of indifference, if not actual hostility, toward the so-called contemplative life, feeling justified in labeling "mystical," and hence suspect, anything beyond their intellectual grasp. Thus it becomes not enough to say, "Deliver us from the mystics!" but, as Bernanos shows us through one of his priest-administrators, one may go all the way and say, "Deliver us from the saints!"

Certainly one could never accuse Jacques Maritain of being against either sanctity or the mystical, yet as he himself says, just because he wrote of such things did not mean that he understood them. So it was that late in life, as he sifted through Raïssa's papers and thought back upon Véra's unobtrusive witness, he did seem to come to a much deeper understanding of the mysteries of the Christian faith. Thus it is not by accident at all that in a book such as *The Peasant of the Garonne* we find Raïssa's presence exceptionally strong, with Jacques quoting her writings as basic reference texts in regard to all sorts of subjects. We thus find Raïssa quoted as an authority on such varied topics as the mystery of the Church's union with Christ's agony for the sins of men; contemplation; the necessity for contemplatives; liturgical music; the one-to-one relationship with God; the humanity of Jesus.[11] And those are only six of a very long list that could be drawn up from *Le paysan de La Garonne* alone.

Moreover, Jacques, not satisfied with the importance he had already given Raïssa's essay "The True Face of God, or Love and the Law," with which he had closed *Journal de Raïssa* in 1963 (pp. 365-70), used it again in 1966 to close *Le*

---

[11]Jacques Maritain, *Le paysan de la Garonne: Un vieux laïc s'interroge à propos du temps présent* (Paris: Desclée de Brouwer, 1966) 272n; 321 and 340-41; 323; 317n; 326; 341-42. Hereafter cited as *LPG*.

paysan (pp. 370-76), thereby revealing the place the questions treated therein played in his own priorities. Yet, this essay notwithstanding, I would maintain that from the evidence we have before us, no aspect of Raïssa's Christian thought actually took on more importance for Jacques at the end than did her reflections on coredemption. Indeed, after he had devoted a dozen pages to it with substantial quotes from Raïssa in *Le paysan*, he came back the following year and, still quoting Raïssa, took up this question again in *De la grâce et de l'humanité de Jésus.*[12]

Might one therefore ask if Jacques perhaps saw this mystery as the one toward which Raïssa was moving in her life of prayer? It was certainly, it would appear, the most precious legacy she left Jacques, and from what one reads one can but conclude that his encounter with this idea, through Raïssa's witness, took on for him, as it should indeed for every Christian, far greater importance than all his many volumes of philosophy, or his social thought, or his excursions into the artistic and intellectual worlds of his time. And let those who are attracted to Jacques Maritain for philosophical, intellectual, artistic, or political reasons, and who sometimes tend to take Maritain's Christianity for granted, not forget that without his Christianity he would be quite worthless to them, as he would be the first to remind them. Therefore, if through Raïssa's witness Jacques's Christian faith were deepened or made richer, all of us are concerned.

Certainly Jacques seems to have grasped through Raïssa's reflections upon the mystery of making up what is lacking in the Passion of Christ—as articulated by Saint Paul in his Epistle to the Colossians (1:24)—that it is more than a rarefied idea reserved for elected contemplatives alone, since Véra too, though never passing for a contemplative, had also moved toward this mystery through her life of prayer. And how was it not possible to see that at the roots of this mystery of coredemption is that very basic and fundamental mystery of the Church as the Body of Christ at work in this world, not only in a visible manner, but also in a hidden, mystic manner? For Christians are all members of that Body and thus are members of one another and, according to the laws of that Body, must thus bear one another's burdens, fulfilling the law of Christ.

Thus what Saint Paul was doing in speaking of "making up what is lacking" in the Passion of Christ was by no means pretending that that Passion was not sufficient but rather that there is significance to be attached to human suffering, which in Him and through Him and by Him is joined to His redemptive action, an idea Raïssa had dwelt upon as early as 1934 (*JR* 228-31). Her explanation made at that time would be taken up by Jacques both in *Le paysan* and in *De la grâce et de l'humanité de Jésus*, as we have already noted. That explanation, faithfully echoed by Jacques, is this: on an eternal plane the Passion of Christ suffices,

---

[12]Jacques Maritain, *De la grâce et de l'humanité de Jésus* (Paris: Desclée de Brouwer, 1967) 34-35.

but it must be continually integrated into the present time in His earthly Body, which is the Church, as member after member of that Body accepts to bear the heat and toil of this earthly life, which can only end in death, and to offer that heat and toil and death, borne for love of Christ, in union with His sufferings, that one may become a living, dynamic member of the suffering Body of Christ at work in the world, a doer of His word and not a hearer only.

Such of course is surely the goal of all Christian life, and this active participation in His work of redemption is much more down to earth than is an ill-defined state called "the contemplative life." Indeed, does the constant, day-by-day, minute-by-minute renewal of our intimacy with God, and of our loving "yes" to all God sends us, be it good or bad, not constitute a goal demanding both a continuous activity on the one hand and, on the other, a deep abiding adoration of the supreme mystery of Christianity—that is, the Incarnation of God in Jesus Christ, of whom we become living, loving, suffering members, glorified in Him, redeemed by His blood that nurtures us, and healed by His stripes that we may well be given to bear in our bodies?

This indeed was to become the fruit of that long, loving attention to the affairs of God that both Raïssa and Véra experienced as they placed themselves at the feet of Jesus Christ while Jacques lagged along behind, as he himself reminds us. For in the last section of *The Peasant of the Garonne*, he writes to praise their choice in contrast to his own, pointing out that his most unmerited gift from God had, in fact, been his fifty-five years lived with the two sisters. And quite categorically he insists that both of them, "never failing a single instant" (*LPG* 286), were faithful to a life of what he, clinging to Western Christian vocabulary, calls "contemplative prayer." But fortunately he elaborates on what "contemplative prayer" has come to mean for him through this double witness when he says that both of them were united in love to Jesus and the love of His cross, as well as to the work that Jesus pursues invisibly in the world through such prayerful souls as theirs. As for himself, he, Jacques, must label himself a laggard, tagging along behind, working with the intellect. This work, he says, would even cause him to think that because he philosophized on certain spiritual things he actually understood them (*LPG* 286).

We see therefore that though the formula on the tombstone may seem exaggerated when we read "RAÏSSA MARITAIN . . . et Jacques," there is indeed a certain acknowledgment being made there of Jacques's debt to his wife, who alone, I believe, was capable of bringing him to an awareness of certain Christian mysteries. His ill-founded and even pompous criticism of the Christianity of both Péguy and Bernanos, French literature's two greatest Christian geniuses in the twentieth century, certainly reveals to anyone who reads the texts of that period that there was plenty of room for Maritain to go much further and much deeper in penetrating the mysteries of the Christian faith.[13] Indeed, for him, as for most of us, I fear, coming to the fullness of truth took a very long time and, as T. S. Eliot says, cost not less than everything. Few of us after all have the spiritual genius of the young Thérèse of Lisieux.

Thus, while it is true that both Jacques and Raïssa Maritain may well have made mistakes and been sometimes even simplistic and naive in regard to their Christian witness, they did both persevere in seeking the saving knowledge of that crucified and resurrected Jewish God whom they had discovered through Léon Bloy and whom they embraced once and for all by their conversion on 11 June 1906. His cross they would then be given to live out in their flesh, for the cross given Jacques, Raïssa, and Véra in their Christian baptism was neither a stunning jeweled ornament nor yet a mere religious symbol nor even a material weapon with which were to be subdued worldly political systems in the illusion of bringing about social justice through manmade utopias where original sin would have disappeared. No indeed, for as many as are baptized into Christ have put on *Christ*. And that Christ is a living Christ. And His cross is a living cross: a dynamic, life-giving spiritual reality, a glowing presence of the Spirit of God hidden within the depths of every Christian's life, which, whether happy or unhappy, must constantly be offered in union with that of Jesus Christ by whose resurrection all human sufferings are finally, in God's mercy, and sometimes only after untold earthly agony, transfigured by the uncreated light of the Holy Trinity.

T. S. Eliot says that the end of all our exploring will be to arrive where we started and know it for the first time. This, I think, is actually what happened to Jacques Maritain, as at the end, he looked back and recalled the little religious community of three souls who, on beginning their novitiate in 1911, were told by their abbot that nothing but their life was to be their work. Thus, at the end, as Jacques Maritain looked back over his own long and sometimes painful pilgrimage across almost three-quarters of the twentieth century, he realized that Raïssa, no less than Dante's Beatrice, had finally led him to the paradise of the saving knowledge of Jesus Christ at work in the world through the mystery of coredemption, a mystery she had made clear to him not only through what she wrote but through the sufferings of her flesh. For this was indeed that truth they had long searched for with such passion and no small number of imprudences, including a suicide pact.

---

[13]See note 8 above; and, in regard to Péguy, see Jacques Maritain's quite extraordinary letters addressed to him in Pie Duployé, *La religion de Péguy* (Paris: Klincksieck, 1965) 641-65.

ERASMO LEIVA-MERIKAKIS

Léon Bloy and Jacques Maritain:
*Fratres in Eremo**

*C'est sur les larmes qu'on sera jugé,
car l'Esprit de Dieu est toujours
"porté sur les eaux."*

I

WHEN HE REEDITED HIS FIRST NOVEL, *Le Désespéré*, in 1913, Léon Bloy dedicated it *ad fratres in eremo*—"to my brothers in the wilderness"—and these brothers are "my very dear godsons, Jacques-Christophe Maritain and Pierre-Matthias van der Meer de Walcheren." The *eremus*, the wild desert meant here, is not the monastic cell but what Bloy considered the spiritual wasteland of Paris and Western civilization at the beginning of our century, an interior desolation that just in the following year, 1914, would become all too graphic a nightmare. For both the interior and the exterior cataclysm Bloy would prove the fitting commmentator; and Pierre van der Meer tells us how he and Jacques sat in a cellar in Versailles in 1918 during a shelling by Big Bertha, all the while reading *Le Désespéré* aloud to one another. Besides the Bible, Bloy's work was to them the only reading "capable of raising the soul above [the] atrocious wretchedness" in

---

*This chapter is dedicated to Michael D. Torre.

which they were immersed.[1] We note that in this dedication Bloy attaches the baptismal names "Christophe" and "Matthias" to his godsons' given names; by this he surely means to stress that at least these two have already undergone regeneration even while remaining in the grips of the world, and by addressing his spiritual children as "brothers" Bloy shows that the spiritual father in Christianity does not encourage any kind of discipleship around his own person but accomplishes his task of begetting when he brings others to Christ as sole teacher.

I suggest that the particular kind of philosopher Jacques Maritain, the more famous of these godsons, later became is attributable in great part to the fact that, for some thirty years before their meeting, Léon Bloy had persevered with his family, in denouncing the self-satisfied niceties of a supposedly Christian society; that he persevered in the task of some miner who, at his own risk, daily society; that he persevered in the task of some miner who, at his own risk, daily went down the sacred shaft to bring up the half-buried treasures of the most vital Catholic tradition. Léon Bloy, the self-styled "naive vociferator" and "hurler of curses," raised a mighty shout in the manner of a Homeric hero on the battlefield, to proclaim what Lautréamont had termed the "good news of damnation"[2] within the hushed sanctuary of conventional Catholicism. Bloy dared call an abomination by no other name, and he thereby threw open the sluices of language and of faith for a bath of violent renewal. And does not Bloy's stance as witness to the truth "in time and out of time" emerge again in Jacques's deliberately gruff persona at the end of his life, that "old layman," the Peasant of the Garonne, who had to "put his foot in his mouth and call a spade a spade" before a church too ready to "kneel before the world"?[3]

I propose, then, that Jacques Maritain owed the shape of his religious destiny to the "phenomenon Léon Bloy" just as he owed the shape of his intellectual destiny to Saint Thomas. Indeed, Jacques found Thomas's love of objective truth anticipated in the very unphilosophical Bloy, whose works Rémy de Gourmont says seem to have been written by Saint Thomas Aquinas in collaboration with Gargantua![4]

---

[1]Pieter van der Meer de Walcheren, O.S.B., *Dieu et les hommes*, 4th ed. (Paris: Desclée de Brouwer, 1957) 136-39. All translations in this chapter are my own.

[2]Jacques and Raïssa Maritain, *Oeuvres complètes* (Fribourg, Switzerland: Editions Universitaires, 1982–) 5:697; hereafter cited as *OC*.

[3]Jacques Maritain, *The Peasant of the Garonne: An Old Layman Questions Himself about the Present Time*, trans. Michael Cuddihy and Elizabeth Hughes (New York: Holt, Rinehart and Winston, 1968) preface; hereafter cited as *PG*.

[4]Henri Clouard, *Histoire de la littérature française du symbolisme a nos jours* (Paris: Albin Michel, 1949) 1:465.

Nor was Jacques Maritain alone in having been crucially marked by Bloy. The name of Léon Bloy appears by rights at the head of that genealogy of artists and thinkers we have come to call the "Catholic literary renascence" of the twentieth century. Thomas Merton, for one, writing from his Trappist woods in Kentucky in 1961, on the occasion of having been sent a book of memoirs by the old Pierre van der Meer, now a Benedictine in Holland, draws a rapid sketch of a remarkable group of people: "Resonances: here is a good choir: van der Meer de Walcheren, Bloy, Green, Chagall, Satie . . . variety and unity . . . Raïssa does most of the singing. . . . Knowing how much I owe to the friendship of the Maritains, how much I owe also to Bloy's books (in those days at Columbia when Raïssa Maritain and I were the only people using Bloy's volumes in the library), I feel perhaps part of the same spiritual family of Bloy, one of his 'converts'. . . . Reading this book in the shadows and cool breezes of the woodshed, I find the place full, once again, of French angels."[5] And again, in the *Seven Storey Mountain*, Merton saw in Bloy an idealized form of his own father's search for spiritual poverty, and of his hatred of naturalism and worldly values.[6]

But Merton is not the only mid-century American conscious of his debt to the nineteenth-century Frenchman who died in 1917. When Flannery O'Connor writes to Cecil Dawkins in 1957, fully sympathetic with Dawkins's repulsion at the "Jansenistic-Mechanical" impression made on him by many Catholics, she says these "don't really have faith but a kind of false certainty. They operate by the slide rule and the Church for them is not the body of Christ but the poor man's insurance system. It's never hard for them to believe because actually they never think about it." And immediately she names the great French Catholic novelists as having helped her to make this distinction between the church as a body of Christ and as spiritual security club and to isolate the question of essential Christianity versus narcotic religious practice. At the head of O'Connor's list there is, naturally, the name of Léon Bloy.[7]

Another close friend of the Maritains, the novelist Julien Green, makes the following entry in his journal during his American exile in 1941, at a moment when he is rereading Bloy's *Mon journal:* "The echo of such a voice makes endless repercussions down the years. None of us who have read Bloy and learned to love him know the extent of what we owe him. . . . He is [still] the bearer of an im-

[5]Thomas Merton, *Conjectures of a Guilty Bystander* (Garden City NY: Doubleday, 1966) 170, 165-66.

[6]Thomas Merton, *The Seven Storey Mountain* (New York: Harcourt, Brace, 1948) 54-55.

[7]Flannery O'Connor, *The Habit of Being: Letters*, ed. Sally Fitzgerald (New York: Farrar, Straus and Giroux, 1978) 230-31.

mense message" (10 Nov. 1941).[8] Anyone familiar with Green's writings knows that his *Pamphlet contre les catholiques de France* is pure Bloy.

Surely the most striking instance of the decisive effect Bloy had on so many, however, is Georges Bernanos's description of his "rolling on the grass on the banks of the Seine" on first reading Bloy during a convalescence in 1917. This vehement bodily reaction at discovering Bloy was accompanied by "literal tears of rage." It was a real spiritual and physical paroxysm mingling joy at finding a kindred spirit with incandescent anger at the way Justice is mocked by the world.[9]

From just these texts—from Merton's French angels and Raïssa's singing to O'Connor's ecclesiology and Bernanos's rage—there already emerges here a rich network of fascinating themes and associations: a sense of urgency of vocation and communality of endeavor, a sense of belonging to a fellowship of mind and heart transcending time and place, a family resemblance uniting vastly diverse individualists, and a joy full of gratitude at having discovered, though Léon Bloy, a depth where Christian faith has a face because its splendor and its fire have been seen to shine on the face of friends. The words of the hugely influential American monk and of the three great novelists especially bear witness to an astonishing fact: that Léon Bloy, barely recognized as having any place at all in literature by the lords of the literary establishment of his day, should evoke such a testimony of spiritual debt from Christian thinkers and writers of the first order half a century after his death.

Particularly since World War II the reputation of Bloy as a critic of bourgeois values, as a writer of great originality, and especially as a prophet of authentic Christianity, has not ceased to grow.[10] His only analogue in this respect in the

---

[8]Julien Green, *Oeuvres complètes,* ed. Jacques Petit (Paris: Gallimard-Pleiade, 1975) 4:625.

[9]Georges Bernanos, *Correspondance inédite*, ed. Albert Béguin and Jean Murray, O.P. (Paris: Plon, 1971) 1:537.

[10]The standard histories of French literature in the twenties hardly mention Bloy at all. There is no reference in the work of the famous *normalien* Gustave Lanson, *Histoire illustrée de la littérature française* (Paris: Hachette, 1923). In the work of Joseph Bédier and Paul Hazard, *Histoire de la littérature française illustrée* (Paris: Librairie Larousse, 1924) 2:296, we find Bloy listed in the section entitled "Matérialisme et pessimisme," and he is defined in one sentence fragment: "Polémiste ardent, écrivain singulier, qui unit la truculence au catholicisme le plus exalté." In the thirties even the standard Catholic attitude toward Bloy is most unsympathetic. A history of modern French Catholic literature, edited by Henri Bremond, *Manual de la littérature catholique en France de 1870 à nos jours* (Paris: Editions Spes, 1939) 283, makes the following judgment: "Insultant ceux qui l'aidaient à vivre et auraient voulu lui être utiles, il a épuisé ses forces a une oeuvre sonore, qu'il aurait voulu *terrible* et qui demeure *vaine*." (The critic is Armand Praviel.)

last two hundred years is Søren Kierkegaard. That he cannot easily be accommodated by the annals of literature under a special genre or particular school of aesthetics results from his stated purpose of using art as an instrument of spiritual truth, as a lash against injustice, and as a means both of purification and mystical embrace. It is no exaggeration to say that Bloy stands quite alone as the undisputed turning point in modern Catholic literature and piety—as the decisive catalyst in that religious and cultural renewal that abandoned many patterns of nineteenth-century bourgeois Catholicism and shattered the canonical forms and conventions that had long imprisoned the fire of God's Word.

Of all the thinkers and artists who were crucially influenced by the work and presence of Bloy, Jacques Maritain presents us with the most interesting case, precisely because their mediums of expression and temperaments were so different. I will attempt in what follows to sketch something of the story of their re-

---

But the perception of Bloy changes drastically after the Second World War. Pierre de Boisdeffre says the following in his *Une histoire vivante de la littérature d'aujourd'hui (1939-1959)* (Paris: Livre Contemporain, 1959): "Chez ces écrivains résolument engagés dans leur temps et qu'on ne saurait pas plus ranger dans le camp de la réaction que dans celui de la révolution [Bernanos, Saint-Exupéry, Simone Weil], si l'on tient à leur trouver des ancêtres, il ne faut pas les chercher dans la seule tradition antidémocratique . . . , mais du côté de ces 'prophètes' chrétiens que furent Léon Bloy et Péguy" (149). Later Boisdeffre adds: "Léon Bloy et Péguy placèrent leur réflexion au niveau des mystères chrétiens, assumant . . . dans leurs oeuvres la métaphysique du catholicisme. . . . Il ne s'agissait plus pour nos [la nouvelle génération d'écrivains catholiques] de défendre respectueusement la politique et la morale de l'Eglise (comme l'avaient fait ces sociologues de bonne volonté qu'étaient Bourget, Bazin, ou Bordeaux), mais de render accessible au monde moderne l'élan vital du christianisme, d'incarner la tension dramatique de la grâce et du péché" (383-84). Most recently we find astounding tribute paid to Bloy (and a surprising amount of text space allotted him) in the prestigious Pléiade history of French literature: Raymond Queneau, ed., *Histoire de littératures*, vol. 3: *Littératures françaises, connexes et marginales* (Paris: Gallimard, 1978). In this work Gaëtan Picon writes: "La fureur avec laquelle [Bloy] dénonce ses contemporains—ecrivains, journalistes, athées, ou bienpensants—n'est que l'envers d'une foi profonde qui lui permet de tout attendre de Dieu, de vivre dans la certitude de l'Apocalypse rédemptrice. Il est le 'pelerin de l'absolu,' plus encore que l'impitoyable accusateur contre lequel s'est formée une 'conspiration du silence' " (1086). Finally, we read in the same work this fitting judgment by Jacques Vier, which quite counterbalances the silences of Lanson, Bedier, and Hazard, as well as the lack of understanding of the established prewar Catholic manuals: "Ce charpentier équarrit quelques-unes des poutres maîtresses de la littérature de son temps. . . . Sa vie fut un scandale permanent selon le siècle. . . . Il entreprenait par l'exhortation orale et le sarcasme écrit une réforme du clergé qui est bien la plus singulière prétention éclose dans la cervelle d'un laïque" (1212).

lationship, highlighting not only the influence of Bloy on Maritain's ideas, but especially the more hidden, intimately human nature of their association, because above all they were *friends in Christ*. Perhaps the most significant result of my reflections on this relationship is that, for the Christian, the specific profession and the specific medium of expression and the specific temperament are always subordinate to the common work of the Gospel. It was not without great scandal to literary and religious sensibilities when Léon Bloy, this "sweeper of the literary horse stables," developed a unique style that dared to introduce the burning and muddy prayer of Saint John the Baptist into the carpeted salons of naturalist and symbolist coteries. Nor was it without offense to "pure" philosophers that Jacques Maritain spent a lifetime writing and speaking a philosophical idiom that is as affective as it is speculative, as full of intuition as of rationality, and as centered ultimately on the beauty and lovableness of the Divine Person as it is eager to understand how the intellectual faculties of man apprehend the ontological structures of reality.

Jacques says of Bloy that "he hated the abjectness of our times just as much as our times hated his thirst for the absolute,"[11] and it is this adversarial state of affairs that explains the necessarily polemical tone of so much of Bloy's writing: he was writing, not from the cloister, but from the marketplace and the café. Like a sleek siren, the age had lulled Bloy's contemporaries into an ominous slumber, into demonic conventionalisms of every sort that are an affront to the holiness of God and to the destiny he intends for his creatures. The disappearance of transcendence produced in society the bourgeois; in religion the *bien-pensant;* in art the one-dimensional naturalist and the decadent symbolist. Therefore, both the artist and the philosopher, if they are Christians, have to break all the classical molds, turn new ground over to go back to the primitive foundations of image and thought (hence Bloy's "Gargantuan" primitivism and scatological symbolism) and take their stance outside the established genres. For this reason, neither Bloy nor Maritain hesitates to use the digression, for instance, as an integral part of his style: exasperating to the stylistic purist and to the hurried, the authors' digressions, references to personal experience, spontaneous expressions of gratitude, and so on, permanently point to their preoccupation with a goal outside of the work itself. This goal is always the person, whether human or divine. The primacy of person shatters every preconceived stylistic mold.

II

But who was Léon Bloy? What in his history and character accounts for the electric effect he had on everyone who met him or read him, an effect that to some

---

[11]Jacques Maritain, *Approches sans entraves* (Paris: Fayard, 1973) 33; hereafter cited as *AE.*

appeared as a long-awaited deliverance, to others (such as Jacques's mother, Geneviève Favre) as the fateful charm of a sorcerer? Nothing can tell us more about Bloy, the interior Léon Bloy, than one of his own texts. I have selected a passage from *Mon journal* (1904), one of the books that led Jacques and Raïssa to seek out the old Bloy in his poor quarters up in Montmartre, under the shadow of the Sacré-Coeur. This text must have been particularly impressive to them. Raïssa includes it in her thick anthology of her godfather's writings, perhaps her chief literary accomplishment during the American exile and still the essential book introducing Bloy to English speakers. And as early as 1912 Jacques quoted it as the conclusion of his article, "The Secret of Léon Bloy":

> At bottom what should you do to avoid being an idiot or a swine? Merely this: you should do something great, you should lay aside all the foolishness of a more or less long existence, you should become resigned to the fact you will seem ridiculous to a race of janitors and bureaucrats if you are to enter the service of Splendor. Then you will know what it means to be the friend of God.
>
> The *Friend of God!* I am on the verge of tears when I think of it. No longer do you know on what block to lay your head, no longer do you know where you are, where you should go. You would like to tear out your heart, so hotly does it burn, and you cannot look upon a creature without trembling with love. You would like to drag yourself on your knees from church to church, with rotten fish strung from your neck, as said the sublime Angela of Foligno. And when you leave these churches after speaking to God as a lover speaks to his beloved, you appear like those poorly designed and poorly painted figures on the Way of the Cross, who walk and gesticulate full of pity, against a background of gold. All the thoughts that had been pent up unknown within you, in the caverns of your heart, run out in tumult suddenly like virgins who are mutilated, blind, starving, nude and sobbing. Ah! Surely at such moments the most horrendous of all martyrdoms would be embraced, and with what rapture. [12]

Such a passage distills for us the essence of Léon Bloy. All of him is here: the forceful rhetoric, perhaps a bit bombastic; the vehemence of emotion; the nobility and heroism of spirit; both his tender love for creation and his contempt for mediocrity; the importance of the religious crisis as breakthrough to joyful self-sacrifice and self-knowledge; the ridiculous and almost abortive figure a believer must necessarily cut in the eyes of the world. Through all this, however, both the fury and the lyricism are vehicles of *love*. What gives the passage, and all his works, a fundamental unity is this passionate love of God, what Jacques would later call *amour fou* (mad, frenzied love) when speaking of the vow of con-

---

[12]Léon Bloy, *Oeuvres de Léon Bloy* (Paris: Mercure de France, 1956) 11:313-14; hereafter cited as *LB*.

tinence he and Raïssa had made early on in their life together: this vow was the particular "block," we might say, on which the Maritains laid their head, for the love of God. In this passage Bloy introduces us with appropriate shock tactics into his all-consuming romance with God as absolute lover, and the authenticity and realism of this love is surely the single most important reason for the attraction he exerted on so many "blind and starving" souls lost in the garishly decorated desert we call the *fin de siècle*.

That as norm for Christian behavior Bloy should take the ecstatic fish-strung mysticism of the thirteenth-century lay Franciscan widow and not the reasonable and moralized Catholicism of the spiritual manuals of Saint Sulpice: this the religious establishment of the day could not bear, for here Christianity was admissible mostly in the form of a "picturesque Catholicism," that is, as the aesthetic construct of a Huysmans or the educational social force proposed by a Paul Bourget, which is to say the church as a teacher of manners and culture. In one loud lament, full of both joy and woe, this "undertaker of demolitions" proclaims from the housetops that the God of Christians has to be *at least* as all-consuming, absolute, inebriating, as the God of Abraham, Buddha, and Al-Hallaj; that the Christian religion, if it is to remain authentic *religion*, cannot fall below the level of the other great visions of God as the supreme Source and End. Indeed, if Christianity has anything unique to offer, it must be that the Gospel, far from backing away from God's burning transcendence, rather draws man right into its furnace in union with the incarnate Word. The shabby figures on Bloy's Way of the Cross, sick with pity and frenzy at the Passion of God *against a background of gold:* such is the metaphysical situation of the Christian who has been sucked by a whirlwind of transforming love into the drama of redemption—the drama of the crucifixion, that is, which is the form God's omnipotence and transcendence take in Christ Jesus. The gold of divinity is the light that sheds its splendor over the distorted features of the Crucified. The Christian, for Bloy, should be drunk with adoration at such an outpouring of God's being and substance, which is why I sometimes think of Léon Bloy as a Hasid dancing for joyful woe at the foot of the cross.

Léon Bloy was born in Périgueux in 1846, the son of one of those typical nineteenth-century French households that symbolize at the domestic level the uneasy truce negotiated between the embattled post-Revolution church and the secularized French state. His father was an employee of the Department of Bridges and Roads, and Monsieur Bloy completely identified himself—almost "mystically," we should say—with the triumphant modernity of his occupation: he was an austere anticlerical who looked on the hocus-pocus of religion as beneath the dignity of a free man, and he believed in a life of service to humanity through progress. Léon's mother, intensely religious by nature, seems to have been a great deal more than a stereotypical *dame pieuse*, if we are to judge from what Madame

Bloy wrote her son in 1866, at the height of Léon's revolt against the pieties of *both* parents: "You are of the small number of people to whom God communicates his love only once they have made an act of humility," and "your heart needs a center it will never find on earth" (*AE* 34-35). The young Bloy moves through a succession of office jobs in Paris and serves as an irregular in the War of 1870. He works as a bookkeeper for the railways and later as a journalist, but the violence of his invectives soon makes him walk the streets. We should carefully note here that this future reformer of Christian art comes from the pedestrian ranks of the unemployed and not from the academy or the seminary.

The exact manner and dates of his definitive return to the faith of his baptism are unfortunately obscure: most of the correspondence of this period is still unedited. But we do know that his drastic about-face in attitude to the church came through the mediation of Jules Barbey d'Aurevilly in the years 1868-1869. With his traditionalist Catholicism, Barbey combined the lifestyle of a contemptuous dandy in the manner of Baudelaire, strutting about Paris covered with lace and writing stories that exploited every element of the fantastic and even the diabolical. Important here is the crucial effect on Bloy of a rebellious and extravagant form of religious faith expressed through the preposterous word and gesture. In Barbey's high-flown disdain for the mediocre, the so-called divine admittedly hovered somewhere between the shockingly grotesque and the authentically supernatural. Bloy would soon leave Barbey behind as he steadily descended to greater depths in his relationship with God; but he would ever be grateful to his master for having taught him that dandyism, purified by humility, can flower as uncompromising heroism, and that the narcissistic word of contempt can be tempered into a tool of justice, once God's honor and not one's own is being defended.

In 1877 Bloy meets the Abbé Tardif de Moidrey, who teaches him to read Scripture as the personal life story of the Holy Trinity contained in a treasure house of symbols that the believer deciphers as a foretaste of the eucharistic nourishment, an approach devastating to the exegetical practice of the day, which primly kept to the moral and edifying sense. An excellent example of such exegesis, and one to which Jacques Maritain refers with admiration, is Bloy's reading of the story of the demoniac in the Gospel. The possessed man who falls now into the water and now into the fire is none other than the incarnate Word himself, who, having assumed a human nature crazed by sin, must fall with it now into the fire of the Spirit and now into the water of the Father so as to have it healed.[13] Such exegesis, for both its visionary daring and its sound doctrinal basis, easily ranks with the best of Origen and Augustine. In anticipation of the

---

[13]Jacques Maritain, *Notebooks*, trans. Joseph Evans (Albany: Magi Books, 1984) 55; herafter cited as *N*.

biblical renewal of our century, Léon Bloy from this time on made the continual rumination on Scripture an extension of his daily communion, a practice that in itself anticipated the exhortations of Pius X to full and frequent particiation in the liturgy by the laity. The method of intense symbolic interpretation that he had learned from Tardif de Moidrey would later be applied by Bloy to the interpretation of history as well, which he considered no less a work of the divine Artist than was Scripture. One of Bloy's favorite axioms was that "everything that happens is adorable," if man but find within the events of his private history and of the public history of the world the hidden involvement of God with man, the "divine conspiracy" into which God invites the believer.

This same year of 1877 brought Bloy into contact with Anne-Marie Roulé, and their relationship has something both of the sublime and the grotesque. She was a poor prostitute whom he converted, and she soon outdid him in mystical zeal. Her innate psychic imbalance finally pushed her religious experiences over the bounds of sanity, and Bloy had to commit her to an asylum. He would call this the great catastrophe of his life, because he loved Anne-Marie intensely and tragically, and he insisted that it was she who effected in him the transition from a Catholic in the revolted style of a Barbey d'Aurevilly to one living a life of habitual prayer centered on the indwelling presence of God. Also in this fateful year, he fled for some weeks to the Grande Trappe at Soligny in an attempt to probe a monastic vocation. He was in fact fleeing from the very sensual love he felt for Anne-Marie and that he could not harmonize with their spiritual relationship. It was in this monastic sojourn, moreover, that his vocation as permanent layman was definitively confirmed.

In 1890 he married Jeanne Molbech, the daughter of a Danish poet and also one of his converts. They had four children, two boys who died in infancy, probably of malnutrition conditioned by their poverty, and two girls who lived to adulthood and were the great consolation of his life.

Aside from the years 1882-1890, when he enjoyed some celebrity as a lampoonist for the *Chat noir*, Bloy's life was quite uneventful externally. Indeed, it would be no exaggeration to say that *suffering* was the only trade he rose to ply every morning, the sole adventure of his existence. His writings, which fill fourteen volumes in the complete edition of the *Mercure de France,* are quite inseparable from the poverty and daily anguish he and his family experienced for many long years. A typical journal entry reads: "January 6, 1903. Epiphany. At 7 in the evening we were in agony. Jeanne and the children were suffering of HUNGER, and so I ran to the charcutier's, who again agreed to give me a few morsels on credit. We have never been so low" (*LB* 12:144). Always, however, he is able to see such unbearable suffering and humiliation as a visitation from God inviting him and his family to share in Christ's Passion, for the sake of both the known and the unknown souls who may urgently need such a capital of sorrow. He writes:

"Jesus passes his cross back and forth from his shoulders to ours and from ours to his, and so one is always weeping, either from pain or from compassion" (*LB* 12:154). And once, in a rare use of analytical idiom, he says of his hero Marchenoir (the man who "walks in darkness"), his fictional self: "Few people have understood that Marchenoir is in *philosophical* despair and not in *theological* despair. In other words, he expects nothing from man, but he expects EVERYTHING from God" (*LB* 12:186).

The forty years, then, between 1877 and 1917, are almost literally spent in three eminently contemplative activities of praying, writing, and "suffering," which in the concrete form it took in Bloy's life meant deciphering agonically, from moment to moment, the work of God in Scripture, history, and his own life. Perhaps the most lucid summary of the meaning of Léon Bloy's life is offered us by his godson, when Jacques speaks of the "mystery of an incomparably painful destiny, where the abyss of God's heart and the abyss of the heart of man never ceased calling out to one another, a destiny whose generosity bears fruit for a long time to come" (*OC* 5:1081-82).

III

The arrival of a letter from Jacques and Raïssa Maritain to Léon Bloy on 20 June 1905 signals the beginning of a deep and constant joy in the life of both the Bloys and the Maritains. Bloy writes in his journal: "They soon became for me like neighbors in Paradise" (*LB* 12:263). And these are his first impressions of the young couple: "The young man is one of these idealists who do not know God but who let themselves be dragged by the hair or by the feet up the staircase leading to the Light. . . . The young woman is a very charming and frail being in which there dwells a soul capable of making the oak trees kneel" (*LB* 12:267). From 1905 to Bloy's death in 1917 the Bloys and the Maritains see each other very frequently, often along with other young men and women. The principal names, besides the Maritains, are Pierre and Christine van der Meer, Georges Auric the composer, Georges Rouault the painter, and Pierre Termier the geologist (who, with Bloy, believed that the Garden of Eden was the lost city of Atlantis).

What was it that attracted the Maritains to Bloy? Certainly, at first, it was the power of his writing. They had read *The Woman Who Was Poor* and some of his *Journal*. But Raïssa keenly notes that after that first dazzling reading of Bloy and its salutary awakening effect, one becomes aware of certain mannerisms that could seriously mar the work of art if it were not for the great religious genius that sustains it. Thus Raïssa distinguishes between the stylistic surface of Bloy's writing and what she calls the "essential ontological value" of his works. [14] I think this means that through the work they were attracted to the man, and in this man they found, in her words, the "constant witness of God (*GA* 397). In Léon Bloy, Jacques, Raïssa, and the others encountered, perhaps for the first time in their lives, a man who lived continually in the presence of God, a man whose sole element was contemplation and who bore all the marks of having wrestled with the Angel.

Bloy appeared to his friends as an extension in their midst of the ongoing drama of redemption. Much as the early Christians viewed their martyrs as living sacraments of the action of God, the friends of Bloy felt privileged in seeing in him a precious reenactment of the Passion of Christ. Bloy brought others to God more by the visible shape of his life than by the persuasiveness of his words. Everywhere we read of the peace that reigned at the Bloys' despite the suffering and the poverty. After spending an afternoon there, Jacques writes in his journal: "Delicious meal at the Bloys'. They now have only 3 francs, but the peace and the fragrances of Paradise inhabit their home" (*N* 47, 5 June 1908). At the Bloys', philosophy was brought in from the cold and seated at a banquet of love. And Pierre van der Meer describes how such afternoons were spent in speaking of the joy of being a friend of God. "Léon would open his big eyes and look out over his friends and say, 'We have become like the Christians of the catacombs; see how we love one another.' "[15]

Jacques, Raïssa, and her sister, Véra Oumançoff, were baptized, with Léon Bloy as their common godfather, less than a year after having met with him. Obviously the speed of the conversions may be attributed to the superior power of lived witness over argumentation. Before they discovered Henri Bergson, Jacques and Raïssa had been nothing if not argumentative and rationalistic, and this path of sheer logical demonstration had led them to despair. But what Jacques and Raïssa could not find even in Bergson's intuitionism, and did find in Bloy's Christian faith, was the living Logos, with all the resonances this word carries for an Origen of Alexandria. Bloy mediated to them not primarily a philosophical principle of spiritual order but a living utterance continually so taken into men's hearts by the Lover of Mankind. Bergson's teachings remained too abstract, too impersonal, and above all too subjective, despite their undeniable merit of having broken through the shackles of contemporary philosophical conventions, which restricted "wisdom" to the ability to measure the data of a historical, sociological, or psychological order and perhaps to combine with this knowledge the living of a decent life. But with Bergson everything hinges on the

---

[14]Raïssa Maritain, *Les grandes amitiés* (Paris: Desclée de Brouwer, 1949) 399; hereafter cited as *GA*.

[15]Van der Meer De Walcheren, *Dieu*, 15.

process, the *élan vital*, the operation of the subject: the object of intuition is still faceless and impersonal, wholly inadequate to satisfy the longing of the human intellect and heart for fullness of knowledge and love. The crucified Logos that was the only absolute in Bloy's life overwhelmingly satisfied this double longing.

To say this means that, by coming into contact with someone steeped in the Christian mystery, Jacques and Raïssa experienced the human presence of God. While many associations of like-minded persons, united on the basis of common ideology, express their convictions by founding schools of thought and publishing manifestos, the converts of Léon Bloy relate to him first of all as friends and not as disciples to a master or as followers to a founder. Despite the great difference of age between them, the Maritains and the Bloys used the familiar *tu* in addressing one another, a rarity that points to equality and intimacy.[16] The two families, upon meeting, immediately plunge into one another's lives with tenderness and mutual responsibility, and if from Léon, Jacques and Raïssa learn stability in faith and ardent love of God, from them he derives immense joy and consolation, and the confirmation of his conviction that contemporary youth was seeking fulfillment ultimately through spirituality and not primarily through scientific and social progress. Now and then we begin hearing in Bloy's words a new playfulness of tone: "How I long to take you and embrace you with my old-lion's paws, my dear godchildren!" And we must admire the ease with which Bloy perfectly blends these new human relationships with his intense spiritual life: "I can hardly express what we feel for one another," he writes in November 1906, shortly after the Maritains' baptism. "This period is for us, from the point of view of *friendship,* what the *Acts of the Apostles* are for Christianity" (*GA* 133).

For the first time in his life, and despite his horror of vacation resorts, where "pleasure is procured with riches," Léon lets himself be persuaded to travel for relaxation. The Bloys, the Maritains, and the van der Meers are often together for weeks at a time either at Bourg-la-Reine (the Bloys' home near Paris), at Bures (at the van der Meers'), or at Saint Piat, near Chartres, where they rent a dilapidated farmhouse. Led by Léon, they would often walk together to the great cathedral for early mass in the crypt. Pierre van der Meer refers to Jacques, Léon, and himself as a "remarkable trio" that never ran out of conversation.[17] This *eclesiola,* or "miniature church," shared all the ordinary concerns of everyday life and all the extraordinary concerns of the life of the soul, and only in this context do they "do philosophy" and write.

From among the many episodes that could be cited to illustrate the friendship of Jacques and Léon, perhaps we are most deeply moved by the young phi-

---

[16]Raïssa Maritain, *Journal de Raïssa,* presented by Jacques Maritain (Paris: Desclée de Brouwer, 1963) 250; hereafter cited as *JR.*

[17]Van der Meer De Walcheren, *Dieu,* 28-29.

losopher's efforts to alleviate the Bloys' poverty, particularly the occasion when he pawns his microscope and gets twenty instead of the expected fifty francs for it. There is also the somber occasion when Jacques accompanies Léon to pawn an item in order to make a payment to the cemetery, in an attempt to keep the body of his little son from being transferred to the common grave. But there are lighter moments as well, like the rumbling sortie the two friends make when urgently summoned by a Protestant who wants to convert and is opposed by family and friends. They rush to his house to find it full of alarmed pastors and a very angry wife.

Léon, for his part, shows great solicitude when Raïssa falls gravely ill, and he naively insists on a certain diet as a sure cure. He corresponds with the Maritains continually during their sojourn in Heidelberg and writes some of his most tender lines in his dedications of his books to them.

When, shortly before Bloy's death in 1917, Raïssa enters in her journal that "men do not communicate among themselves unless they go through *being* or one of its qualities" (*CA* 47), I believe she is making a categorical statement that is a reflection not so much on any philosophical doctrine as on the experience of faith lived in the circle around Bloy. Friendship at this level is the converging of individuals in the full reality of God. And I would suggest that the famous "Sundays at Meudon" at the Maritains' home in the twenties and thirties are but a more organized and more formally intellectual continuation of what the Maritains had experienced more spontaneously at Montmartre and Bourg-la-Reine with the Bloys. What both gatherings have in common is the unabashed communal search for God by every means available—whether philosophy, art, or prayer. Rather than aiming at any particular ideological platform, this common pursuit sought the most direct path for individual and communal union with God. It is interesting to compare with the statements by Jacques and Pierre already quoted, describing an afternoon at the Bloys', this passage in a letter of 1963 to Jacques from Olivier Lacombe, who frequented the Maritain home in the thirties: "Everyone left your home moved to the bottom of his soul for having been accepted and recognized personally, with a solicitous friendship which went straight to the center of one's being" (*GA* 377).

IV

Friendship in the absolute: if Jacques Maritain clung with such fidelity and affection to Léon Bloy throughout his life it was because Bloy had "begotten him in the faith" by introducing him to a wholly unexpected way of perceiving the truth. "You are *seeking*, you say," Léon writes to his future godson with gentle irony shortly after their first meeting. And he continues: "O professor of philosophy, O Cartesian! You believe, with Malebranche, that truth is something *one seeks!* . . . I declare that I never sought or found anything, unless one wishes to describe as a discovery the fact of tripping blindly over a threshold and being thrown flat on one's stomach into The House of Light."[18] This violent reversal of the conventional coordinates of perception, this being shattered in one's learned ignorance by an overpowering force irrupting from outside one's expectations, this deliverance from a doomed reliance on one's own natural lights: such was the healing revolution Léon Bloy brought about in his godchildren. Through Bloy and his family the Maritains experienced in the concrete the reason why the truth of Christianity is the *non plus ultra:* in the church, the ontological absolute takes on form as a "House of Light" into which God pushes one with the wise violence of his love. The saint is he who has let himself be overpowered by God. In his most famous aphorism Léon Bloy said that "the only sadness is not being a saint," and with this the philosopher's quest is burst open from within because, paradoxically, the philosopher who had set out to seek the truth "finds it" only when *Truth finds him.*

The whole secret of Léon Bloy, and the incredible transformation it effected in the souls of those who exposed themselves to it with docility, is the realization that the very heart of the Christian religion consists of entering into a "conspiracy" with God: beyond all the moralizing and aestheticizing fashions of the day, Bloy demonstrated that to be a Christian meant to let oneself be done over by God in the image of Jesus Christ. Man obeys God when he "conspires" with him for his own salvation and that of the world, by allowing God to achieve the terrible work of ontological transformation in his creature—not in heaven, but already here, in the midst of a world of politicians, littérateurs, landowners, and, yes, parish priests, who are often more in love with rank and promotion than with the Christ who has anointed their hands. Jacques Maritain learned from Bloy not only that God—Truth with a Face—pulls his chosen ones up by the hair against all expectation but that the fullness of the divine life exists as a continual flow of grace communicating itself to the saints both on earth and beyond.

On the last page of *The Peasant of the Garonne* Jacques introduces Bloy, as he does so often in the middle of a theological discussion. Here the philosopher wants to propose one of Bloy's favorite and most original themes, namely, that "in reference to men, and not only to God, the communion of saints unites in charity the human members of the Church through a mysterious interdependence . . . and hence constitutes the *body* of the Church, its visible aspect" (*PG* 276). "Interdependence" is here a more neutral term for Bloy's bolder "reversibility," which makes both the merits and the sins of all to be common spiritual property, mysteriously circulating and affecting all the members of the Body throughout space and time, both for joy and for sorrow.

---

[18]Léon Bloy, *Pilgrim of the Absolute,* ed. Raïssa Maritain, trans. John Coleman and Harry Lorin Binsee (New York: Pantheon Books, 1947) 278.

To an age, however, that largely gives the lie not only to the primacy but to the very existence of the supernatural, Jacques says in the *Peasant* that a "burning and purified faith, a passion for the absolute, a whole-hearted longing for the perfection of charity" will be found in "tiny flocks"—the communion of saints in the visible concrete, the *ecclesiola* as he and Raïssa had experienced it at the Bloys' in 1905. And he has not forgotten it sixty years later (*PG* 5). At the end of his life Jacques Maritain echoes his godfather, affirming that he has toiled with writing all his life long, and obstinately, because it had been a task entrusted to him by God, not to develop and systematize a philosophical and theological program of any sort, but in order to be an "imprudent talker" who stammers out truths that are not welcome for the benefit of a small number of known and unknown friends who might listen.[19]

The decisive influence of Bloy on Jacques, on a subject such as the communion of saints, becomes apparent first because we must marvel at the degree to which Jacques was never—and by choice—a "pure philosopher." He everywhere puts the existential before the abstract, and greatly delights in crossing and recrossing the hypothetical borderline between philosophy and theology. Who would have guessed that, beginning with the interiorism and subjective vitalism of Henri Bergson, he would end his life talking more and more about a *body* of believers with its heart in heaven and its feet on earth? But his debt to Bloy extends even to the manner in which he develops his understanding of the intercommunion of the redeemed. For both of them, *suffering* is the primary activity engaged in by the saints as lovers of God for so long as the work of redemption remains incomplete; and this not because of some hankering after Baroque dolorism but because they have clear insight into the necessary bond of identity uniting the believer to the Savior and his redemptive work.

But their meditation on suffering, beginning with the existential evidence gleaned from the lives of the saints, does not stop at the Passion of Christ. If Jesus suffered, Bloy would say, it was not ultimately becauese he was man but because he was God. In Christ Jesus not only the man but God suffered. Bloy did not hesitate to let his own experience of God prolong that of the great mystics, and it was from these, and not from theologians, that he came to see and feel in his flesh that, in the words of Pascal, "Jesus *is* in agony until the end of time."

Decisive for Bloy in this regard was the apparition of the Blessed Virgin to Mélanie Calvat in 1846, the year of his own birth. That this poor shepherdess saw the immaculate Queen of Heaven, "Beatitude itself," weeping within the splendor of the beatific vision for the sins of her Son's people: this was to Bloy a

---

[19]Jacques Maritain to Julien Green, in their *Une grande amitié: Correspondance (1926-1972)*, ed. J.-P. Piriou (Paris: Plon, 1979) 108. See also *PG* 232-33.

living revelation congruous with the deepest scriptural doctrine of Saint John and Saint Paul. Had not Jesus, after all, spoken of his crucifixion as a "glorification"? As a young philosopher Jacques Maritain devoted two years of his life to writing a huge tome on the apparition at La Salette, a subject of such urgency to him that he went to speak to Benedict XV about it.

Nor was this part of the fling with illuminism we are willing to grant a recent convert, for again toward the end of his life, in 1968, he delivers a talk to the Little Brothers of Jesus in which he says that, if it is human virtue to suffer because of the evil and loss we see in one we love, this suffering is but a reflection of an awesome mystery, a *passionis affectus* that exists exemplarily in God himself and that Scripture calls the *viscera misericordiae Dei:* and in this phrase from the Benedictus the very Hebraic "bowels of God's compassion" is not to be taken as a metaphor but as a literal reality; God's inner being *does* quiver and go out with tenderness to his fallen creature. Jacques goes on to probe with patient philosophical questioning how the attribution to God of suffering may be understood. But as the last word, and as the source for his daring speculation, he here quotes his godfather's dictum: *"Tous les viols imaginables de ce qu'on est convenu d'appeler la Raison peuvent être acceptés d'un Dieu qui soffre"* (All imaginable ravishments of what we have agreed to call Reason are acceptable if they come from a God that suffers [*AE* 307-308]).

I think Jacques saw in this more than just another typical hyperbole of Bloy's. What Bloy calls the "ravishments" (*viols*) of reason are not only "violations" of its normal functioning but also the forceful "fertilization" by God of a too-proper, virginal reason who furtively resists the advances of even the Lord in the name of philosophical consistency. What deep satisfaction they would have both derived from knowing that, in pursuing such an unusual contemplation on the nature of God, they are joining company with a giant among the Fathers of the church, one who could write the following:

> The Father himself and the God of the whole universe is "longsuffering, full of mercy and pity" (Ps. 86:15). Must he not then, in some sense, be exposed to suffering? . . . The Father himself is not impassible; . . . he shows in some sort the passion of love, and is exposed to what he cannot be exposed to in respect of his greatness. . . . As our good actions and our progress in virtue produce gladness and rejoicing for God and the angels, so I feel does our evil way of life bring about lamentation and mourning not only on earth but also in heaven; and it may well be that men's sins afflict with grief even God himself. . . . It is the cry of God lamenting over mankind, when the prophet says: "Woe is me, for I am like one who gathers stubble in the harvest" (Mic. 7:1, 70).

It is the most Greek of all the Fathers, Origen—according to Harnack, one of those who distorted the purity of the Gospel with Hellenistic categories—who can provide such commentaries for Ezekiel and Numbers from this very non-philosophical perspective at the feet of the crucified God;[20] and, like him, neither do Léon Bloy and Jacques Maritain hesitate to violate the Aristotelian categories, which do not admit the conjunction of suffering and beatitude—to violate them, but only on the basis of the revelation of God's nature manifested in the drama of Christ's Passion.

Further influences of Léon Bloy on the thought of Jacques Maritain remain to be explored in detail. This example of the communion of saints, leading to a bold meditation on the suffering of God, offers but one instance of Bloy's forceful and original impact. There is also much significance in the fact that, with the group around Bloy, we are dealing with a markedly *lay* movement within the church, the category of Christians Jacques good-humoredly calls the *genus laicorum* (*PG* 173). Nor has anyone probed the extent to which Bloy's lifelong invectives against bourgeois Christianity shaped Jacques's social thought, especially in *Integral Humanism*. Another fertile area of inquiry would be the manner in which Bloy demolished the aesthetic *apologetics* for Christianity rooted in Chateaubriand (the orderly beauty of Christian dogma and tradition) and instead helped develop a truly aesthetic *theology*.[21]

Although this list of themes for research could be greatly extended, I will conclude with three brief texts without comment, which will allow Jacques and Léon to sketch a quick portrait of one another and of this generation of God-seekers. The first text is from Bloy:

> October 17, 1912. Read in the *Revue Thomiste* an article by my godson Jacques Maritain: "Les deux bergsonismes." It's known I have little taste for philosophy, in my eyes the most tiresome way of wasting the precious time of life, and its Hyrcanian patois discourages me. But, with Jacques, all this changes singularly. I knew this beloved godson of mine to be superior, and in so many ways! But I didn't expect such a strong arm to come out from under the tattered rags of philosophy. An athlete's arm and the high voice of a lamenter. I felt something like a wave of painful poetry over me, a powerful wave emerging from the depths and coming from far away. (*LB* 13:319)

The other two texts are from Jacques, the first from a conference given at Dax on the Bay of Biscay in 1968 and entitled "En hommage à notre cher parrain Léon Bloy":

> I remember the sweetness and tenderness of this terrible man, the marvelous hos-

---

[20]Henry Bettenson, ed. and trans., *The Early Christian Fathers* (Oxford: Oxford University Press, 1956) 186-87.

[21]Hans Urs von Balthasar, *Herrlichkeit: Eine theologische Ästhetik* (Einsiedeln, Switzerland: Johannes, 1961) 1:91.

pitality of his poor family, in whose home the wings of miracle seemed to beat noiselessly. That house on Montmartre, in the rue Chevalier de la Bare, a shelter for so much suffering, was also a place where dwelt a supernatural peace. (*AE* 41)

The final text is taken from Jacques's foreword to Raïssa's *Journal:*

To be sure, we founded and established nothing: in the end, we see everything vanishing into smoke. But the reward for our trouble is that something better now exists in the world—this marvel of the friendships which God has brought about [*fratres in eremo!*], and the pure fidelities he has inspired and which are like the mirror of the gratuity and generosity of his own love. (*JR* 13-14)

Addendum: A letter of Georges Bernanos

Jacques Maritain says that Léon Bloy was simultaneously a "terrible" and a "tender" man. No doubt the best commentary on the abrasive and seemingly intrasigent side of Bloy's character is his own statement: "My anger is the effervescence of my pity." Nevertheless, much of Bloy's writing is finally rejected by people who would be sympathetic if it were not for the violence of Bloy's invectives and his continually exasperated tone. By way of a "guide to the use of Léon Bloy," I here reproduce a remarkable letter on the subject of Bloy written by one of his most ardent and yet careful admirers, Georges Bernanos:

La Rade (Toulon)
[April-May 1931]

My very dear M . . . [a woman],
Don't go starting anything foolish with that old Bloy! In the first place, I'm jealous. And then a long experience with prophet friends entitles me to tell you with what attitude one ought to approach such a ravisher of souls. Finally, I'll tell you in a brief how *I* go about it. In any event, I am sure you'll do exactly as you please (which reassures me).
So, as long as the Old Man is quarrelling and hurling invectives from his mountaintop, I leave him to his thunder. I join him more humbly on his descent, when he's run out of words and is intent on unburdening his old and heavy heart to a friend. I probably first kneel next to him for about five minutes in some dark corner of the church at Bourg-la-Reine and then we go to the bistro, where I buy him a glass of white wine (which he loved, as he did billiards). Then he puts his elbows on the table, his big face in his hands (he thought they were aristocratic, but that's bosh), and he expresses to me, and me alone, something of that naive pity, that childlike pity, that unreasonable pity out of which he drew his most firm, most terrible, and also most loving curses. Afterwards, I lend him a hundred *sous*, and he lets me have it because the fruiterer's bill is 20 francs. But the next day we're again friends anyway, in front of another glass of white wine. . . .

There is still too much revolt in you, dear friend. As for me, I'm done with revolts. . . . We must yield to God, dear M . . . ; you must loosen your armor. Better to take it off altogether before some messenger from the Most High, some seraphic blacksmith, blows it to smithereens. . . .

Your unworthy friend,

G. Bernanos[22]

---

[22]Bernanos, *Correspondance* 1:415-16.

PETER REDPATH

Romance of Wisdom:
The Friendship between Jacques Maritain
and Saint Thomas Aquinas

In HIS INTELLECTUAL AUTOBIOGRAPHY, *The Philosopher and Theology*, Etienne Gilson described what he considered to be the day on which one becomes aware of being a Thomist:

> A man becomes aware of being a Thomist on the day he realizes that from then on he will no longer be able to live without the company of St. Thomas Aquinas. He feels in the *Summa Theologiae* as a fish in the sea; away from it he feels out of his element, and cannot go back to it. More deeply, this is what gives the Thomist the joyous feeling that he is free. Essentially a Thomist is a free mind. His freedom does not consist in having neither master nor God but rather in having no master other than God. And indeed God is for man the only bulwark against the tyrannies of other men. God alone delivers from fears and timidities a mind that otherwise would die of starvation in the midst of plenty. Left to itself, it will be unable to choose and will die either from starvation or from indigestion. The happiness of a Thomist is the joy he experiences in feeling free to welcome all truth from whichever side it may come. The perfect expression of this liberty of the Christian man is that of Saint Augustine: *Dilige et quod vis fac: Love and do what you will*. Like charity, faith is a liberator. Incidentally, this is a reason why the Christian should willingly accept being considered as a rather unusual specimen by non-Christian thinkers. [1]

Certainly the day that Gilson described was the sort Jacques Maritain experienced when he first came into contact with the theological writings of Saint

---

[1]Etienne Gilson, *The Philosopher and Theology*, trans. Cecile Gilson (New York: Random House, 1962) 204; hereafter cited as *PT*.

Thomas Aquinas. From that time on there was to begin between Maritain and Aquinas a romance of wisdom that was to last until Maritain's death in 1973. That Maritain had the sort of day described by Gilson is evident from what Maritain himself reports about his first encounter with Saint Thomas.

> It was in 1908 . . . while I was deliberating in the country near Heildelberg whether or not I could harmonize Bergson's critique of the concept and formulas of revealed dogma, that the irreducible conflict between the "conceptual" pronouncements of that theological faith which had recently opened my eyes and the philosophical doctrine to which I had had such a passionate devotion during my student years, and to which I owed my delivery from the idols of materialism, appeared to me as one of those all too certain facts from which the soul—once it begins to admit it—immediately knows that it cannot escape. The effort, obscurely pursued for months, to realize a reconciliation—which was the goal of all my desires—suddenly ended in this undeniable conclusion. I had to choose, and hence to admit that all the philosophical work with which I had busied myself had to be begun anew. . . . At that time I had not as yet become acquainted with Saint Thomas. My philosophical reflection leaned upon the indestructible truth of objects presented by faith in order to restore the natural order of the intelligence to being, and to recognize the ontological bearing of the work of reason. Thenceforth, in affirming to myself, without chicanery or diminution, the authentic value as reality of our human instruments of knowledge, I was already a Thomist without knowing it. When, several months later, I was to meet the *Summa Theologica*, I would erect no obstacle to its luminous flood. [2]

That Maritain's romance with wisdom through friendship with Aquinas lasted until the end of his life is evident from the spirit that pervades his writings from 1910 onward. This friendship and spirit, as he himself noted above, began some time before his exposure to the *Summa* of Saint Thomas. To get some idea of when his "romance" with wisdom began, and how it brought him to friendship with Aquinas, it is necessary to consider Maritain's first exposure to philosophy as a young man at the Lycée Henri IV and at the Sorbonne.

Raïssa Maritain tells us that the quest for wisdom, for metaphysical truth, that she and Jacques shared during their whole adult life was deeply influenced by the experience they underwent through their exposure to the philosophers of the Faculté des Lettres at the Sorbonne and to the philosophers at the Lycée Henri IV. Their teachers, she says, "were philosophers, yet they had in fact lost all hope in philosophy" (*WHB* 67). Even at the young age of sixteen, Jacques Maritain experienced an appetite for metaphysical truth that descended to the very roots

---

[2]Quoted in Raïssa Maritain, *We Have Been Friends Together: The Memoirs of Raïssa Maritain*, trans. Julie Kernan (New York: Longmans, Green, 1945) 198-200; hereafter cited as *WHB*.

of his life, and that was frustrated by his teachers. "Young Jacques," Raïssa states, "would hurl himself in despair on the rug of his room, because to all his questions—*there was no answer*" (*WHB* 67).

Jacques Maritain experienced the same type of frustration at the Sorbonne. While his teachers were "personally men of great merit," whose "learning was broad and deep," while "they were keenly alive to the demands of scientific research," nonetheless, in Raïssa's opinion, the spirit that dominated their philosophical pursuits was not philosophical but was, rather, historical and mathematical:

> [T]hey bent their energies, as to their main task, to the endless analysis of the detail of historical matters, reducing almost to this alone that study of wisdom which their name and their philosophic profession imposed upon them as duty. Their whole learning was in the direction of historical erudition, or toward the mathematical sciences. In none of them did we find rooted a positive theory of knowledge; the conclusions which they believed they could formulate provisionally, under the influence of the rationalistic and idealistic tradition to which they still clung, fell into dust under the influence of positivism and an empiricism which were at once dogmatic and ineffectual. (*WHB* 67)

For them, as Raïssa saw it, history replaced metaphysics as the queen of the sciences and assumed for itself the rights of the genuine metaphysics that they repudiated. Because they unwittingly falsified the subject of history into a model of an exact science and sought to obtain from it the ultimate explanation of life and thought, they made history "so much the more arrogant" (*WHB* 68). By seeking to verify everything by methods of material learning and empiricism these thinkers wound up despairing of truth. As a result, Raïssa says, "the only practical lesson to be had from their conscientious and disinterested instruction was a lesson in integral relativism, intellectual skepticism, and—if one was logical—in moral nihilism" (*WHB* 68).

Jacques Maritain's friendship with wisdom and with Aquinas must be understood within the context of his reaction to the relativism, skepticism, and moral nihilism that were the consequences of the antimetaphysical and reductionistic spirit of his early teachers of philosophy. Indeed, not only must Maritain's romance with wisdom be understood within this context, but the whole of his adult intellectual life, as well as the scope of his contribution to twentieth-century philosophy and theology, can only be appreciated from within it. Philosophers and theologians are not born into an age devoid of intellectual presuppositions, but rather into a time that is dominated by an intellectual spirit in which certain intellectual principles and problems predominate. To understand and appreciate the greatness of a philosopher or a theologian is not simply to understand and appreciate the truth that is within his teaching but to understand

and appreciate the evolution of his teaching as a response and solution to the intellectual spirit and problems of his age.

The intellectual age into which Maritain was born was, and still is, as his wife tells us, one dominated by an antimetaphysical spirit and by historicist, idealistic, and positivist reductionism, that is, an age in which thinkers attempt to view all problems as historically determined facts to be studied from the perspective of methods of reasoning employed in the physical sciences—methods that find their ultimate raison d'être in philosophical rationalism and idealism. It was, and still is, an age that, because of its dominating antimetaphysical spirit, has its own set of problems—relativism, intellectual skepticism, moral nihilism. Jacques Maritain can be completely understood and appreciated only when viewed in the light of his age with its particular spiritual problems and his quest for metaphysical truth.

Maritain's romance with wisdom began before his encounter with Aquinas. It began at the very latest with his early friendship with Raïssa at the Lycée Henri IV. As with most romances, Maritain's metaphysical romance had its ups and downs. The early part of the romance was quite rocky. It was, by and large, one of anguish, and, as Raïssa notes, "this metaphysical anguish, going down to the very roots of the desire for life, is capable of becoming a total despair and of ending in suicide" (*WHB* 74). Indeed, at one point in his early metaphysical romance, the anguish experienced by Jacques, and by Raïssa, too, gave rise to the well-known suicide pact made in the Jardin des Plantes (*WHB* 77-78).

Luckily, Maritain's metaphysical romance was saved by the pity of God and Henri Bergson (*WHB* 79). Through Bergson, Jacques and Raïssa became convinced that they were capable of knowing what is (*WHB* 83). "By means of a wonderfully penetrating critique Bergson dispelled the anti-metaphysical prejudices of pseudo-scientific positivism and recalled to the spirit its real function and essential liberty" (*WHB* 84).

The romantic reconciliation effected by divine pity and Henri Bergson between Jacques Maritain and Dame Metaphysics was to rest undisturbed until the year 1908, two years after his conversion to Roman Catholicism. By this time Maritain's metaphysical romance had been overtaken by the "spirit of Thomism," a spirit that pervades the mind of the genuinely Catholic Scholastic theologian.[3] Trained as a philosopher, yet recently converted to Catholicism,

---

[3] I am using the phrase "spirit of Thomism" in a sense similar to that employed by Etienne Gilson in his book *The Spirit of Thomism* (New York: Harper and Row, 1964) 9. Gilson says, "I think the true spirit of Thomism illumines a certain way to understand and practice theology, namely, the way of scholastic theology." As I understand it, the spirit of Thomism is a theological principle that measures the whole order of objects discoverable by light of natural reason and rational argumentation against the background of the authority of revelation. Hence one need not consider oneself a Thomist to be possessed of this spirit.

Jacques Maritain was confronted by a problem. As a philosophic spirit in the tradition of thinkers such as Socrates, Plato, and Aristotle, Maritain had realized that what was presented to him in his youth by his teachers as philosophy was a cheap imitation of the real thing. Philosophy for the Greeks had always taken its principles of reasoning from the world of sense experience, the origin of our inclination to wonder, and had ascended through stages of abstraction from the physical world to God.[4] Starting as it had from the common human experience of the sense world, the philosophy of the Greeks had begun with a public object and could thereby maintain its impartiality, its objectivity, and its realism. It was these qualities of impartiality, objectivity, and realism that Maritain recognized to be missing from the antimetaphysical, rationalistic, subjectivistic spirit that had been set free to roam about the modern world by the dream of Descartes.[5] Maritain recognized the dream for what it was—a gross hallucination, a nightmare—a nightmare from which he had been luckily set free by grace and Henri Bergson.[6] As a Catholic, however, he experienced a new conflict—how to reconcile his authentic philosophical spirit with his newly found faith?

Already that faith was presenting him with spiritual conflicts. It was causing him to question the validity of the very Bergsonian philosophy that had just recently helped to save him from physical and metaphysical suicide, for he found in his revealed dogma formulas that he could not harmonize with Bergson's philosophical view that the concept is a mere practical device for cutting up the continuous flow of reality, but which in and of itself is incapable of transmitting reality to our minds. As a Catholic, Maritain knew this view of the concept had to be inaccurate. Christian revelation had taught him that,

> since God proposes to us in concepts and conceptual propositions (which reach us streaming with the blood of martyrs; in the times of Arianism men knew how to die for the sake of one iota) truths which are the most transcendent and inac-

---

[4]This is true even of as ethereal a thinker as Plotinus, who, in his *Enneads*, does not begin his reasoning from the One and then descend to the physical world. Plotinus starts his reasoning from sensation, from "sense beauty," then ascends to the One and returns to the sense world. See Plotinus, *Enneads* 1, and Joseph Owens, *A History of Ancient Western Philosophy* (Englewood Cliffs NJ: Prentice-Hall, 1959) 397-403.

[5]For some of Maritain's views regarding the impact of Descartes's thought upon the modern world, see his *The Dream of Descartes*, trans. Mabelle L. Andison (New York: Philosophical Library, 1944).

[6]Maritain himself does not, to my knowledge, speak of Descartes's dream as a "gross hallucination," or as a "nightmare." For something he does say about the "cerebral episode" of Descartes that founds modern philosophy, something that, I think, justifies my rather severe judgments about Descartes's dream of a new science, see Maritain, *Dream of Descartes*, 15-16.

cessible to our reason, the truth even of His own Life, His own abyss, this means that the concept is not a mere practical instrument which is incapable in itself of transmitting reality to our minds, serviceable only for artificially cutting up ineffable continuities, and which lets the absolute escape like water through a sieve. (*WHB* 199)

Yet this conflict was beginning to ripen in Maritain a spirit of intellectual analysis that would characterize his thinking for the rest of his life. Already, before being formally introduced to Saint Thomas Aquinas, Maritain was utilizing the method of the Angelic Doctor, for he was changing the natural investigation of the light of human reason from the water of philosophy into the wine of theology. Already in its fetal stages of development was the realization in Maritain's mind that in order to restore philosophy to realism, he would have to restore the order of human intelligence in philosophy to the natural order of learning, to the being of sensible objects, as its proper base of operations. To do this, however, Maritain realized that he could reason like neither a Descartes nor a Bergson. In Maritain's mind,

a slow ripening process was thus made possible, during which the principal outlines of a philosophy of being and of spirit took shape before his eyes, and also the conviction that truth attained in any degree whatever of reality should be the friend and companion of the truth in any other degree of being. The Angel of the Schools could not unveil his presence to this mind silently prepared to receive the eternal message of intelligence and faith. (*WHB* 202)

From this time on Maritain would no longer study either philosophy or the things around him from the perspective of natural reason alone but would instead study everything in light of the grace of faith, which, just as it perfects nature, perfects the natural light of reason in its pursuit of truth.

Of course, in doing this he was bound to run into problems. Maritain himself soon found this to be the case, for, as someone known to be a philosopher, his joining together of philosophy and his faith could not have failed to look to philosophers like a bastardization of the purity of natural reason. And, as someone known to be a convert, actually studying *ad mentem sancti Thomae*, for the purpose of solving the problems of his own age, he could not have helped but look like a heretic to some Scholastics, whose Thomism was the carcass of a once-living theology become manualized into a set of easily memorized formulas resembling a pseudo *sacra doctrina* of its own. Hence, both to many Catholics and to many philosophers Maritain appeared quite odd, so odd in fact that Etienne Gilson could not help but relate how Maritain was viewed at a meeting of the French Society of Philosophy and how he was viewed by some French theologians.

Regarding the appearance of Maritain at the philosophical meeting, Gilson recalls:

how could I forget the twenty-first of March, 1936, the day when this noble mind honored with his presence a meeting of the French Society of Philosophy? He spoke there his usual language. A philosopher who had come from Mars would not have been less understood. The excellent Bouglé was the least fanatic among the representatives of secular philosophy. He was most anxious that his Catholic colleagues should feel they were trusted by him, and as a result he strove to prove it to them by courageous decisions. He came out of this meeting visibly preoccupied, even worried. "Say," he whispered in my ear, taking me by the arm in a friendly way, "what is the matter with him? I think he is crazy." (PT 203)

Regarding Maritain's appearance to French theologians, Gilson relates a different, but equally telling, story of how Maritain had the appearance of someone not quite normal, of someone so abnormal, in fact, as to occasion the wrath of some fellow members of God's Church on earth. As Gilson puts it:

He who enters upon this road [Thomism] must be ready for some surprises. The first one is that from this moment one will be treated by the "Thomists" according to their customary ways, which are not always gentle. Should he be French, he can expect to become the object of particular attentions on the part of integrists whose theological fanaticism is matched by the intolerance so common among Frenchmen. The only Thomist in contemporary France whose thought was lofty, bold and creative, capable of meeting the most urgent problems and, so to speak, to stand ever ready before all emergencies, was rewarded for his zeal by incessant, active and venomous hostility of unhappy creatures who have little else to put in the service of God than their hatred of their neighbors. (PT 201-202)

That Maritain should appear a misfit to many of his contemporaries both in theology and in philosophy is a credit to his own wisdom, for he has as predecessors in oddness such giants in theology and philosophy as Saint Thomas Aquinas himself, the Christian theologian's Christian theologian, and Socrates, the perennial philosopher's perennial philosopher. Thus, like Aquinas and Socrates, Maritain was among his contemporaries what Homer said Teiresias was among the dead, like someone real, possessed of mind, among shadows.[7]

Indeed, this characterization of Maritain as a misfit, as someone abnormal, even a little crazed, has more than a bit of truth to it. For Maritain himself was fond of speaking of his *amour fou* ("mad," boundless love) for God.[8] And Saint Thomas recognized that one of the effects of love is to make a person mentally ecstatic, that is, such a person is placed outside his normal mental activity. This

---

[7]Homer *Odyssey* 10.494; see Plato's *Meno* 100a.

[8]René Vouillaume, preface to *Raïssa's Journal,* presented by Jacques Maritain (Albany: Magi Books, 1974) xiii.

can happen, as many parents of teenagers might readily recognize, when a person in love has his mental activity lowered to a state of understanding beneath his own or the norm of other humans. Or it can happen, as many mystics might attest, when a person in love has his mental activity elevated to an understanding above the apprehension of reason to which he or another is normally accustomed.[9]

It is in this latter sense that Jacques Maritain was a misfit, crazed and abnormal, for his was the reasoning of a man elevated by grace to a condition of thinking beyond that of normal theologians and philosophers. Yet it is precisely by understanding Maritain as just such an "abnormal" thinker that one can get a sense of his distinctive contribution to twentieth-century intellectual life and one can understand the truth of Gilson's observation:

> It is not necessary to read many pages from Jacques Maritain to realize that one is dealing with one of the best French writers of our time. He is not always easy to understand and the high quality of his style escapes the readers who do not grasp his thought. But for those who understand him the incessant fecundity of his imagination creates a delightful conspiracy between metaphysics and poetry. (*PT* 202)

To understand the precise sense in which Jacques Maritain's thinking is abnormal is, also, to understand something more; it is to understand the exact nature of the romance of wisdom between Maritain and Aquinas. For the romance between these two men was a romance of Catholic theologians, and, to be precise, a romance of Scholastic theologians of the highest order. The greatness of Jacques Maritain lies precisely in his being the premier Scholastic theologian of the twentieth century, just as the greatness of Saint Thomas Aquinas lies in his being the premier Scholastic theologian of the thirteenth century. In my estimation, Maritain's single greatest achievement has been the restoration of Scholasticism in theology, reflecting the spirit of Pope Leo XIII, *ad mentem Sancti Thomae.*[10] Hence what better phrase can be used to describe the nature of the romance between these thinkers than "a romance of Scholastic Theologians"?

Yet no sooner do I write this phrase than I suspect that it might not sit well with some contemporary Thomists, in particular with the disciples of Maritain. While it hardly can be seriously disputed that Saint Thomas was a Scholastic theologian, there are those who might take issue with the claim that Jacques Maritain was one. Some might point out that Maritain himself, in all likelihood, would have protested against that description, preferring instead the title

---

[9]St. Thomas Aquinas, *Summa theologiae* I-II.28.3, Respondeo.

[10]Pope Leo XIII's encyclical *Aeterni Patris* is subtitled *De philosophia christiana . . . ad mentem Sancti Thomae . . . in scholis catholicis instauranda.*

"Christian philosopher."[11] In addition, these disciples might remind me that no less a man than Yves Simon, one of Maritain's dearest friends, has claimed, "Maritain was the first non-scholastic among the disciples of Saint Thomas."[12]

I think it is fitting to refer to Maritain as a Scholastic because I am using the term "Scholastic" in a way that is different from the way it is used by Yves Simon. In addition, I do not think it is fitting, *without serious qualification*, to refer to him, *or to anyone*, as a "Christian Philosopher," because I consider the idea of a Christian philosophy, as an exercise of natural reasoning distinct from revealed theology, to be a self-destructive (indeed contradictory) notion.

Yves Simon objects to the use of the term "Scholastic" to refer to Maritain because "[a] scholastic philosophy is a philosophy of professors, and Maritain holds that a professor is precisely the worst enemy of St. Thomas' philosophy. A scholastic culture is centered on what takes place between teachers and students, with little or no concern for what goes on in public affairs, in art and literature, and in spiritual life."[13] If the term "Scholastic" refers to what is professorial, as opposed to that which is concerned with public affairs and so forth, then I would have to agree with Yves Simon that Maritain was no Scholastic. I use the term in a different sense, however. I take my understanding of the term from the procedure described by Saint Thomas in his "Introduction" to his *Commentary on the de Trinitate of Boethius.*

In that work Saint Thomas described two methods of investigating the Trinity. One mode, employed by such church fathers as Ambrose and Hilary, was to set forth conclusions based upon reference to authorities. The other mode, employed by Boethius, was *first* to accept, as presuppositions, conclusions based upon authority, *and then, having done this*, to proceed according to reasoned arguments.

As I understand the term *Scholastic*, it refers precisely to this theological method of reasoning used by Boethius in his *De Trinitate* and by Saint Thomas in his own writings. It is the distinctive use of argumentation according to natural reasoning within the context of revealed theology that formally distinguishes reasoning as Scholastic, not the fact that reasoning is professorial, as Simon asserts.

---

[11]Regarding Maritain's view on Christian philosophy, see his *An Essay on Christian Philosophy*, trans. Edward H. Flannery (New York: Philosophical Library, 1955), hereafter cited as *ECP*; *Science and Wisdom*, trans. Bernard Wall (London: Sheed and Ward, 1938), hereafter cited as *SW*; and *The Peasant of the Garonne: An Old Layman Questions Himself about the Present Time*, trans. Michael Cuddihy and Elizabeth Hughes (New York: Holt, Rinehart and Winston, 1968).

[12]John H. Griffin and Yves R. Simon, *Jacques Maritain: Homage in Words and Pictures* (Albany: Magi Books, 1974) 3-4.

[13]Ibid., 4.

Of course, having shown that my understanding of a Scholastic is different from that of Yves Simon, I do not seem to be any better off than I was before. For if Maritain was a "Scholastic," according to my understanding of the term, this would entail that he be a Christian theologian. To this he would no doubt, as I have already noted, object—just as he would object to being described as a "professor." He would prefer to be described as a Christian philosopher; and such a designation may seem especially fitting, since, along with Etienne Gilson, Maritain has been one of the chief advocates of the idea of Christian philosophy in the twentieth century.

Such a designation, however, is infelicitous in my estimation, in particular since neither the defense of Christian philosophy given by Gilson nor that given by Maritain is adequate. This can be shown, I think, from a brief consideration of some things each has to say about the reality of a Christian philosophy.

In his *Spirit of Medieval Philosophy* Gilson makes the following statement, quoted approvingly by Maritain in his own *An Essay on Christian Philosophy:*

> Consider any given philosophic system. Now ask if it is "Christian," and if so by what characteristics you can recognize it as such? From the observer's standpoint it is a philosophy, therefore a work of reason. The author is a Christian and yet his Christianity, however telling its influence on his philosophy has been, remains essentially distinct from it. The only means at our disposal for detecting this inner action is to compare this data which we can outwardly observe: The philosophy without revelation and the philosophy with revelation. This is what I have attempted to do. And since history alone is capable of performing this task, I have stated that history alone can give meaning to the concept of Christian philosophy. . . . I may say, then, that Christian philosophy is an objectively observable reality for history alone, but that once its existence has been thus established, its notion may be analyzed in itself. This ought to be done as Mr. J. Maritain has done it; I am in fact in complete agreement with him. On the other hand, if . . . Christian philosophy is not a historically observable reality, or . . . the Christian character of philosophy is in no wise indebted to revelation, my position must be considered false. (*ECP* x, n. 1)

There are several weaknesses in Gilson's position. First of all, as Anton Pegis rightly notes:

> Philosophy is not some sort of Avicennian absolute essence, inhabiting a pure philosophical heaven, before it is realized in the world of existence. There are philosophers and there are theologians. Philosophers philosophize, and then philosophy exists in its proper autonomy; and theologians, in using philosophy, theologize, and when they do the wine of theology exists.[14]

---

[14]Anton C. Pegis, "Sub Ratione Dei: A Reply to Professor Anderson," *New Scholasticism* 39 (1965): 154.

As a historically observable reality, what Gilson is talking about, as he himself notes elsewhere, is a theological essence, not a philosophical one. The phrase "Christian philosopher" is used by Gilson to express a "theological notion of a reality observable in history." The phrase, as he sees it, characterizes a historical event, a certain way of using philosophy within the context of theology that is distinctive to the Middle Ages.[15] The first weakness of Gilson's position is to assume that philosophy as used by the theologians of the Middle Ages was, or could have been, present prior to its exercise in theology as an essence or nature in a Christian distinct from its existence or state in revealed theology. In looking at philosophy in this way, Gilson gives to it a kind of *esse essentiae* of its own, distinct from its *esse existentiae* in theology.[16] Such a way of viewing philosophy is a mistake.

Similarly, it is a mistake to think that such a theological notion is observable in history. At least it is a mistake to think that it is observable in history by anyone other than a Christian historian versed in theology. To suggest otherwise smacks of historicism, and it confounds the orders of theological and historical research, for how is one supposed to recognize revelation in history except through the grace of the Holy Spirit present through the theologically infused virtue of faith?

Gilson himself seems to have recognized the awkwardness of his own use of the phrase "Christian philosophy"—and no wonder. Why should one use the term "philosophy" to describe such a theological idea? Is this not somewhat odd, in fact quite misleading? Indeed, even Gilson admits he was somewhat disconcerted by the characterization:

> I felt somewhat embarrassed to have to characterize the philosophy of the middle ages by a formula of which the history of that philosophy provided practically no example. Indeed, a master in theology teaching in the thirteenth century would never have considered himself as having a philosophy, even a Christian one. (*PT* 178)

Furthermore,

> [Gilson] notes that in Thomas's time the theologian who used philosophy in his work was normally not described as a philosopher, but as a philosophizing theo-

---

[15]Etienne Gilson, *The Christian Philosophy of St. Thomas Aquinas*, trans. L. K. Shook (New York: Random House, 1956) 441 n. 20.

[16]These phrases were commonly used by famous Thomistic commentators such as Giles of Rome, Cajetan, John of St. Thomas, and Francisco Suarez. For an introduction to the problems concerning the use of these phrases, see Gilson's *Being and Some Philosophers* (Toronto: Pontifical Institute of Medieval Studies, 1955).

logian, or more simply as a philosophizer (*philosophans*). The term "philosopher" was usually restricted to pagan thinkers. The thirteenth-century theologians do not seem, according to Gilson, to have considered explicitly the possibility of a person who would be at one and the same time a *philosophus* and a *sanctus*, that is, one sanctified by baptism.[17]

If such be the case, if no master in the thirteenth century would even have considered himself as having a philosophy, even a Christian one, if the Scholastic theologian of the Middle Ages was normally not described as a philosopher but as a philosophizing theologian or as a "philosophizer," if the term "philosopher" was usually restricted to pagan thinkers, and if the thirteenth-century theologians do not seem explicitly to have considered the possibility of a person simultaneously being a philosopher and a Christian, how then can it be considered fitting to describe the spirit of "philosophy" of this period as Christian philosophy? Indeed, the spirit of the medieval "philosophy" is not a philosophical spirit at all. Rather, it is a theological one. There is no philosophy as such in the Christian Middle Ages at all.

At best, the notion of Christian philosophy, as used by Gilson, is an analogous one, standing for a part of Scholastic theology; a notion that he was prompted to adopt because of a curious event that he had witnessed in the history of Christian theology in the Middle Ages and in what he refers to as "modern philosophy":

> [W]hat other name could one find for this body of doctrines so deeply marked with the seal of the Christian religion? Since, indeed, such a large portion of it was so truly rational that modern philosophy has appropriated it, one could rightly call it a philosophy, and since this philosophy was quickened by a genuinely Christian spirit, there was no escape from calling it a "Christian" philosophy. (*PT* 179)

Yet there was an escape from calling this body of doctrines a "Christian philosophy." One could just as easily, and better, have called it a "Christian theology," or, more exactly, a "Scholastic theology." Where Gilson went wrong was in making several unwarranted assumptions. First of all, he assumed that a person can be a Christian and can simultaneously have an autonomous philosophy, that is, a philosophy formally distinguished by its object alone. This is not possible. Secondly, he thought that something he recognized to be *actually* present in what he calls "modern philosophy" had to be *actually* present during the Middle Ages, when it was only present there potentially. Third, he confused the notions of rational and philosophical, when in fact they are not identical. Finally,

---

[17]John F. Wippel, "Thomas Aquinas and the Problem of Christian Philosophy," in *Metaphysical Themes in Thomas Aquinas*, ed. John F. Wippel (Washington: Catholic University of America Press, 1984) 16.

he assumed there is such a thing as modern philosophy, when in fact there is not. What poses under the banner of modern philosophy is, in actuality, a rather poor imitation of theology, what Maritain called "ideosophy,"[18] and what I call "psychotheology." For, in reality, the pretender to the throne of philosophy in the modern and contemporary age, that antimetaphysical, materialistic spirit attacked so vigorously by Jacques Maritain, is actually a secular Scholastic theology, a bizarre imitation of the Christian Scholastic theology of the Middle Ages.[19]

Toward the end of his life, Gilson seems to have realized the inadequacy of his earlier view, as stated, for example, in his *Spirit of Mediaeval Philosophy*. Thus, in his late work, *The Philosopher and Theology*, Gilson no longer sees that philosophy maintains an essence independent from Christianity, such as he thought in the former work. Hence, in the latter work, he says, "what becomes of philosophy in this venture? Can it thus be used by theology toward ends that are not its own without losing its essence in the process? In a way it does lose its essence, and it profits by the change" (*PT* 100).

Gilson notes that Saint Thomas himself had been reproached for mixing "the water of philosophy with the wine of Scripture," but that Saint Thomas's reply was, "Those who resort to philosophical arguments in Holy Scriptures and put

---

[18]Maritain, *The Peasant of the Garonne*, 98-102.

[19]I call modern philosophy "psychotheology" because its act of philosophizing has as its object not the being of things known by the natural light of reason but the human psyche known by the light of Absolute Perfection. The act of modern philosophizing reasons from "God" to the world, using the authority of God and a purely subjective conviction of certitude as its supreme criteria of truth. It regards its matter (the human psyche) *sub ratione Dei*. My thesis is that if Descartes was a Christian then his "philosophy" must derive its principles, in some way, under the light of his faith. If the history of modern philosophy is a footnote to Descartes (that is, if it derives its first principles from him), then it, too, must derive its principles under the light of faith. Since Descartes derives his principles from a personal self-revelation, from his own psyche "divinely" considered, his supreme criterion of truth is the authority of God (just as a theologian's is), and he uses reasoned arguments within the context of his method (just as a Scholastic does). Modern philosophy tends to proceed in the same fashion. Is it not then appropriate to call this reasoning a secular Scholastic theology? Since Descartes's object of speculation has no evidential foundation *in re* but is woven out of his own divinely illuminated subjective spirit, is it not appropriate to call his reasoning both "secular" and "psycho" theology?

While my claim regarding the nonexistence of modern philosophy might strike some readers as outlandish, it should be noted that Maritain holds a somewhat similar position in *The Peasant of the Garonne*, 122. Furthermore, Maritain notes in *The Dream of Descartes*, 27-29 and 69-90, the penchant of Descartes to model philosophy after the pattern of theology.

them in the service of faith, do not mix water with wine, they change it into wine." By this Gilson understands Saint Thomas to mean, "they change philosophy into theology, just as Jesus changes water into wine at the marriage feast of Cana. Thus can philosophical wisdom, imprinted in the mind of God as the seal of God's knowing, include the totality of human knowledge in its transcendent unity" (*PT* 100-101).

Gilson's view in *The Philosopher in Theology*, while different from his earlier one, is still inadequate. When the Christian theologian studies the works of philosophers as part of his subject matter, this treatment of philosophy does not change the essence of philosophy. It does not turn philosophy into theology. Philosophy is philosophy, and theology is theology; just as water is water, and wine is wine. Philosophy can no more become theology than blue can become green. Just as Jesus, at Cana, changes the "material" that is water into the "material" that is wine, so the Scholastic theologian changes the purely rational arguments that are philosophical in the context of natural reason unaided by faith into the purely rational arguments that are theological in the context of natural reason working under the supernatural light of faith.

Just as grace perfects rather than destroys nature, so faith perfects rather than destroys natural reasoning. The essence of philosophy does not change when philosophy is studied from the perspective of the theologian, any more than the essence of theology changes when it is studied as part of the subject matter of the philosopher. Both the philosopher and the theologian use natural reasoning, but the natural reasoning of the theologian proceeds under the light of faith and uses primary principles derived from *authority* (*sub ratione Dei*),[20] whereas the natural reasoning of the philosopher proceeds under no other light than its own and uses primary principles derived from the being of physical objects (*sub ratione mundi*).[21] The arguments of the theologians are not precluded from being "purely" rational because they are illuminated by faith any more than the nature of a human being is precluded from being "purely" human because it is infused with grace.

Of course, if what one means by "purely" is "only," then this is not the case, for theological reasoning is not "only" rational any more than nature infused by grace is "only" natural. On the contrary, theological reasoning is not "only" rational, it is "more" than rational; and nature infused by grace is not "only" natural, it is "more" than natural. Yet being "more" than natural or "more" than rational does not prevent nature and reason from being "purely" natural and rational in the sense of being "completely" rational and natural. What is filled to excess certainly is filled completely, just as a glass that is filled to over-

---

[20]Pegis, "Sub Ratione Dei" 151; St. Thomas Aquinas, *Summa theologiae* Ia.1.7.

[21]*Sub ratione mundi* is my expression.

flowing is absolutely full, and just as a person who exceeds normality because of the perfection of his ability is both completely normal and supernormal.

So much for Gilson's view of Christian philosophy. Now to Maritain's. The defense that Maritain gives of Christian philosophy is, I am sorry to say, no more adequate than Gilson's; it is, however, much more complex. Maritain treats the nature and existence of Christian philosophy in several works—in *An Essay on Christian Philosophy*, in *Science and Wisdom*, and in *St. Thomas Aquinas: Angel of the Schools*, to mention a few. The theme running throughout these works remains more or less the same and is founded upon principles derived from *An Essay on Christian Philosophy*, principles that are of a rather dubious and non-Thomistic character.

Foremost among these principles is the distinction that Maritain makes between the *nature* and *state* of philosophy (*ECP* 11-12), in order to answer the questions, "Does a Christian philosophy exist? Is a Christian philosophy at all conceivable?" (*ECP* ix). Maritain seeks to answer these questions, as he puts it, "in the light of Thomistic theory," by appealing to what he refers to as "the classical distinction between the *order of specification* and the *order of exercise*" (*ECP* 11). As Maritain employs this "classical" distinction, "the order of specification" is replaced by the term "nature," and the "order of exercise" by the term "state." For Maritain, "This means that we must distinguish between the *nature* of philosophy, or what it is in itself, and the *state* in which it exists in real fact, historically, in the human subject, and which pertains to its concrete conditions of existence and exercise" (*ECP* 11-12).

In *Science and Wisdom* Maritain qualifies this distinction more completely. There he adds:

> Considered in its pure *nature*, or essence, philosophy, which is specified by an object naturally knowable to reason, depends only on the evidence and criteria of natural reason. But here we are considering its absolute nature. Taken concretely, in the sense of being a *habitus* or a group of *habitus* existing in the human soul, philosophy is in a certain *state*, is either pre-Christian or Christian or a-Christian, which has a decisive influence on the way it exists and develops. (*SW* 79)

To consider philosophy in its "pure" nature is, for Maritain, to consider its absolute nature. It is to consider the nature of philosophy "in itself," as he puts it, "by means of an abstraction" (*ECP* 12). Thanks to this abstraction, Maritain thinks, the human turns its gaze from the existential conditions of the nature of philosophy and "lifts it to the order of essences; it posits a possible before our thought; in sum it disregards the *state* to ponder the *nature*" (*ECP* 12). In *An Essay on Christian Philosophy* Maritain further elucidates his distinction between the nature of philosophy and its state under two separate headings, one entitled, "The Nature of Philosophy," and the other, "The Christian State of Philosophy."

Within the context of the section dealing with the nature of philosophy, Maritain contends that for Saint Thomas, substances are "specified absolutely" by virtue of themselves, their powers of operation are "specified absolutely" by virtue of their acts, and these latter acts are "specified absolutely" by their objects. From this he concluded, "it is uniquely in function of the object that philosophy is specified, and it is the object toward which it tends by virtue of itself (by no means the subject in which it resides) that determines its *nature*" (*ECP* 13-16).

For Maritain this means, "whether the form of knowledge which of itself is directed to the understanding of this universe of naturally attainable objects is actually achieved in the human minds or not, and even if it is achieved with more or less deficiencies and flaws, its essence is clearly marked out: it is intrinsically a natural and rational form of knowledge" (*ECP* 14).

As he sees it, "Thomistic philosophy" (not, however, Thomistic theology) is wholly rational. That is, no reasoning springing from faith enters into its inner fabric. For him, "Thomistic philosophy" issues from reason and rational criticism alone, basing its soundness as a philosophy entirely upon logical proof plus experimental or intellectual evidence (*ECP* 15).

From his consideration of the nature of philosophy, a nature, one should recall, that he states exists solely in the order of essences as an "abstract nature," Maritain concludes:

> Since the specification of philosophy hinges entirely on its formal object, and since this object is wholly of the rational order, philosophy considered by itself—whether in the pagan or Christian mind—depends on the same strictly natural or rational intrinsic criteria. So that the designation *Christian* which we apply to a philosophy does not refer to that which constitutes it in its *philosophic essence:* simply as a philosophy, *reduplicative ut sic* [considered formally in itself], it is independent of the Christian faith as to its object, its principles, and its methods. (*ECP* 15)

Under the heading "The Christian State of Philosophy," Maritain considers certain benefits that philosophy, in its concrete existence, receives from its state in the Christian mind, existing in *Faith*. These elements include objective data, which consists primarily of revealed truths of the natural order (*revelabilia*), and subjective reinforcements, such as the inspiration philosophy receives from superior theological lights that rectify and purify the philosophical habitus in the soul. These elements, he thinks, in no way alter the essence of philosophy in itself. Rather, they enhance conditions under which it exists (*ECP* 13-16; *SW* 79-81). As he states in *Science and Wisdom*, Christian philosophy "indicates not an essence in itself but a complex: an essence taken in certain states, under conditions of performance, of existence and of life, for or against which one is in fact obliged to make a choice" (*SW* 81).

The enhancement of philosophy due to its conditions is especially evident to Maritain in the case of moral philosophy, which, he contends, "would not only fail to reach its maturity, but it would even fail to exist as a science, in the precise Aristotelian sense of the word, would fail to exist as practical knowledge stabilized in truth in an organic and sufficient manner, unless it recognized the truths of faith. Moral philosophy adequately considered would then only be a philosophy 'subalternated' to theology" (*SW* 80-81).

For Maritain, therefore, theology acts as both a negative and a positive norm of philosophy. Negatively, it exercises control over the conclusions of philosophy, both speculative and practical.[22] Positively, it exercises control over practical philosophy, namely the science of ethics, with respect to its goal (*IP* 99). The premises of philosophy, however, are independent of theology, being based upon primary truths that are self-evident to human understanding (*IP* 95).

"Speculative philosophy," for Maritain, "becomes Christian not through its specifying object, but through its state" (*SW* 97). Practical philosophy, on the other hand, "must be Christian not only because of its state but also because of its very object; in other words it is in a relationship to theology of *subalternation* and not only of *infraposition*. Because here the object—human acts—is taken in its actual existence and as needing direction in its concrete movement toward its concrete ends" (*SW* 107).

Practical philosophy is lifted up and ceases to be purely philosophical by being subalternated to theology. It has to be lifted up by theology, however, because its final object as the object of "science" is essentially speculative. For science, or philosophy, as Maritain understands it, is essentially speculative! (That is, for him philosophy *is* speculative philosophy.)[23] And as speculative, philosophy is unable to visualize its proper object without grace, for the "final" object of moral "science" is "knowledge" of human acts, that is, the "universal" and abstract consideration of human acts (*IP* 202-203), while the object of "moral," or practical, science is moral conduct (*EE* 47).

---

[22]Jacques Maritain, *St. Thomas Aquinas: Angel of the Schools*, trans. J. F. Scanlan (London: Sheed and Ward, 1931) 130-31; and Jacques Maritain, *An Introduction to Philosophy*, trans. E. I. Watkin (1930; reprint, New York: Sheed and Ward, 1959) 99; hereafter cited as *IP*.

[23]In *An Introduction to Philosophy* (regarding art) Maritain says, "The province of philosophy thus defined is indeed practical, since it is concerned with making, and its object is to order from above the branches of practical instruction. Nevertheless, since it is in the strict sense a science, it cannot be essentially practical, but remains essentially speculative in virtue of its object and procedure (199)." And in his *Existence and the Existent*, trans. Lewis Galantière and Gerald B. Phelan (New York: Pantheon, 1949) 47 (hereafter *EE*): "Practical philosophy remains speculative in its mode (since it is philosophy), and practical by reason of its object (which is moral conduct)."

As Maritain sees it, that is, speculative philosophy is *truly* philosophy, is *truly* scientific, because it looks at things from the perspective, or "eidetic visualization" (*EE* 30), of abstract universal essences; because it looks at things according to their "intelligible values" rather than according to their "actual conditions of contingence and singularity" (*SW* 108). Practical philosophy, on the other hand, considers things according to their actual conditions, and, in doing so, precludes itself from being genuinely scientific qua practical. The object of *to praktikon* is action and, as such, being singular and contingent, is for Maritain no fit object for science (*SW* 107).

For the "practical science" of ethics to know its proper object it must consider the "knowledge" of human acts (its final goal qua science according to the basic and universal conditions that are imposed upon man in point of existence here below) (*SW* 109). Such a consideration, however, according to Maritain, is not possible unless one knows the existential relation in which a person is placed to his end. "And what science knows this save theology?" Hence, as he sees it, "theological truths are indispensable for the full constitution of ethics and the object of morals is only adequately known in light of these truths" (*SW* 109). Nevertheless, moral philosophy, for Maritain, is not formally theological. Moral philosophy adequately considered is for him "a formally philosophic science subalternated to theology" (*ECP* 86).

The reason Maritain thinks that moral philosophy is formally philosophical rather than formally theological lies in what he considers to be the "ultra-formal determination upon which the specification of sciences properly depends" (*ECP* 66). This ultraformal determination for him "is a certain mode of immateriality or abstracting and defining" (*ratio formalis sub qua*) under which a subject (*ratio formalis quae*) can be scientifically known. That is, it is an abstract and universal essence through the light of which a concrete essence can be intellectually apprehended in a scientific way (*ECP* 12, 68). As he sees it, the formal determinants of moral philosophy and of moral theology are different. Consequently, moral philosophy and moral theology must be distinct sciences, for the formal determinant of moral theology is the light of divine revelation (*ECP* 79). The formal determinant of moral philosophy, however, is the "ordinability" of voluntary human action by practical human reason suitably completed (that is, by a human reason with the habitus of practical philosophy elevated and completed by subalternation to theology) (*ECP* 12, 71, 103 n. 13.) Thus, while both moral philosophy and moral theology share the same subject (*ratio formalis quae*), namely, the ordination of human acts to their end, moral philosophy studies this subject through the ultimate formal perspective (*ratio formalis sub qua*) of what it is in human acts that can be so ordered by a suitably completed human reason. Moral theology, on the other hand, studies this same subject, the ordination of human acts to their end, through the ultimate formal perspective of what is divinely revealable.

In short, for Maritain, moral philosophy cannot be part of moral theology because the two have different ultimate formal objects. They are distinct because sciences are distinguished by just such formal objects (*ECP* 66). Still, because the final object of moral philosophy as a "practical" science cannot be adequately known qua practical without the mediation of a suitable science, capable of grasping both theoretical and practical objects (with all their detail) under its ken, moral philosophy must be subalternated to theology. Hence a Christian moral philosophy adequately considered is, in Maritain's view, inseparable from revealed theology but formally distinct from it in its own object and procedures (*ECP* 86).

Having thus considered Maritain's treatment of Christian philosophy, what are we to conclude? Does his teaching regarding Christian philosophy refute the claim that Maritain himself was a Scholastic theologian? To put it bluntly, "No, it does not." While Maritain's view of Christian philosophy is a marvelously orchestrated melange of fine distinctions that is as entertaining to attempt to unravel as is the dance of the dialectic of the Hegelian *wesen*, it is not sustainable according to the principles of Saint Thomas.

Maritain's view of Christian philosophy suffers from many weaknesses, among which can be included: (1) an all-encompassing essentialism, (2) a misunderstanding of Saint Thomas's teaching on the specification of habits, (3) a misunderstanding of his teaching on the abstraction and the division of the sciences, and (4) speculativistic and metaphysicistic reductionism. That these faults, and others, actually are present in Maritain's teaching can be shown by reflecting upon what Maritain tells us about the nature and state of philosophy.

Maritain draws this distinction to answer the questions, Does a Christian philosophy exist? Is a Christian philosophy at all conceivable? The way he answers these questions is inadequate, proceeding *a posse ad esse*[24] and assuming the existence of a philosophy "in itself,"which necessarily exists by virtue of its own intrinsic intelligible necessity (that is, having an *esse essentiae* of its own) prior to its existence in an individual human mind (*esse existentiae*).[25]

For Maritain the *nature* of philosophy (its *esse essentiae*) must be distinguished from its *state* (*esse existentiae*). The nature of philosophy, as he sees it, is specified by its object "toward which it tends by virtue of itself" whether or not this nature "is actually achieved in human minds or not" (*ECP* 12-16). *Intrinsically, in itself*, philosophy, for Maritain, is "a natural and rational form of knowledge" (*ECP* 14).

---

[24]Pegis, "Sub Ratione Dei," 150.

[25]Maritain seems to me quite clearly to be deriving his distinction of nature and state from these principles taken from John of Saint Thomas and Cajetan. His *Essay on Christian Philosophy* is filled with references to the latter.

Such being the case, Maritain can be asked the question, Where does philosophy exist *in itself?* Maritain, like Gilson before him, stands convicted of his own essentialism when faced with this question and with Pegis's observation: "Philosophy is not some sort of Avicennian absolute essence, inhabiting a pure philosophical heaven, before it is realized in the world of existence."[26] Apart from its *state,* that is, philosophy has no existence at all. The distinction between the nature of philosophy and its state, as drawn by Maritain, is illicit, and can in no way be used to defend his view of a Christian philosophy. It is a distinction that is drawn not from Saint Thomas but from John of Saint Thomas and Cajetan,[27] and it weakens the whole of Maritain's case for a Thomistic philosophy independent of Thomistic theology.

The specification of philosophy in itself and as a habitus, according to Maritain, is determined entirely by its formal object (*ECP* 13). This, however, is inaccurate. Philosophy *in itself* has no specification because it has no existence, and philosophy as a habitus, properly speaking, receives its specification from its act and not from its object. For Saint Thomas, operative powers are specified by their acts. These acts, in turn, are specified by their objects. But when the act of one habit is under the direction of another, the directed act receives its form from the directing habit.[28] This is illustrated by the directing of the appetitive power by reason through which appetite apprehends its object.

Saint Thomas's principle of the specification of an operative power's acts means, in the case of the act of natural reasoning, that what for the Greeks was called an act of philosophy becomes for a Christian an act of theology. In the state of Christian existence, the theological habitus acts as a formal determinant of philosophical activity inasmuch as the subject matter of philosophy can be considered under the aspect of the more universal formal *ratio* of revelabilia of the theological habitus.[29]

As a result of conceiving philosophy as a nature specified by its object alone, Maritain has created a monadic essence, closed in upon itself, and unreceptive to formal determination from any higher lights. It is for this reason that he thinks theology acts only as a negative norm for speculative philosophy, whereas in actuality it acts as a positive norm for both speculative and practical reason. As

---

[26]Pegis, "Sub Ratione Dei" 154.

[27]See note 16.

[28]St. Thomas Aquinas, *On Charity,* trans. Lottie H. Kenzierski (Milwaukee: Marquette University Press, 1960) a3, Respondeo ("it is necessary to judge habits according to acts. Wherefore, when that which pertains to one habit is as a form in regard to the act of another habit, then that one habit is related to the other as a form"). See also *Summa theologiae,* I-II.51.2, and Pegis, "Sub Ratione Dei," 53.

[29]St. Thomas Aquinas, *Summa theologiae,* Ia.1.3, Respondeo, and ad 2.

Saint Thomas tells us, "understanding" is always the first principle of any science.[30] Yet it was precisely the understanding of theology that revealed to Saint Thomas the principle of *esse* and to Maritain the inadequacy of the Bergsonian version of the same concept by shedding its light on the being of things.

As Maritain has conceived it, the essence that is speculative philosophy has no windows through which the light of theology can enter. Hence, at best, he sees this light as sneaking in through cracks in the walls.

In the case of the essence that is practical philosophy, Maritain involves himself in a maze of theologico-philosophical confusion in order to open the doors of practical reason to the light of faith. Yet, one could take issue with his interpretation of Saint Thomas's moral teaching. The problem with Maritain's moral teaching has been demonstrated quite clearly in an excellent but shamefully underread book by Richard Geraghty entitled *The Object of Philosophy According to St. Thomas Aquinas*. As Geraghty shows, and the words of Maritain himself display, Maritain conceives of moral philosophy as speculatively practical. For Saint Thomas, however, moral philosophy is thoroughly practical.[31] But Maritain is forced to view philosophy in his way because of his reduction of philosophy to a thoroughly speculative essence, and worse still, a metaphysical one (*ECP* 13). Moral philosophy, for him, moreover, is specified by two objects, not one. As *philosophy*, practical reason is specified by an abstract universal (the *knowledge* of moral conduct) (*SW* 109), and, as *practical,* it is specified by the doing of the moral deed in the contingent circumstance (moral conduct) (*IP* 201 and *SW* 107).

Maritain attempts to escape from the exigencies of his own principles of conceiving of moral philosophy as subalternated to theology; in doing so he misinterprets Saint Thomas's teaching regarding subalternation and regarding abstraction and division of the sciences (following the interpretation of the latter by Cajetan and John of Saint Thomas—an interpretation criticized as inadequate by Armand Maurer in his *Division and Methods of the Sciences*).[32]

---

[30]St. Thomas Aquinas, *Expositio super librum Boethii de Trinitate*, ed. Bruno Decker (Leiden: E. J. Brill, 1955) q2, a2, ad7.

[31]Richard P. Geraghty, *The Object of Moral Philosophy According to St. Thomas Aquinas* (Washington: University Press of America, 1982) 25-31, 46-47, and 49-81. For Saint Thomas the division of ethics into speculative and practical is not made on the basis of its end. To call some part of ethics "speculative," therefore, is not to place that part under speculative philosophy divided in view of man's end. In other words, the speculative part of ethics is formally determined as part of a practical science by the practical goal that is the end of this science. See St. Thomas Aquinas, *Expositio super librum Boethii de Trinitate*, q5, a1, ad 4.

[32]See Armand Maurer, *The Division and Method of the Sciences* (Toronto: Pontifical Institute of Medieval Studies, 1963) xxvi-xxvii and xxvii n. 31.

Moral science is not subalternated to theology because subalternation requires that one science be inferior to another and that it borrow principles from another, principles that it cannot explain by itself but that can only be explained by the superior science.[33] Moral science does not borrow principles from revealed theology either in its state in a pagan mind or in a Christian mind. In the pagan mind it takes its principles from human choice unaided by revelation, and in the Christian mind it derives its principles from its own source of theology, examining human choice under the aspect of revelabilia.[34]

Failing to realize how practical reason functions *in faith*, Maritain compounds his confusion by drawing upon a specification of the sciences and by bringing in levels of abstraction and formal determination (such as that which *formally determines the object as thing* and that which *formally determines the object as object*) that simply do not exist in the writings of Saint Thomas.

It should be clear by now, I hope, that neither Etienne Gilson nor Jacques Maritain has adequately defended the notion of a Christian philosophy as autonomous by virtue of its object from revealed theology. Neither thinker was able to do this because it was something that simply could not be done. Either the term "philosophy" is a universal term referring to a self-enclosed habitus deriving its principles from the being of things by natural reason alone—unaided by any other lights; or it is an analogous one referring to an open-ended habitus able to derive its principles *sub ratione Dei*. In the former case, one cannot simultaneously be a Christian and a philosopher for the simple reason that a Christian can have only one master, which is God, and one criterion for the truth—the word of God. A philosopher (univocally so-called) can have only one master and one criterion of truth—the being of physical things. A Christian can be a philosopher only in the sense that the habitus, whereby the pagan Greek was able to derive principles of natural reasoning from an understanding of the being of physical things, can exist in the Christian. The Christian qua Christian does not lose the skill to reason according to principles derived from the natural world. The habitus that the Greeks called philosophy is, properly speaking, for a Christian the habitus of "Scholastic theology." Only as such a theology can it be analogously called a "Christian philosophy." So, if there is such a thing as "Christian philosophy," it is something whose existence can be demonstrated only theologically. From the standpoint of the principles of secular philosophy, its existence

---

[33]Ibid., 15 n. 42.

[34]See Joseph Owens, "The Grounds of Ethical Universality in Aristotle," in *Aristotle: The Collected Papers of Joseph Owens*, ed. John R. Catan (Albany: State University of New York Press, 1981) 148-65.

is no more demonstrable or nondemonstrable than the existence of creation in time.[35]

It is only in an analogous sense, therefore, that Jacques Maritain can be said to be simultaneously both a Christian and a philosopher. This is in the sense that he is a Scholastic theologian. Maritain the Christian can no longer be Maritain the "secular" philosopher. Yet in this dichotomy lies the key to understanding the greatness of Jacques Maritain.

Etienne Gilson, commenting upon the distinctive contributions to metaphysics that began when Saint Thomas first started to understand problems of essence in terms of problems of existence, once said: "a decisive metaphysical progress or, rather, a true metaphysical revolution was achieved when somebody began to translate all the problems concerning being from the language of essence into that of existence."[36] The same can be said *mutatis mutandis* of both the Scholastic theologians of the Middle Ages and of Jacques Maritain in the twentieth century: a decisive intellectual progress, or rather, a true metaphysical revolution was achieved when these Scholastic theologians began to translate all problems concerning being from natural reason unaided by faith to natural reason illumined by faith. What the medieval Scholastic theologians did to natural reason and philosophy in the Middle Ages, Jacques Maritain, the premier Scholastic theologian of the twentieth century, did for natural reason and philosophy in his own day.

Once one understands this, one can understand the distinctive character of Maritain's thought. One of the greatest dangers one can face in studying Maritain's thought is to think that one is studying a faithful disciple of the principles of Saint Thomas, or a Thomistic philosopher. For the Thomism of Maritain is no more a philosophy, or a simple exposition of Thomistic theology for that matter, than Saint Thomas's Scholastic theology was an Aristotelian philosophy or an Augustinian theology. Indeed, Maritain, at times, changes the thought of Saint Thomas to suit his needs in the same way that Saint Thomas "improved" upon Aristotle to make him, at times, say what was "right." Hence to study Maritain as a simple twentieth-century interpreter of Aquinas is to misunderstand both Maritain and Aquinas. The friendship between Aquinas and Maritain was not one of teacher and faithful student. Indeed, at times it is easier to read Aquinas in order to understand Maritain than it is to read Maritain in order to understand Aquinas. The friendship between Maritain and Aquinas was a romance between Scholastic theologians whose wisdom, as wisdom ought, transcends all ages.

---

[35]See St. Thomas Aquinas, *Summa theologiae*, Ia.1.4.

[36]Etienne Gilson, *God and Philosophy* (New Haven: Yale University Press, 1970) 67.

Part II

Contemporary Themes

JOHN HELLMAN

The Humanism of Jacques Maritain*

Each OF THE CHAPTERS in this volume is concerned with an aspect of the unique humanism of Jacques Maritain—his distinctive philosophical concern for the interests and ideals of people. This chapter, in contrast, will focus on Maritain's humanism in the first sense of that word—his quality of being human. For he was a very unusual and distinctive human type, who lived through the profound transformation of a religious culture in which he played during his lifetime a singular, unrivaled role as a prototype.

Maritain was at least as important for what he was and did as for what he wrote and thought, for he lived his Roman Catholicism in a way in which no one had before or has since. He was a model, an archetype, for a generation that lived through a remarkable mutation in religious belief and practice.

"I am a convert," Jacques Maritain wrote to Jean Cocteau, "a man whom God has turned inside out like a glove."[1] The notorious "convert," as opposed to the brilliant but inaccessible metaphysician, had far more influence and importance as a "humanist" than many of his philosophical disciples imagined. Jacques Maritain had an impact far beyond the circles who could grasp his sometimes turgid philosophical writings. The Maritains—bright, perspicacious, uncompromising—converted to Catholicism at a time when, and in a milieu where, that institution represented the epitome of obscurantism to a great many men and women of culture and intelligence. Yet the young couple insisted that their intentions were humane and lucid, their behavior altruistic and enlightened. "If

---

*The author wishes to thank the Social Sciences and Humanities Research Council of Canada for its research support.

[1]"Réponse a Jean Cocteau," in *Jacques Maritain: Oeuvres (1912-1939)*, ed. Henry Bars (Paris: Desclée de Brouwer, 1975) 363. All translations into English are mine.

it has pleased God to hide His truth in a dunghill," the young Jacques remarked to Raïssa, "that is where we shall go to find it."[2]

Conversion

During the late nineteenth century, according to Nietzsche, Western European Christianity began to lose moral intensity, to enter into what he called a period of "weightlessness." He discerned a process of secularization: a general blurring of moral and cultural boundaries, a loosening of emotional ties, a weakening of the conviction that certain principles, certain standards of conduct, must remain inviolable—a loss of the gravity imparted to human experience by a supernatural framework of meaning. With the decline of Christianity, Nietzsche had predicted, "it will seem for a time as though all things had become weightless."[3] Jacques Maritain offered an example of this, when, as a student, he hurled himself in despair on the floor of his room over his inability to find answers for his "big" questions and when he effected the suicide pact with Raïssa should they fail to find the absolute truth they so ardently desired. The Maritains' passion for an invisible reality, for an ultimate explanation of the universe, made them part of that general revolt against the "scientism" or "positivism" of French intellectual life early in this century. This movement set the stage for the "intuitionist" philosophy of Henri Bergson, who, in his eloquent lectures in the Collège de France, defended the various ways of knowing, the rich variety of perceptions, that escaped those of narrow scientific mentality. The mutual affinity of Maritain and Bergson helped establish Maritain's philosophical genius. The philosophy of intuition promised "weight" to the two young *sorbonnards*. Bergson's philosophical "spiritualism" led the Maritains' friend Charles Péguy toward an eloquent celebration of the peasant Catholic *mentalité* of his illiterate grandmother; it persuaded Péguy's older friend, Georges Sorel, of the importance of spiritual factors in social change. Bergson's sensitive philosophical analysis of nonscientific perceptions was somewhat paralleled in the celebrated novels of his contemporary Maurice Barrès, which, with the author's new perception of *la terre et les morts*, provided weight for a generation of *déracinés*. While the new, quasi-religious nationalism of Barrès was of rather limited appeal for the cosmopolitan, and increasingly ultramontane, Maritains, they did retain their passion for experiencing a solid and serious certitude.

---

[2]Raïssa Maritain, *We Have Been Friends Together: Memoirs*, trans. Julie Kernan (1945; reprint, Garden City NY: Doubleday, Image Books, 1961) 138; hereafter cited as *WHB*.

[3]Cited by T. J. Jackson Lears, *No Place Of Grace: Antimodernism and the Transformation of American Culture, 1880-1920* (New York: Pantheon, 1981). Lears's portrait of the turn-of-the century American intelligentsia is suggestive for our purposes.

Several passages in Raïssa Maritain's memoirs echo these themes: the young couple, off to render the decisive visit to the hovel of the prophet Léon Bloy on the hill of Montmartre, mounted "that eternal stairway which leads up to Sacré Coeur," she wrote, with "that distress which is the only serious product of modern culture." And when they met Bloy in all of his domestic squalor they likened him to "a firestained and blackened cathedral . . . the purity was within, in the depths of the tabernacle." In meeting Bloy, Raïssa recalled, "all values seemed reversed, as by an invisible switch" (*WHB* 61, 72, 80, 97-98). In this hovel they found the blinding purity and certitude they were so desperately seeking. Bergson had given them an appreciation for significant realities discerned by non-scientific methods. The Maritains, disgusted with their education, their social class, and modern life, were fascinated by the absolute conviction with which Bloy (in a weightless period) prophesied the end of the world. Jacques later confided how deeply impressed he was when attending mass in the Basilica of Sacré Coeur with Bloy: "A woman usher arrived in front of him with the collection plate precisely at the moment of the elevation of the host. Furious, he turned his enormous terrible eyes and pointing his finger, hissed 'On your knees, brigand!' The poor woman, flabbergasted, fell to her knees in worship."[4] The Maritains experienced what Raïssa later described as "the rude shock of conversion" (*WHB* 316). A scholar who studied the prominent literary converts of the century has described a generation suffering from something like the weightlessness Nietzsche described, finding gravity in the radical "otherness" of Roman Catholicism; he found the role of the intransigent convert Paul Claudel in the conversion of the writer Jacques Rivière quite similar to the role played by Bloy in the conversion of Maritain: "In each case a brilliant intelligence was converted by someone of essentially simple, violent opinions."[5]

The Basilica of Sacré Coeur on Montmartre in which the Maritains were baptized was of symbolic importance in France in general, and in the Maritain family in particular. Jacques's grandfather Jules Favre had negotiated the ignominious armistice with the Prussians that had helped precipitate the violent rebellion of the Paris Commune (18 March-28 May 1871). The basilica was subsequently erected by national subscription, by a *Gallia poenitens et devota*, on the site where the communards first shed the blood of the counterrevolutionary forces. At the time when the Maritains encountered Catholicism in its neo-Byzantine portals, the basilica was among the most prominent counterrevolutionary symbols in the country. The erection by "Catholic France" of an architecturally exotic, expia-

---

[4]Emmanuel Mounier, *Entretiens* 2, 9 February 1930, unpublished part of his diaries kindly made available to me by Mme. Mounier.

[5]Richard Griffiths, *The Reactionary Revolution: The Catholic Revival in French Literature, 1870-1914* (London: Constable, 1966) 33.

tory edifice dedicated to Christ's suffering heart where the diabolical communards had sinned was at once romantic, patriotic, and popular (at least in Catholic regions of the country). The bleeding heart was a vivid example of that ancient doctrine of vicarious suffering so important to Bloy; the imposing church a monumental reaffirmation of law and order. Like their godfather Bloy, the Maritains developed a keen interest in the anguished, disquieting—and counterrevolutionary—prophecies of the Virgin at La Salette in 1846, as well as (via Father Clérissac) the authoritarian and disciplined antimodernism of Charles Maurras and the Action Française. In an inhuman world the Maritains found a paternalistic, authoritarian, and certitudinal "Christian humanism" in the church.

The Maritains entered into a world in which apparitions and prophecies were interpreted by ascetical celibates who served as intellectual, spiritual, and moral models. Soon the Maritains imitated, in their *mariage blanc*, the chastity of their clerical mentors and began a rarefied life in, but not of, a polluted and corrupt society—steering clear of what their friend Péguy denounced as the "world of money." They befriended religious, philosophical, and aritistic elites who shared their sympathy for the religion of all of the people: Catholicism. And they soon came to enjoy an unrivaled place in those circles as a surprising number of individuals found their example attractive (*their* example—not necessarily that of those medieval saints held up for imitation by the Maritains).

Jacques Maritain's "humanism," like that of most other Roman Catholic intellectuals who were nurtured by the church shaped by Pius IX, was inspired by hostility to the modern world. The Maritains located "that distress which is the only serious product of modern culture" in that rootless individualism that had resulted from capitalism's destruction of the old medieval hierarchies and communities. (When he visited Canada for the first time in 1933, he found his contact with the Anglo-Saxon Protestant world, "the heart of the capitalist system," "a bitter and disgusting experience."[6]) Maritain became adamantly anti-individualistic, anti-Protestant, antibourgeois, and antirevolutionary with strong feelings and sophisticated reasonings. His humanism grew from his effort to find a "third way" between capitalism and communism.

In his important *Integral Humanism: Temporal and Spiritual Problems of a New Christendom* (1936), Maritain would provide a quite accessible and internationally popular *haute vulgarisation* of his thinking on humanism. Westerners were living, he charged, through "the *bourgeois* moment of our culture," and the materialistic bourgeois man was "as displeasing to the Christian conscience as he is to the Communist conscience." The bourgeois liberalism of the nineteenth century, which viewed the individual as "a little god" possessing absolute freedom

---

[6]Letter to Emmanuel Mounier, 6 March 1933, in *Maritain/Mounier, 1929-1939*, ed. Jacques Petit (Paris: Desclée de Brouwer, 1973) 75-76.

of ownership, was a "practical atheism." Whereas capitalism claimed to represent "a spirit of exaltation of the active and inventive powers, of the dynamism
of man and of the initiatives of the individual," in practice it had diffused "a
spirit of hatred of poverty and of scorn of the poor man," who exists not as a
person, but as an instrument of production.[7]

Jacques Maritain's humanism grew directly out of his loathing for the bourgeois culture in which he had been raised, his rejection of the "individualism"
of modern life in the West. The prominent America liberal Sidney Hook was
troubled by the evidence in this book of Maritain's tolerance for the violence in
Marxism if only the revolution, "harsh as may be its means, will uproot the
'bourgeois man' whom Maritain loathes with an almost unchristian contempt."[8]
Hook found this an incongruous theme in the thinking of an ascetic Christian
philosopher whose governing value was charity. But the violence in Jacques Maritain's humanism grew directly out of the intensity of his abhorrence of the un-
charitable *individualism* of modern life in the West.

Antimodern

In his widely read book *Three Reformers* (1926) Maritain attacked Luther,
Descartes, and Rousseau for engendering the antihumanism of the modern
world—for fostering that "individualism," that "imbalance" that followed the
High Middle Ages. Although Maritain later disavowed the polemical excesses in
this work, it did constitute an eloquent, meditative analysis of what was wrong
with the capitalist world engendered by Protestantism, and of what had been
sound, well-founded, in traditional Catholic culture. The communitarian character of Catholicism was celebrated by Maritain, as he clarified the role of authority, community, and orthodoxy in a "true humanism." Maritain had been
drawn to a church with a strong notion of mystical communion among its members, rich and poor, living and dead, in the mystical body of Christ, and he considered these communitarian linkages of great importance throughout his life.[9]

In 1936 Maritain caught the attention of the Catholic world with his call for
a "true humanism" that would transcend the baneful individualism of the mod-

---

[7]Jacques Maritain, *Integral Humanism: Temporal and Spiritual Problems of a New Christendom*, trans. Joseph W. Evans (New York: Scribner, 1968) 79, 115.

[8]Sidney Hook, *Reason, Social Myths, and Democracy* (New York: Humanities Press,
1950) 79.

[9]He often remarked, matter-of-factly, in his letters to his friend Yves Simon after
Raïssa's death that she continued to be "amused" or "pleased" by events in his life. Simon, in turn, prayed to her (from the unpublished Maritain-Simon correspondence, in the
possession of Anthony O. Simon).

ern world. Almost contemporaneously his fellow Thomist Etienne Gilson denounced the epistemological individualism of modern philosophy in his William James Lectures at Harvard (later published as *The Unity of Philosophical Experience*)—a *philosophical* denunciation of the individualism of the modern world since Descartes, and a celebration of the true humanism that had flourished earlier.[10] Both of these important books by the two most eminent Catholic scholars of their generation were profound denunciations of the modern world. Maritain had isolated the spiritual and religious, Gilson the philosophical, roots of that alienating individualism both descried. Both of them offered implicit retrospective justification for Pius IX's disdainful mid-nineteenth-century proclamation that "if anyone suggest that the Roman Pontiff could or should be reconciled with progress, liberalism, and the modern world let him be anathema." Gilson was lionized at Harvard (where a certain aesthetic medievalism had been in vogue since Henry Adams's *Mont St. Michel and Chartes*), Maritain at the University of Chicago (where Maritain's friends and students flourished under the Great Books classicism of R. M. Hutchins) and Princeton's Institute for Advanced Study (where Maritain finally settled as a prestigious scholar-in-residence). Both men offered immensely learned defenses of the well-foundedness and wisdom of the ancient, precapitalist, prebourgeois, Catholic cultures; thus they lent support to Nietzsche's remark that the Reformation was "the rebellion of the simpleminded against something complex."

Throughout all of these years, the Maritains "lived" their philosophy—and in such a thorough, even spectacular, way that it significantly contributed to their influence. Jacques Madaule described the Maritains' salon at Meudon before World War II:

> At Meudon, a bit lower than the plateau, in a region where the houses almost, but not quite, touched one another, Jacques and Raïssa Maritain lived in a house where they had visitors Sunday afternoon. . . . Maritain spoke in a very soft, almost inaudible, voice which did not at all resemble his style, which was assertive and sometimes violent—cutting to be exact. One had to cut off the false, to prune, to prune. . . .
>
> Pale, a bit swollen, with something cat-like in the skull and shoulders which he always covered with a carelessly fixed muffler, Jacques Maritain had the physique of his voice rather than that of his style. Nevertheless his eyes, a bit globular and very clear, which seemed to observe nothing and no one—they were fixed on the infinite—gave away the gentle, but inflexible intransigence of the Thomist philosopher. . . .

---

[10]See Laurence K. Shook, *Etienne Gilson* (Toronto: Pontifical Institute of Medieval Studies, 1984). This study offers a wealth of detail on the subject.

. . . [O]ne of the intellectual chapels of Paris. There are the young—younger than I—who speak. They seem, themselves, initiated. From time to time, one or the other noiselessly left the salon and went up to the next floor where the Chapel, the true one, was. . . .

. . . [T]he most furtive allusion was sufficient for those lively intellects. It was in fact a communion. It was the reflection in light, brilliant, self-effacing words of the silence above, on the first floor.

Certainly the atmosphere at Meudon was a bit rarefied. Perhaps that came from the *mariage blanc* of Jacques and Raïssa. They were imitated by a few other couples. It was like a convent with walls of dazzling whiteness, where all was of an irreproachable and audacious good taste.[11]

The Maritains became living examples of a heroic ideal and of a disdain for modern society partially inspired by a contempt for sexual permissiveness. At the time when the Maritains were converted to Catholicism (by a man whose obsession with modern impurity was expressed in vivid sexual imagery), the intellectual life of the church was dominated by priests who undertook the spiritual direction of married couples. The Dominicans Humbert Clérissac and Reginald Garrigou-Lagrange played this important role in the lives of the Maritains. The couple maintained a discreet silence about certain aspects of their marriage, but they did not publicly dissuade other couples from adopting their notion of chastity. Jacques Maritain displayed contempt for Martin Luther's inability to conquer his sexual desires and maintain his celibacy vows. Clearly the austere lifestyle of the Maritains—which sometimes prompted the accusation of "angelism"—was part of their rejection of contemporary self-indulgence and materialism, and of their affirmation of what Jacques called "the primacy of the spiritual."[12] Jacques derided psychiatry and psychiatrists and described Freudianism as the particular scourge of Protestant consciences and cultures.[13]

The Maritains obliterated their "individualism" by entering the French Catholic community at one of its most sacred pilgrimage places. They pained friends and family, rejected "their own" for strangers, and rigorously affirmed in word and deed the supernatural veracity of the community to which the "shock of conversion" had led them. For the rest of his life one of Jacques's most significant and important preoccupations was his reflecting on the relationship between the "person" and the "community."[14] The Maritains' friend Péguy suggested that an important element of the truth of Catholicism was in its link

---

[11]Jacques Madaule, *L'absent* (Paris: Gallimard, 1973) 11-14.

[12]See his *Primauté du spirituel* (Paris: Plon, 1927).

[13]The Maritain-Simon correpondence offers several examples.

[14]See his *The Person and the Common Good*, trans. John Fitzgerald (New York: Scribner, 1947) chapter 4 and passim.

with the Catholic peasant masses, and this romantic populist element played some role in the couple's Catholic sensibility—particularly in North America,[15] where the immigrant and working class constituency of the church represented an element of distance from what Maritain saw as the individualistic or "bourgeois" character of much of American Protestantism.

A Humanism

Before World War II, by special permission, the Maritains had a private chapel, a tabernacle containing the sacred host, in their home. Thus they created a sort of parish for intellectuals at Meudon during the interwar years that drew philosophers, writers, artists, and musicians of all—or even little—faiths (although Thomists and "white Russian" Orthodox were particularly well represented). Thus although the Maritains joined "the Catholic Community" one met the Parisian—then American—intellectuals and artists rather than the common run of Catholics in their salon. Only the Russian philosopher Nicholai Berdyaev at his home in Clamart held gatherings similar to those in Meudon, alternating his own for a time with them.

The Maritain salon was integrally "Catholic" yet ecumenical—inviting participants representing a variety of belief and nonbelief. The couple seemed to believe that although Roman Catholicism was "the Truth," serious representatives of other traditions, Christian or non-Christian, were worthy of respect. While Jacques developed close friends among various non-Catholics and nonbelievers, his Catholic friends tended to be monks, priests, or ascetical lay people (Fathers Journet, Garrigou-Lagrange, Clérissac; Julien Green) who were rigidly orthodox in their Catholic doctrine and practice. Apparently he drew from Bergson the notion that there was a particular genius in each religious tradition as long as its particular "mystique" was lived "integrally" and "authentically." And so the Maritains frequented the intellectual, artistic, and spiritual elites of literary and aesthetic schools and religious traditions ("they want to be in on everything," a cynic remarked) while maintaining a certain contempt for the slackers and heretics,[16] and relative ignorance of the foot soldiers, in their own adopted tradition.

---

[15] An important example was Maritain's close friend the American Catholic radical and convert Dorothy Day, who often celebrated the plebeian nature of the church to which she had adhered.

[16] Nicholai Berdyaev was sometimes shocked to find how harsh the soft-spoken Maritain could be toward sincere Catholics who wandered from what Maritain considered to be Catholic orthodoxy. Even Jean Cocteau became "excrement" for Maritain after reneging on his conversion to the church. See John Hellman, "Maritain versus Mounier," *Review of Politics* 32:2 (April 1980): 152-66.

The intense and intuitive "conversion" of the Maritains had been to the Roman church—not to a milieu, a metaphysics, or a political and social philosophy. This was spectacularly demonstrated when Maritain, then considered the most brilliant young philosopher of the Action Française school, broke with it out of fidelity to Roman discipline. Thus his Catholicism stood beyond all "modern" notions of progress, beyond all political and social considerations; its doctrines were unquestioned and unquestionable.

The humanism of the Maritains was based upon their faith commitment to the veracity of a particular dogmatic community—one that had come under attack again and again but, somehow, had survived. The life-style of the Maritains grew out of the distinctive roles of the spiritual and intellectual elites in that community. As one of the church's most prominent married couples, they attempted to embody that ideal in highly visible, efficacious positions.

Why did the relatively austere humanism of the Maritains strike such a responsive chord? The authoritarianism and anti-intellectualism of the religion shaped by Pius IX seemed to place it in a holding action against the contemporary world. That such a highly intelligent couple freely chose to adhere to it at the time and place they did, that they maintained their commitment and regularly defended it with great intelligence and eloquence, was truly remarkable: this was a time when "anti-catholicism was becoming the anti-semitism of the liberal intellectual."[17]

Jacques Maritain regularly defended an organization, a *mentalité*, that was basically hierarchical, dogmatic, illiberal, intolerant. During his lifetime he often passed for a liberal, or even a leftist, as he broke ranks over Mussolini, Franco, or Pétain. But this gave him all the more prestige among non-Catholics, who were surprised to see a liberal, an intellectual, prominent within a community that seemed so overwhelmingly illiberal and anti-intellectual.

Aquinas

Jacques Maritain, like his fellow Bergson student Etienne Gilson, had a gift for making thirteenth-century texts seem comprehensible, "timeless," relevant to present-day concerns. This effort had some unavoidable reactionary implications, for it assumed that a medieval man—albeit one of unusual intellectual and spiritual gifts—had penetrated the truths of the universe, had grasped the nature of things in the thirteenth century, in a way comparable to the best efforts of our own best scientific, philosophical, and technological minds. Despite the fact that Aquinas was an Aristotelian and an eminently logical thinker, was it any more rational to look for the *truth* in those ancient texts than to seek it out in the hovel

---

[17]I first heard this old saw from Martin J. Corbin, former editor of the *Catholic Worker*.

of a scatological novelist on Montmartre, or in the "secrets" of the Virgin's prophecies at La Salette? It was radically "antimodern" to try to grasp the thought processes and insights of a man who had philosophized when men still thought the earth was flat, stars were moved by angels in a divinely ordained way, and man was the center of the universe. Then, too, the retrospective celebration of Aquinas also entailed a certain legitimation of Aristotelian politics recommended by the saint that had little sympathy for revolutionary social and political transformations.

Medievalism

At the turn of the century there was a fashionable "medievalism" in some Western countries; it is part of the background to Maritain's legitimation of Scholastic philosophy. J.-K. Huysmans was an example as he tried to project himself, through a powerful effort of the imagination, into a "weightier" age— one in which beliefs, commitment, values, feeling, and sensibilities were more intense and less complicated. He adorned his novels with medieval symbols. The Maritains participated in Georges Rouault's effort to recapture the simple intensity of stained glass in his art; they knew the monks who revived Gregorian chant and duplicated the architecture of the Middle Ages in the spirit of Dom Gueranger at the Abbey of Solesmes. Etienne Gilson, devotee of the romantic adventurer-novelist Pierre Loti and Wagnerian opera, learned to study the medieval texts in a new way after the course taught by Bergson ("the most important event in my life") and contact with the pioneers of the *histoire des mentalités*, Lucien Febvre and Marc Bloch. [18]

Maritain was not a trained historian like Gilson, and his moralistic monograph *Humanisme intégral* made certain generalizations regarding the Middle Ages, [19] inferred from his reading of Saint Thomas, which suggested that the quality of life, then, was superior to our own in several respects. As the distinguished Cambridge medievalist G. G. Coulton pointed out, Maritain "drew some of [his] important conclusions by rigid logic from unverified assumptions." The Thomist philosopher implied, for example, that a general authenticity, purity, intensity, and integrity characterized the religious *mentalité* of men and women in the Middle Ages, that the integrated religious perceptions of those times fostered attitudes toward nature, toward one's fellow human beings, that were a healthy contrast to our own "bourgeois" alienation. Coulton juxtaposed a num-

---

[18]Valuable background is provided by Father Shook in *Etienne Gilson*, and John E. Craig, *Scholarship and Nation Building: The Universities of Strasbourg and Alsatian Society, 1870-1939* (Chicago: University of Chicago Press, 1984).

[19]See *Integral Humanism*, especially chs. 1 and 5.

ber of period authors, including Saint Thomas, on themes such as slavery, serf-
dom, relic veneration, and social hierarchy as an antidote for the sanguine rhetoric
about the medieval quality of life. The medieval historian found Maritain's "true
humanism" based upon "a comparatively narrow specialization in medieval
metaphysics," and, at bottom, "little more than an old theology refurbished."[20]

Etienne Gilson's method for studying "the medieval mind" also entailed the
culling of texts for precious philosophical and religious insights, rather than examining the "popular religions" of the masses. But Gilson, distrusting "contemporary readings" of Saint Thomas, avoided speculating about current
applications of the antique texts or considering himself a historian of philosophy
rather than a philosopher; "the only task of history is to understand and to make
understood," he wrote, "whereas philosophy must choose."[21] But Gilson, too,
chose to understand a lost world through its intellectual and spiritual elites.

At the time when Maritain and Gilson were discovering the riches of medieval Catholicism, the Catholics of the United States seemed to represent the
antithesis of higher culture in North America—a church of the untutored, often
illiterate, masses of newer immigrants from Ireland and southern Europe. Protestants had tended to denigrate the "Dark Ages," but nineteenth-century ro-
manticism had celebrated the beauties of the Age of Faith—spirituality, art, and
architecture—suddenly fashionable among the educated in both France and the
United States.

Jacques Maritain's inference from his reading of Saint Thomas that a "true
humanism" had been experienced in the Middle Ages met a receptive audience
in the North American intelligentsia—he was a learned celebrator of a lost world
that pretended to survive in certain ethnic groups' veneration of Mary and the
Sacred Host, pilgrimages, concern for the souls in Purgatory, and reverence for
sacred relics. What had seemed so primitive, obscurantist, and superstitious to
non-Catholics was now presented as part of a remarkably complex, harmonious
edifice that could be properly appreciated by the initiated. Training in medieval
metaphysics, under Maritain or Gilson, drew the most talented Catholics of the
younger generation to these teachers who legitimized the philosophy of an entire
religious culture, one in which medieval texts continued to dominate the educational formation. American Catholics did not produce "intellectual" spokes-
men for their community as did the Protestants or Jews, and their church remained
singularly unattractive to the cultural aristocracy. Henry and Brooks Adams,
Ralph Adams Cram, and most of the American intelligentsia who "converted"
to a love for the Middle Ages preferred a "High Anglican" affiliation. American

---

[20]G. G. Coulton, "The Historical Background of Maritain's Humanism," *Journal of
the History of Ideas* 5 (October 1944): 415-33.

[21]Shook, *Gilson* 115, 278.

Catholics imported their intellectuals from the old continent, men who had established their reputations making the Middle Ages "understood" (such as Gilson, the historian of medieval philosophy; Christopher Dawson, historian of an organic medieval culture and holder of the first Stillman Chair of Catholic Studies at Harvard; and Maritain, interpreter of Saint Thomas Aquinas). Thus in a higher culture in which Catholics were conspicuous by their absence, distinguished Europeans arrived with vast, complex, arcane intellectual baggage to fill the void. G. G. Coulton's charge that the heritage of Protestant unfairness to the Middle Ages led to an overcompensation in favor of the neo-Thomist revival may be supported by the relatively uncritical reception of Maritain, Dawson, and Gilson, at Princeton, Chicago, and Harvard, where—despite the noncomformity of their approaches—they remained relatively unchallenged champions of medieval culture. In Roman Catholic intellectual circles, such as they were, Gilson and Maritain were honored as living saints. Controversial and much less influential figures in their own country, they became "prophets" in the New World. Their legitimacy was confirmed by secular institutions (where no native-born, self-conscious, Catholic intellectual would surface for some time to come). Moreover Maritain, with his Protestant background and Jewish wife, and Gilson, with his *gourmandise* and sociability, often seemed more comfortable in the liberal atmosphere of secular campuses, among their intellectual peers, than in the Catholic universities, where they were fawned upon in a rather naive and embarrassing way.[22]

Demise

The heyday of Jacques Maritain's influence in North America came during the 1950s, as the "bricks and mortar" American Catholic church constructed a vast network of parishes, convents, seminaries and educational institutions. The Maritains at Princeton were reassuring symbols of the ultimate good sense of this immense effort, as the American Roman Catholics retained their traditions of hierarchy, authority, dogmatic coherence, and distinctiveness in Protestant North America.

In France, World War II marked a significant decline in interest in the great prophetic and apocalyptic miracles such as Notre Dame de La Salette, the casting of a certain discredit on the "medievalism" of Catholicism in France, and a decline in the authority of the Catholic episcopacy. While certain Catholics were prominent in the Resistance, many others sympathized with the early Pétain regime's traditionalist rhetoric, corporatist social projects, and pro-Catholic policies. The hierarchy showed enthusiasm for the marshal's *prise de pouvoir* at the

---

[22]This is vividly reflected in several letters in the Maritain-Simon correspondence.

outset and counseled obedience to legitimate authority thereafter. Vichy propaganda suggested that un-Catholic phenomena such as liberalism and individualism were responsible for France's defeat and were now doomed. Several old friends of the Maritains—Action Française associates such as Henri Massis, a number of priests—had come from political limbo to play important, if fleeting, roles in their country. In 1945 a number of "Thomists" were discredited along with their antimodern moralistic rhetoric.

Our understanding of the origins of the Maritains' humanism has been shaped by Raïssa's eloquent memoirs, *Les grandes amitiés*—published in 1941 when Jacques was an isolated "Catholic of the Resistance" cut off from the majority supporting the Revolution Nationale. Raïssa explains how she and Jacques had taken their distances from the philosophy of Bergson, the Action Française, and those right-wing Catholics who had found Pétain a providential figure. The Maritains' defection from the Right, disapproval of Vichy, and pro-Americanism were abrasive to significant figures in the church back home, and the couple, admired as champions of freedom in the New World, were considered traitors to their church and to their friends in the Old.

But World War II, in retrospect, hastened the doom of that traditional Catholicism that the Maritains had found so attractive: it accelerated fundamental alterations in Catholic religiosity, sense of the sacred, and community. There were, for example, important changes in Catholic burial practices. Whereas for centuries the dead had been buried in close proximity to, if not inside, the churches, graves now began to be shunted outside of town, while the dead began to play a far less important role in the lives of the living. This weakened not only the local sense of community but also that cosmic juncture with the souls in purgatory and the communion of saints that Jacques always found so important. The veneration of local saints and their relics, healing shrines in general (Lourdes excepted), also went into decline. The melting away of "the magical" in ancient religious practices accelerated the decline of certain forms of popular piety and of the church's authority. The disappearance of Latin from philosophical and theological discourse and the liturgy fostered a new pluralism in philosophy, theology, and liturgical practices and eroded that coherent and unified religious culture that had been so important to Jacques and Raïssa Maritain.

The erosion of Thomism's status as the orthodox Catholic philosophy and theology undermined the prestige of the Thomists, who suddenly became intellectuals "like the others." The new pluralism in these fields encouraged an ecumenical and tolerant attitude toward other systems of belief. Some prominent Thomists defended the notion of freedom of conscience; after some vigorous debate, it was legitimized at the Second Vatican Council. Even clerical celibacy, that basic traditional Catholic difference from Protestantism, came into question—along with the conception of sexuality that inspired the traditional ideal of chastity. After encountering Léon Bloy, Raïssa Maritain recalled, "only one thing mattered: to be of the saints." The role of asceticism, contemplative withdrawal, the interior life, penance, in the traditional way toward saintliness, came to be displaced by admiration for intense, altruistic, efficacious social action.

The rapid and wide-ranging changes within Roman Catholicism after World War II swept away not only the distinctive, colorful features of the nineteenth-century French Catholic church but also several centuries-old facets of Catholic religious culture.

The Roman Catholic church that had answered Jacques Maritain's desperate turn-of-the-century quest for certitude seemed, by the 1960s, to have been altered beyond recognition. Would he have been tempted to be "turned inside out like a glove" by the pluralistic, dissension-ridden institution that saddened his last years? A cultural anthropologist might wonder if it was even the same religion! Maritain's humanism had been inspired by a counterculture that, in his twilight years, seemed to disintegrate around him. Maritain and Gilson were, in their devout old age, living relics of a church in which the veneration of relics had long been of great importance. As old men they prayed to the dead, and awaited death as a passage unto eternal life—while the dead, and death, were disappearing from their religion.

Karol Wojtyla, soon after his election to the papacy, acknowledged his debt to Jacques Maritain. As a seminarian in Rome immediately after World War II, he had been formed by Maritain's mentor, then sometime political adversary, Reginald "the rigid" Garrigou-Lagrange, "the sacred monster of Thomism."[23] The great Dominican, decisive in the intellectual formation of the new pope, was held up by the latter as a model of priest-scholar for worldwide emulation. Karol Wojtyla's "Thomist Personalism," his distinctive personal philosophy, displayed an approach to Saint Thomas that seemed to ignore the incidents of political divergence and drew from the ideas of both Maritain and Garrigou-Lagrange.

Father Wojtyla absorbed a notion of humanism quite similar to that of Maritain. His Polish Catholic Church (a religious culture, "preserved as in a time capsule," resembling that of late-nineteenth-century France) was the kind to which Maritain had been originally attracted: integrated, distinctive, national, popular, and plebeian. It celebrated mass pilgrimages to shrines of the Virgin, a rich sense of the sacred, conservative sexual mores, hierarchical authority, and an anti-individualistic community spirit. Thus Pope John Paul II is a reincar-

---

[23]François Mauriac used this term to describe the philosopher. Maritain attacked Father Garrigou-Lagrange's support for the Franco and Vichy regimes. See his letter to the priest of 1946, reprinted in Bernard Doering, *Jacques Maritain and the French Catholic Intellectuals* (Notre Dame IN: University of Notre Dame Press, 1983) 222-23.

nation of the Maritain paradox: he proclaims a "new humanism"—which has much of an old medievalism to it; he proclaims human liberation—while reinforcing authoritarian structures in the church; he upholds the dignity of women—while defending male-dominated religious institutions and sexual comportment. Like Maritain, John Paul II uses his brilliant, well-trained, and logical mind to celebrate the virtues of popular religious practices such as the veneration of the Black Madonna or national hero-saints. While denouncing the unhealthiness of contemporary sexual morality, John Paul II defends ideals and life-styles attacked by psychologists and psychiatrists as fostering neuroses. While celebrating the populist and democratic nature of the Catholic culture, he fights to reestablish the role of spiritual and intellectual elites within that culture. John Paul II is out to convert the world to a new humanism, to turn it inside out like a glove, the way Léon Bloy, at the beginning of this century, converted Jacques and Raïssa Maritain.[24]

[24]See John Hellman, "John Paul II and the Personalist Movement," *Cross Currents* 30:4 (Winter 1980-1981): 409-19 and, more generally, the same author's *Emmanuel Mounier and the French Catholic Left* (Toronto: University of Toronto Press, 1981).

MATTHEW J. MANCINI

Maritain's Democratic Vision: "You Have No Bourgeois"

I

BY 1641 RENÉ DESCARTES felt prepared to reveal at last the great secret he had discovered two decades before. Human beings, he announced, consist of two distinct and separate substances, the mind and the body. These two substances coexist in single individuals, of course, but remain distinct. The Scholastic philosophers of old had reasoned that human persons were made up of a single substance—a fusion of intellect, spirit, and matter—but Descartes, shrugging off the heavy burden of the past, denied the traditional doctrine. My mind alone shall be the judge, he said, and from that time man's nature was thought to be twofold. Believing it to be so, men acted as though two utterly different kinds of being—minds and bodies—were the objects of different kinds of investigation—that of thoughts and that of things.

Jacques Maritain considered Descartes's severing of human nature to lie at the root of the modern confusion about man and man's relation to God, nature, and society. He called it "the original sin of modern philosophy."[1] By rending the fabric of human nature, Descartes created within man the two domains of intellect and "extension," or the properties of bodies. For Descartes, knowers are sundered from the world of objects; all they can grasp of that world are its appearances. If it were not for their faith in God, human beings would despair of there being any congruence between what they think they know and the nature

---

[1]Jacques Maritain, *Three Reformers: Luther, Descartes, Rousseau* (London: Sheed and Ward, 1928) 77; cited hereafter as *TR.*.

of the world of extended bodies outside of them. Maritain labeled the Cartesian doctrine "angelism," since it is a philosophy of clear ideas independent of material things, a philosophy of pure intellectual apprehension—such as Descartes had learned about when he studied what the Scholastic philosophers had had to say about angels.

A century later, Descartes's spiritual "angelism" engendered its material counterpart in the self-absorbed individualism of Jean-Jacques Rousseau. With his belief in individual self-sufficiency, primitive natural liberty, the "General Will," law as merely the numerical expression of a majority, and a social contract emanating solely from human will rather than from nature, Rousseau was the progenitor of the great modern myth of "Democratism."[2] This myth perverted democracy at the very moment of its modern formulation, and so sent it staggering off under a burden of near-truths, and in the wrong direction.

Maritain might be said to have viewed Rousseau's ideas as the dialectical counterpart of angelism. Rousseau's precept of "be yourself" meant, in his case, following the "inclinations of his material individuality"; if it felt good he did it. And so, Maritain said, in a phrase that throws a flash of illumination upon the problem, "Rousseau is Descartes's angel acting like a beast" (TR 99). Descartes, in other words, had separated bodies and intellects and chose to live in the intellect. Rousseau chose the body. Together these two stand like colossi at the gate of modern thought and feeling, testifying to the divorce between matter and spirit that Descartes had triumphantly announced in the midst of the Thirty Years War.

This chapter is an attempt to elucidate Maritain's understanding of democracy—not just democracy as a tenet of a political philosophy but as a theme in his life and work as well. In it Rousseau and Descartes appear as touchstones, men whose obscure glimpses of shrouded truths pointed the way to a profounder understanding of this most noble and difficult of political ideas. This is not a study in political philosophy per se (for that huge subject see the chapter by Paul Sigmund in this volume) but rather an attempt to unravel the democratic thread from that larger coherent fabric. Its aim is simple: to make plain what Jacques Maritain's understanding of democracy was; how that understanding developed; and how, when properly understood, democracy was seen to have emerged from the heritage of the Gospels. Several themes will be developed along the way: how Maritain's customary approach to philosophic problems of all sorts was especially suited to the examination of democracy; how he saw democracy as part of the larger task of creating an integrally human civilization; and finally how Chris-

---

[2]Jacques Maritain, *The Things That Are Not Caesar's*, trans. J. F. Scanlan (New York: Scribner, 1930) 135-36.

tianity illuminates both the failure of the bourgeois democracies and the possibilities for their regeneration in other, quite different forms.

By the 1920s Maritain saw clearly that his philosophic labors would have to be directed toward the reconstruction of the human personality, its restoration to wholeness: its reintegration. But no such effort could remain exclusively philosophical, not in the France of the interwar years; and so his calling would thrust him into the fiery world of political and social controversy. He would emerge with many scars but having accomplished, with a sort of fierce charity, a great task of intellectual synthesis.

His work was social and political because, in France particularly, the ideas of Rousseau were bound inextricably with the development of democratic ideas and institutions. In Maritain's time and place, many religious persons suspected the rationalist, agnostic basis of democratic ideas. The reputed origins of such notions in the likes of Locke and Montesquieu (not to mention the man his worshipers dubbed "Nature's Saint") helped to create a continuing hostility to democracy, and a great bitterness permeated the harsh polemics of the republicans and the clericals. To criticize Rousseau would therefore mean to attack a whole constellation of political and social attitudes associated with the great and unruly tradition of French republicanism. "What the ecclesiastical history of this century shows above all," Theodore Zeldin writes, "is a crisis of communication: churchmen and free-thinkers were so carried away by the bitterness of their disagreements that they became incapable of understanding each other, and hopelessly confused as to what their quarrels were about."[3]

How, in such an atmosphere, could the task of philosophic reconstruction proceed? The answer to that question had first been revealed to Maritain in 1910, when he turned the first pages of the works of Thomas Aquinas. Maritain's task was to be achieved not by the rigid imposition of the letter but by the dynamic application of the spirit of Saint Thomas to the problem of the derailment of modern thinking that stemmed from the dream of Descartes.

The correspondences are intriguing: four hundred years before Descartes, Friar Thomas d'Aquino had confronted a condition remarkably similar to Jacques Maritain's. In the thirteenth century, two groups of zealous revolutionaries seemed to be at each other's throats. These were the voluntary poverty movement, exemplified in the new mendicant orders founded by Saint Dominic and Saint Francis, and the followers of the newly rediscovered pagan sage, Aristotle. Pieper tells us that Thomas was destined to span these two seemingly antagonistic view-

---

[3]Theodore Zeldin, *Intellect, Taste, and Anxiety*, vol. 2 of *France, 1848-1945* (Oxford: Clarendon, 1977) 983.

points. Thomas's thought was like an "arc," he says; or like Odysseus's bow, which required a strength that few men possessed to string the two ends together.[4]

What was characteristic—and exemplary—in Thomas's reaction to these impassioned groups was his "refusal to choose," that is, to judge the situation to be one that demanded his embracing one movement and absolutely rejecting the other. "Both [movements] appeared in extremist form—theologically speaking, in the form of heresies," Pieper writes.

> The remarkable thing about St. Thomas . . . is that he recognized and accepted the rightness of both approaches; that he identified himself with both; that he affirmed both, although they seemed mutually opposed to one another; and that he attempted to incorporate both in his own spiritual and intellectual life. . . . He "chose" both—and did so not by merely tacking one onto the other in a mechanical fashion, but by grasping and demonstrating their inherent compatibility; in fact, by showing the necessity for fusing these apparently contradictory and mutually exclusive approaches to the world.[5]

Here then are a series of striking parallels. Two views of man's heritage and destiny, each presented in radical form, each after its own fashion true; an overheated religious and political atmosphere that forced people into one or the other of two hostile camps; a resounding No to the imperative of choice: such features characterized the milieu of Jacques Maritain no less than that of his great thirteenth-century mentor. Indeed—to use a phrase that Maritain himself might favor—Thomas's situation was *existentially analogical* to Maritain's. Not only, then, was Maritain to employ the strong and supple instrument of Thomism to understand and try to rectify the dislocations of post-Cartesian man; he was also to sense the existential links between Thomas's predicament and his own. "Saint Thomas's struggles against the pseudo-Augustinians and the Averroists [that is, the mendicants and the Aristotelians] will have to be taken up again and again," he wrote in 1924.[6]

We can discern in these remarks the broad outlines of Maritain's approach to philosophical problems generally. It was to search out the truths latent in opposing philosophical positions he considered erroneous, then to synthesize these partial truths in a higher truth. *Distinguir pour unir*—the title of his *magnum opus* of 1932—provides a description of Maritain's method as well as his goal.

Maritain gave this method a graphic, deliberately oversimplified illustration in a handbook he wrote during World War I for the purpose of introducing sem-

---

[4]Josef Pieper, *Guide to Thomas Aquinas* (New York: Mentor-Omega Books, 1964) 27.

[5]Ibid., 106.

[6]Jacques Maritain, *Bergsonian Philosophy and Thomism,* second ed., trans. Mabelle L. Andison in collaboration with J. Gordon Andison (New York: Philosophical Library, 1955) 21.

inarians to the discipline of philosophy. The book is full of diagrams like this one, which explains the different answers to the problem of substance (the very important problem that, as we saw, Descartes attempted to solve with a form of dualism):[7]

Philosophy of Aristotle and St. Thomas (Animism)

Two principles each incomplete in itself, one of which (the rational soul) is spiritual, form together a single substance (the human composite).

Error of Defect	Error of Excess
The human soul does not exist (*materialism*) or is unknowable (*phenomenalism*).	Man is a spirit accidentally united to a body (*exaggerated spiritualism*); the soul and the body are two substances each complete in itself (*dualism*).

This sort of diagram appears thirteen times in 160 pages. If it seems quaintly simplistic, almost droll, the reader should recall the didactic, introductory nature of the book in which it appears. And there comes at the end of this *Introduction to Philosophy* a calm and eloquent justification of his Thomist approach:

> The truth, indeed, is not to be found in a philosophy which keeps the mean between contrary errors by its mediocrity and by falling below them, being built up by borrowing from both, balancing one against another and mingling them by arbitrary choices made without the light of a guiding principle (*eclecticism*): it must be sought in a philosophy which keeps the mean between contrary errors by its superiority, dominating both, so that they appear as fragments fallen and severed from its unity.[8]

II

How do these considerations about Descartes, Rousseau, and Thomas help to illuminate Maritain's encounter with democracy? Quite simply, by establishing a general framework in which democracy occupied a specific position. Descartes and Rousseau exemplify a deviation at the outset of modern man's journey, and Thomas shows how to regain the right road. Such a formula as this is too simple, of course; a fuller investigation of the origins of the modern world's affliction would link several other names: Machiavelli—Luther—Descartes—

---

[7]Jacques Maritain, *An Introduction to Philosophy*, trans. E. I. Watkins (New York: Sheed and Ward, 1930) 176.

[8]Ibid., 270.

Rousseau—Hegel.[9] But it may be useful to begin with to portray Descartes and Rousseau as we have seen them thus far: as incarnations of the two distinct substances that, in Descartes's view, constituted human individuals.

The book containing Maritain's great polemic against Descartes and Rousseau was *Three Reformers*—a work that, if not one of Maritain's masterpieces, nevertheless occupies a crucial place in the evolution of his thought. Here were presented two men whose thought reflected the angelic and the material in very pure, almost clinical forms. (I do not fully endorse his portraits, but they must be acknowledged to be painfully penetrating.) Maritain held, at least in later days, that such a crystallizing of error was beneficial. "Even when they are wrong," he explained in a 1960 lecture, "philosophers are a kind of mirror, on the heights of intelligence, of the deepest trends which are obscurely at play in the human mind at each epoch of history." And all great doctrines develop from "a central intuition" that "truly gets hold of some aspect of the real." Far better to have these ideas clearly and systematically articulated than diffuse, vague, "anonymous and unrecognizable."[10]

Three Reformers appeared in 1925. It marks a milestone in Maritain's career. Here was an explicit formulation of themes that had been scattered in his earlier works. Yet, central as it is, it says little directly about democracy. In fact, before 1926 Maritain had had few words to say about political subjects. But in that year came the magisterial papal condemnation of Action Française, and Maritain's experiences during the crisis of this odious organization turned his thoughts toward political questions.

Action Française was an antirepublican, proto-Fascist organization founded during the turmoil of the Dreyfus Affair as a vehicle for undermining France's Third Republic. The catchphrase of its leader, Maritain's friend Charles Maurras, was *politique d'abord*—politics before all else, or the primacy of politics. (More telling, perhaps, was the slogan of Vaugeois, a prominent early leader: *réaction d'abord*.) Maritain responded to Maurras with a book called *The Primacy of the Spiritual*.[11]

---

[9]Jacques Maritain, *Christianity and Democracy*, trans. Doris C. Anson (New York: Scribner, 1944) 14-15; hereafter cited as *CD*.

[10]Jacques Maritain, *On the Use of Philosophy* (Princeton: Princeton University Press, 1961) 27, 5.

[11]*Primauté du Spirituel* appeared in English as *The Things That Are Not Caesar's*. The definitive study of Action Française is Eugen Weber's *Action Française* (Stanford: Stanford University Press, 1962). See especially 219-39.

It is not necessary to rehearse here the sorry tale of Maritain's oblique connections with the royalist posturers who constituted the group's leadership.[12] It is enough to note that those connections were real, if later regretted (and, as the papal action loomed closer, ever more critical); that Maritain defended the condemnation at the cost of bitter personal attack; and that the episode made him more fully aware of politics, and most especially of democracy, its promise and its heritage. He was at this time in his mid-forties, entering his intellectual prime with a thorough mastery of a multitude of fields of thought; he could direct his formidable and superbly trained intellect toward this new object and proceed with the well-earned gracefulness of full maturity.

And how did he proceed? In the manner his entire previous career had shown him to be right: by dissecting the errors, the "central intuitions" of thinkers with whom he disagreed, displaying the missteps of Machiavelli, of Descartes, of Hobbes, of Rousseau, revealing their misguided metaphysical assumptions, demonstrating how such mistakes, no matter how tragic their consequences might be, are "as fragments fallen and severed from" a lost unity; in sort, by distinguishing in order to unite.

Now it happened that a parody of such a method was ingrained in the French educational system. Saint Thomas and his "refusal to choose" aside, Maritain had been instructed as a schoolboy to philosophize in a similar way—one that Claude Lévi-Strauss sardonically described in his memoirs as pure artifice: the student introduced one common view of a disputed question, then disproved that view by recourse to a second, which, alas, proved to be inadequate as well. The impasse could then be overcome by the presentation of yet a third position, which disclosed how incomplete were the first two and showed them to have been different facets of a single reality. To Lévi-Strauss such a method was mere verbal gimmickry, an empty sophistry.[13]

But Maritain's mind was congenial to this sort of dialectic. The rhetoric of "neither . . . nor" and "on the one hand . . . on the other hand" defines the outward form of so much of what Maritain wrote that the reader sooner or later becomes attuned to the cadence of his writing, begins to anticipate the form of the coming argument. I am neither to the right nor to the left, Maritain asserted in his *Lettre sur l'indépendance* of 1935. And again, "Thomism belongs to no party

---

[12]The clearest exposition and analysis of this troubling episode appears in Bernard Doering, *Jacques Maritain and the French Catholic Intellectuals* (Notre Dame IN: University of Notre Dame Press, 1983) 6-59 and especially 6-16. Also useful is Julie Kernan, *Our Friend, Jacques Maritain: A Personal Memoir* (New York: Doubleday, 1975) 70-76.

[13]Claude Lévi-Strauss, *Tristes Tropiques*, trans. John and Doreen Weightman (New York: Atheneum, 1975) 51. See also Zeldin's comments on this passage in *Intellect, Taste, and Anxiety*, 226-27; and his remarks on French philosophy generally, 205-27.

either of the 'right' or of the 'left' ";[14] *Sept*, the Dominican periodical deeply influenced by Maritain, was "Neither of the Right nor of the Left."[15] One might cite dozens of similar examples, but to note only the most important, there were Maritain's definitions of Christian humanism, neither anthropocentric nor antihumanist;[16] of the person, neither a mere atom in a larger social mass nor a sovereign individual;[17] and of Christian equality, neither empiricist ("anti-Christian") nor idealist ("pseudo-Christian") in orientation.[18] Bringing such ideas together in a higher synthesis was a task of integration; and so Maritain's humanism was an "integral humanism." It was a call for integration that shocked and angered the proponents of other, quite different "integral" movements in France, which came from the political Right: the integral Catholics, the integral nationalists of Action Française. *"Marxiste-chrétien,"* murmured the *intégristes,*[19] but Maritain meant what he said: he was neither a rightist nor a leftist, and he regretted the iron grip of those "worm-eaten" categories on people's political outlooks.[20]

Maritain's labors would be directed toward the articulation of a democratic philosophy that would incorporate the legitimate truths latent in the yearnings of a bitterly divided France, the Right's passion for order and civilization, for example, and the Left's hunger for social justice and human dignity. Though he envisioned his task as one of building, others thought it more akin to walking on a tightrope. So inured were the French to the worm-eaten categories that many were not equipped to interpret his work, save by recourse to them. So it was that politics in the interwar years actually presented a situation appropriate to the method he had perfected. This method was far more rigorous and subtle than Lévi-Strauss's caricature.

---

[14]Jacques Maritain, *St. Thomas Aquinas: Angel of the Schools,* trans. J. F. Scanlan (London: Sheed and Ward, 1931) xi; cited hereafter as *STA.*

[15]Quoted in Doering, *Maritain,* 78.

[16]Jacques Maritain, *The Twilight of Civilization,* trans. Lionel Landry (New York: Sheed and Ward, 1943) 12-13; Jacques Maritain, *Integral Humanism: Temporal and Spiritual Problems of a New Christendom,* trans. Joseph W. Evans (New York: Scribner, 1968) 21-34 and passim; cited hereafter as *IH.*

[17]Jacques Maritain, *The Person and the Common Good,* trans. John J. Fitzgerald (Notre Dame IN: University of Notre Dame Press, 1966) chap. 3 (cited hereafter as *PCG*); Maritain, *The Rights of Man and Natural Law,* trans. Doris C. Anson (New York: Scribner, 1943) pt. 1; cited hereafter as *RMNL.*

[18]Jacques Maritain, *Ransoming the Time,* trans. Harry Lorin Binsse (New York: Scribner, 1941) 1-29; cited hereafter as *RT.*

[19]Doering, *Maritain,* 89.

[20]Maritain, *Twilight of Civilization,* 57.

III

In the decade before World War II, Maritain found that the democratic garment had been handed down in a worn and tattered state. The original fabric—the classical and Christian inspiration animating its message—was hardly recognizable.

Democracy, of course, has arisen in and from specific historic circumstances. It is not a universal phenomenon; it is absent from most of the vast compass of human history and therefore pertains to specific times and places. So it can be said that democracy is rooted more in material conditions than in eternal principles. Maritain, the arch-opponent of idealism, would have been the last to deny these assertions. But true as they may be, it must also be remembered that democracy is rooted in spiritual soil as well, and particularly in the message of Christ. It is these tidings of love, human worth, and dignity that Maritain so often referred to as a "leaven" of Christian inspiration active in the profane world. At the heart of this Christian inspiration there resides the notion of the person.

Maritain followed Saint Thomas in defining the person as "a universe of spiritual nature endowed with freedom" (*IH* 9).[21] A universe, and therefore a "totality" or whole; spiritual in nature rather than essentially material; and free: this is the human person. Men and women so considered are radically unlike the "individuals" who have inhabited society in the minds of political thinkers since Locke, as we shall have occasion to see.

Two facts about Maritain's notion of the person require emphasis: its wholeness and its intrinsic relation to the common good. First, persons are not mere components but rather are themselves (in essence) complete. Though persons are creatures, owing their existence to God, yet "each exists for its own sake, not as a cog in the machinery of the world" (*PCG* 17). Democracy, in its lurching, uncertain progress, has been the record of the attempt to recognize this wholeness; yet its crabbed individualist and materialist philosophic base has served to frustrate its own interior thrust.

Thus it is that human beings find themselves between two poles—that of individuality, a "material pole," and the "spiritual pole" of personality (*PCG* 33). What we have here is a familiar being: it is pre-Cartesian man, the human person of the Scholastics before Descartes tore the human substance asunder and declared body and spirit to be completely distinct. Of course, persons are also individuals, parts in a greater whole, and as such they have obligations to the state. But the state's obligation is to human persons, their fullest development as persons—to the task, that is, of civilization. We might express it in a formula:

---

[21]See also Jacques Maritain, *Freedom in the Modern World*, trans. Richard O'Sullivan (London: Sheed and Ward, 1930) 30n.

while individuals may be subordinated to the needs of the state, the state must remain subordinate to the needs of persons.

But (and here is the second point to be stressed) the idea of the person is inseparable from that of the common good. "Personality tends by nature to communion" (*PCG* 47). In other words, though each person is a whole he is an "open" totality, and naturally inclines toward social life. Yet the person's concern for the common good involves more than the gregariousness acknowledged by the classical philosophers. This common good is an ethical idea, not a sociological datum. It means the good of the social body as a whole, but in such a way that the concrete person is maximally liberated from "the servitudes of nature" (*PCG* 54). Maritain thus defined the common good specifically as

> the collection of public commodities and services—the roads, ports, schools, etc., which the organization of common life presupposes; a sound fiscal condition of the state and its military power; the body of just laws, good customs and wise institutions, which provide the nation with its structure; the heritage of its great historical remembrances, its symbols and its glories, its living traditions and cultural treasures. The common good includes all of these and something much more besides. . . . It includes the sum or sociological integration of all the civic conscience, political virtues and sense of right and liberty, of all the activity, material prosperity and spiritual riches, of unconsciously operative hereditary wisdom, of moral rectitude, justice, friendship, happiness, virtue and heroism in the individual lives of its members. These things . . . constitute the good human life of the multitude. (*PCG* 52-53)

This sketchy outline of Maritain's observations on the person is perhaps just enough to throw into relief the reveries of the solitary Rousseau on the subject of the individual and democracy. For the individual imagined by Rousseau was, in nature, self-sufficient; then he transformed himself in society, through the alchemy of the Social Contract, into a fragment of the whole. Individuals, then, were for him material components or atoms in civil society. Rousseau's self-sufficient individuals set out by sheer force of will to form a social state based on the specious and entirely artificial notion of the General Will—an act that gave rise to the equally contrived concept of the sovereignty of the people, which is the very wellspring of the confusion between democracy as a myth and as a form of government (*TR* 136). Since sovereignty means a supreme power that rules separate from and above the body politic, Maritain argued,[22] the inherent contradiction of Rousseau's formula is apparent from the outset. The people can never exist above and separate from itself. But beyond that, no legitimate form of po-

---

[22]Jacques Maritain, *Man and the State* (Chicago: University of Chicago Press, 1951) 34, 26-53; cited hereafter as *MS*.

litical power can exist in such a fashion, whether in monarchies or aristocracies or any other structure of government. Legitimate political power always resides in the people.

But these "people"—who are they? Considered collectively, "the people" is far from the aggregate of self-sufficient atoms who agree to depart from Rousseau's state of nature. They are rather, as Maritain described them in one of his most evocative essays, the "moral community made up of the bulk of those who labor with their hands, farmers and workers, and also of the various elements which in point of fact are socially and morally bound up with them."[23] The French term, *le peuple*, conveys shades of significance absent from its direct translation into English. Since it is in fact a community, *le peuple* embraces more than any social class, a social and economic category; and certainly more than "race," a biological concept of dubious validity. Instead it is at bottom an ethical idea, one that involves distinct ways of living in and thinking of the world. In 1937, amid the tragedy of the civil war in Spain and the anxiety it engendered in France, Maritain proclaimed in this essay his vocation of living and suffering with this community of manual labor. The proclamation marked also his existential embrace of the democratic promise.

Human beings, then, comprise both individuality and personality. But, in Maritain's view, with the rise of modern misconceptions of the human substance, the idea of the human being as individual had grown to enormous proportions, generating by way of reaction various doctrines of collective salvation, some pseudobiological or racist, others pseudosocial, like the Soviet version of Marxism. These deviations share an unyielding materialism. The one, bourgeois individualism with its refusal to recognize the communal basis of any form of good life and its shameful scorn for the poor; and the other, a monstrous compensatory myth of the submergence of the individual in the mass, which alone is seen to possess reality—both find their foundation in a notion of humanity as a material thing.

Thus were defined the terms that Maritain considered essential to any significant discourse about democracy: the person, entailing the notion of the common good; and, in sharply etched contrast, the individual and his or her accompanying ideology of self-interest. We may now turn to the substance of Maritain's scathing critique of democracy as it had developed in the nineteenth and twentieth centuries and to his vision of a genuine, integrally human democracy.

---

[23]Jacques Maritain, "To Live with the People," in *The Range of Reason* (New York: Scribner, 1952) 122; cited hereafter as *RR*.

IV

Maritain's turn toward democracy was gradual, even reluctant,[24] precisely because the common understanding of the term was so full of errors. These mistakes were associated with the narrow individualism of the bourgeoisie and with the development of capitalism (*CD* 48).

In 1956 Maritain dryly informed what I imagine to have been a roomful of raised eyebrows at a Chicago seminar: "You have no Bourgeois. That is one of the blessings of this country."[25] His mordant remark contains a world of meaning, for the bourgeoisie were the social embodiment of the illusions to which the Rousseauist conception of democracy had given rise. Those errors, he wrote, "correspond to the advent of the bourgeois class and ideology," and are "deadly" to democracy (*CD* 48). The task ahead, then, must be "passing from bourgeois democracy, drawn dry by its hypocrisies and by a lack of evangelical sap, to an integrally human democracy, from abortive democracy to real democracy" (*CD* 20).

The passage just quoted will reward an attentive pause. In it are ranged two sets of terms:

bourgeois/dry/	real/sap/evangelical/
hypocrisy/abortive	integrally human

That is to say: a genuine democratic faith contains a life-giving sap (this metaphor permeates all Maritain's democratic writings). The sap is evangelical, that is, derived from the Gospels. And genuine democracy is integral; it recognizes the fusion of matter and spirit that human beings comprise. By contrast, the blighted form of democracy that the bourgeoisie has brought in its train is dry, lacking in sap, hypocritical, and a failure. Let us take a moment to investigate these themes.

At the dawn of the modern era, after Descartes split human nature, man could function under two guises, as a natural creature and "a believing double" (*IH* 22). This partition left him free to pursue his material self-interest while keeping a separate sphere in his life reserved for such spirituality as he deemed necessary. Such was individualism, the creed of the emergent bourgeoisie, and democracy developed to the extent it coincided with the interests of this social class. The idea of the individual, then, was far removed from the whole "person" we have

---

[24]Doering, *Maritain*, 178-79.

[25]Jacques Maritain, *Reflections on America* (New York: Scribner, 1958) 87; cited hereafter as *RA*. Maritain argued that the United States, though "middle class," was not a "bourgeois" nation, since its class system is not bound up with a sense of fatalism (ibid., 177-78).

described; he was instead a material component or atom in civil society. And, just as the notion of the person entailed that of the common good, so that of individualism was stamped with the doctrine of self-interest. In other words, bourgeois individualism gave rise to a society without a common task (*RMNL* 24-25.)

Moreover, just as it knew no common good, bourgeois democracy "had no real common thought—no brains of its own, but a neutral, empty skull clad with mirrors" (*MS* 110). This striking image, with its implication of narcissism, helps to pinpoint the characteristic malady of bourgeois man, a certain arid detachment and superficiality. The syndrome is due not only to his preoccupation with himself but also to his aloofness from the world of real objects. Paradoxically, that world is of no real interest to this relentless accumulator of things, because he is actually more concerned with the *signs* of things than with things themselves. "A whole idealist and nominalist metaphysic underlies his comportment," Maritain said. "Hence in the world created by him, the primacy of the sign: of opinion in political life, of money in economic life" (*IH* 78). Such a valuation of the sign over the signified characterizes capitalism, a society "not of men but of money and paper, of symbols of wealth, a society whose soul is the desire to produce more titles of possession" (*IH* 164). The fundamental principle of capitalism, a return to capital of a share of income, is itself unexceptionable, but it too becomes distorted, "the *sign,* money, predominating over the *thing,* commodities useful to mankind."[26] Values are stood on their heads as money, rather than feeding productive activity, is instead fed by it.

In practice, then, democracy seemed to Maritain as confused and vitiated as its muddled theory would lead anyone to expect. And indeed in the thirties and forties the world's floundering democracies provided little enough evidence to the contrary. "The tragedy of the modern democracies," Maritain wrote in the darkest hours of the Second World War, "is that they have not yet succeeded in realizing democracy" (*CD* 17).

The reasons for the tragic failure come under two principal headings. First, though in varying degrees embedded in the sphere of politics, democracy remained unfulfilled in the social sphere; that is, the democratic nations have evolved a political but not a social democracy. The second reason is spiritual: democracy's break with its past, its losing track of its roots in the Gospel. Let us examine both these sources of breakdown further.

To begin, then, with the failure of democracy in the social sphere: democracy cannot be realized in an artificially compartmentalized arena of men's and women's lives labeled "politics," and then sealed off from the rest of human activity.

---

[26]Jacques Maritain, *Religion and Culture*, trans. J. F. Scanlan (London: Sheed and Ward, 1931) 56-57.

It is essential that it be a vital part of social life generally. And so it leads us to confront the difficult subject of equality, a subject on which the mind can easily be led astray by the deceptive clarity of geometric metaphors. While social democracy entails equality, equality must not be perceived as a willful blindness to the motley richness of human variety.

As may be expected, two different sorts of errors, each of which provides a fugitive glance at truth, characterize thinking about equality. "On the one hand . . . on the other hand": there are the nominalist philosophers of enslavement, and the idealist apostles of geometric sameness. The first, seeing that equality is not perceived by the senses, conclude that it cannot exist. So they divide humankind into unequal, pseudoscientific social and biological categories and declare that the favored groups absorb all the dignity of human nature. The second treat the abstraction "mankind" as the only reality. The nature of man resides, according to them, in the species, and justice in the law of numerical superiority.

Standing apart from these two distortions is the Christian knowledge of the unity of mankind, a wisdom activated only by love: "As long as love does not call it forth, that unity slumbers in a metaphysical retreat where we can perceive it only as an abstraction" (*RT* 15). That unity entails individual inequalities, since "No man is man in essence"; that is, no single person exhausts the potential of humanity. Finally, equality, activated by love, is realized only in society. So it, like political democracy, is an activity, not a thing merely. It is something men and women do as well as something they "are."

And so Maritain came to recognize more clearly than many of his contemporaries a great lesson of the twentieth century: democracy is the only way, not for all time but for our time, of solving "*the* basic problem in political philosophy" (*MS* 54), the problem of ends and means. Politics can be rationalized in one of two ways, he wrote, the technical-artistic or the moral. The first of these is familiar to us all. It is the solution of Machiavelli, of Hobbes, of the modern apostles of technocratic rationalization. The second is democracy; Maritain calls it "the only way of bringing about a *moral rationalization* of politics" (*MS* 59). And indeed, after the sterile selfishness of the bourgeois democracies, the mad Soviet drive for industrial domination at any cost, the vile racist fantasies of Nazi Germany, nothing could be clearer than the fact that democracy is not just a luxury, or simply one in a group of political values neutral in themselves, but a moral necessity in a world uncertain of its own survival.

The second, deeper reason for the failure of the modern democracies to realize democracy was that they had forgotten its origins in the Christian message of the person's infinite worth and the unity of mankind. Maritain employed a remarkably consistent family of metaphors when he discussed those origins. Surprisingly, these richly allusive tropes have attracted little direct comment. One finds that Maritain nearly always (in this political context) represented Christianity as a "leaven," or "sap," a "ferment" in society. These figures describe an immanent, vitalizing action or substance. The leaven causes bread to rise and imparts to it a sensory pungency, without which it remains insipid. The vintner adds yeast to his wine to induce fermentation, providing the wine with its flavor and its power to raise our spirits. Sap is to plants as lifeblood is to animals; where it flows, deep inside and scarcely perceptible—we know it chiefly by its effects—there is health. And an infusion is something beneficial poured into another mixture, as nutrients may be infused into the veins of a sick patient.

The evocatively Christian connotations of these metaphors enhance their aptness. Leaven and ferment call to mind bread and wine, food and drink for a sustenance both material and spiritual. And "infusion" is also the technical term used in Christian theology to explain the presence of spiritual grace in human beings. This connotative, anagogic quality is fitting, too, because Maritain took pains to point out that the democratic leaven often operated independently from the explicitly institutional structure of the church. Indeed it operates obscurely in the secular order, "in the depths of the profane, temporal conscience" (*RT* 204), "in the obscure depths of human history" (*MS* 111). We see it as through a glass darkly, but we should recognize and acknowledge its source and affirm that "the democratic impulse has arisen in human history as a temporal manifestation of the inspiration of the Gospel. The question does not deal here with Christianity as a religious creed," he insisted, "but rather with Christianity as a leaven in the social and political life of nations" (*CD* 25). And the Christian's vocation (not as a representative of his church but as a human being who is Christian) is that of "infusing into the world, wherever I am, a Christian sap" (*IH* 294).[27]

In the plainest terms, this sap, this leaven, is simply fraternal love, that force in the temporal order whose meaning was dimly understood by the great classical writers, Sophocles and Cicero in particular, and the full meaning of which is immensely clarified by the exemplary sacrifice of Christ and its explanation in the Gospel. Obviousy, Christianity is not a requirement for social justice to exist in the world—there was justice before Christ!—but the fuller unfolding of a social order directed to the common good awaited this news about charity—that virtue, Aquinas says, that gives form to all the other virtues and without which no genuine virtue exists.[28]

But clearly Maritain thought that the Christian origins of the democratic impulse had been lost, and that the price of that loss could be reckoned by examining the bourgeois democracies.

The diseased state of bourgeois democracy, then, manifests itself in a multitude of symptoms: it stands for a society whose members have lost a commit-

---

[27]See also Doering's discussion of this distinction in *Maritain*, 78-79.

[28]*Summa theologica* II-II.23.7-8.

ment to the common good, and as often as not even an awareness of it; a society without a center, either moral or intellectual. It lacks even a knowledge of its own origins, Christian and pagan alike. It treats of society as solely comprising self-interested, self-contained individuals. And it inverts the order of values. No wonder Maritain called the liquidation of capitalism a precondition for the construction of an integrally human democracy (*IH* 190).

But there is more; Maritain's analysis sliced even deeper. This form of civic life also produces its own contrary, in the form of the freedom-destroying totalitarian regimes so assiduously cultivated in the twentieth century.[29] He saw that, like the bourgeois democracies, those regimes too are hypocritical and dry: spiritually empty cities swept by the acrid winds of materialism. And it is this point exactly—the common materialist assumptions of both forms of rule—that kept Maritain aloof from the sterile contentions of Left and Right; this point, too, that was most easily and frequently misunderstood by his many critics.[30]

Yet it is important to emphasize the obvious point that bourgeois democracy *is* democracy and as such is precious. Maritain deplored its selfishness and confusion, but that did not mean that he put it on the same plane with its even more hideous offspring. On the contrary, democratic ideas and practices could be restored to health in a way that communism, for instance, was far less likely to be. Democracy's roots in the Christian and natural-law doctrines of the human person's dignity had to be reclaimed; like feuding brothers desperately in need of mutual forgiveness, "Christianity and democracy must recognize each other and become reconciled" (*CD* 19). And only on such a mutual recognition and reconciliation could be constructed—slowly, no doubt, and with many false steps along the way—a truly human, democratic common life.

V

After having seen the essential points in Maritain's critique, let us now examine his democratic vision, what he called an integrally human democracy. In a series of works extending from the late 1920s to the early 1950s, Maritain can be observed winnowing the democratic grain, so that at last we are presented with a democracy purged of its debilitating myths. Only a democracy thus purified, as Henry Bars remarks, "of the parasitic errors sucking at its life," is a fit vehicle for civilizaton.[31]

---

[29]Jacques Maritain, *Scholasticism and Politics*, translation ed. Mortimer J. Adler (Garden City NY: Doubleday, Image Books, 1960) 96.

[30]Brooke W. Smith, "The Jacques Maritain Controversy in Perspective," *Thought* 50:4 (December 1975): 381-99.

[31]Bars, quoted in Doering, *Maritain*, 182.

Civilization, in this context, means the development of persons. Taking issue with the German ideologists of *Bildung*, who had constructed an elaborate wall between the terms "civilization" and "culture," Maritain instead equated the two terms. Civilization was for him the culture of persons, their development in freedom of their artistic, intellectual, and spiritual powers.

In these deeply felt meditations on civilization, one can distinguish echoes of Maritain's own early life, for Maritain was himself a deeply civilized man. Born and raised in *fin de siècle* Paris, he received a superb education in philosophy, literature, and languages. If it was marred by a doctrinaire positivism, his training nonetheless served to cultivate the dormant seeds of his young intellect. He followed avidly the Parisian literary and artistic struggles that took place as the approach to art known loosely as "modernism" came to be born. Moreover, as Stanley Jaki points out in this volume, Maritain was also an accomplished student of the natural sciences, having undertaken formal postgraduate training in biology in Heidelberg under the distinguished Hans Driesch. Several of Maritain's friends remarked that this comfortable familiarity with twentieth-century trends in both science and the arts helped him in his role as observer, analyst, and, not least, Thomist philosopher. He could be a Thomist critic from the inside, as it were.

Maritain was, moreover, an urban creature. Keenly sensitive to the products of civilization, he seems to have had little appreciation for nature in the sense of wilderness or the countryside. His friend and translator Harry Lorin Binsse once said that, to Maritain, the country was just "a necessary evil . . . from which, mysteriously, the city draws its sustenance."[32] (Perhaps we have here a hint that Maritain's aversion to Rousseau was partly temperamental.) This strong mental and emotional feel for civilized life is reflected in Maritain's democratic vision. Like Pindar, he knew that "we must become who we are"[33]—that becoming human was a rigorous task possible only in civilized society.

Just as important, Maritain insisted that civilization was natural. It is the product of a kind of nature, human nature, but nature cultivated: "A civilization is truly deserving of the name only if it is a culture, a truly human and therefore mainly intellectual, moral, and spiritual development" (*STA* 50n). Culture is best understood by reference to its root meaning, "inciting nature by some human labor to produce fruits which nature left to herself would have been incapable of producing."[34]

---

[32]Harry Lorin Binsse, "Jacques Maritain: A Biographical Impression," *The Maritain Volume of the Thomist* (New York: Sheed and Ward, 1943) 6.

[33]Jacques Maritain, *Education at the Crossroads* (New Haven: Yale University Press, 1943) 1. This was one of Maritain's favorite aphorisms. See also *PCG* 44.

[34]Maritain, *Religion and Culture* 3; see also *IH* 95-96.

Among those fruits is civil society. It is a natural product, the nature in question being human. Maritain rejected radical notions of statecraft, the belief that the body politic is an unnatural, purely mechanical construct. Rousseau had argued that men and women leave nature behind and build society by an act of will. Before him, Hobbes based his grim masterpiece *Leviathan* on the idea of the state as a gigantic artificial concoction explicitly dissociated from man's natural condition. And before Hobbes, the great preceptor of Renaissance statecraft, Machiavelli, portrayed the state as a conscious work of art. This distinction between nature and art, itself highly artificial, serves to obscure the vital fact that social and political life precedes the arrival of any given individual and that civilization is *what men do* by nature. Reason and will are important for the development of any polity. But that does not make the City unnatural.

Democracy does run against nature's grain, Maritain conceded. "Democracy is a paradox and a challenge hurled at nature, at that thankless and wounded human nature whose original aspirations and reserves of grandeur it evokes" (*CD* 43). But this fact does not entail a violation of nature; rather it means an attempt to "straighten" it (*RMNL* 32). Just as education, for example, requires "taming the irrational to reason" but does not negate nature, so too democracy means nature must be straightened by reason and justice, raised by Christian inspiration as by a leaven. Jacques Maritain was a master of the fine distinction, but he used the words "democratic," "humanist," and "civilized" interchangeably.[35]

The activity appropriate to politics, then, is the development of civilization, or culture. But this misson is related to democracy at a profound level, for civilization becomes the political task in a specifically *democratic* political philosphy (*CD* 45). Here we approach the heart of Maritain's democratic vision. Persons in society, conscious of their essential unity and of a common good, no matter how differently that common good might be defined, recognize the task of civilization. It is a political and social task varyingly defined. Lincoln endowed it with its classic political expression: a government of, by, and for the people. Maritain's definition, if less aphoristic, is nevertheless elegant: "a rational organization of freedoms founded on law" (*MS* 59).

Affirming explicitly the source of this inspiration was to him a matter not just of intellectual fairness but of the very capacity of democracy to endure.

A time will come [he warned], when people will give up in practice those values about which they no longer have an intellectual conviction. . . . These remarks apply to democracy in a particularly cogent way, for the foundations of a society of free men are essentially moral. There are a certain number of moral tenets—

---

[35]*CD* 85; *IH* 95; *STA* 50. The humanism spoken of in this manner is always an "integral" humanism, distinguished from other, "anthropocentric" versions.

about the dignity of the human person, human rights, human equality, freedom, law, mutual respect and tolerance, the unity of mankind and the ideal of peace among men—on which democracy presupposes a common consent; without a general, firm, and reasoned-out conviction concerning such tenets, democracy cannot survive.[36]

VI

The metaphors that Maritain used to describe democracy lean heavily on a sense of prolonged duration: the democratic leaven works its way slowly in human history. It is not hard to detect in this sensitivity to duration the influence of Maritain's old teacher Henri Bergson. In his perception that the Gospels' power "unfolds in a measure of duration quite different from the rhythm of time" (*RT* 201); in his sense of human progress, remote though it was from the cult of progress worshiped in the nineteenth century;[37] and in his explanation of how, when measured by the span of "political duration," Machiavellianism does not succeed (*RR* 134-64), we can see how Maritain was able to extract from Bergson something truly valuable.

To a far greater degree, Maritain was indebted to Saint Thomas, yet his enterprise was always to incorporate the spirit of Thomism into his works. Where Saint Thomas was too directly tied to an anachronistic cosmology or polity, Maritain probed for the guiding spirit behind the letter. As Gerald McCool reminds us, most of Maritain's Thomist contemporaries opposed democracy because Thomas had favored a mixed form of government, comprising aristocratic, oligarchic, and democratic elements.[38] Saint Thomas could hardly have been for or against "democracy" as we know it, since it had not developed. But Maritain detected Thomas's deeper purpose, which was his claim that political legitimacy resides in the people. The specific form that that legitimacy takes will vary in different cultural and historical circumstances.

It is by virtue of the same dynamic spirit that Maritain's immensely rich body of work can serve to help us reflect about the direction of the lives we are called upon to live now. If, as Marshall McLuhan ruefully noted more than thirty years ago, Maritain's signposts are often mistaken for park benches,[39] it is nevertheless also true that Maritain himself teaches us by example the value of seeking out the essential spirit of a great thinker's work.

---

[36]Maritain, *Uses of Philosophy*, 12.

[37]Jacques Maritain, *On the Philosophy of History*, ed. Joseph W. Evans (London: Geoffrey Bles, 1959) ch. 1; *RMNL* 20.

[38]Gerald A. McCool, "Maritain's Defense of Democracy," *Thought* 54:2 (June 1979): 135.

[39]H. Marshall McLuhan, "Maritain on Art," *Renascence* 6:1 (Autumn 1953): 44.

PAUL E. SIGMUND

Maritain on Politics

A HUNDRED YEARS FROM NOW, I would venture to say, the political philosophy of Jacques Maritain will still be read. Those who read him will do so not so much for the intrinsic content of his arguments, although they do have a certain persuasiveness. It will rather be because his writings marked an important development of Thomist and Catholic political thought in relation to moden politics and society that helped to overcome the long-standing alienation between the Catholic church in Latin countries and democracy and the free society. A second reason that Maritain's political thought will be read is that he was the one primarily responsible for reformulating the Thomistic theories of natural law and the ideal state in ways that made them applicable to modern political conditions and that gave life to the political application of neo-Thomism. A third important impact of his political thought has been ideological. It provided the theoretical underpinnings for the important Christian Democratic parties and movements of Europe and Latin America. These contributions were made over a period of fifty years, during which his political thought underwent a certain internal development that I would also like to examine in this chapter.

First, a brief word about Maritain's personal political evolution. He only began to write on politics in middle age, catalyzed by the political shock of the papal condemnation of the right-wing French movement, Action Française. This led to his first specifically political work, published in Paris in 1927 and translated into English as *The Things That Are Not Caesar's*, a discussion of the role of the church in politics and the relations of church and state. That discussion was formulated in fairly traditional terms, focusing on the meaning of the so-called indirect power of the papacy in temporals and obviously relevant to the action against Action Française. In the book he criticized the excessive individualism of contemporary "bourgeois" liberalism and, while accepting democracy as one of several possible political forms, gave greater emphasis to the divine origin of all political power and to the church's metapolitical role "to lead all nations." Part of his criticisms of excessive democracy ("democratism") echoed his earlier attacks on Rousseau in *Three Reformers: Luther, Descartes, Rousseau*, the original French edition of which had been published two years earlier in 1925. Rousseau was criticized for adhering to a fundamentally flawed view of human nature in his admiration for the "natural man" and for supporting a false concept of the sovereignty of the people, the omnipotent "General Will." In both these works traces were still evident of the earlier political attitudes, summarized in the title of his 1922 work, *Antimoderne*, that had led him to sympathize with the conservative monarchism of Action Française. [1]

Under the impact of world depression and the rise of fascism and nazism, Maritain began to develop his political thinking in a more systematic way. In 1934 he published the French version of the book that was to be published in the United States as *Freedom in the Modern World* (*Du régime temporel et de la liberté*, 1934), [2] but his most important political work originated as a series of lectures delivered in Santander, Spain, in 1934, that is, two years before the outbreak of the Spanish Civil War. Published in English in 1938 as *True Humanism* (*Humanisme intégrale; problèmes temporels et spirituels d'une nouvelle chrétienté*, 1936), [3] it was the best known and most influential statement of Maritain's political thought until his Walgreen Lectures at the University of Chicago in 1950, published as *Man and the State*. [4] In *Integral Humanism* the fundamental elements of Maritain's Christian political thought were outlined, including his argument for integral

---

[1] *Antimoderne* (Paris: Revue des Jeunes, 1922). A bibliography of the works of Jacques and Raïssa Maritain (containing 7,423 items!), entitled *The Achievement of Jacques and Raïssa Maritain: A Bibliography, 1906-1961*, has been published by Donald and Idella Gallagher (Garden City NY: Doubleday, 1962). It is, of course, incomplete, since Maritain continued to publish until 1973, the year of his death. The most useful short bibliography appears on pp. 164-69 of John M. Dunaway, *Jacques Maritain* (Boston: Twayne Publishers, 1978). The only full-scale biography is Julie Kernan, *Our Friend, Jacques Maritain: A Personal Memoir* (New York: Doubleday, 1975). When a book that is mentioned in the text has been translated into English, the original French title and Paris publication date will appear in parentheses. If no French title appears, the book appeared originally in English. The two books mentioned above are *Three Reformers: Luther, Descartes, Rousseau* (New York: Scribner's, 1929) [*Trois Réformateurs: Luther, Descartes, Rousseau*, 1925] and *The Things That Are Not Caesar's*, trans. J. F. Scanlan (New York: Scribner's, 1930) [*Primauté du spirituel*, 1927].

[2] Trans. Richard O'Sullivan (New York: Scribner's, 1936).

[3] Trans. Margot Adamson (New York: Scribner's, 1938). Later retranslated by Joseph W. Evans and published as *Integral Humanism* (New York: Scribner's, 1968); cited hereafter as *IH*.

[4] Chicago: University of Chicago Press, 1951; cited hereafter as *MS*.

(that is, theocentric) humanism as superior to liberal or socialist humanisms; his theories of personalism, communitarianism, and political, economic, and juridical pluralism; his claim that the Gospel message is the "leaven" that has produced human freedom; and his initial revisions of the classical Catholic theory of church and state in the form of the theories of a "new Christendom" and the distinction between the spiritual and temporal planes. At this time (1935) he also wrote "Letter on Independence" (of Left and Right), which, as discussed below, had a very important influence on Latin America. Two other topics that engaged his attention in the later 1930s were anti-Semitism (*A Christian Looks at the Jewish Question*,[5] originally *Les Juifs parmi les nations*, 1938) and shorter introductions and polemical pieces opposing the Franco regime.

Maritain visited the United States in 1936 and 1938, in the latter case delivering lectures later published as *Scholasticism and Politics*.[6] He spent the war years in New York, where he published in French (Editions de la Maison Française) two short books in 1942 and 1943 that appeared in English a year later as *The Rights of Man and Natural Law*[7] and *Christianity and Democracy*.[8] In the first book he developed, out of the Thomistic theory of natural law and his own theory of personalism, a full list of rights of the human person, of the citizen, and of the social being, especially the worker. In the second, he argued once more for the evangelical (i.e., Christian) basis of democracy and against the errors of individualistic liberalism.

At the end of the war, Maritain was appointed French ambassador to the Vatican, and he remained in Rome until 1948. At that time he moved to Princeton, where he lectured in the philosophy department. He also spoke frequently at the University of Chicago, which, under the influence of Robert Hutchins and Mortimer Adler, had long been a center of neo-Thomism. His Walgreen Lectures at Chicago in 1950 marked a significant development of his political thinking and produced *Man and the State*, probably his most important work in the field. It included one of the most influential modern restatements of the Thomistic theory of natural law—now linked even more directly to natural rights—a more profound analysis of his theories on church and state, as well as a discussion of the possibilities of world government. Some of the themes developed in *Man and the State* were also discussed in several of the earlier essays collected in *The Range of Reason*,[9] including an important discussion of how the natural law can be known

---

[5]New York: Longmans, 1939.

[6]Translation ed. Mortimer J. Adler (New York: Macmillan, 1940); cited hereafter as *SP*.

[7]Trans. Doris C. Anson (New York: Scribner's, 1943); cited hereafter as *RMNL*.

[8]Trans. Doris C. Anson (New York: Scribner's, 1944).

[9]New York: Scribner's, 1952.

and a criticism of modern Machiavellianism. Maritain's enthusiasm for his adopted country was expressed in his *Reflections on America*,[10] but after hs wife's death in 1960 he left the United States and retired to a monastery in Toulouse, where he died in 1973. He continued to write in his retirement, and one of his books, *The Peasant of the Garonne*,[11] originally published in French in 1966, created a considerable furor because of its criticisms of the movement away from Thomism during and after the Second Vatican Council (1962-1965). His criticisms had political implications, since already radical theologians were drawing on new European theologies to produce a major challenge to his political thinking.[12]

This brief summary mentions only Maritain's most important political works. For an initial introduction to Maritain's political thought, *The Social and Political Philosophy of Jacques Maritain*[13] is a useful collection of excerpts from his major works, while *Man and the State* is the most accessible expression of his mature views. *Integral Humanism*, although more diffuse and undeveloped, should also be consulted because of its wide influence in Europe and Latin America.

As this account indicates, Maritain's political philosophy moved from a traditional rightist position in the early 1920s to a third position that was critical of capitalism and of communism in the 1930s to a position that we (although not he) might describe as natural rights liberalism in the 1940s to a close identification with the American version of liberal democracy in the 1950s, ending with an increasingly critical attitude toward radical tendencies in Catholic theology and political thought in the 1960s. Yet underlying those apparent shifts in position were certain common elements and an overall goal—to apply Thomistic thought to modern politics and to show the unique relevance of the Christian message for the solution of contemporary political, economic, and social problems. Typically he did this in classic Thomist fashion, by demonstrating that the position that he upholds occupies a middle position between two extremes in modern thinking. Let us examine some examples of Maritain's arguments along these lines.

---

[10]New York: Scribner's, 1958.

[11]Trans. Michael Cuddihy and Elizabeth Hughes (New York: Holt, Rinehart and Winston, 1968).

[12]See the criticisms of Maritain's "New Christendom" in Gustavo Gutierrez, *The Theology of Liberation* (Maryknoll NY: Orbis Press, 1973) ch. 4. The drafts of the original chapters were written by Gutierrez in the late 1960s and were directly influenced by German and French theologians. See my forthcoming study *Liberation Theology at the Crossroads: Democracy or Revolution?*

[13]Ed. Joseph W. Evans and Leo R. Ward (Notre Dame IN: University of Notre Dame Press, 1976); cited hereafter as *SPP*.

Whereas earlier Catholic writers and popes had condemned liberal democratic freedoms (for example, Pius IX in his encyclical *Quanta cura* and the *Syllabus of Errors* [1864]), and the Catholic church had been in conflict with the Italian and French republics since the 1870s, Maritain accepts and even endorses modern freedoms and especially democracy as the form of government most in keeping with the nature of man. Earlier "sacral" civilizations, such as that of the Middle Ages, he asserts, did not yet realize the implications of the Gospel message of freedom. Those civilizations recognized the spiritual aspect of man, but they had not yet developed adequate institutions for the expression of the freedom of the temporal side of man's nature. It is only in the modern age that "the order of terrestrial civilization and of temporal society has gained the complete differentiation and full autonomy . . . required by the Gospel's very distinction between God's and Caesar's domains" (*MS* 159; *RMNL* 23n). The problem that emerged, however, in this process of gaining political autonomy and freedom was that it has been accompanied by "a most aggressive and stupid process of insulation from, and finally rejection of, God and the Gospel in the sphere of social and political life. The fruit of this we can contemplate today in the theocratic atheism of the Communist state" (*MS* 159). In Maritain's thinking, then, already anticipated as early as his writings on Rousseau in the 1920s, the problem of modern politics is that in working out the implications of the Gospel message of human freedom, modern man has denied the spiritual side of his personality, leading to an excessive individualism, materialism, and egalitarianism that finally leaves the way open to totalitarian solutions, whether of Rousseau's legislator and general will or of modern communism. A properly based theory of democracy will reject the "anthropocentric" conceptions of Rousseau and Kant that have led to the disappearace of the idea of the common good so that

> the social divinization of the individual, inaugurated by "bourgeois" liberalism, leads to the social divinization of the State, and of the anonymous mass incarnate in a Master, who is no longer a normal ruler but a sort of inhuman monster. . . . True political emancipation, or the true city of human rights, has for its principle a conception of the autonomy of the person that is in conformity with the nature of things and therefore "theocentric." (*SPP* 19-20)

Our conception of man must be theocentric because

> man is truly alone and acts truly alone if God does not exist; and even against God, I mean against whatever in man and the human milieu is the image of God. This . . . demands the organization of humanity into one body whose supreme destiny is not to see God but to gain supreme dominion in history. It is a position which declares itself humanistic, but it is radically atheistic and it thereby destroys in reality the humanism which it professes in theory. (*SP* 6)

[margin note: Modern Freedoms & earlier sacral civilizations]

In what has been described as a reformulation of Aquinas's argument that natural law and politics need in practice to be supplemented by revelation (*Summa theologica* I-II.91.4), Maritain argues that a successful democracy must be based on "right instincts" and these can only be developed on the basis of religious values, so that "a general Christian education for the nation, a general development of Christian habits and Christian instincts is, in fact, a condition for the political success of democracy" (*SP* 90). "The supreme ideal towards which modern democracies are aspiring and which has been betrayed by a false philosophy of life . . . requires the climate of a heroic conception of life, fixed on the absolute and upon spiritual values . . . with the development of law and of civic friendship."

> Justice and law by ruling man as a moral agent and appealing to reason and free will [will] transform into a relation between two wholes—the individual and the social—what must otherwise be a mere subordination of part to the whole. And love, by assuming voluntarily that which would have been servitude, transfigures it into freedom and into free gift. (*SP* 60)

The modern state then is a positive development in terms of the increased opportunity that it offers for the exercise of human freedom, but without the "leavening" of religious values, it is always in danger of falling into the extremes of individualism or collectivism. That leavening is to take place through the action of Christian citizens who do not act as church members as such but act under the influence of Christian values, including those formally defined by the church as revealed truths and those mixed areas that both involve the earthly city and affect the "supratemporal goods of the human person and the common good of the Church of Christ" (*IH* 297). Thus Maritain has asserted both the autonomy of the temporal and the need for political action by Christian citizens to promote the values that undergird and strengthen democracy and (much more controversially) to protect the interests of the Catholic church as an institution. Leaving for subsequent consideration the question of the role of the institutional church in a free society, let us consider Maritain's arguments for certain Gospel-based values that will support a free society that is neither individualist nor collectivist. In this connection three concepts keep recurring in his writings—*personalism, communitarianism*, and *pluralism*—and each is defended as a mean between extremes.

Personalism. A central distinction is made in Maritain's thought between the "individual" and the "person." An individual is simply a narrow ego separated from all other men and tending to disintegration as a result of the operation of physical laws. A person, on the other hand, is "a reality which subsisting spiritually, constitutes a universe unto itself, relatively independent within the great whole of the universe and facing the transcendent Whole which is God" (*SPP*

21). Personality is thus rooted in a transcendent and spiritual conception of humanity that will affect the way the society is organized, leading it to recognize the rights of persons as beings who are free, social, and spiritual. Those rights, as Maritain describes them in his short wartime work *The Rights of Man and Natural Law,* appear almost as an anticipation of the United Nations Universal Declaration. The difference, of course, is that they are specifically related in the book to a Thomistic and "personalist" conception of human nature. A second difference would appear to be that Maritain claims that his personalism is capable of transcending or resolving the conflict between the individual and society. "To say then that society is a whole composed of persons is to say that society is a whole composed of wholes." In a perfect society such as that of the Trinity, "each one is in the other in an infinite communion," while

> far below the city of men . . . there is a "society" of material individuals which are not persons, which are so isolated each within itself that they do not tend toward any communion and have no *common* good. . . . Human society, located between these two, is a society of persons who are material individuals who are isolated each within himself, but who nonetheless ask to commune with one another as much as possible here below, before perfectly communing with one another and with God in life eternal. (*SPP* 86)

Communitarianism. As these excerpts already indicate, Maritain's personalist democracy has a strongly social content. This is further developed in what I shall call the "communitarian" aspects of his political thought. This is not a term that is frequently used in English, and the 1968 translation of *Integral Humanism* uses "communal" for *communitaire* (*IH* 133). The terms "communitarian" and "communitarianism" have been used so frequently by Maritain's followers in Europe and Latin America, however, that I feel justified in making use of them. I stress this usage because Maritain speaks often about a conception of "the common good" (the term is, of course, Aristotelian and Thomistic) as what is lacking in modern democratic thought, and his followers have used his writings in this area to defend a wide range of social welfare laws, as well as to develop what they consider to be a concept of the good society that is superior to that of Marxism and of liberalism. In describing his communitarianism Maritain emphasizes that while he believes that the common good is something distinct from the sum of individual goods, it is not in any sense totalitarian, since it is subordinated to the ultimate spiritual end of man, and he quotes in this connection the famous statement of Saint Thomas, "Man is not ordained in all that he is and has to the political community but to God" (*Summa theologica,* I-II.21.4.ad3).

Is this simply a religious expression of the social nature of man? Or, given the existence of an institutional church, is it something more sinister as in the view of liberal democrats, an opening for the imposition of theocratic totalitarianism? (See the discussion of "Integral Humanism" in Sidney Hook, *Reason, Social Myths, and Democracy,*[14] which begins, "Catholicism is the oldest and greatest totalitarian movement in history.") To answer this question, it is necessary to review in some detail his discussion of pluralism and the specific institutions that he proposes to embody it.

Pluralism. In his discussion of the political aspects of pluralism in *Integral Humanism*, Maritain specifically calls for "an organic heterogeneity in the very structure of civil society." This would include autonomy for regional and minority groups, decentralization, and diversification of public functions. He quotes in this connection Pius XI's principle of "subsidiarity," enunciated in his encyclical *Quadragesimo anno* (1931), which asserted that "It is an injustice, a grave evil, and a disturbance of right organization for a larger and higher organization to arrogate to itself functions which can be performed efficiently by smaller and lower bodies" (*IH* 164). In one case, that of Pinochet's Chile, this principle has been cited to defend the rigorous implementation of a free market economy and privatization of areas that had been under government control. For Maritain, however, it appears to be an endorsement of the promotion of federalism, political parties, cooperatives, unions, professional organizations, and a multiplicity of interest groups in the political life of the society.

A few pages later in a footnote (*IH* 175n), Maritain argues for what appears to be a Gaullist conception of political institutions that would replace "the out-of-date parliamentary regime which was suitable for the age of liberal individualism" with a weakened legislature and a strong indirectly elected executive, advised by various consultative groups—the latter presumably as an expression of pluralism. The footnote was added to the text in 1946 and clearly reflects some of the French constitutional debates of the time, which led to the creation of an advisory Economic and Social Council. (When a plebiscite De Gaulle called on establishing such a system was defeated in 1969, he resigned.)

When Maritain discusses what he calls "economic pluralism," he endorses cooperatives and the family farm in the area of agriculture, but he reserves most of his attention for the analysis of an alternative form of industrial organization that is more in keeping with the personalist and communitarian conception of society. He outlines an industrial structure based on "an associative form of industrial ownership" comprising a "society of persons (workmen, technicians, investors), entirely different from the societies of capital," which would involve "the co-ownership of material goods (means of production)" (*IH* 187). Maritain is referring to proposals in Catholic social thought for worker shares in ownership and management and even in some cases worker-owned and managed firms. Those proposals have influenced a number of Latin American experiments, especially

---

[14](New York: John Day, 1940) 76-104.

in Chile and Peru—none of which has been particularly successful. Once again the discussion illustrates Maritain's effort to find a middle way, in this case between capitalism and socialism.

A third and very important discussion of pluralism is devoted to what Maritain calls "juridical pluralism" (*IH* 165-68). What he means by this is in reality the relationship between church and state. Here he makes a clear break with the older European Catholic theories reflected in his writings in the 1920s. In *Integral Humanism* Maritain argues that the legislator who wishes to pursue the common good must take into account "the various spiritual families and lineages which makes [*sic*] up the people" (*IH* 166). This would be done by tolerating differing "ways of worship more or less removed from the true one." At the same time, however, "it is toward the the perfection of natural law and Christian law that the pluriform juridic structure of the body politic would be *oriented*" (*IH* 167). Fifteen years later Maritain extends the requirements of the temporal common good much further. In a striking rejection of the establishment of a state religion or granting privileges to one religion over another, he writes in *Man and the State*,

> the fact of inserting into the body politic a particular or partial common good, the temporal common good of the faithful of one religion (even though it were the true religion), and of claiming for them, accordingly, a privileged juridical position in the body politic, would be inserting into the latter a divisive principle and, to that extent, interfering with the temporal common good. (*MS* 175-76)

It is true that he calls for the state to acknowledge the existence of God as the basis of rights and liberties and to promote public morality and to cooperate with the various "religious communities historically rooted in the life of the people" but he seems at this point to have completely abandoned the older notions of "thesis" and "hypothesis" in church and state and "toleration of a lesser evil," which had been used in European Catholic and papal writings to give reluctant acceptance to the secular democratic state. This was an important development, since along with writings by other authors such as Rev. John Courtney Murray, S. J., it prepared the way for the reversal of Catholic teaching on religious freedom, which took place in the encyclicals of John XXIII and especially in the *Declaration on Religious Freedom* adopted by the Second Vatican Council in 1965. Maritain's argument was made, be it noted, by using traditional Thomistic categories to argue to a conclusion that would have horrified Saint Thomas. (It is true that Aquinas, as Maritain frequently notes, would tolerate such non-Christian rites as Judaism and Islam "in order to avoid worse evils," but as Maritain does *not* point out, Aquinas's recommendation for heresy was that the obstinate offender be handed over to the secular arm "to be exterminated from the world by death" [*Summa theologica*, I-II.11.3]).

There is still a heresy problem, but it is with the political heretics, those who deny the basic doctrines of what Maritain calls the "democratic secular faith." In dealing with what we would call subversive groups, he distinguishes between action and expression of ideas. For the first he recommends punishment of illegal activities like the use of violence. Speaking and writing by subversive groups should not be penalized, only overt actions, since "the State is not equipped to deal with matters of intelligence" (*MS* 118) and a better remedy is the use of the mass media by democratic groups for education in democracy.

For all his earlier attacks on liberalism, Maritain is thus a liberal and opposed to restrictions on freedoms of religion and expression. He differs somewhat from contemporary liberals in his greater emphasis on the social aspects of human existence and his greater readiness to use social groups and the state to promote "the common good," particularly in the areas of private property and social welfare legislation. There still remains a faint trace of his early conservatism in his use of terms such as "integral" and "organic," which sound somewhat suspect to liberal ears. Nevertheless he found Anglo-American liberalism congenial and said so in *Reflections on America* (1958), and there are good reasons in his political philosophy for him to have done so.

There is an important difference from contemporary liberalism, however, in Maritain's philosophy of natural law and natural rights. Ever since the attacks by Hume and Mill on the derivation of moral claims from nature, most modern liberals have looked elsewhere for the basis of value than to human nature—although one can observe in some recent writings such as those of John Finnis and Alasdair MacIntyre a certain revival of interest in this approach. As a Thomist, however, natural law is central to Maritain's political philosophy. It is a bit surprising how long it took him to get to a discussion of this theme, however. It does not appear in his political writings of the thirties, and it is only when he feels the need to discuss human rights during World War II that he writes *The Rights of Man and Natural Law*. Even in that book he does not initiate the discussion of natural law until he has spent the first half of the book reviewing familiar earlier themes such as his view of society as personalist, communitarian, and pluralist—to which he now adds that a free society should also be one that is theist or Christian, "not in the sense that it would require every member of society to believe in God and to be a Christian but in the sense that it recognizes that in the reality of things God, principle and end of the human person and prime source of natural law, is by the same token the prime source of political society and of authority" (*RMNL* 21). When he finally gets to the discussion of natural law, he simply assumes that there is such a thing as a human nature that is common to all people, which includes a capacity to use intelligence to perceive the ends that are common to all and to perceive that these ends constitute "an order or disposition" in accordance with which they should act (*RMNL* 61). Maritain then derives his theory of human rights from this structure of obligations, asserting that the ideas of rights and of moral obligations are correlative and related to a universal order established by God. Natural law then, he says, concerns the rights and duties that follow from the first principle, to do good and avoid evil, "in necessary fashion and from the simple fact that man is man" (*RMNL* 63).

Maritain does not cite Saint Thomas here, but he is clearly influenced by Aquinas's discussion of natural law in the *Summa theologica* (I-II.94). Still, he has added to it a neo-Thomist interpretation that derives from Aquinas's belief in a universe ordered in teleological fashion by God in a hierarchy of ends, an application of that conception to human ends that forms the foundation of a theory of human rights. In the course of his explanation of this theory, he once again attacks the Enlightenment theories of rights, especially those of Kant, because they are based on an erroneous theory of human autonomy that does not ground human rights in human nature. The attack is rather general and does not specify any writers other than Kant. In the case of Locke, for example, Maritain is clearly in error, since more and more recent commentators on that writer have recognized the theistic basis of his natural rights theories.[15] Arguing from duties to rights, Maritain then develops a summary list of rights of the person, the citizen, and the social being, especially the worker. These include religious and family rights, property rights, rights to freedom of expression and association, and rights to a job and to a salary, "and wherever an associative system can be substituted for the wage system, the right to joint ownership and management of the enterprise" (*RMNL* 113).

Partly as a result of his writing on the subject, Maritain was active after World War II in various United Nations groups that contributed to the formulation and adoption of the Declaration of Human Rights. The experience of working with men of widely differing philosophical and religious outlooks on the preparation of the Declaration seems to have had an effect on his natural law theories. His next major discussion of the question, the chapter "The Rights of Man" in *Man and the State*, opens with a recognition that in this area men of opposing ideologies can come to agreement on a list of human rights. In his discussion of his own theory he also seems to make some important modifications, which may have been influenced by his recent experience. Although he repeats his attack on "the eighteenth century conception of the rights of man," it now includes not only his earlier criticism of Kantian notions of the autonomy of the will but also the

Nat l.
law

---

[15]See ch. 5 of my *Natural Law in Political Thought* (1971; reprint, Washington: University Press of America, 1981) as well as recent discussions of Locke by John Dunn, James Tully, Richard Ashcraft, and John Finnis. The argument is reviewed in my forthcoming Norton Critical Edition of Locke's "Second Treatise" and "Letter on Toleration."

argument that it was too rationalistic and deductive in character. This discussion is followed by an important distinction between the ontological basis of natural law and rights in the "ends which necessarily correspond to man's essential constitution" (*MS* 86) and the "gnoseological" element in natural law, that is, how it is known. In this latter discussion, Maritain picks up Aquinas's discussion in the *Summa* (I-II.94.2) of man's "natural inclinations" as the basis for the precepts of the natural law and uses it to develop a theory of "knowledge through inclination" or natural tendencies to explain the general consensus among man on the basic principles of morality. He adds that this kind of direct knowledge of morality has operated in a dynamic and progressive fashion through history so that "human knowledge of natural law has been progressively shaped and molded by the inclinations of human nature, starting from the most basic ones." Thus Maritain has added two elements to his earlier theory—the importance of historical development in our moral knowledge and his description of a nonconceptual way of knowing natural law through "natural inclinations."

The importance of the latter element becomes clear when he discusses the *jus gentium*, or "law of nations." In 1944 in the *Rights of Man* he had described this as the principles that follow from natural law "in a given state of civil society or relationship among peoples" (*RMNL* 70), but in *Man and the State* it becomes the basic principles of morality as known "not by inclination but through the conceptual exercise of reason or through rational knowledge" (*MS* 98). Thus, as Paul Ramsey has pointed out, Maritain's natural law theory moves toward a kind of moral intuitionism with every attempt to express its insights in a rational way resulting in something less than natural law.[16] Maritain appeals to Saint Thomas's description of *jus gentium* as "conclusions" from the natural law, but he clearly seems to have altered Aquinas's theory by de-emphasizing its rational character. (For Aquinas, for example, all law is "an ordination of reason," but for Maritain "the only reason on which natural law depends is divine Reason" [*MS* 98].)

Having spent most of the chapter on a discussion of natural law and having in a way undermined (or at least called into question) any attempt to give the kind of list of rights that he had produced in his earlier book, Maritain then concludes with a short discussion of particular rights, which is mainly devoted to an analysis of the increasing tensions between the so-called "new" social rights and "old" civil rights. He also notes that, although "advocates of a liberal-individualist, a communistic, and a personalist type of soceity" may agree on the same list of rights, they will not apply them in the same way (*MS* 106).

A year after *Man and the State* appeared, Scribner's published *The Range of Reason*, a collection of earlier articles by Maritain, which included a discussion of international political ethics that once again argued for a middle position be-

---

[16]*Nine Modern Moralists* (Englewood Cliffs NJ: Prentice-Hall, 1962) ch. 8.

tween "hypermoralism" and "Machiavellianism" based on a political ethics that has both an "authentic moral character" and a "genuinely realist quality" (*RR* 160). This essay, as well as his discussions of the possibilities of international cooperation in both books, demonstrates a certain optimism about the future even as the clouds of the Cold War grew thicker. A similar optimism pervades *Reflections on America*, which sees in the pluralism, fluidity, and grass-roots community orientation of the United States, as well as its continuing religious vitality, an application of his political principles.

His later writings were not directly concerned with politics, but his influence as a political philosopher was perhaps at its height in the 1950s and 1960s. This was mainly because his writings on politics had become the principal ideological underpinning for the important Christian Democratic parties that emerged in postwar Europe, as well as for similar parties that were beginning to be established in Latin America. The Christian Democratic Mouvement Républicain Populaire in France, which for a time was the largest party in postwar France and formed the central core of most French governments between the end of the war and the collapse of the Fourth Republic in 1958, consciously appealed to his writings, and the Christian Democratic party in Italy, which has been the most important government party since World War II, supports institutes and study groups on Maritain's thought. While the interdenominational character of the German Christian Democratic Union makes a specifically Catholic and Thomist theory less applicable, he was also studied in Germany, where *The Rights of Man* was translated in 1949 and *Christianity and Democracy* in 1951.

The European postwar parties underwent an evolution in their economic theory and practice that was similar to that in Maritain's own thinking—moving from a position that argued that Christianity could be applied in a way that would transcend both capitalism and socialism to a social-welfare-oriented but basically capitalist economy, best described in Ludwig Erhard's term, "the social market economy." In Latin America, however, the criticism of capitalism in Maritain's writings in the 1930s and mid-1940s and his concern with the proletariat (which he described in a controversial passage in *Integral Humanism* as "the bearer of fresh moral reserves which assign to it a mission in regard to the new world; a mission which will be . . . truly a mission of liberation" [*IH* 235] fell on responsive ears. Eduardo Frei, the cofounder of the Chilean Christian Democratic party and future president of Chile (1964-1970) heard him give the lectures that were to be the basis of *Integral Humanism* when he traveled to Europe as the representative of the Chilean National Association of Catholic Students (ANEC). Maritain traveled to Latin America in 1936 and again in 1938, lecturing in Rio de Janeiro and in Buenos Aires. *Integral Humanism* was published in Spanish in Madrid in 1935 before it appeared in French, and Maritain's "Letter on Independence" was published in Buenos Aires in 1936. I have verified the important impact of the latter work, which was reprinted in a conservative newspaper in Chile just at the time that the youth wing of the Conservative party had split off to form the Falange, the ancestor of the present Christian Democratic party of Chile. Jaime Castillo, the chief ideologue of the party, later minister of justice under the Frei government and currently chairman of the Chilean Human Rights Commission, was converted to Maritain by reading the "Letter," which, in its discussion of the need to reach out to the workers with a message that transcended the categories of Right and Left, corresponded precisely to the needs of the new party. (Even today the symbol of the Chilean Christian Democratic party is a vertical arrow that pierces too crossed lines, symbolizing the way that the party cuts through the Right and the Left.) Frei and Castillo have written articles and books about Maritain's thought, and until it was suppressed by the Pinochet dictatorship, *Politica y Espiritu*, the party's theoretical journal, devoted many articles and special issues to his thought. When Maritain died in 1973 the Chilean Congress held a special session recalling his contributions. Elsewhere in Latin America the numerous Christian Democratic research institutes that sprang up in the 1960s studied his thought and used it to support the programs of the important Christian Democratic parties that emerged in Venezuela, El Salvador, Guatemala, Costa Rica, and Panama.

On the other hand, Latin American conservatives viewed his political thought as a threat to their links to the church, and there is a considerable polemical literature, arguing for and against the orthodoxy of his political theory. In particular, the conservatives objected to his arguments for religious pluralism and for limits on property in the interests of "the common good."[17]

The attack from the Catholic Left took place after the opening associated with the Second Vatican Council made it possible for a radical Catholicism to be expressed and after the disappointment with the reform efforts of the 1960s associated with the Alliance for Progress had radicalized a sector of the Latin American

---

[17]See, for example, the attack on Maritain by Jorge Ivan Hubner, a Chilean professor of law, for "professing a true idolatry of democracy, liberty, and human rights inspired directly by secularist liberalism," in opposition to "conservatism which proclaims its faith in God, the church, and religion," in Frederick B. Pike, ed., *The Conflict between Church and State in Latin America* (New York: Knopf, 1964) 181, and the writings of the Argentine theologian Julio Meinvielle, especially *De Lamennais à Maritain* (Buenos Aires: Nuestro Tiempo, 1945; French translation, Paris: La Cite Catholique, 1953; 2d ed. Buenos Aires: Ediciones Theoria, 1967). Replies to Meinvielle include Julio Jimenez Berguecio, S.J., *La ortodoxia de J. Maritain* (Talca: Ediciones Cervantes, 1948), and Jaime Castillo, *En defensa de Maritain* (Santiago: Politica y Espiritu, 1949). For an example of the application of Maritain's communitarianism to Latin America, see Jaime Castillo, "Natural Law and Communitarianism," translated in Sigmund, *Natural Law*, 198-200.

clergy and Catholic students and intellectuals. The early writings of liberation theologians such as Gustavo Gutierrez saw that they called "developmentalism" and "reformism" as approaches to be rejected because of their evident failure to resolve the problems of poverty and dependence. Gutierrez and others after him denounced what they called the model of the "New Christendom" (the term is quoted from Maritain's *Integral Humanism*) as "timid and basically ambiguous" because although it encouraged political participation by Christians it was not willing to propose "radically new social forms"—(i.e., socialism) for Latin America. While Maritain's "distinction of planes" allowed the Christian citizen to make political choices on the basis of conscience, Gutierrez accused him of an "ecclesiastical narcissism" that placed the church in a special and separate position that prevented it from directly attacking the fundamental social and structural problems of society. Conciliatory approaches like those taken by Latin American Christian Democratic parties he characterized as "naive reformism" that provided "a justifying ideology . . . for the few to keep living off the poverty of the many." Writing in the late 1960s Gutierrez observed that "apostolic youth movements have gone more radical in their political stance" and "no longer gravitate toward the Social Christian parties."[18]

Maritain himself, of course, was not an exponent of the developmentalism espoused by many Latin American Christian Democrats in the 1960s, but he was strongly committed to democracy and human rights—two concerns that emerged only later in the writings of the liberation theologians and that even today receive less emphasis in such writings than the need for a "total" change of economic and social structure to benefit the poor. The flirtation of the early liberation theologians with Marxist categories would also have been denounced by Maritain as opening the way to a dangerous statism that tends to emerge once his more balanced personalism and communitarian approach is abandoned in favor of the commitment of the church to social revolution. That commitment has been considerably modified by the liberation theologians in recent years in favor of the promotion of grass-roots basic ecclesiastical communities, but they remain suspicious of Maritain and Christian Democracy as too willing to accept the exploitative structures of capitalism in the name of Christianity and democracy.

---

[18]Gustavo Gutierrez, "Notes for a Theology of Liberation," *Theological Studies* 31: 2 (June 1970): 250. The earlier quotations are taken from chs. 3 and 4 of *A Theology of Liberation*. For the liberation theologians' movement from Marxist-influenced structuralism to grass-roots populism, see Sigmund, *Liberation Theology at the Crossroads*, and compare Gutierrez, *We Drink from Our Own Wells* (Maryknoll NY: Orbis Press, 1984), with his earlier writings. For a critique of the economic assumptions of the liberation theologians that quote Maritain as an exponent of "the dynamism of North American liberation philosophy," see Michael Novak, *Will It Liberate? Questions about Liberation Theology* (New York: Paulist Press, 1986) 255 and 262.

There are many reasons why there is less specific discussion of Maritain in Latin America. First, the opening to the other viewpoints that resulted from the Second Vatican Council, especially the *Declaration of the Church in the Modern World* (*Gaudium et spes*), made it less imperative to have a specifically Catholic base for party programs. In addition the experience in power of the Christian Democratic parties in Venezuela and Chile demonstrated that the vision of the middle way that Maritain outlined could not be applied in its entirety—although in both those countries as well as in El Salvador the neo-Thomist argument for "the social function of property" was cited in favor of important land reform laws. In Peru as well, an effort by the military to draw on Christian Democratic ideas about worker participation and ownership under the Velasco government between 1968 and 1975 had only limited success. Finally one can also note a general decline in ideological utopianism among Latin American democrats as a result of some of the bitter experiences of the 1960s and 1970s.

In the United States, too, Maritain is no longer the byword among Catholic intellectuals that he was in earlier periods, and his influence has disappeared from universities like Princeton and Chicago, where he had considerable visibility three decades ago. Still, there is a Maritain library at Notre Dame, an active Maritain Association holds annual meetings, as does an international organization of such associations, and a center has been established in Italy for the study of his work.

Those organizations formed by his ideas continue to be active in the intellectual and political life of Latin America and Europe, especially in the Christian Democratic parties, and in a way his basic political ideas, which once were so controversial, have become part of the conventional wisdom of Catholic social and political thought. In particular, the adoption of the Declaration on Religious Freedom (*Dignitatis humanae*) by the Second Vatican Council in 1965 and the publication of the encyclicals *Pacem in terris* (1964) and *Populorum progressio* (1967), the latter of which specifically cites Maritain, marked the incorporation into the mainstream of Latin and worldwide Catholicism of the ideas for which Maritain fought so long.

His specific contributions to political thought then can be summarized: (1) he established a Thomistic basis for democracy, religious pluralism, and human rights; (2) he moved the traditional Catholic critique of liberalism in a more positive direction, ultimately adopting most of liberalism's mental positions, while claiming to provide a more socially oriented alternative—personalism; (3) he provided a theoretical justification for the welfare state and for agrarian reform and experiments in worker participation in Latin America; and (4) he helped to open what had been a ghettoized Catholicism to other religions and philosophies while maintaining a strong loyalty to the Thomist tradition.

What about the negative side? First, one must remark that often the effort to demonstrate that one holds the middle position is forced, exaggerated, or based on a stereotyped view of those he is criticizing. This is particularly true of his attacks on liberal individualism, which ignore the considerable social content that liberalism has developed over the last several centuries and fails to distinguish among different kinds of liberals.

Second, that middle position is often not helpful as a guide to policy. As the Christian Democrats in Chile discovered in the 1960s, "communitarianism" can be interpreted in ways that are quite radical or rather conservative. On the other hand, this can be a virtue, since it can be used to construct broad "umbrella parties" of the European variety that include both business and labor groups and make a strong appeal to the middle class. The middle way, then, may be unappealing to those who see revolutionary transformation as the only solution, but it seems to work as a basis for centrist parties.

A third problem is the question of the relation of church and state. Maritain seems to think that theism is necessry to the maintenance of a free society, but he never makes a convincing argument for this proposition. He seems to believe, citing the example of Rousseau, that the atheism or secularism of Enlightenment liberalism will lead down a slippery slope to totalitarianism, but the argument as to why this should be the case is either not made or is very superficial. Yet it is an important element in his thought because he wishes the democratic state to acknowledge the existence of God and to cooperate with various religious groups—for secular reasons, because religious values are important for the development of the integral humanism that undergirds democracy. He does not face the problem that has vexed the U.S. Supreme Court, the rights of atheists or agnostics and the implications of the First Amendment for generalized programs of aid to all religions. Perhaps this is a problem it is not possible to resolve, but many secular liberals would make a counterargument that a free society can function only when religious conflicts are muted by a decline in religious zeal and a general commitment to freedom and toleration, and that historically it was not the Gospel but the Enlightement, including its antireligious or nonreligious elements, that produced the modern free democratic state. It is difficult to say how Maritain would respond, but given his well-known openness to those who hold opposing views he might acknowledge the sincerity of those of a more secularist persuasion but point to the current religious revival in the United States as proof of the need for a religiously based response on the question of freedom, human rights, and the welfare state.

Finally, there is a problem with his theory of natural law as known by natural inclination. Which inclinations are natural, and what happens when they come { Natural in conflict? Aquinas has a list (*Summa theologica* I-II.94.6; 94.2) and he believes { inclinations in a harmony of divine purposes in the universe. Maritain shares this view but does not develop the implications of his natural rights theory to demonstrate its applicability.

The religious revival in the United States and elsewhere has had political implications. In the 1960s it was often radical in content, while in the 1980s the most visible religiopolitical movements in the United States seem to be conservative in character. This view can only conclude, therefore, with a plea for renewed efforts to carry on the tradition that Maritain represented of reinterpreting the ancient Christian and Thomist message in a balanced moderate way that supports, promotes—and criticizes—the achievements of liberal (Maritain would say "free") democratic politics as an activity in which the claims of authority and participation, community and the individual person, and politics and religious belief can be joined together in a cooperative, rather than conflictive, mutually reinforcing relationship.

RICHARD FAFARA

Angelism and Culture

SIMONE WEIL DEFINED CULTURE as "an instrument wielded by professors to manufacture professors who when their turn comes will manufacture professors."[1] Actually, the term "culture" has rather earthy origins. From referring to the tilling of the soil, the term was broadened to include other objects that required much time, energy, and exercise. Ovid speaks of the culture of the body, Varro of the culture of the home. In addition to the material sphere, "culture" gradually made its way to include the spiritual. Cicero, for example, speaks about the culture of the mind and of morals. Eventually, culture came to signify all human goods and operations—a kind of universal excellence of human nature. Maritain expands this awareness more fully. For him culture means the perfecting of man's physical, intellectual, and moral nature.[2]

As with other philosophers, Maritain's approach to culture presupposes a specific conception of man. He defines man as "a spirit united in substance to the flesh and engaged in the universe of matter"[3] and agrees with Aristotle that to propose to man only the human betrays man and wishes his misfortune. Both claim that because man is principally spirit, man is called to something more than a purely human life. As a Christian philosopher, Maritain maintains that faith enables man to lay hold of the Supreme Truth. But since faith requires the working of reason, it normally presupposes rational preliminaries such as the nat-

---

[1] Simone Weil, *L'enracinement: Prélude à une déclaration des devoirs envers l'être humain* (Paris: Gallimard, 1949) 65, my translation.

[2] Jacques Maritain, "Religion and Culture," in *Essays in Order*, ed. Christopher Dawson and J. F. Burns (New York: Macmillan, 1940) 8; Jacques Maritain, *Some Reflections on Culture and Liberty* (Chicago: University of Chicago Press, 1933) 1-3.

[3] Jacques Maritain, *Moral Philosophy: An Historical and Critical Survey of the Great Systems* (New York: Scribner, 1945) 2, 452.

ural and demonstrated certainty of the existence of God. Indeed, much of Maritain's long philosophical career was dedicated to showing how human reason can demonstrate that the nature and destiny of man as seen in the Gospels have an ontological foundation. Faith also demands to be completed by theology, by a certain intellectual grasp—imperfect though it may be—of the ineffable mystery of God and of things divine. The conception of culture adequate to Maritain's conception of man is "theocentric." Only a culture that is centered on the divine and assimilates the cultural to the spiritual can give us a true conception of human nature and allow for a full or integrated human life.[4]

I do not now intend to elaborate on Maritain's rich and fertile conceptions of man and culture—at least, not directly. Rather, I wish to focus on Maritain's critique of Descartes and, thereby, cast into relief one fundamental philosophical requirement of the theocentric conception of culture that Maritain advocates. According to Maritain, it is Descartes who commits "the great French sin in the history of modern thought" and who bears much of the responsibility for the disease of the mind affecting the modern world. The disease results in an anthropocentric conception of culture, ordered to purely terrestrial ends. Because this type of culture affirms human nature as absolutely self-sufficient, God and the supernatural are irrelevant to it.[5]

At this point, some questions might arise: Should not this chapter more properly be titled "Descartes and Culture," and what do angels have to do with all of this? The answers lie in Maritain's neologism "angelism." Admittedly, this term does not refer to the angels per se; Maritain uses it to designate the specific character of the Cartesian influence in the metaphysical realm. Although the original version of "angelism" is found in Descartes,[6] it is not re-

---

[4]Maritain, *Some Reflections on Culture and Liberty* 1-8, 20; *The Twilight of Civilization*, trans. Lionel Landry (New York: Sheed and Ward, 1943) 4-8; "Religion and Culture" 8-13, 28-34; *The Peasant of the Garonne: An Old Layman Questions Himself about the Present Time*, trans. Michael Cuddihy and Elizabeth Hughes (New York: Holt, Rinehart and Winston, 1968) 84-87; *The Range of Reason* (New York: Scribner, 1952) 194-95.

[5]Jacques Maritain, *Three Reformers: Luther, Descartes, Rousseau* (New York: Scribner's, 1929) 86, 77; *St. Thomas Aquinas*, trans. and rev. Joseph W. Evans and Peter O'Reilly (New York: Meridian, 1958) 89-93. L. J. Beck views the sin as being less grievous: "Some of the subtle and insidious mistakes made by Descartes sent generations of philosophers on a wild goose chase that still continues. *To this extent only*, can one accept Maritain's statement that 'Descartes (or Cartesianism) has been the great French sin in modern history' " ("Descartes, René," *New Catholic Encyclopedia*, 16 vols. [New York: McGraw-Hill, 1967] 4:787; emphasis mine).

[6]Jacques Maritain, *The Dream of Descartes*, trans. Mabelle L. Andison (New York: Philosophical Library, 1944) 28. Maritain is "perfectly well aware that Descartes is nei-

stricted to Descartes, for it finds expression both in the speculative and practical aspects of other systems of thought.[7] But what specifically constitutes this Cartesian metaphysical reform? In brief, it is a refusal to accept the human condition by imitating the angels and attempting to usurp angelic prerogatives. By refus-

---

ther the only one, nor the first one responsible for the morbid elements which encumber our philosophical heredity. These morbid elements were fermenting well before his time. But he gave them a form, a countenance—all the energy which comes from a powerful systematization" (ibid., 185; see also, *Three Reformers* 54, 83). Anton C. Pegis locates the beginning of anthropocentric humanism in the doctrinal decline of medieval thought and its "failure to reconcile Christian belief with the philosophical lessons taught by Aristotle and his Greek and Arabian disciples." See his "Toward the Rediscovery of Man," *Proceedings of the American Catholic Philosophical Association* 17 (1943): 8-17.

[7]In *Three Reformers* and, to a lesser extent, in *The Dream of Descartes*, Maritain traces the consequences of angelism in modern thought to Kant, Hegel, and beyond. See Charles Fecher, *The Philosophy of Jacques Maritain* (Westminster MD: Newman Press, 1953) chaps. 19 and 20; Mortimer J. Adler, *The Angels and Us* (New York: Macmillan, 1982); and the magisterial treatment of this theme in the context of modern philosophy and science in Stanley L. Jaki, *Angels, Apes, and Men* (LaSalle IL: Sherwood Sugden, 1983).

For Maritain's criticism of angelism in contemporary art, especially painting and poetry, see his *Art and Faith: Letters between Jacques Maritain and Jean Cocteau*, trans. John Coleman (New York: Philosophical Library, 1948); *The Situation of Poetry*, trans. Marshall Suther (New York: Philosophical Library, 1955); *Art and Scholasticism* and *The Frontiers of Poetry*, trans. Joseph W. Evans (New York: Scribner's, 1962); and *Creative Intuition in Art and Poetry* (New York: Pantheon Books, 1953).

Angelism in French literature has been admirably studied by Maritain's godson, Wallace Fowlie. See his *Rimbaud* (Chicago: University of Chicago Press, 1966) 225-58; and *Jacob's Night: The Religious Renascence in France* (New York: Sheed and Ward, 1947). For a bibliography of Fowlie's works, see *Symbolism and Modern Literature: Studies in Honor of Wallace Fowlie*, ed. Marcel Tetel (Durham: Duke University Press, 1978) 275-92. According to Fowlie, Maritain's "perceptive comments on the work of Baudelaire and Rimbaud and Cocteau are among the most precious he has bequeathed to future students of French poetry." See his "Maritain the Writer," in *Jacques Maritain: The Man and His Achievement*, ed. Joseph Evans (New York: Sheed and Ward, 1963) 57.

I am grateful to Rev. John McIntyre, S.J., for referring me to Allen Tate's discussion of Edgar Allan Poe's "surrender" to angelism. See Tate's essay, "The Angelic Imagination," in *The Forlorn Demon* (Chicago: Regnery, 1953) 56-78. My thanks also to Deal Hudson, who, in commenting on an earlier version of this chapter, delivered at the annual meeting of the American Maritain Association, 12 October 1985, indicated the recent literary treatments of angelism in the works of Walker Percy. See Percy's *Love in the Ruins* (New York: Farrar, Straus and Giroux, 1971) and *Lost in the Cosmos* (New York: Farrar, Straus and Girous, 1983).

An interesting sidelight to the issue of angelism is the attempt of Ann Lee, founder of the Shakers, who in 1774 brought eight followers to New York from Manchester, England,

ing to accept the properly human condition of being able to know only by the senses and the intellect working together, Descartes plays "pure spirit." He models human thought after angelic thought.[8]

We know from medieval theological doctrine that angels, lacking bodies, are without sense perception and imagination.[9] This means that they know not by means of concepts abstracted from experience or otherwise formed. According to the classical doctrine, angels know through the archetypal ideas infused in them at their creation by God. Not being immersed in time and motion, angels do not reason or think discursively as men do by reasoning from premises to conclusions. Angelic knowledge is intuitive and immediate: from the knowledge of a known principle, angels straightaway perceive, as known, its consequent conclusions. What happens when Descartes attempts to transfer this teaching to man?

---

to establish a "new order of beings more like angels than men," free from war, greed, poverty, lust and intemperance. Over the years, the Shakers did produce marvelous houses, furnishings, and utensils. Thomas Merton attributed "a particular grace" of the Shaker chair to the maker's belief that "an angel might come and sit in it." See June Sprigg, *Shaker Design* (New York: Whitney Musuem of American Art, 1986) 12, 21.

[8]Maritain, *Three Reformers* 54-55, 79-81; *Moral Philosophy* 454. Gassendi, in his *Fifth Set of Objections* to the *Meditations*, was the first to accuse Descartes of angelism. The charge was also leveled in 1657 by the Polish Socinian Wolzogen. See Jan Ludwik Wolzogen, *Annotationes in meditationes metaphysicas Renati Des Cartis*, trans. and ed. L. Joachimowicz and D. Gromska (Warsaw: Panstwowe Wydawnictwo Naukowe, 1959). This work may constitute an eighth set of objections to the *Meditations*. See Richard J. Fafara, "An Eighth Set of Objections to Descartes' *Meditations*?" *Modern Schoolman* 52:1 (November 1979): 36.

[9]St. Thomas Aquinas, *Summa theologiae* I.50-64 and 107-14. See J. D. Collins, *The Thomistic Philosophy of Angels* (Washington: Catholic University of American Press, 1947). A good bibliography on the subject of angels can be found in Adler's *Angels and Us*. For other aspects of Maritain's philosophical speculation on angels, see his *The Sin of the Angel: An Essay on a Re-interpretation of Some Thomistic Positions*, trans. William L. Rossner, S.J. (Westminster MD: Newman Press, 1959), and "A propos de l'instinct animal," *Approches sans entraves* (Paris: Fayard, 1973) 163-84, in which, nine years before his death in 1982, Maritain proposed that the properly intellectual knowing presupposed by animal instinct is transmitted by the angels.

The fashionable dismissal of angels serves as an effective tactic to have Christians cease taking Satan seriously (see Maritain, *Peasant of the Garonne* 6) and was recently addressed by Pope John Paul II in his catecheses on angels. The pope made it clear that denying the existence of angels radically revises sacred scripture itself and the entire history of salvation. See *L'Osservatore Romano*, weekly edition in English no. 28 (946), 14 July 1986, through no. 33 (950), 18 August 1986. In its coverage of one catechesis, which gave "Roman Catholics lessons about the dangers of forgetting religious practices and concepts that many thought were cast into religious history's waste basket after the Second Vatican Council in the early 1960's," the *New York Times* reported that "the Pope *startled* several thousand listeners . . . by insisting that angels exist" (18 July 1986, sec. A, 2, col.3; my emphasis).

Although Descartes has a body, he resolves at the outset to begin philosophizing as if he did not. [10] In employing a method of doubt that dismisses all sense knowledge, Descartes arrives at the self revealed in the *cogito* as purely spiritual and distinct from the body. The "self" or "I" is a thinking thing, that is to say, a mind, or, as Frans Burman pointed out, an angel. [11] Since Descartes makes an angel out of the soul, it is not surprising that its knowledge discloses the three key characteristics of angelic knowledge: it is intuitive, innate, and independent of things.

The Cartesian mind has one function: intuition or vision. Everything known is reduced to the fixing of the intellect on an object of thought, fully and completely grasped. In totally isolating thought from the body and bypassing the

---

[10]Although Maritain cites Gilson's overall interpretation of Descartes as confirming his own (*Dream of Descartes,* 194-95 n. 31; 212 n. 158), Gilson's interpretation of the relation of Descartes' physics to his metaphysics eventually becomes "more flexible and more carefully shaded" (ibid., 194-95 n. 33). Maritain, however, did not modify his position that the *Meditations* were written to justify Descartes's physics. See Henry Bars, "Gilson et Maritain," *Revue Thomiste* 79:2 (April-June 1979): 251. On the evolution of Gilson's interpretation, see Jean-Luc Marion, "L'instauration de la rupture: Gilson à la lecture de Descartes," *Etienne Gilson et Nous: La philosophie et son histoire,* ed. Monique Couratier (Paris: J. Vrin, 1980) 13-34. General assessments and references to reviews and articles dealing with both Maritain's and Gilson's interpretations can be found in Gregor Sebba's *Bibliographia Cartesiana: A Critical Guide to the Descartes Literature 1800-1960* (The Hague: Martinus Nijhoff, 1964).

Commentators sometimes fail to see beyond the impassioned and even "violent" language of Maritain's critique of Descartes. See Sebba, *Bibliographia* 48 and Fecher, *Philosophy* 233. Maritain's own assessment of the style of his youthful works in which he "did not hesitate to rush in where angels fear to tread" can be found in the foreword to the English translation and preface to the second edition of *Bergsonian Philosophy and Thomism* trans. Mabelle L. Andison and J. Gordon Andison (New York: Philosophical Library, 1955). Maritain admits that he is generalizing and that these generalizations should be taken not so much a critique of Descartes himself as of the "spirit" of Descartes, namely, the consequences logically following from the ideas Descartes sets down but not necessarily intended by Descartes himself. It is not a question of denying the genius of Descartes or of trying to destroy all that he left us, for his contributions to the physical and mathematical sciences and to reflexivity carving out its own niche in philosophy do constitute progress. Still, Descartes's angelistic starting point in philosophy leads to intellectual suicide and cultural depravity. See *Dream of Descartes,* 35-36, 164-65; *Religion and Culture* 24; *Peasant of the Garonne* 100-102; *Moral Philosophy* 448.

[11]Maritain, *Three Reformers* 81; Jaki, *Angels* 12-13. On the question of the authority and use of Burman's philosophical interview with Descartes in interpreting the work of Descartes, see *Descartes' Conversation with Burman,* trans. John Cottingham (Oxford: Clarendon Press, 1976) xvi-xviii, and Ferdinand Alquié's comments in his edition of *Descartes: Oeuvres philosophiques,* 3 vols. (Paris: Garnier, 1973) 2:765-67.

senses and imagination, Descartes endows the mind with innate ideas. He must; what other source can he find for them? Maritain locates the core of Descartes's angelism in the curious view—at least when applied to humans—that the intuitive knowledge possessed by the human intellect, in virtue of its innate ideas, is possessed independently of man's having any acquaintance with really existing things. This view stems from the Cartesian theory of ideas that asserts that ideas are the *objects* that are known, rather than the *means by which* things are known or understood. Descartes separates the idea, the known, from what it represents, from reality as existing in itself independently of the mind. In short, thought attains nothing but itself; it is no longer ruled by things but only by its own exigencies. Thought, sealed off in an impenetrable world, shut in and fixed upon itself, develops science from the seeds of truth latent within itself.[12]

Since, for Descartes, what is true of the idea of a thing is true of the thing itself, and since the mind—like an angel—has a clear and distinct idea of the essence of matter, the innate idea of matter as nothing but geometrical extension defines material reality and allows for the a priori derivation of the shape, structure, and laws of that universe. Needless to say, the universe fabricated in such a way and the science of such a universe remain very fallible constructions indeed. In developing the intuition of the "foundations of the admirable science" revealed to him in the famous dream of 10 November 1619, Descartes understood that all science is one—"the sciences taken altogether are identical with human wisdom, which always remains one and the same, however applied to different subjects."[13] This is the idea of a universal knowledge, mathematical in type, achieved by applying the criterion of clear and distinct ideas to all reality—science, with a capital S, or the notion of science that the modern world would come to worship. Moreover, everything that cannot be brought under this criterion of clear and distinct ideas must be rejected. Since man has no clear and distinct idea of matters proposed to us by theology—the Incarnation and Redemption, for example—theology as a science is impossible. Descartes tries to safeguard faith by isolating it from the intelligence and making the objects of faith completely inaccessible to our minds. He precludes philosophy's being ordered to theology as to a superior science and theology becomes "an exercise of ignoramuses chattering about the unknown."[14] Thus, the Cartesian revolution secularizes wisdom by separating philosophy from everything in man that comes from above man.

---

[12]Maritain, *Three Reformers* 66, 77-78; *Dream of Descartes* 39-40, 170-71.

[13]René Descartes, *Rules for the Direction of the Mind*, vol. 1 of *The Philosophical Works of Descartes*, trans. Elizabeth S. Haldane and G. R. T. Ross (Cambridge: Cambridge University Press, 1967) 1.

[14]Maritain, *Dream of Descartes* 81; *Peasant of the Garonne* 15; "What I Believe," in *What I Believe: Thirteen Eminent People of Our Time Argue for Their Philosophy of Life*, ed. Mark Booth (New York: Crossroad, 1984) 51.

In upsetting the order between philosophy and theology, the hierarchy proper to philosophy itself is also subverted. Unlike the speculative philosophy of the ancients and the Middle Ages, Descartes's new philosophy is practical. To be sure, it studies wisdom, but wisdom defined as the perfect knowledge of all that man can know to conduct his life, preserve his health, and invent arts and techniques. The famous Cartesian philosophical tree of the *Principles* has metaphysical roots and a trunk constituted by physics that branches into all the other sciences, which can be reduced to three main ones: medicine, mechanics, and ethics.[15] Metaphysics, that brief body of a priori principles, does nothing more than ground the true fruit of philosophy. The Cartesian reform degrades metaphysics by ordering it to practical science. Descartes's metaphysics exists only for the sake of his physics. Speculation on the highest truths accessible to reason ceases to be an end and, henceforth, becomes a means for construing knowledge of the sensible world. Here there appears a latent naturalism by which we arrive by reason alone at a perfect knowledge of all that man can know, including practical wisdom, or ethics. Science, by itself, will provide "the sovereign good of human life" in giving us mastery of ourselves and of this world.

Maritain contends that Descartes's distortion of human reason and lust for pure spirituality in making an angel of the soul, along with the new Cartesian philosophy of nature, spoiled as it was by the illusion that it possessed an exhaustive knowledge of the essence of bodies, secretly causes the breakdown of our culture. Since the mind is no longer oriented toward God, it turns toward the world. Human intelligence, even in a philosophy like Descartes's, which does leave room for religion, nevertheless begins functioning in a way that is atheistic. Instead of longing for and possessing being or reality, the mind eliminates reality by nullifying it. The intellect, restricted to the realm of thought, becomes fascinated and content with concepts, with signs and symbols, with the productive activity of the intellect, and not with the real being made manifest by this productive activity. Man goes to meet reality with a gust of formulas, with mechanical thinking eager to utilize and control being, while avoiding having to submit to it or be regulated by it.[16]

---

[15]René Descartes, *The Principles of Philosophy*, preface to the French edition, in *Rules for the Direction of the Mind* 211. See Maritain, *Dream of Descartes*, 20-29, 167-68.

[16]Maritain, *Three Reformers*, 79; *Distinguish to Unite or The Degrees of Knowledge*, trans. from the French edition under the direction of Gerald B. Phelan (New York: Scribner's, 1959) 3-5, 108-109; "The Ways of Faith," in *Range of Reason*, 206-207. For provocative remarks and criticism of the fields of artificial intelligence and cognitive science within the world of computer technology as part of Descartes's mathematical project to codify the laws of thought, see Theodore Rozak, *The Cult of Information* (New York: Pantheon, 1986) 210-20.

Cartesian idealism is characterized by optimism. How could it not be? When things and the extramental stability whereby they regulate our thought are carefully rejected, human thought is that around which all objects revolve. In Maritain's words, "Either there is no being to be set off against thought or there is only being completely docile to thought."[17] The proximate and remote consequences of Cartesian idealism are likewise filled with optimism. Salvation becomes attainable by science and reason. Progress that is technological in nature, automatic, and necessary is seen as leading to the earthly realm of peace. Freedom becomes centered on the exterior freedom of power. This freedom is achieved by technique, by a means extraneous to man, rather than by the self-determination or self-mastery characteristic of the freedom that imposes the law of reason on the universe of man's own inner energies. Morality likewise becomes technological. An appropriate technique then enables us to rationalize human life, to satisfy our desires with the least possible inconvenience, to elude any interior reform of ourselves. As Maritain notes, however, "what such a morality subjects to reason are material forces and agents exterior to man, instruments of human life; not man, nor human life as such." Such a morality, according to Maritain, weakens rather than frees man, rendering him a slave to the universe and especially to his own egoism.[18] In addition to atheism, Maritain sees the final stage of anthropocentric humanism in communism.[19] It is the ultimate logical development of a metaphysics that sees the world exclusively in terms of men and history. Here man works out his salvation completely by himself. But this salvation involves the giving up of personality and the organizing of collective man into one body whose supreme destiny is to gain dominion over matter and human history. Intoxication with matter sacrifices the human person to the titanism of industry.

The dualism initiated by Descartes's philosophy, whereby the things of the world—man's social, economic, and political life—are separated from God and the demands of the Gospel, results, Maritain maintains, in an intensification of materialism in all these realms. Everything becomes evaluated in terms of quantities, ultimately measured by economic value. The Cartesian reform causes a dualism within man's world because it first creates a dualism within man himself. The union of the human mind and body proves to be a philosophical embarrassment for Descartes; he never could reconcile the two satisfactorily into a unity. Before long, an extremist spiritualism that regards every psychic function as angelic, as purely spiritual, will precipitate such sciences as medicine and neurology into materialism. Practitioners of these sciences will forget that man's life

---

[17]Maritain, *Dream of Descartes*, 171.

[18]Ibid., 182; *Culture and Liberty*, 8-10.

[19]Maritain, "Christian Humanism," in *Range of Reason*, 187-92.

is not only corporeal but also moral and spiritual. By emphasizing pure thought and disregarding the affective life, angelism also causes a contempt for both the body and the senses. But the body and its affectivity will have their say via psychologies, like Freud's, that submerge everything under the affective and instinctive. Rational and free behavior are nothing more than illusions emerging from the unconscious and instinct. Spiritual feelings and activities, artistic creations, and religious faith are only the sublimation of the sexual libido or an outgrowth of matter. This hatred of reason in the form of a mysticism of instinct and life has as its fruits the "will to power," the "death of truth," and the "death of God." The human species, as well as its ideas of values, becomes an epiphenomenon of social evolution. In this reaction against reason with its animalization of the image of man, we see the pessimistic side of angelism.[20]

The philosophical principles provided by Aquinas are, in Maritain's opinion, the only remedy for counteracting the effects of angelism. Only those principles can restore order in the mind, and, therefore, in culture, because only they allow for a realism grounded in the sensible and measured by the objective, by which the scope of human knowledge is defined and accurately mapped. "Critical realism" serves as the basis for a theocentric culture. It leads to wisdom conceived not in terms of power and the domination of nature but as terminating in the truth that is the perfect good of the human intellect. By subordinating all material goods and progress in technology necessary for man's good to the goods of the spirit, such wisdom answers man's intellectual hunger for certainty and truth. This wisdom also answers the human search for beatitude, since it terminates in the truth that is the perfect good of the human intellect.[21]

Late in his life, Maritain formally adopted the attitude of a peasant, of "un homme qui met les pieds dans le plat, ou qui appelle les choses par leur nom [A man who puts his foot in his mouth, or who calls a spade a spade]."[22] He argued that idealism is utterly incompatible with Christianity. Then he went on to emphasize that he was neither crazy nor speaking lightly in denying that Descartes and (with few exceptions) his successors are philosophers. They are actually "ideosophers," who begin with thought and remain within it, concerned with ideas and their phenomenal relations. Since ideosophers absorb reality into thought, they impugn the absolutely basic foundation of philosophical knowledge and research, namely, reality as seized by the senses. What is new is not this thesis but the stark clarity with which Maritain formulates it. He maintains that those imbued with idealism dismiss reality from the beginning and are not

---

[20]Ibid., 190-92; *Dream of Descartes*, 179-84; *St. Thomas Aquinas*, 60-62, 67-68.

[21]Maritain, *Peasant of the Garonne*, 104-107, 127-32; *Degrees of Knowledge*, 71-136.

[22]Maritain, *Le paysan de la Garonne* (Paris: Desclée de Brouwer, 1966) 7.

doing philosophy. Ideosophers, in other words, cannot provide us with the basis of a fully human culture because of their truncated view of man.[23]

The accusation that ideosophers embark on a path of research and thought other than the philosophic one was immediately viewed as too contentious or contemptuous of others; it even caused anxiety and dismay among those sympathetic to Maritain's thought.[24] And this, no doubt, is what Maritain would perceive as the most alarming symptom in the struggle between anthropocentric and theocentric conceptions of culture.[25] It indicates the pervasiveness of anthropocentric humanism within our society and the lack of faith and confidence in the principles needed for a theocentric culture. In his essay "Christian Humanism," written in 1942, Maritain depicts the situation we find ourselves in today: "Human reason lost its grasp of Being, and became available only for the mathematical reading of sensory phenomena, and for the building up of corresponding techniques—a field in which any absolute reality, any absolute truth, and any absolute value is of course forbidden."[26]

One may quibble with some of the details in Maritain's treatment of angelism in Descartes and its consequences for modern culture, or with the tone in which Maritain couches his analysis. Still, one is, I believe, forced to admire the adroit manner in which Maritain forges angelism, or the fallacy of attributing to man attributes or powers that belong only to a spiritual substance, into a keen philosophical tool used to delineate the limitations of human nature and the actual conditions of human life on earth. Although it is Descartes who commits the "original sin" of angelism, Maritain throughout his philosophical career identifies various versions and effects of angelism not only in other thinkers but also in writers and artists.

Early on in this chapter I indicated that one of Maritain's main concerns is the conception and development of a culture that is true to the nature of man, a nature that Pascal described as neither brute nor angel. By considering man from the perspective of the angel to whom he is inferior, Maritain arrives at a more accurate determination of man's proper stature and needs. Likewise, he arrives at a better understanding of the character of the culture that can meet those needs.

---

[23]Maritain, *Peasant of the Garonne*, 98-102.

[24]See Yves Congar, "Souvenir sur Jacques Maritain," *Notes et Documents* no. 27 (April-June 1982): 5-7; James Collins, "Maritain Asks Some Questions," *America* 118:2 (13 January 1968): 29-32; and the excellent treatment of this topic in Henry Bars, "A propos de *Paysan de la Garonne*," *Revue Thomiste* 68:1 (January-March 1968): 89-100.

[25]Maritain, *Range of Reason*, 189.

[26]Ibid., 186; *Degrees of Knowledge*, 3.

PART III

Philosophical Foundations

STANLEY L. JAKI

Maritain and Science*

"FEW SPECTACLES are as beautiful and moving for the mind as that of physics thus advancing toward its destiny like a huge throbbing ship." Such are the
words that introduce Maritain's discussion of "The New Physics."[1] Almost exactly half a century old,[2] that discussion should for that reason be worth considering at this celebration of the centenary of Maritain's birth. Praising the new
physics was by 1932 a useful foil for philosophers, and for physicists waxing
philosophical, to treat with a pretense to originality of difficult topics without
saying anything profound about them. Space, time, causality, external reality,
motion, and matter—so many crucial issues for physics—have always been difficult topics for philosophers who were scrupulously exacting of themselves. Such
a philosopher was Jacques Maritain. According to his own admission he dwelt at
some length on the new physics "not to indulge in any rash prophecies on the
future of its theories, but to see whether its scientific progress confirms or in-
validates the epistemological principles we have been trying to establish up to
this point" (DK 155).

---

*This chapter was originally presented at the meeting of the American Maritain As-
sociation held at Princeton University, 28-29 October 1983, in commemoration of the
centenary of Maritain's birth. Since shortly after that meeting I was able to consult the
archives of Lycée Henry IV and of the Sorbonne, and relevant dossiers in the Archives
Nationales, I felt it appropriate to rewrite and expand the section dealing with Maritain's
student years.

[1] Jacques Maritain, Distinguish to Unite or The Degrees of Knowledge, translated under
the direction of Gerald B. Phelan (New York: Scribner's, 1959) 154; cited hereafter as
DK.

[2] The French original was first published in 1932.

That a serious metaphysician ought to be seriously concerned with physics in particular or with knowledge about sensory nature in general should seem obvious.[3] Such concern is almost like a somber warning to the metaphysicians of modern times. Science, especially physics, has increasingly taken over the center stage of intellectual interest for the past three hundred or four hundred years. To be sure, the intellectual talent needed to cultivate metaphysics is not exactly the same as the bent of mind needed in the exact sciences. There is, however, no doubt that during the last three hundred or so years science kept drawing to itself talented minds who in former times most likely would have ended up as metaphysicians if not plain theologians.[4] Whatever one may think of the intrinsic merits of Hegel's philosophy, which was all metaphysics, he displayed extraordinary mental powers. A man with similar powers has not since appeared on the metaphysical scene. Tellingly, Hegel finished his career when Faraday started his with the discovery of electromagnetic induction. It was a discovery that in a sense was more instrumental in ushering in the new physics, that is, electromagnetic theory, relativity, and quantum mechanics, than were all the scientific discoveries prior to 1832, including the discoveries of Newton and Galileo.

From the mid-nineteenth century on scientists began to feel an undisputed sense of superiority over metaphysicians. Of course, the metaphysics they mostly knew was the metaphysics of German idealism,[5] which precisely because it presented itself with so superior an air could readily appear in its very lowly nature. It certainly deserved the sarcasm of James Maxwell, who about 1870 spoke "of the den of metaphysicians, strewed with the remains of former explorers, and abhorred by every man of science."[6] In the early 1930s, just about the time when Maritain's reflections on the new physics saw print, no less a prominent physicist than Max Born brushed aside what he called the "dry tracts of metaphysics."[7]

---

[3] If metaphysics is indeed a move, nay a jump, beyond physics, its soundness should seem to depend on the measure in which the metaphysician's hold on the jumping board is firm and secure. That hold is inconceivable without a fair grasp of physics, the par excellence study of empirical nature, or *physis*.

[4] For example, Jacob Bernoulli, Leonard Euler, Jacques Ozanam. For further details, see my *The Relevance of Physics* (Chicago: University of Chicago Press, 1967) 462.

[5] Or its logical fruit, Naturphilosophie. Because of the campaign led by Naturphilosophes in the 1820s and 1830s against genuine scientists, such as George Ohm, the latter did not spare the former of well-merited invectives. For further details, see ibid., 334.

[6] J. C. Maxwell, "Address to the Mathematical and Physical Section of the British Association" (1870), in W. D. Niven, ed., *The Scientific Papers of James Clark Maxwell*, 2 vols. (Cambridge, 1890) 2:216.

[7] Max Born, *Atomic Physics*, 6th ed. (New York, 1957) 312; originally published 1935.

Still another half a century later, the physicists' dislike of metaphysics is as strong as ever. That there is no metaphysics whatsoever in physics was the flat dismissal of a set of questions that I posed two years ago, I believe, to a world-renowned physicist well known for his work on scientific cosmology. Strangely enough the same physicist failed to remember that he hardly ever fails to cite with approval Bishop Berkeley's idealist metaphysics, the logical outcome of which is solipsism, the supreme form of misguided metaphysics.[8] It would be mistaken to see a bellwether in the often-quoted statements with which Einstein, from his fifties on, endorsed realism and metaphysics. However enlightening, those statements impressed at most only a few philosophers of science but hardly the body scientific.[9]

Such is the general background against which Maritain's appraisal of the new physics should be seen. It is not an appraisal that, however just and incisive, would turn the thoroughly antirealist and therefore thoroughly antimetaphysicist tide that flows back and forth over the entire intellectual landscape of our times. Such tides are fashions against which, just as against huge tidal waves, no argument, however rational, has ever proved convincing. Maritain, it is well to recall, was not only fully aware of this situation but also described it in phrases characteristic of his unsparing incisiveness.

The particular background against which Maritain's dicta on the new physics should be seen concerns Maritain himself. While a great deal is known about most aspects and phases of Maritain's career, few specifics are available in the printed record about Maritain's two years at the Lycée Henri IV, one of France's prestigious lycées, and about his six years at the Sorbonne, 1900-1906. The primary published source on those years has been Raïssa's account of her and Jacques's spiritual odyssey. There we are told about the precocious philosophical anxieties that beset Jacques as a student at Henri IV and about the good prospects that he had at the Sorbonne owing to the esteem in which he and Raïssa were held by Felix Le Dantec, their teacher of zoology. Raïssa also recalled the names of teachers whose courses in the life and earth sciences they followed at the Sorbonne.[10]

Had Jacques ambitioned a study of the exact sciences (mathematics and physics) at the Sorbonne, he should have spent two more years at Henri IV, the years

---

[8]I refer to Robert H. Dicke of Princeton University.

[9]No wonder. Those statements collected by G. Holton in pioneering studies could but lose their impressiveness by his and also Einstein's efforts to secure them a purely "rationalist" character. For details, see my Gifford Lectures, *The Road of Science and the Ways to God* (Chicago: University of Chicago Press, 1978) 185, 193.

[10]Raïssa Maritain, *We Have Been Friends Together: The Memoirs of Raïssa Maritain*, trans. Julie Kernan (New York: Longmans, Green, 1942) 67, 64, 39; hereafter cited as *WHB*. The list, as far as the names are concerned, is accurate.

known as *mathématiques élémentaires* and *mathématiques spéciales*. The two years preceding these were called *rhétorique* and *philosophie*, which a typical student attended in his sixteenth and seventeenth years. In both of these years the classes were the ones prescribed by the ministerial decree of 14 February 1885, which set the pattern, a rather rigid one, of French secondary education for decades to come.[11] In the *rhétorique* the courses included algebra with trigonometry and a mostly descriptive physics with astronomy. The registry of examinations in Henri IV contains only the marks that Jacques obtained in Latin, French, German, and history.[12] They reveal a student who impressed his teachers not so much with his actual performance as by his inquisitive mind. According to his French teacher he was "very intelligent, somewhat distracted, not the student type, one who could do better by not thinking also of matters other than those discussed in class."[13] His Latin teacher described him as an "esprit net, de la finesse," no small praise coming as it did from Georges Félix Edet, a renowned classicist.[14] For his history teacher Jacques was "intelligent, un peu inégal." Only the German teacher found his scholastic achievement above any criticism.

As to the *philosophie* year the entries in the registry are very incomplete concerning Jacques. One finds there only the marks that he received in philosophy in all three trimesters and the mark given him in physics and chemistry in the third trimester. For the philosophy teacher, Hector Dereux, Jacques was an "excellent student, with an adventurous though fine and distinguished mind, a searching spirit worthy indeed of esteem and sympathy."[15] The intellectual profile of Maritain is clearly forecast in these observations. Jacques had to take a course in natural history as well, in addition to German, history, and a review course

---

[11]See *Bulletin administratif du ministère de l'instruction publique Tome XXXVI I Année 1885*, Nos 630-654 (Paris: Imprimerie Nationale, 1885) 219-20.

[12]It is my pleasant duty to express my gratitude to Mme. Rivaud, director of the Library of Lycée Henri IV, for making that registry and other documents available to me.

[13]"Très intelligent, un peu distrait, n'est pas assez écolier; pourrait encore mieu faire en ne pensant pas à autre chose qu' à la classe."

[14]Edet (1855-1903) was also giving courses in Latin composition at the Sorbonne and is mentioned by Raïssa (*WHB* 69) as the "superlative Latin scholar whose corrections of Latin themes were such masterpieces that the students eagerly vied to get hold of them."

[15]"Excellent élève, d'esprit parfois aventureux, mais fin et distingué, il a beaucoup gagné sous le rapport de la méthode" (first trimester); "élève distingué, tout à fait digne d'estime et de sympathie" (third trimester). It tells something of young Jacques's mischievousness that apparently he kept recalling later a speech defect of Dereux to Raïssa, for whom Dereux was Jacques's only teacher at Henry IV to be mentioned by name: Dereux "who was called Dereuf because he always added an *f* to the ends of words" (*WHB* 67).

of algebra and trigonometry (calculus was reserved for *mathématiques élémentaires* and *spéciales*). The *Annuaire* of Henri IV for 1899-1900 reveals that Jacques took first prize in natural history.[16] Clearly, he was well prepared to matriculate in the Sorbonne either in the Faculté des Lettres or in the Faculté des Sciences. He entered both in November 1900. On 26 July 1902 he obtained his *licence* in philosophy in the Faculté des Lettres.[17] Obtaining *licence* in the life sciences was a longer affair, partly because of the laboratory work involved.

For *licence ès sciences* one had to obtain three certificates in any of the three major fields—mathematics, physics (chemistry), and biology (geology), in each of which, especially in the latter, a fair choice of subjects was available. Jacques obtained a certificate in botany in July 1901, one in physiology in July 1903, and one in minerology in July 1906. His personal card[18] also contains references to his attending a course in geology in 1902-1903. Of course, he may have audited other courses as well, and, as will be clear shortly, he must have attended courses in evolution and embryology. His marks were *bien* and *assez bien*, which put him in the top fifth of his class. In botany his teachers were Professor Gaston Bonnier (1853-1922) and his associate, Louis Matruchot (1863-1921). The physiology courses were taught by Professor Jules Dastre (1844-1917) and his assistant, Louis Lapicque (1866-1948), who became professor in 1919. Minerology was taught by Professor Emile Haug (1861-1927) and his assistant, Louis Gentil (1868-1925).

Such was a distinguished group of scientists, most of whom have received a special article in the *Dictionary of Scientific Biography* in witness of the lasting value of their contributions. The same is true of Felix Le Dantec (1869-1917), assistant during Jacques's Sorbonne years to Alfred Giard (1846-1908), professor of zoology, both of whom taught courses on evolution as well. Le Dantec, who became professor of biology in 1908, taught also a course in general embryology. A widely read popularizer with a vibrant and warm personality, Le Dantec made quite an impression on both Jacques and Raïssa, who obviously felt that Le Dan-

---

[16]*Année scolaire 1899-1900; Lycée Henri IV; Distribution solennelle des prix faite le 29 juillet 1899* (Paris: P. Dubreuil, 1900) 52.

[17]See Dossier AJ[16] 4785 (p. 489) in the Archives Nationales (Paris). There is no similar documentation available for the *procès-verbaux* for *licences ès sciences* for the years 1899-1919. I would like to express my appreciation to Laurent Morelle, archivist of the Sorbonne, for his kind help in guiding me to this and other documents relating to Maritain's years there.

[18]Or *fiche scolaire*. See Dossier AJ[16] 5712 in the Archives Nationales. The only information on the *fiche scolaire* of "Mlle Oumançoff, Raice" (AJ[16] 5716) is that she failed (*éliminée*) in the three examinations that she took in geology (October 1901), in botany (October 1901), and again in geology (July 1902).

tec had a great and influential scientific career ahead of him. Such is the background of Raïssa's remark that Le Dantec held out for Jacques the prospect of a brilliant scientific future. But then Jacques would have had to commit his life to Le Dantec's chief aim, namely, producing living and conscious matter in vitro (*WHB* 64-65). While Le Dantec was an outspoken materialist,[19] his two favorite students had by then got beyond that stage of intellectual perception in which eating is simply taken for proper nourishment. By 1906 both Jacques and Raïssa had suffered an intellectual hunger that drove them at one point almost to suicide (*WHB* 72-78). Their first move to satisfy their hunger consisted in embracing a study of biology, which plainly acknowledged the insufficiency of physics to deal with the immense richness and adaptability of organic life. The academic years 1906-1907 and 1907-1908 found Jacques and Raïssa in Heidelberg, where Jacques studied with Driesch, a leading German biologist of the time and the head of the neovitalist movement.[20] Jacques became the first in 1910 to introduce Driesch's work and thought to the French intellectual world, which was not, however, to pay attention to an article published in a Catholic philosophical monthly.[21] Ten years later he wrote an introduction to the French translation of Driesch's magnum opus on the science and philosophy of organism,[22] first delivered as Gifford Lectures at the University of Aberdeen in 1907 and 1908.[23]

Maritain's article published in 1910 was his first and last article that could be considered a scientific paper. Quite possibly, if the scholarship that took him to Heidelberg had not included an obligation to present in a publication his studies there, that article might not have been written. Actually the two years that separated Maritain's return from Heidelberg and the publication of that article, a mere twenty-five pages, suggest that Maritain's heart was no longer in the sciences.[24] Science as a professional study ceased to exist for Maritain at almost the

---

[19]Among the publications of Le Dantec (1869-1917) are such titles as *L'athéisme* (1906), *La lutte universelle* (1906), *Contre la métaphysique* (1912), in witness to the antimetaphysical creed into which Le Dantec turned Darwinism, in itself a mere scientific method.

[20]Hans A. E. Driesch (1867-1941) was at first a convinced mechanist, a fact that made his turning to vitalism, about 1884, all the more significant and newsworthy.

[21]"Le néo-vitalisme en Allemagne et le Darwinisme," *Revue de philosophie* 17 (1910): 417-41.

[22]Hans Driesch, *La philosophie de l'organisme*, trans. M. Kollmann, preface by J. Maritain (Paris, 1921) i-xi.

[23]Hans Driesch, *The Science and Philosophy of the Organism* (London, 1907-1908). Driesch wrote and delivered these lectures in English, of which he had a full command.

[24]Jacques and Raïssa returned "for good" from Heidelberg in May 1908. They first went there on 25 August 1906 (*WHB* 180, 198). Their stay in Heidelberg was made possible by a grant from the Michonis Fund.

very moment he had completed that year in Heidelberg. Moreover, what Anatole France (that is, Jacques Thiébault) had by then described with a literary finesse, which was persuasive in the measure of its professed cool detachment, almost happened to Maritain. France spoke of his own love turned into hatred as he made one of his heroes, Jerome Coignard, state: "I hate science for having loved it too much after the manner of voluptuaries who reproach women with not having come up to the dream they formed of them. I wanted to know [through science] everything and I suffer today for my culpable folly."[25] Indeed that former lover of science was to speak of it in terms of vibrating contempt: "The universe which science reveals to us is a dispiriting monotony. All the suns are drops of fire and all the planets drops of mud."[26]

Maritain never despised science, not even under the impact of transferring his intellectual loyalties to metaphysics in general and to Thomism in particular. Nothing would have been more natural for him than to follow, say, Ferdinand Brunetière, certainly a leading figure about 1900 on the French intellectual scene, whose phrase, the "bankruptcy of science" had become a byword and a battle cry by the time Maritain entered the Sorbonne.[27] While even Brunetière failed to see the difference between science and scientism, young Maritain unerringly put his finger on scientism as the true cultural culprit and curse.[28] He did so in an article

---

[25] Anatole France, *The Opinions of Jerome Coignard*, trans. W. Jackson, in *The Works of Anatole France* (New York: Gabriel Wells, 1924) 4:114.

[26] France made that remark in the late 1880s in his review of Flammarion's once famous popularization of astronomy, *Uranie*. See Anatole France, *La vie littéraire* (Paris: 1882-1892) 3:212.

[27] Brunetière's phrase could but incense the scientistic establishment of the Third Republic for more than one reason. First, Brunetière had made his scholarly reputation with a study in which he interpreted the development of belles lettres in terms of Comte's law of three phases, a widely accepted basis of scientism. Second, Brunetière's position as editor-in-chief of the *Revue des Deux Mondes* assured him of a worldwide hearing. Third, Brunetière's stated preference of talking of the "bankruptcy of science" instead of seeing in it the hope for the future appeared in an article in which he described the Vatican as that very hope, following an audience with Leo XIII ("Après une visite au Vatican," *Revue des Deux Mondes* 127 [1895]: 97-118; see 98).

[28] The *Dictionnaire alphabétique et analogique de la langue française*, part 7 R-Z (Paris: Presses Universitaires de France, 1951-1970), a work as authoritative as the big *Oxford Dictionary of the English Language*, is in conflict with Raïssa's remark that Jacques coined the word scientism (*WHB* 72). In the *Dictionnaire*, 1911 is given as the first appearance of "scientism," and Le Dantec, of all people, is given the credit. In view of the friendship between the Maritains and Le Dantec, the latter was most likely the recipient of a reprint of Jacques's article published a year earlier. One cannot help thinking of Chesterton's dictum: "Catholics first and forgotten," or simply ignored.

published in June 1910, which was in fact his first publication and carried the title: "La science moderne et la raison" (modern science and reason),[29] an article yet to be published in English translation. Some of the major themes of what Maritain was to say later on the subject in his most mature works are fully stated in that article. Unlike those works, that article vibrates with the unabashed fiery élan of the one who at the age of twenty-seven, a rather youthful age, finds the long-sought answer and who is suddenly seized with a missionary consciousness to share his find with his fellowmen.

That Maritain was already at the age of twenty-seven the kind of thinker he wanted to be remembered as, and who is in fact remembered as such, has a partial explanation in a reminiscence of Raïssa about their Sorbonne years. What would have happened, Raïssa asks, if "we had directed our studies toward the physico-mathematical rather than toward the natural sciences," that is, botany, physiology, embryology, and geology? It would have been a very mixed blessing. On the one hand, "We would undoubtedly have been fascinated by the magnificence of the discoveries of so great a galaxy of scientific genius; . . . it would have been wonderful, for instance, to attend the classes of Paul Appell, or of Marie and Pierre Curie, scientists of genius and heroic workers, who had opened the way to a new science." On the other hand, fascination by what was presented about the latest marvels of physical science "would for a long time have hidden from us our hunger for metaphysical knowledge" (WHB 63-64). The gist of this remark is that the exactness of physical science is more effective than is the partially descriptive character of other empirical sciences in distracting one from questions about the causes, essences, and purposes of empirical reality. This is not to suggest that professors in the faculty, or rather departments, of natural sciences at the Sorbonne cared for such questions. When Raïssa posed such questions to Professor Lapicque, he brushed her aside with the words: "But that is mysticism" (WHB 39-40).

Mysticism was to become a legitimate and integral subject matter in the metaphysics of Maritain. The last third of his Degrees of Knowledge is about the contemplation of the highest truth, God. To try to answer questions about cause, essence, and purpose has always been an enterprise that inevitably conjures up

---

[29]Jacques Maritain, "La science moderne et la raison," Revue de philosophie 16 (1910): 575-603. That Maritain attributed some importance to that article is evident from its having been selected by him as the first chapter in his Antimoderne (1922), which appeared in German translation in 1930. This is, of course, not the only detail that has readily come to my attention from The Achievement of Jacques and Raïssa Maritain: A Bibliography 1906-1961 (Garden City NY: Doubleday, 1962), an epitome of meticulous scholarship, for which any student of Maritain should feel much indebted to its authors, Donald and Idella Gallagher.

questions about the ultimate cause, the ultimate essence, and the ultimate purpose. The philosopher may, of course, rush to the ultimate. Indeed, as they tried to gain hold of the ultimate, many philosophers jumped one or two if not all the intermediate degrees of knowledge. Descartes was one such philosopher. Convinced that God's nature was an open book to him, Descartes thought, and very logically, that he had therefore a privileged access to the entire observable nature. The result was not a science about the universe of things, but a mere novel, to recall the biting remark of Christiaan Huygens, a younger contemporary of Descartes and of incomparably greater stature as a physicist than Descartes was. In the case of Hegel the result was the *Enzyklopädie der philosophischen Wissenschaften*, a horror story about science. [30] The other side of the coin is no less instructive. Philosophers, whose principal reasoning was aimed at establishing man's inability to know the ultimate, or God, fared just as badly with respect to their legislation about science. The dicta and at times lengthy discourses of a Hume, a Kant, a Mill, a Spencer, a Mach, and a Carnap on how science should be cultivated amount to a scheme of how to put science into a straitjacket. [31]

With both extremes, the rationalist and the empiricist, the source of the fiasco lies with the concept of reality. In their discourse on reality the modern rationalists as well as the modern empiricists were heavily conditioned by what they thought to be the doctrine of the science of their day about reality. They all failed to see the difference between the science of their day and the prevailing fashionable views about it. Those views were not science but philosophy or metaphysics, and all too often a very corrupted form of metaphysics. Maritain never made that mistaken identification. In fact, in the page that in a sense is the first page of his *Degrees of Knowledge*, he begins with a clear-cut distinction between science and philosophy, that is, a critico-realist philosophy. He did not make that distinction in order to get science out of the way. On the contrary, he was eager to show that whereas the positivist scheme does not at all accord with science exactly, the critico-realist philosophy "corresponds more exactly to the vast logical universe of whose modern development the sciences offer us some picture" (*DK* 21). Maritain added in the same breath that a setting forth of their correspondence would require an entire book, a book that he described as a sort of history of science. Maritain never wrote that book, a fact about which the historian and philosopher

---

[30]Since the publication in 1970 of Hegel's *Enzyklopädie* in a three-volume English translation by M. J. Petry (*Hegel's Philosophy of Nature* [London]), none of the countless Hegel experts who read only English can pretend the unavailability of a work in which Hegel provided a far more destructive exposure of his own philosophy than any critic of it could ever write. For some eye-opening details, see my *Angels, Apes, and Men* (LaSalle IL: Sherwood Sugden, 1983) 37-38.

[31]As argued in the respective chapters of my Gifford Lectures (see note 9, above).

of science, such as myself, can only feel a deep frustration. Of course, around 1920, let alone earlier, the writing of such a book would not have been an easy task—except for its pre-Galilean part, which had been brilliantly interpreted by Pierre Duhem, with whose work Maritain was fairly familiar.[32] Histories of science available until recently were top-heavy on clichés forged by the Enlightenment and by its heir, positivism. Most of those histories were conspicuously void of positive facts. While such an imbalance could and did in fact mislead most readers, Maritain would have unerringly seen the difference between the grain and the chaff.

This last appraisal would easily pass for hero worship were it not for the evidence that Maritain's reading of the literature on the new physics was very judicious. It was a literature in the sense that Maritain, from all the evidence, never read strictly scientific publications relating to the new physics. His scientific education at the Sorbonne was centered on the biological sciences. Whatever free time he had, he spent it, not by reading calculus and rational mechanics, but by attending Bergson's lectures and by being a student activist. In fact, he met Raïssa as he gathered signatures for a protest against Czarist pogroms. In writing about the new physics Maritain had to rely on what the French felicitously call *haute popularisation*. They included books and lectures by British, German, and French men of science.[33] Among the British were Arthur Eddington, Whitehead, Bertrand Russell, W. R. Thompson; among the Germans, Einstein, Hermann Weyl, Ernst Herzfeld, Werner Heisenberg; among the French, Charles Picard, Paul Langevin, Henri Poincaré, Georges Urbain, Louis De Broglie. Mention should also be made of first-rate presentations of the philosophy of physics and mathematics by Émile Meyerson, Pierre Duhem, and Ferdinand Gonseth. The latter's book on the foundations of mathematics and the four-dimensional space-time manifold[34] was on a level even higher than the very highest popularization. Last but not least, mention should be made of Maritain's personal contacts with scientists, such as his conversation with P. N. Lebedev (*DK* 183), the first to measure the pressure of light, and of Maritain's close following of the lectures that Einstein gave in Paris in April 1922 (more on this later). The footnotes of *The*

---

[32]Maritain did not seem to know about the series of articles that Duhem published between 1891 and 1894 in the *Revue des questions scientifiques*. There Duhem put a much greater emphasis than he did in his classic work, *La théorie physique* (1906), on a realist epistemology (metaphysics) that alone can make meaningful the positivist methodology of science. It is in this corrective light that one should read Maritain's strictures (*DK* 44) of Duhem's theory of scientific knowledge. For further details, see my book *Uneasy Genius: The Life and Work of Pierre Duhem* (Dordrecht: Nijhoff, 1984) 321-22.

[33]The following list is gathered from the footnotes of *DK*.

[34]F. Gonseth, *Les fondements des mathématiques* (Paris: Blanchard, 1926).

Degrees of Knowledge also contain references to several books and articles published in 1930 and 1931, in proof of Maritain's resolve to remain abreast as much as possible with the latest about the new physics.

The new physics, it is well to recall, was about 1930 a mere dwarf compared with what it was to become in the following half century. To give only two examples: nothing was known in 1930 about the antimatter that now plays a central role in theories relating to the earliest phases of the universe. The first evidence of antimatter was discovered only in 1932. Again, nothing was yet known about the neutrino, first postulated in 1934 by Enrico Fermi, which today is the hottest topic in fundamental particle physics. Today when atoms, to say nothing of molecules, can be directly observed through electron microscopes, and when atomic energy has entered countless households as a source of electricity, it is difficult to recall the time, only fifty years ago, when one could say as Maritain did that "atoms are symbolic images of the primordial parts of the spatio-temporal organization of matter." Such was his answer to the atomic nucleus and their subconstituents. Maritain expected precisely that type of development illustrated by the ever-receding fundamental level among elementary particles, whose never-ending proliferation could in 1932 appear but a dream.

Maritain's expectation was based on what he called "the real being as an inexhaustible source of effectuable measurements" (*DK* 139-40), that is, a subject that permits an ever more detailed mathematization. With this we have arrived at the central problem of a critico-realist philosophy with respect to science, even the new physics. The problem is the extent to which the mathematical models built by the theoretical physicist correspond to reality. Such is also a problem for the theoretical physicist. Yet the respective concerns of the realist philosopher and of the theoretical physicist have a different dynamics. The difference relates to the primary meaning they respectively attach to the term "real." The difference, as Maritain put it in a memorable paragraph that renders graphically the respective thinking of the two, is a matter of emphasis. The philosopher must put the emphasis on the difference between a real being and a mere being of reason, such as a mathematical function. The latter is, however, for the physicist the real thing, provided it works.

> Doubtless, replies the philosopher. That is what they are made for, even those among them which are most obviously *entia rationis* [beings of reason]. And, not to be outdone by his colleague, the physicist will immediately add that these real entities are "shadows" or allusions from which it would be silly to expect anything concerning the intimate nature of matter. (*DK* 140)

Such a graphic hint of the unity of the two viewpoints is a priceless example of the gist of Maritain's *Degrees of Knowledge*, a title that in its full form begins, *Distinguish to Unite.* Of course this full title made sense only if there was an ontological ground for unity. Not that Maritain would have ever made that unity depend on an opinion poll, be it the polling of leading physicists. But he knew all too well that in a scientific age the words of scientists carried a special weight. He was among the first to see the significance of Einstein's increasingly numerous votes on behalf of ontological reality as presupposed by physical theory (*DK* 156).[35]

The relation between reality and mathematical symbolism used in physics was only one of the great problems that imposed itself with a renewed force on the philosophical consciousness. Another was the true sense of the relativity of time and motion, in other words, the possibility of simultaneity. Curiously, none of the physicists and philosophers of science, who have in ever-greater number discussed this question since the 1930s, has cared to seize upon an astute remark of Maritain that first appeared in the wake of Einstein's lectures at the Sorbonne in 1922. The remark concerned Einstein's continual return to the question, What does the word *simultaneity* mean for me the physicist? He always replied, Maritain recalled, by falling back on the methodological theme: "Give me a definition that will tell me by what ensemble of measurements, concretely realizable in each case, I can verify that two events deserve to be called simultaneous or not; only then will I have a definition of simultaneity which can be handled by a physicist and have value for him" (*DK* 158).[36] In other words Einstein implicitly acknowledged the irrelevance of the empiriometrical method to ontological questions about simultaneity and even about the speed of light. Ontological questions had therefore to be referred to that much misunderstood and much abused common sense with which fewer and fewer intellectuals were willing to appear in public. Physics, especially the Einsteinian physics of relativity, may have liberated itself completely of common sense, Maritain remarked, but only at a price. The bargain meant a complete renunciation of any assertion about the real, a renunciation to which no physicist could consistently subscribe. Furthermore, the complete relativization of empiriometric procedures depended on keeping in the same form all basic equations of physics, regardless of their reference system. What this meant was an absolutization far more profound than,

---

[35]*DK* 156. Maritain was not disturbed at all by the fact that he had found those statements quoted by Langevin, a leading French physicist and also a professed Marxist. Precisely because Marxism insisted on the reality of matter as a primary datum, Maritain (as was the case with Gilson as well) saw in it a lesser danger than in the phenomenologists' methodical avoidance of questions relating to reality as such.

[36]There is a complete *procès-verbal* of the question-answer period that followed Einstein's lecture on 6 April 1922 before the Société française de philosophie in its *Bulletin* 17 (1922): 91-113.

say, the postulating of an absolute space in Newtonian physics.[37] In 1930 or thereabouts very few physicists and philosophers of science saw Einstein's physics in that absolutist light.[38] Maritain's insight was not acknowledged by those who in recent years have spoken and written as if they were the "discoverers" of their absolutist aspect. Even today a mere mention of that aspect often leaves dumbfounded the scientific and intellectual community, thriving as ever on hollow clichés as to what Einstein's relativity is really about.

Another such cliché covering a major problem raised by the new physics is the question of causality. That quantum mechanics in general and the uncertainty principle in particular have given the coup de grâce to causality is an assertion that saw print in countless contexts. It has in fact become a climate of opinion ever since that principle was formulated by Werner Heisenberg, who rushed to give it that anticausal interpretation.[39] It shows something of the philosophical poverty of the scientific world that it fails to realize the obvious, namely, that empiricism, even if it is mathematico-physical in the most refined form, is incapacitated by its professed empiricism to say anything about causality. While empiricists are not different from anyone in that they can *observe* only sequences, empiricists as such can *know* only mere sequences. "Causation," Maritain recalled the elementary truth, "is not *observable* as such or insofar as it is an intelligible relation" (*DK* 160). Moreover, Maritain also pointed out another elementary truth: failure to measure an interaction exactly in an operational sense could not mean that the interaction could not take place exactly in an ontological sense.

There were some well-meaning physicists, Heisenberg himself and Eddington in particular, who tried to undo their destruction of causality with the claim that the freedom of the will might therefore be rehabilitated in a world that is noncausal. Maritain (we are in 1931, or only four years after the enunciation by Heisenberg of the principle of indeterminacy) tersely noted that not only does the principle have no bearing on the freedom of the will, but it has no bearing whatever on purely physical causality (*DK* 189). In substance, Maritain charac-

---

[37]This perspective of Einstein's physics, mentioned but fleetingly by Maritain (*DK* 157), is developed in ch. 12 of my Gifford Lectures (see note 9 above) and in my paper "The Absolute beneath the Relative: Reflections on Einstein's Theories," *Intercollegiate Review* 20 (Spring/Summer 1985): 29-38.

[38]The only major exception was Max Planck, whose lectures, widely read in Germany, did not apparently come to Maritain's notice.

[39]For details and documentation, see my "Chance or Reality: Interaction in Nature versus Measurements in Physics," *Philosophia* (1980-1981): 85-105; the first essay reprinted in my *Chance or Reality and Other Essays* (Washington: University Press of America, 1986).

terized as nonsense any abolition of causality and any reinstatement of freedom on the basis of the uncertainty principle. He did so four years before Eddington, who had even tried to calculate the physical measure of freedom allotted to the human will by the new physics, came to the conclusion that such a calculation was sheer nonsense.[40]

Space does not allow us to review and appraise, however briefly, Maritain's analysis of what the new physics offered by 1932 on space, multidimensions, and space-time manifold (DK 165-71). Nor can we review his strictures of those physicists who in the name of quantum mechanics had abolished individual reality (DK 151-52 and 181-84). It should, however, be pointed out that Maritain did not spare from criticism those of his fellow Thomists who were swayed by some apparent similarities between the ideology of the new physics and several basic doctrines of Aristotelian realism.[41] One of these is hylomorphism, according to which actual reality is the actualization of a purely potential entity called *materia prima* by a so-called substantial form. Just as the latter is not the observable shape, the former is not a matter that would have any even indirectly observable features. In defense of that often vilified doctrine of hylomorphism, let me recall only the fact that any philosophical school that tried to cope in terms of another doctrine with the problem of identity through change either had to deny change, or had to throw consistency and coherence to the winds, or to pretend that change represents no problem at all. But let me return to the *materia prima* to which Aristotelians of all times have been tempted to give some observable properties. The temptation was either that of some misguided realism, or, what is worse, the temptation to be in agreement with the latest intellectual or scientific fashions. Thus it happened that in the 1920s several prominent Scholastic philosophers began to talk about the Bohr atom as an illustration of hylomorphism. The nucleus of the atom was taken for the *materia prima* and the arrangement of the electrons around it for the substantial form. Maritain had no use for a policy that by marrying the fashions of its own age is bound to become widowed in the one to follow.

In those intellectual fashions Maritain saw topics for the sociology of knowledge, a point that should seem quite original in view of the rather recent trend to see in all intellectual activity, including scientific activity, a mere matter for sociology. Not only original but also far more profound. This should be very clear in view of the latest phase of the sociologization of the analysis of scientific thinking: Its proponents are interested only in ever-varying social patterns, or to use

---

[40]Details are given ibid.

[41]Most appropriately some of those strictures (DK 183, 188) were administered in a section that Maritain entitled "Dangerous Liaisons."

the prevailing jargon, in revolutions and mutations.[42] The utter superficiality and, I should add, irresponsibility of this allegedly scholarly interest becomes all too evident when it comes to the imperative of seeing connections among those successive patterns or paradigms. The imperative is imposed by the widespread belief in scientific progress. Nothing shows better the superficiality of paradigmists than their failure to show evidence of progress in the succession of paradigms. The root of their fiasco is their extracting philosophy from the new physics without seeing that in fact they exploit not the new physics or the new biology but the pseudophilosophy grafted onto it. This would not have happened if the sociology of science had observed a judicious remark of Maritain:

> From the epistemo-sociological point of view science is no longer considered *in itself*, that is, in respect to what is true or what is false, nor in respect to the determinations which necessarily result from the exigencies of science in the knowledge of things. Rather, it interests us as a collective attitude or spirit engendered *hic et nunc* in the mind of men. So considered, it influences the evolution of the mind as a ferment or a center of organization of various activities belonging to an associative, rather than a rational order and accidental in relation to the essence of science itself. (*DK* 189)

The gist of this remark is that a climate of opinion engendered by the science of the day was not philosophy, let alone a valid and good philosophy. Consequently, change in such a climate was not to be considered an obvious progress, an unmitigated blessing. To be sure, as Maritain observed, the ideology surrounding the new physics certainly discredited the mechanistic ideology grafted on classical physics. He viewed that outcome as "a considerable result from the viewpoint of the sociology of the intellect." But, as he added prophetically:

> The new physics will influence the common intellect in the same irrational fashion as classical physics did. Through some sort of associative influence or subintellectual induction, it will probably give birth in its turn to an inchoate philosophy, a new "scientific tableau of the cosmos" which will save us from the former errors only at the price of illusions of another type. (*DK* 191)

As a chief example of those new illusions in the offing, Maritain singled out the saving of freedom by quantum mechanics through its destruction of causality. Then he turned to his other major topics of the analysis of modern science, namely, the respective roles of ontology and empiricism in the study of living organisms.

Those respective roles, as one can easily guess, related to the questions of what is life or living matter, and what is the purposiveness apparent in such a matter. In this very year, when the twenty-fifth anniversary of the discovery of the dou-

---

[42]For a discussion, see chap. 15, "Paradigms or Paradigm," in my Gifford Lectures.

ble-helix structure of DNA is being celebrated and heavy investments are attracted by the gene-splicing industry, it may sound almost irrational to hint that anything but sheer physics is involved in living matter, including its conscious kind. Yet it is well to recall that a very different kind of irrationality was seen by Sir Andrew Huxley to encroach upon biological research when three years ago he warned the scientific community against taking the origin of life as solved and against shoving the problem of consciousness under the rug, a still greater problem for biology.[43] Indeed if the charge of irrationality is to be brought against any trend, it is the trend according to which the purely physicochemical account of life has for some time been completed. Anyone familiar with the world of biology could easily do today what was done in 1932 by Maritain, who cited quite a few biologists who, although authorities in the latest phase of research, expressed their conviction that life is more than a mere physicochemical mechanism (DK 195-96 and 198). The survival for the past 150 years within biology of a prominent dissenting minority is in fact a unique phenomenon in modern science, which witnesses the opposition party die out within a generation or so.

This opposition party in biology is usually referred to as the party of vitalists or neovitalists, terms rather misleading because they seem to imply that some sort of mysterious vital fluid is at work in living organisms. The vitalism Maritain defended was never of this sort. He insisted on the validity of a never-ending extension of the physicochemical method and renounced a vitalism that would thrive on an observable area denied to that method. Maritain wanted no part in more subtle forms of vitalism either, such as the one proposed by Bergson, or the one generated by phenomenology (DK 192-98). The latter was especially dangerous in Maritain's eyes because of its professed emphasis on doing justice to all phenomena. Among the latter in the biological realm was the observation that irresistibly imposes on the mind the conviction that living matter works for an end. But working for an end, and the teleology it prompts, is never a mere phenomenon. And since it is more than that, phenomenology can cope with it only by erecting its professedly nonmetaphysical status into pseudoprofessional metaphysics.

It is in this light that one should see Maritain's mixed feelings about the rise of criticism in the 1920s against the purely materialistic biology of the late nineteenth century. Appreciative as he was of that reaction he saw an even more dangerous irrationalism entering the scene in its wake. In fact he saw that irrationalism fomented by what he called the "re-entry of intellect into science" (DK 196). He had in mind the ever more fashionable philosophizing by scientists in terms of phenomenology. Not science, he warned, but "only good philosophy

---

[43]He did so in his presidential address to the Royal Society in 1981. See *Supplement to Royal Society News* 12 (November 1983): v.

can drive out bad philosophy" (*DK* 191). Insisting as he did that the future, nay, the salvation of biology lies in a full attention given to the physicochemical as well as to the intuitive account, he urged that the interpretation of such intuition be assigned to a separate field, the philosophy of nature.[44]

Such a stance was in full harmony with his basic contention that unless one has carefully distinguished, unless specific roles have been carefully kept distinct, their unification would result in confusion. The deluge of words that for the past three decades has been poured out on the unification of two cultures, scientific and humanistic, fully justifies Maritain's concern; for if anything has been produced by that deluge it is the steady dilution of humanities. Humanities have either been turned into mysticism as was done in Michael Polanyi's doctrine of personal knowledge, in which science too becomes ultimately mystical, or they have been turned into mere epiphenomena as shown by the writings of Jacob Bronowski, or they were merely given charming literary lip service as illustrated by the oracular utterances of the late high priest of two cultures, C. P. Snow. The common delusion of the last two efforts is the inability of their proponents, or their lack of courage, to recognize and to proclaim that science is a limited knowledge.

Once Maritain had seen the intellectual light in which he found full meaning, he no longer suffered from that inability or lacked that courage. It took enormous courage, as it still does today, to say, as he did in that first article of his, that science was a "diminished knowledge" whose accuracy grew in the measure in which its objective becomes more and more restricted. It took and still takes enormous courage to stand up to scientism because one becomes thereby, to quote from Maritain's first article, as isolated in modern culture as "were the few just men in Sodom and Gomorrha." It took and still takes courage to call upon reason to protest "against nine-tenths of what arrives to the public in the name of science." It took and still takes courage to state that there would be no opposition between faith and science if science were to be of philosophical "good faith."[45]

Yet it is on a point closely related to that harmony between faith and science, a harmony all too dear to Maritain, that a puzzling question arises concerning his interpretation of science in general and his survey of the new physics in particular as both stood about 1930. By then the expansion of the universe or rather the recessional velocity of galaxies was a widely discussed topic. The expansion of the universe in turn was universally connected with Einstein's general theory of rel-

---

[44]This is also the gist of the octogenarian Gilson's book, *D'Aristôte à Darwin et retour* (1974), published in English as *From Aristotle to Darwin and Back Again*, trans. John Lyon (Notre Dame IN: University of Notre Dame Press, 1984).

[45]"La science moderne et la raison," 599, 587, 603.

ativity. Maritain himself could not be unaware of the shock that Einstein created in 1922 in the Sorbonne by insisting on the finiteness of the universe as the most acceptable among various possibilities offered by his cosmology.[46] Yet Maritain ignored both the finiteness of the universe and its expansion, although he spoke of the universal increase of entropy and even allowed it to be a somewhat imperfect but valid pointer to an absolute origin (*DK* 187). What is especially puzzling is that Maritain nowhere speaks to any notable extent of the universe as such.[47] It is impossible to assume that he was unaware of the very gist of Kant's disparagement of the notion of the universe, the very gist of the Kantian criticism of the proofs of the existence of God. Consequently, Maritain should have more than welcomed the twentieth-century discovery of the universe by the new physics.

He did not, and the fact is perplexing for two reasons. One is the ever-stronger reliability of the confidence that science has indeed become a valid discourse about the quantitative interaction among the totality of material things, or the universe. Maritain did not make prognostications about the special directions of the future progress of science, but he expected the unveiling by science of the quantitative aspects of things on an ever-larger scale. As this process unfolds, the material universe shows itself to be more and more specific. The consequences in this respect of the $3°K$ cosmic background radiation are simply breathtaking. But this overall cosmic specificity that manifests itself in all parts, big and small, early and late, of the universe, is precisely the ground on which the critical realist philosophy has always staked its basic claims.[48] Herein lies the second of those reasons concerning Maritain's puzzling silence. For it is the specificity of things that is their most gripping pointer to their existence and also to their possibly existing in some other way, and if so, to their possible nonexistence or, rather, nonnecessary existence and therefore radical contingency. Maritain, if I may conclude on a slight note of criticism, did not seem to realize how right he was when he spoke of the progress of new physics as one of the most beautiful and moving spectacles the modern mind is privileged to contemplate.

---

[46]For details on that shock, see my *The Paradox of Olbers' Paradox* (New York: Herder and Herder, 1969) 224-25.

[47]In *DK* the few references to the universe (pp. 130, 132, 137, 187) are fleeting indeed.

[48]The contributions that modern scientific cosmology can make to philosophical cosmology and natural theology are set forth in my article "From Scientific Cosmology to a Created Universe," *Irish Astronomical Journal* 15 (March 1982): 253-62.

RAYMOND DENNEHY

Maritain's "Intellectual Existentialism": An Introduction to His Metaphysics and Epistemology

IN *Notes from the Underground,* Dostoyevski's narrator observes that "Two plus two equals four is nice, but two plus two equals five is nicer." This remark expresses the perennial tension between knowledge and life. The growing dominance of science appalled Dostoyevski, who saw that scientific knowledge is incapable of accounting for the realities and values most important to human life, such as autonomy, self, and God. Because science had come to be regarded, in too many influential circles, as the standard of all knowledge, he could see no alternative for the preservation of those values but the rejection of rational knowledge and the consequent embrace of irrationalism; hence, "two plus two equals five is nicer."

But the adulation of science was only an expression of the deeper philosophical outlook known as rationalism. This outlook, which was the propelling force behind the Enlightenment, derived its primary inspiration from an excessively optimistic view of the human mind's capacity to know. Relying on the mathematical criteria of clear and distinct ideas—thanks to the assumptions of René Descartes—to determine which propositions were intellectually defensible and which were not, much that had traditionally been regarded as valid knowledge was relegated to the dustbin of the irrational and the sentimental. It was hardly surprising then that writers of Dostoyevski's stature should reject "reason": Kierkegaard, for example, vilified philosophy to protect Christianity, and Freud insisted that human behavior had its ultimate explanation in the dark, irrational forces of the unconscious.

Maritain grew up in such a milieu. His early master, Henri Bergson, taught that conceptual knowledge distorts reality by representing it as static and stereotypical, after the manner in which a motion picture depicts events, when in fact it is dynamic, diverse, and unpredictable. Only intuition, argued Bergson, could give us a direct and undistorted knowledge of reality, and this is accomplished through the will rather than the mind.[1] Many members of Maritain's generation appealed to Bergsonism and other forms of anti-intellectualism in the hope of putting themselves in touch with "life."[2] Maritain too saw early in his career that a philosophy that failed to account for the dynamic, diverse, and unique, and—on the level of the person—for autonomy and self, was indefensible. But he also quickly came to see that a philosophy that was truly in touch with reality must furnish a rational justification for the aforementioned features of reality. He was persuaded that if irrationalism prevailed, then anything was possible, and reality, including man himself, would suffer monstrous distortions.

Accordingly, Maritain would come to characterize Thomistic philosophy— of which he is beyond all doubt the twentieth century's greatest exponent—as an "intellectual existentialism."[3] This characterization encapsulates his distinctive contributions to metaphysics and epistemology: (1) the intuition of being, (2) the primacy of the act of existing, (3) the metaphysical doctrine of the subject, and (4) the integration of intuition with the conceptual functions of judgment. The first three of these themes will be treated in part 1 of the present chapter; the fourth in part 2, on Maritain's epistemology. The resulting philosophy is one that acknowledges the dynamism, diversity, and uniqueness of reality and also the autonomy and selfhood of the person, while at the same time affirming its intelligibility and the mind's capacity to know it.

Maritain's Metaphysics

1. Maritain's metaphysics is at the very heart of his philosophy. All his philosophical writings—whether treating of sociopolitical topics, education, philosophy of man, aesthetics, or epistemology—can be traced back to a single inspiration, the intuition of being. This intuition is the binding link between his metaphysics and his epistemology. His characterization of Thomistic philosophy as an "intellectual existentialism" expresses the radical influence of the intuition of being.

---

[1]Henri Bergson, *Creative Evolution*, trans. Arthur Mitchell (New York: Modern Library, 1944) 8-9, 34-35; Raymond Dennehy, "Understanding Maritain," *Notes et Documents* 7 (July-September, 1984): 123-41.

[2]Henri Massis and Alfred de Tarde, *Les jeunes gens d'aujourd hui* (Paris: Plon, n.d.) 46-49.

[3]Jacques Maritain, *Existence and the Existent*, trans. Lewis Galantière and Gerald B. Phelan (New York: Doubleday, 1947) 70; hereafter cited as *EE*.

The best sources to consult for an understanding of Maritain's metaphysical thought are his *A Preface to Metaphysics*[4] and *Existence and the Existent*. The former is the more foundational and systematic, whereas the latter represents a more mature reflection that reveals the distinctive nature of his thinking in addition to exemplifying the vital connection between his metaphysics and epistemology.

Maritain affirms the view that philosophy is the love of wisdom. Because wisdom in the strict sense is a knowledge that pertains to all reality, only the investigation of being *insofar as it is being* can confer it. "Being" refers to that which exists or can exist. Because everything is either a being (actual or possible) or an aspect of being, it follows that a knowledge of being and its principles constitutes a foundational knowledge of reality itself. Metaphysics is the apex of philosophy because its charge is the investigation of being *insofar as it is being.*

Maritain begins *A Preface to Metaphysics* by adverting to the unchanging yet progressive nature of wisdom. When he proclaims the contemporary relevance of Thomistic metaphysics, he does not wish to suggest that philosophy must be made palatable or congenial to the contemporary world but rather to demonstrate its capacity to address the basic perplexities and correct the philosophical errors that beset the age. As he put it, "For more than thirty years I have remarked how difficult it is to persuade our contemporaries not to confuse the philosopher's faculty of invention with the ingenuity that inspires the art of the dress designer" (*EE* 11). The expression "living Thomism" reflects Maritain's conviction that, in accordance with the demands of authentic wisdom, Thomistic metaphysics is ever young and anything but a historical curiosity (*PM* 9-10).

Obviously wisdom must pertain to truths that are permanent. But how can the permanent be progressive? Maritain's answer is that without permanence genuine progress is impossible. He illustrates the point within the context of the terms "mystery" and "problem." Scientific advance cannot accurately be called progress because the latter term implies development: to develop, a thing must change while remaining the same in some important respect. In contrast, science advances by *"substitution"*: "Einstein's system has dethroned Newton's, as the Copernican had dethroned the Ptolemaic astronomy." Science makes its way by addressing problems. A problem lends itself to a solution; the mind then proceeds to another problem. Because problems are solved by the discovery of new data, it is always possible that propositions and theories thought to be true now will be falsified by future discoveries.

The data in question are the sensible properties of things to which the empiriological approach of the sciences is restricted. Because science observes measurable data, it does not study things directly but rather studies their sensible

---

[4]Jacques Maritain, *A Preface to Metaphysics* (New York: New American Library, 1962); hereafter cited as *PM*.

properties; only the material and the sensible are measurable. Philosophy, on the other hand, employs the ontological approach, which is to say it investigates the being of things and thus studies them directly, that is, as being. Philosophy accordingly knows things in their mystery.

A mystery does not lend itself to a solution. It is not a case, as in the solution of a problem, of finding all the pieces to the puzzle, for there are no pieces. A mystery allows only an ever-deepening understanding, a progressive penetration of reality. Only in the understanding of a mystery do we have the two essential elements of progress, permanence and change. What is known, as the penetration increases, is the same reality; no new data are discovered. The truth of it never changes, but one's understanding of it does change as the mind acquires an ever more profound understanding of it.

Wisdom allows for progress in knowledge. By its very concern with the real, it confers permanence; by its constant assault on reality, its knowledge changes, but it does so by deepening already existing knowledge.

If metaphysics operates in the realm of mystery, its object is, for all that, "intelligible mystery." This is not a contradiction in terms. What makes it seems so to the modern mind is the rationalist influence. Descartes introduced the criteria of truth, properly belonging to the domain of mathematics, into philosophy and accordingly maintained that only those propositions that the mind beholds as "clear and distinct" are rationally acceptable. He thereby created an unreal opposition between intelligibility and mystery. Maritain observes that the proper object of the mind is being and that

> being is a mystery, either because it is too pregnant with intelligibility, too pure for our intellect, which is the case with spiritual things, or because its nature presents a more or less impenetrable barrier to understanding, a barrier due to the element of nonbeing in it, which is the case with becoming, potency and above all, matter. (*PM* 12-13)

Every act of knowing is a combination of mystery and problem. It is because knowing has for its object that which is, being, that it contains mystery. And it is because the human mind is such that it can penetrate being only by means of concepts that knowing contains the problem. One or the other of these two aspects predominates, depending upon the kind of knowledge in question. Where knowledge is most ontological, the mystery aspect predominates. This is the case with metaphysics, whose direct object is being as such.

Being alone can satisfy the intellect's thirst for knowledge. Other disciplines—mathematics, the empirical sciences, the philosophy of nature and so on—furnish important kinds of knowledge, but by themselves they cannot slake this thirst. Because the ontological riches of being are inexhaustible, the intellect must turn to the science of being, metaphysics, to drink its fill (*PM* 15-16, 19-23).

Given the widespread misunderstanding of being, Maritain is at pains to make clear what being is not. It is not the "particularized being" of everyday experience and the empirical sciences. The being that underlies the sensible phenomena investigated by the empirical sciences and that is implicit in the objects of our daily experience is not being as such but rather the particular being that these phenomena and objects imply. Nor is it the "vague being of common sense." To be sure, this being is materially the same being as that studied by metaphysics, but it is concretized by and hidden beneath material properties and forms. Because it is the same being materially as that studied by metaphysics, common sense can and does ascend from the things of its experience to the existence of God. But this ascension is not the result of philosophical reasoning. If the vague being of common sense were the subject of metaphysics, everyone would be a metaphysician.

Nor is it "being divested of reality," which is to say, it is not the being studied by the logician. The latter deals with being, for all concepts are reducible to the concept of being and all concepts are ways of being in the mind. But the being of the logician is what is called a being of second intention, for it is a mental construct designed to lay bare the mechanisms by which the mind moves from premises to conclusion. Its constructs are, for example, genus and species. *Animal*, as a generic category referring to no specific animal, does not exist in the world but only in the mind.

Nor is it "pseudo-being," by which Maritain means being regarded as the ultimate in the hierarchy of categories or genera, so that it is the concept with the broadest extension but the least content or intension. Such a concept of being is so empty of content as to be indistinguishable from nothing. It is because Hegel construed being thus that he was led to identify it with nonbeing. Finally, the being of metaphysics is not the being of dialectics. The latter is coextensive with the being studied by the metaphysician in that it is coextensive with real being. But it differs crucially because its being is being as it exists in the mind, being as it enjoys a conceptual life. Consequently, the being of dialectics is not concerned with the real causes of being but only with being as shaped and governed by the conceptual mechanisms of the mind (*PM* 34-47). It is because being is thus erroneously construed that many modern philosophers conclude that metaphysics is a pseudoscience.

In contrast, the true subject of metaphysics is being as such, and it is known by intuition. This means that the understanding of metaphysics requires a discussion of the intuition of being as such, and it is here that Maritain's originality as a metaphysician manifests itself. Consider the following passage:

> This is the ultimate object to be attained by the intellect, which it attains at the summit of its natural knowledge. It boxes the compass. For it sets out from being, but from being as it is immediately apprehended when the mind first awakes in

the sensible world. That is the starting point. And at the end of its course it arrives at being, but being envisaged in itself, disengaged from its matrix, viewed in its own light and in accordance with its own type of intelligibility. (*PM* 48-49)

The intuition of being, in presenting to the intellect being as such, discloses the "transcendental character and analogical value" of being. The transcendality of being proclaims itself in the confrontation with being as such in that the intellect sees that being is not a category or a genus but instead overflows all categories and genera, for there is nothing outside being and therefore nothing to limit being: being is all there is; outside being there is nothing. The analogical value of being proclaims itself in the intuition because being as such pertains simply to what things have in common: however they may differ in their essences and way of being, they are all beings insofar as each is a *that which is or which exists*.

The following passage is Maritain's attempt to explain what he means by the "intuition of being":

[It] is a perception direct and immediate. . . . It is a very simple sight, superior to any discursive reasoning or demonstration, because it is the source of demonstration. It is a sight whose content and implications no words of human speech can exhaust or adequately express and in which in a moment of decisive emotion, as it were, of spiritual conflagration, the soul is in contact, a living, painstaking and illuminating contact, with a reality which it touches and which takes hold of it. . . . [I]t is being more than anything else which produces such an intuition. (*PM* 50-51)

One does not have to be a metaphysician to have the intuition of being, this "revelation, this species of intellectual shock" (*PM* 51), but without it one cannot be a metaphysician. The intuition visits anyone who one day suffers the shock of realizing that things exist or that he himself exists, as when one suddenly realizes the contingency of one's own existence: "I exist, but suppose my parents had never met or the car speeding towards us yesterday had not swerved in time!" The intuition is not given to everybody, not even to all who engage in philosophy; not even to all those who desire to be or believe they are metaphysicians. Maritain says that Immanuel Kant, despite his stature in the history of philosophy, never had the intuition. The difficulty of attaining the intuition is not a difficulty in executing a technique; it is not a matter of skillful application. Rather, it is one of achieving a sufficient degree of intellectual purification to enable the intuition to take place in us, a degree "at which we become sufficiently disengaged, sufficiently empty to *hear* what all things whisper and to *listen* instead of composing answers" (*PM* 52-53).

Perhaps it will be helpful in attempting to grasp the significance that Maritain attaches to the intuition of being to recall his early discipleship under Henri

Bergson and his own constitutional sensitivity to the real. Bergson's great contribution to contemporary philosophy was to remind it of what it had forgotten owing to the influence of rationalism, namely, that the real and the conceptual are two quite different things.[5] Although eventually repudiating Bergsonism because of its rejection of conceptual knowledge, Maritain never relinquished the Bergsonian insight into the real. Add this to his own sensitivity to the real—one that led him to dissociate himself from the title of "professor" because the latter's knowledge is too often drawn primarily or entirely from books at the expense of the world of things and events, and to associate more often with artists, missionaries, and mystics than with professors and students.[6] These two forces prepared Maritain's intellect and indeed his very soul for a profound understanding of being and the primacy that Thomas Aquinas accorded the act of existing as "the act of all acts and the perfection of all perfections."[7] It was not the intuition of being precisely that Maritain saw as primary but, as he put it in his final metaphysical treatise, the "intuition of the act of existing" (*EE* 12).

What comes through Maritain's prose, time and again, is his frustration in trying to express the meaning of the real, of being, of the act of existing. He struggles unceasingly to break free of the constraints of language and concepts, but despite his search for the right words, these words themselves confess his sense of failure. Consider the following two passages, written almost a half-century apart:

> There is but one word by which we can express our discovery, namely being. Let us have the courage to require our intellect, acting as such, to look the reality signified by the term in the face. It is something primordial, at once very simple and very rich and, if you will, inexpressible in the sense that it is that whose perception is the most difficult to describe, because it is the most immediate. Here we are at the very root, at last laid bare, of our entire intellectual life. You may say, if you please, for I am here attempting to employ a purely descriptive terminology as a preliminary to the formation of a philosophic vocabulary, that what is now perceived is, as it were, a pure activity, a subsistence which transcends the entire order of the imaginable, a living tenacity, at once precarious—it is nothing for me to crush a fly—and indomitable—within and around me there is a growth without ceasing. By this subsistence, this tenacity, objects come up against me, overcome possible disaster, endure and possess in themselves whatever is

---

[5]Henri Bergson, *An Introduction to Metaphysics*, trans. T. E. Hulme (New York: Bobbs-Merrill, 1955) 32-35.

[6]Yves R. Simon, "Jacques Maritain: The Growth of a Christian Philosopher," *Jacques Maritain: The Man and His Achievement,* ed. Joseph W. Evans (New York: Sheed and Ward, 1963) 18.

[7]Thomas Aquinas, *Disputed Questions on the Power of God* VII.2, reply obj. 9.

requisite for this. *These are metaphors, lamentably inadequate, which attempt to express not so much what my intellect sees, which is superempirical, as my experience of the vision, and do not themselves enter the domain of metaphysics but which may make us aware that to the word 'being,' when it expresses a genuine metaphysical intuition, there must correspond a primary and original datum, of its essence above the scope of observation.* (PM 56-57; emphasis added)

[A]t the root of metaphysical knowledge, St. Thomas places the intellectual intuition of that mysterious reality disguised under the most commonplace and commonly used word in the language, the word *to be;* a reality revealed to us as the uncircumscribable subject of a science which the gods begrudge us when we release, in the values that appertain to it, the act of existing which is exercised by the humblest thing—that victorious thrust by which it triumphs over nothingness. (*EE* 28-29)

Small wonder, then, that Maritain feels obliged at one point to say: "If I am asked about this concept of being, called upon to explain it, I shall say and can only say—and this is not a definition but a simple designation—that being is 'that which exists or can exist.' And this designation possesses meaning only because it thus refers to a primary intuition" (*PM* 66).

The primordial nature of the intuition of being is such that one does not have to study philosophy to experience it. But Maritain is emphatic in his rejection of the position that it is therefore a nonrational or irrational experience. The intuition of being is an "intellectual intuition" (*PM* 51). It works in tandem with a "confirmatory rational analysis." By this expression Maritain means that it is both possible and necessary to show analytically the inevitability of arriving at the intuition of being. Rational analysis establishes "the necessity of being . . . as the supreme object of our knowledge" (*PM* 58). The analytic proof rests upon the commonsense judgment and epistemological confirmation of the ontological basis of knowledge and the primacy of being. Because all our concepts are reducible to the concept of being, being is the first of all our concepts; all other concepts are determinations of the concept of being, for they are ways of being in the mind. It follows that being is what the intellect apprehends first of all, though it is implicit in our concepts and judgments rather than explicit (*PM* 58-59).

The interdependence between the intuition and the analysis, upon which Maritain insists, amounts to this: lacking the rational necessity; lacking the intuition, the analysis, although demonstrating the necessity of arriving at the intuition of being, cannot produce the intuition. The analysis leads by logical necessity to the threshold, but only the intuition carries us across it to the apprehension of being as such (*PM* 59).

Not only does the intuition of being occur in conjunction with a rational analysis, but it also results in a conceptualization. Thus Maritain calls the intuition of being as such an "eidetic intuition" or "ideating visualization." By these terms he means "an intuition producing an idea":

> The intellect by the very fact that it is spiritual proportions its objects to itself, by elevating them within itself to diverse degrees, increasingly pure, of spirituality and immateriality. It is within itself that it attains reality, stripped of its real existence outside the mind and disclosing, uttering in the mind a content, an interior, an intelligible sound or voice, which can possess only in the mind the conditions of its existence one and universal, and existence of intelligibility in act. (PM 61)

To say that the intuition of being is eidetic is therefore to assert the condition for the investigation of being as being. Were being the object of a concrete intuition—for example, the intuition furnished by the external senses or by introspection—it would be bound to a reality apprehended as concrete and singular. This would in turn either destroy all intelligibility by fragmenting reality into "a pure phenomenalist pluralism" or reduce the diversity and dynamism to "a pure ontological monism" (PM 61). But apprehending being under the aspect of eidetic existence preserves the analogous nature of being, and the principle of identity protects the irreducible diversities of reality. For the unity conferred on being by eidetic visualization is a relative unity—a unity based upon the apprehension of being—accomplished by intellectual abstraction from the diversities of being in order to focus on what is common to all beings, namely, that being is. This relative univocity dissolves as being returns to the existential plane from the conceptual (PM 61-62).

Maritain's defense of the intuition of being as an intellectual intuition can fully be appreciated only when viewed within the context of his reaction to Bergson. Like Bergson he understands quite well the imperatives of the real and the consequent inability of the concept itself to grasp the real as such; but like intellectualists, chiefly Thomas Aquinas, he also understands that the objectivity of knowledge and thus the apprehension of being as being is possible only through the intellect's elevation of the intuition to its own level of immateriality.

Moreover, Maritain's critique of existentialists like Sartre, who in their desire to affirm the primacy of existence deny the reality of essence (EE 13-17), harks back to his earlier criticism of Bergson, although the latter criticism was advanced on the epistemological level primarily. It is clear that, for Maritain, the metaphysical intuition of being abstracts from the confrontation with being in the concrete and thus apprehends being as such. Being is thus presented analogously, for the apprehension of being as being is the apprehension of being insofar as it is: being is represented both in its unity and its diversity. In other words, the apprehension of being as such, although focusing on what all beings have in common—namely, actual or possible existence—does not exclude the diversity of being.

2. Underlying this diversity is the reciprocal influence of existence and essence. What exists is not existence but things, specific things. What specifies things, beings, existents, is essence. The apprehension of a thing as being, as that which exists either actually or possibly, is implicit in our experiences. If being is characterized as that "which exists or which can exist," a judgment, albeit implicit also, must occur, which asserts *this being is*. From this judgment follows, argues Maritain, the principle of identity, "being is what is." This being that I now apprehend is a specific being, that is, a tree, a dog, a man, and what specifies it as a *this* or *that* is essence.

The principle of identity is not a principle of the mind only but is also, and primarily, one of being and reality. And because being is all there is and nothing is outside being, being is the basis of intelligibility. If then the principle of identity belongs to the mind, it is because it is first a principle of being. As such it safeguards both the intelligibility and the diversity of reality; otherwise we would be forced to adopt either the position of Heraclitus and emphasize the diversity of being to the point of fragmenting reality unto chaos and unintelligibility, or that of Parmenides and stress the unity of reality at the cost of its diversity. But these are both false options. Being, and thus reality, is intelligible precisely because every being is what it is and not another thing and because no matter *how* things differ, they have in common *that* they exist or can exist; this is being as such.

To reiterate, Maritain characterizes being as "that which exists or can exist." Essence, or *what* a thing is, is a potency for existing, whereas the act of existing actualizes that potency. Because existence is an act that is exercised, it does not exist by itself; rather it is the actualization of a potency to be, and to be a *this* or *that*. Maritain agrees with the existentialist in maintaining the primacy of existence, but, as noted above, for him this does not mean the exclusion of essence; what it means is that existence comes before essence in the sense that the act of existing makes the essence *to be* and that without that act essence would be nothing. Thus, if it is true that an existing lion is better than an existing ant, it is also true that an existing ant is better than a merely possible lion (*EE* 46).

The intuition of being conceived as an intellectual intuition furnishes the basis for the so-called first principles. These may be regarded as the preepistemological justification for the objectivity of knowledge. From the concept of being implicit in all our knowledge is derived the principle of identity, "Being is being" or "Every being is what it is." The second of these formulations elucidates the first, thereby making clear that the principle is not a tautology. For the knowledge that a thing exists depends not only on the judgment that it exists but also on the apprehension of *what* it is, on the apprehension of its essence. Thus the elm in the front yard is an elm and not an oak or a dog. In the formulation "Every being is what it is," the subject, "Every being," expresses the thing's existence (either actual or possible), while the predicate, "what it is," expresses its essence. Thus the formulation "Being is being" contains the statement "Every being exists (either actually or potentially) according to what it is, that is, according to its essence or nature" (*PM* 91-94).

The principle of noncontradiction, "It is impossible for a being to be and not be at the same time and in the same respect," Maritain regards as the logical expression of the principle of identity (*PM* 91). Like all the first principles, this is self-evident, for its truth presents itself to the intellect as soon as the meaning of the terms is known.

Allied principles are those of sufficient reason ("Every being has the reason for its being either in itself or in something outside itself"), of efficient causality ("Every being that has the reason for its being outside itself is caused by another being"), and of finality ("Every agent acts for an end"). Although incapable of direct demonstration, since every proof presupposes them, they can be demonstrated indirectly by showing that their denial leads to self-contradiction inasmuch as they cannot be denied without at the same time being assumed and therefore affirmed (*PM* 90). To deny any of these principles is to tumble into absurdity, since it is to deny the principle of identity. For if it is denied that a being whose sufficient reason is outside itself is caused by another, then the principle of sufficient reason must be denied, since it must then be admitted that the being lacks a sufficient reason for being. But that which lacks a sufficient reason does not exist. The elm in the front yard would both exist and not exist at the same time: it does exist; it proclaims its existence to all the world, but it cannot exist, for it lacks a raison d'être; it has no reason to be. This, in turn, constitutes a denial of the principle of noncontradiction insofar as it affirms that the elm both exists and does not exist. And since this principle is but the logical formulation of the principle of identity, what is ultimately denied is "Every being is what it is."

The indefectibilty of these principles has its ground in being. They are as certain as our knowledge that being is. This ontologically grounded certitude not only furnishes the rationale for the principles of all branches of knowledge but also for the human mind's capacity to rise from a knowledge of the sensible world to a knowledge of immaterial, transcendent being. This can be demonstrated by reconsidering the second formulation of the principle of identity, "Every being is what it is." The formulation expresses a real distinction between essence and existence. An examination of the essences of the existents we perceive reveals that their existence cannot be explained by their essences. Take the essence man, for example. It constitutes the sufficient reason for man's rationality, capacity to teach and learn, to laugh, and so forth—for his essence is rational animal—but not for his existence. This means that, although the existence of things is undeniable, they themselves cannot furnish the sufficient reason for their existence. That must be found in a being outside themselves, a being whose very essence is to exist, a being in whom essence and existence are identical (*PM* 96-98).

3.   Considerations such as the actualization of essence by existence and the analogical value of being bring us face to face with what is perhaps the most distinctive aspect of Maritain's metaphysical thought, his notion of the subject. His book *Existence and the Existent* is the culmination of his lifelong effort to reconcile thought and reality. An examination of the book's structure reveals the notion of the subject to be at the heart of the reconciliation, for it is there that Maritain characterizes Thomism as an "intellectual existentialism" (*EE* 70). This rubric distills Maritain's claim that the existentialism of Sartre and others denied the reality of essence, thereby creating an anti-intellectual and "apocryphal existentialism," while Thomism is an "authentic existentialism" (*EE* 13). It is impossible to grasp the significance of all this apart from what Maritain means by "subject":

> Precisely because of the existentialism of . . . [Thomistic] philosophy, the notion of subject plays a capital part in it; we may even say that *subjects occupy all the room there is in the Thomist universe, in the sense that, for Thomism, only subjects exist, with the accidents which inhere in them, the action which emanates from them, and the relations which they bear to one another. Only individual subjects exercise the act of existing.* (*EE* 70)

The essence of the thing *as known* is, in all its universality and immateriality, an abstraction from the concrete existent or subject. The operation of judgment has for its goal to reunite the abstracted essence with the existent; in this operation the existent is grasped as an existent because it is seen by intuition as exercising an act: only a subject, a center and source of activity, can exercise an act.

Maritain accordingly sees the subject as the point of reconciliation between the uniqueness and dynamism of the real, on the one hand, and the intelligibility of the real, on the other. Each subject exercises its act of existing according to the specifications of its essence. Because each is a unique embodiment of essence, it exercises its act of existing in a unique way, issuing forth unique actualizations of its essence on the existential plane. But Maritain insists that the essence and existence in themselves are not enough to account for the subject. In addition to them, a positive mode or perfection is needed to render the subject capable of exercising its act of existing:

> What we call subject Saint Thomas called *suppositum*. Essence is *that which* a thing is; supositum is *that which* has an essence, *that which* exercises existence and action . . . —that which subsists. Here we meet the metaphysical notion which has given students so many headaches and baffles everyone who has not grasped the

true—the existential—foundation of Thomist metaphysics, the notion of subsistence. (*EE* 70-71)[8]

Maritain justifies his notion of subsistence by appealing to the observation
that when existence actualizes an essence's potency to exist, it does not thereby
simply make the possible to be real, as though the essence were "pinned outside
of nothingness."[9] Because, on the contrary, existence is an act that is exercised,
a positive mode or perfection is needed to render the subject capable of receiving
existence, which is to say, rendering it capable of exercising the act of existence.
Subsistence is thus the mode which transfers the subject from the possible to the
existential order. Just because subsistence renders the subject capable of receiving existence, it is neither a property of essence nor the act of existence (*DK* 437).

The consequences that the notion of the subject and its ground, the theory
of subsistence, have for Maritain's philosophy of man and sociopolitical philosophy are considerable. This should not be surprising. Although he is perhaps
best known as a political philosopher and although he wrote extensively in the
fields of aesthetics and educational philosophy, not to mention ethics, he is first
and foremost a metaphysician. Thus the rational foundation of the dignity and
autonomy that he ascribes to the human person is metaphysical, as it has its ultimate rationale in his theory of subsistence:

> And when the subject or supposit is a person, subsistence, from the fact that the
> nature which it "terminates" or "sur-completes" is an intellectual nature . . .
> brings with it a positive perfection of a higher order. Let us say it is then a state
> of active *and autonomous* exercise, proper to a whole which envelops itself (in this
> sense, that the totality is in each of its parts), therefore interior to itself, and pos-
> sessing itself. Such a whole, possessing itself, makes its *own* in an eminent sense,
> or re-duplicatively, the existence and the operations that it exercises. They are
> not only *of it*, but *for it*—for it as being integral parts of the possession of the self
> by the self characteristic of the person. All the features we have just indicated
> belong to the ontological order. They refer to the ontological depths of subjec-
> tivity. Precisely here lies the ontological basis of the properties of the person in
> the moral order, of the mastery that it has over its acts by free choice, of its as-
> piration to liberty of autonomy, of the rights it possesses. (*DK* 438-39)

Thus, Maritain's metaphysical notion of the subject not only provides the rationale for his philosophy of man and sociopolitical philosophy, but it also contrib-
utes in a major way to the formation of a philosophical view of reality that is at

---

[8]See Raymond Dennehy, "Maritain's Theory of Subsistence: The Basis of 'Existentialism,' " *Thomist* 39:3 (July 1975): 542-74.

[9]Jacques Maritain, *Distinguish to Unite or The Degrees of Knowledge,* trans. under the
direction of Gerald B. Phelan (New York: Scribner's, 1959) 436; cited hereafter as *DK*.

once intelligible and open to reality as diverse, dynamic, and unique. For, as noted, earlier, things could not exist unless specified by intelligible structures known as essences, but what is real is not the essence itself, or its act, existence; it is the subject that is real: only subjects exist.

Maritain's Epistemology

I have said that the intuition of being is at the very heart of Maritain's philosophy and that it is the binding link between his metaphysics and epistemology. His characterization of Thomistic philosophy as an "intellectual existentialism" has its completion in his epistemology; for if the "existentialism" portion refers to the primacy of the act of existing in his metaphysics, the "intellectual" portion refers to the integration of intuition with the conceptual functions of judgment in his epistemology. This integration reflects Maritain's previously-alluded-to recognition that the real is intelligible and as such is knowable by means of concepts. Another way to express the tie between his metaphysics and epistemology is to say that if metaphysics studies being *as being*, epistemology studies being *as known*.

Maritain's major opus, *The Degrees of Knowledge*, is the primary source for his epistemology, but important expositions of it will also be found in his *Bergsonian Philosophy and Thomism*[10] and *Existence and the Existent*. As is true of his entire philosophy, Maritain's epistemology stands in the tradition of Thomistic realism. The basic tenet of epistemological realism may be expressed thus: things are the measure of mind, not mind the measure of things. As opposed to the mainstream of modern philosophy, the realistic tradition maintains that, rather than colliding with each other, common sense and philosophy are mutually complementary: philosophy grows out of, purifying and rationally developing, the spontaneous judgments implicit in commonsense knowledge. Examples of such judgments are that things exist independently of our knowledge of them and that we can know what they are, sometimes with a knowledge that is certain. Contrast this with modern philosophy's view that our knowledge of extramental reality, no matter how eminently plausible it often may be, must always remain probable and therefore open to doubt. Recall Maritain's position on the intuition of being and his claim that the judgment "Being is" is implicit in all our knowledge. Although it is impossible to demonstrate that things outside our mind enjoy an existence of their own independent of our knowledge of them, their existence is known by us with certitude, and indeed this primal knowledge is the source of all our knowledge, even our knowledge of possible beings.

---

[10]Jacques Maritain, *Bergsonian Philosophy and Thomism,* second edition, trans. Mabelle L. Andison in collaboration with J. Gordon Andison (New York: Philosophical Library, 1955); cited hereafter as *BPT.*

Maritain recognizes two realms of knowledge, the natural and the supernatural. What differentiates them are their respective criteria of truth. In natural knowledge the criterion is the evidence of the object;[11] for example, what validates the claim that salt dissolves in water is the observation of the behavior of salt when immersed in water; what validates the claim that man is a rational animal is the observation of human behavior. In supernatural knowledge the criterion of truth is not the object to which assent is given but divine veracity. For example, the claim in Genesis that the world was created in time cannot be verified—or falsified—by unaided reason; believers assent to this claim on the principle that God has revealed it to them, and because he is all good he would not deceive them, nor could he convey erroneous information to them, because he is all-knowing. Maritain insists that religious belief, the object of which is divine revelation, constitutes the valid, objective knowledge that cannot be obtained by unaided reason.[12] He also has much to say about mystical knowledge, by which God, through the infusion of the theological virtues faith, hope, and charity, draws the individual ever closer to him in mystical union (*DK*, part 2).

The realm of natural knowledge contains three important levels of knowing: scientific, philosophical, and connatural. Although all three have the same criterion of truth, namely, the evidence of the object, philosophical and scientific knowledge differ from connatural knowledge by virtue of having a *formal* object. It is the different formal objects that, in turn, differentiate these two levels of knowledge from each other. Accordingly, Maritain coins the terms "dianoetic," "perinoetic," and "ananoetic" to indicate the different kinds of knowledge yielded by philosophy and science. (The terms are derived from the Greek *nous*, for "mind" or "intellect"; *dia-*, meaning "through"; *peri-*, meaning "around" or "about"; and *ana-*, "a moving upward.")

By "dianoetic intellection," Maritain means knowledge that the intellect attains of the nature of the essence of a thing through the latter's sensible properties. By means of "dianoetic intellection, substantial natures are to some degree known *in themselves, by signs* that are proper accidents, properties in the philosophical sense of the word" (*DK* 207). Aristotle's observation that in the beginning children call all men father until they learn the difference is an example of what Maritain intends in this passage. Repeated experience of concrete, particular things—individual men, in this case—is required for a true understanding of what individual things essentially are. Through the perception of a thing's sensible properties and behavior, the human intellect arrives at a knowledge of

---

[11]Jacques Maritain, *An Introduction to Philosophy*, trans. E. I. Watkin (Kansas City: Sheed, Andrews, and McMeel, 1957) 64.

[12]Jacques Maritain, *Science and Wisdom*, trans. Bernard Wall (New York: Scribner's, 1954) 79.

its essential being *as presented through those sensible properties and that behavior:* the knowledge that man is a rational animal follows from the knowledge, gained through our sense perceptions, of the morphology, speech, laughter, creations, and so on, of individual human beings.

By "perinoetic intellection" Maritain intends the kind of knowledge attained by the sciences through the observation of measurable properties. It is "a knowledge of essences by the 'signs' . . . which are known *in place of* the natures themselves" (*DK* 206). For example, the electron as represented in scientific discourse refers to actually existing entities, but the knowledge it gives of them is a knowledge only of certain of their measurable, operational properties rather than their essence or substance, and these properties are expressed in the language of mathematico-empirical signs.

And by "ananoetic intellection" Maritain means a knowledge by analogy. This kind of knowledge enables our intellect to go from knowledge of sensible things to knowledge of immaterial being, such as God.

> The Divine Essence, constituted as object for us not in itself but by means of the objectification of created subjects (considered in those of their perfections which belong to the transcendental order) is attained and known in things which at the same time resemble and infinitely differ from it. . . . In God, what they signify escapes, without our being able to know how, our mode of conceiving. The Divine Essence is, therefore, really attained by our metaphysical knowledge, but without delivering itself; it is known, but its mystery remains intact, unpenetrated. To the very degree that we know it, it escapes our grasp, infinitely surpasses our knowledge. (*DK* 229)

Thus, from the observation that the activities of beings in the sensible world are purposive, that is, act for an intelligible end, as the spider spins its web to catch insects for food, we arrive at the conclusion that the world is governed by an Intelligence and accordingly that God, along with His other perfections, is Perfect Intelligence. But since this inference is drawn from the observation of sensible beings, the only things of which we have direct knowledge, we have no direct knowledge and hence no conception of this Perfect Intelligence as such. Knowing of the existence of the latter, however, as the necessary inference from what is intelligible in finite beings, we nevertheless do attain an analogical knowledge of God as Perfect Intelligence.

Finally, by "connatural knowledge" he means "a kind of knowledge which is produced in the intellect but not by virtue of conceptual connections or by way of demonstration."[13] It is knowledge by inclination rather than by concept: the

---

[13] Jacques Maritain, *The Range of Reason* (New York: Scribner's, 1952) 22; cited hereafter as *RR*.

intellect does not operate alone but in conjunction with the emotions, appetites, and the proclivities of the will; indeed, these other faculties guide and govern the will. Consider, for example, Aristotle's advertence to the virtuous man who, by love of virtue rather than by theoretical knowledge, makes the correct moral judgment in the concrete situation. He inclines toward virtue because he is, owing to his love for it, "co-natured" with it. This kind of knowledge plays an immense part in our everyday experience and practical activity, particularly with regard to our knowledge of the concrete particular and relationships with other persons.

Art and morality are two areas where connaturality figures prominently. For example, Maritain describes poetic knowledge as "nonconceptual and nonrational" and as originating in the "preconscious life of the intellect." Working through emotions that, in turn, enter the preconscious life of the intellect, this "unconceptualizable knowledge," Maritain writes, "becomes intentional and intuitive," producing there a vague apprehension of an existential reality as identical with the self. This apprehension blossoms as a sign: "so as to have the self known in the experience of the world and the world known in the experience of the self, through an intuition which essentially tends toward utterance and creation" (RR 25).

Maritain points to moral experience as the most common example of knowledge through connaturality: "It is through connaturality that moral consciousness attains a kind of knowing—inexpressible in words and notions—of the deepest dispositions—longings, fears, hopes or despairs, primeval loves and options—involved in the night of subjectivity" (RR 26). Natural law is the primary case in point. To say that it is naturally known is to say that it is known through inclination or through connaturality rather than through conceptual knowledge and reasoning. Maritain argues that the natural law expresses itself to practical reason in judgments that spring from a connaturality or congeniality that enables the intellect to grasp as good what harmonizes with the essential inclinations of human nature and as evil what collides with them. Through historical and social experience man gains an ever-deepening understanding of human nature and thereby understands more clearly how to respond to these inclinations. Maritain does not deny that moral philosophy or moral rules are discovered by and through concepts and reasoning. What he has in mind here are the primary rules of the natural law *as they express themselves through the spontaneous human inclinations*, such as the urge to preserve one's life, to know truth, to live with one's fellowmen in society, and the like. Reason's reflection on, and elucidation of, these primary principles carries us from the domain of the natural law to that of moral philosophy. Although admitting that connatural knowledge is not rational knowledge, Maritain bases his claim that it is genuine knowledge nonetheless on the observation that it is co-natured with man, and man is a rational animal.

Thus, as the title of his book *The Degrees of Knowledge* implies, Maritain seeks an epistemology that embraces the full range of human knowledge, from the connatural to the supernatural. The observation was made at the outset of this chapter that Maritain's lifelong labor was to harmonize philosophy with "life," intellect with reality. The result of his labor can be summarized as follows.

Modern science, to be sure, does not supply us with the whole or only intellectually respectable knowledge about reality, but it does supply us with important knowledge that cannot be obtained from other disciplines. Metaphysics and theology also supply us with important knowledge of reality, knowledge that is beyond the grasp of science. Maritain points to Descartes as the thinker who must bear the heaviest responsibility for modern philosophy's rejection of metaphysics and theology from the realm of the intellectually respectable. As noted in the introduction to this chapter, Descartes's criteria for an idea's acceptability—clarity and distinctness—constitute the importation of mathematical criteria into philosophy. Because metaphysics relies upon ananoetic knowledge and because such knowledge cannot furnish ideas that are clear and distinct, Descartes and, increasingly, subsequent modern philosophers could only conclude that metaphysics lacks the precision to qualify as an intellectual discipline. Similarly, by making the human intellect the standard of all knowing, Cartesian rationalism sired a tradition that found divine revelation an increasingly indefensible source of knowledge. Moreover, Descartes's definition of man as a "thinking-being"—in obedience to the injunction imposed on philosophy by the criteria of clear and distinct ideas—leaves no place for nonrational knowledge such as knowledge by connaturality.

The rationalists' subservience to mathematical criteria of truth was a major cause of the decay of respect for natural law theory in the eighteenth and nineteenth centuries. They supposed that the principle of the natural law was known a priori and could be applied with all the universality and necessity of geometrical theorems. Divergent moral practices among the different peoples of the world falsified that view. Paul Ramsey is correct in observing that Maritain's major contribution to natural law theory has been to rescue it from the clutches of rationalism.[14] Knowledge by connaturality, besides having an experiential grounding in human nature and action, explains the divergent moral practices in terms of the inchoateness of nonconceptual and nonrational knowledge and the variation in historical and social circumstances needed to elicit and clarify that knowledge. Maritain's theory of connaturality powerfully expresses the meaning of his epistemological realism. For if the natural law is *natural*, then it must be grounded ontologically, that is, in reality. The ground of this law must be independent of the knowledge of it. Reason, whether the spontaneous reason of

---

[14]Paul Ramsey, *Nine Modern Moralists* (New York: New American Library, 1962) 263.

common sense or the reflective reason of moral philosophy, elucidates that which is already present in the human subject and manifests itself through inclinations and strivings. The charter of epistemological realism, recall, is the principle "Things are the measure of mind," and not "Mind is the measure of things."

It is "angelism" that Maritain cites as the most damaging of the Cartesian errors. Descartes's conception of man as a pure intellect, whose capacity for clear and distinct ideas amounts to an angelic intuition, would attribute to the human intellect the capacity to lay bare immediately the essences of sensible beings,[15] thereby discounting the importance of sensory knowledge and the need of the human intellect, owing to its imperfections, to derive its knowledge from the sensorial perception of things.

In contrast, the discrimination of the levels of human knowledge attests to what Maritain regards as at once the glory and the misery of the human intellect. Its glory is to know the essential being of sensible things and to ascend from there to a knowledge of immaterial being and ultimately God. Its misery is that man is a diminished intellectual substance the weakness of whose powers of understanding evinces itself in the necessity of wrestling with sensible things to attain a dim, albeit true, knowledge of them (perinoetic intellection) and a dark, analogical, albeit true, knowledge of supersensible things (ananoetic intellection).

For an understanding of the persistence with which Maritain criticizes Cartesian "angelism," it is necessary to look to the latter's aggrandizement of the human intellect. Maritain does, indeed, also criticize empiricism—for reducing all knowledge to sensation and entertaining a pessimistic view of the human intellect's power to know;[16] but the scant attention he gives to it suggests that he regards it as a lesser force to contend with than rationalism. The reason seems to be that the latter's excessively optimistic view of the human intellect's capacity to know—celebrated in the appeal to the clear and the distinct as the criteria of truth—leads in the first instance to idealism and subjectivism[17] and in the second to empiricism and scientism. It leads to the first set of consequences because clarity and distinctness, being mathematical criteria, are to be found not in extramental being but in intramental being and personal experience. It leads to the second set of consequences because the retention of these criteria, along with the assertion (made by the empiricists against the rationalists) that primary knowledge is of the extramental world, inevitably leads to considering sense data and

---

[15]Jacques Maritain, *The Dream of Descartes*, trans. Mabelle L. Andison, (Port Washington: Kennikat Press, 1969) 39-40.

[16]Jacques Maritain, "The Cultural Impact of Empiricism," *From an Abundant Spring, The Thomist,* ed. staff (New York: Thomist Press, 1952) 448-66.

[17]Maritain, *Introduction to Philosophy*, 131.

the measurement of sensible phenomena as the fulfillment of the "clear and distinct" criteria.

In contrast, Maritain seeks to vindicate the capacity of the human intellect to know by unfolding the full expanse of human knowledge.[18] In doing so he reveals that the various levels are hierarchically ordered: science for example is subordinate to metaphysics in virtue of the latter's more comprehensively ontological view of being. The hierarchy allows for diversity in knowledge without conflict. Unlike rationalism, which excludes important aspects of human experience and knowledge by virtue of demanding too much of the human intellect, and unlike irrationalism, which in order to protect what is valuable among these excluded things, rejects, root and branch, the validity of rational knowledge, the intellectualism advocated by Maritain is capable of sheltering under the canopy of reason the full expanse of reality and human experience.

So much for overall considerations. What about the specific aspects of Maritain's epistemology? The answer must include attention to his "critical realism." I observed earlier that, since Descartes, philosophers have regarded the existence of things outside the mind as problematic, and that, as a realist, Maritain holds that we know certainly that things exist independently of our knowing them. This knowledge is spontaneously evident and certain. But Maritain is not a naive realist, hence his reference to his epistemology as a "critical realism."

He supports the position, held by some contemporary Thomists, that philosophy has the responsibility of turning its critical apparatus onto its own act of knowing, thereby validating the human mind's capacity to know extramental reality. Since other Thomists, notably Etienne Gilson, reject the idea of "critical realism" as a contradiction of terms, a case can be made for placing this aspect of Maritain's epistemology under the heading of what is distinctive about it.[19] Specifically, Gilson's objection is that whereas realism holds that the mind enjoys a spontaneous and certain knowledge of extramental being, and while the critical approach holds that such knowledge is doubtful and thus in need of verification, a "critical" realism would lead Thomism into the very idealism that entrapped Descartes—the idealism that realism denies by forcing it to philosophize inside the mind rather than with extramental being. And as Descartes's "I think, therefore I am" demonstrated, to start philosophizing inside the mind is never to get out of it: "One does not form a passing acquaintance with idealism."[20]

---

[18]Jacques Maritain, St. Thomas Aquinas, trans. Joseph W. Evans and Peter O'Reilly (New York: World, 1962) 94, 98.

[19]Etienne Gilson, Réalisme thomiste et critique de la connaissance (Paris: Librarie Philosophique J. Vrin, 1947).

[20]Etienne Gilson, "Vade Mecum of a Young Realist," Philosophy and Knowledge, ed. Rolande Hande and Joseph P. Mullally (Chicago: Lippincott, 1960) 387.

Maritain's reply to the objection is that philosophy is a wisdom and it is one of wisdom's tasks to defend itself rationally. Although it is true that we have a spontaneous and certain knowledge of extramental being, it is no compromise of realism's principles to advance an elucidation of this knowledge and accordingly a philosophical defense of realism (DK 73-75).

The error in the idealist critique of knowledge is that committed by Descartes. By starting with the proposition "I think, therefore I am," Descartes failed to see that to think is to think about *some* thing. The first object of knowledge is not the self but some thing outside the self; then what is known is the act of knowing and through that the self who knows. The correct reformulation of the proposition, insists Maritain, is *"I am aware of knowing—I am aware of knowing at least one thing, that what is, is; not: I think" (DK 76)*. Thus it is being, some thing, that the intellect first knows. I discussed earlier Maritain's defense of the principle of identity as a principle of the real rather than of the mind alone. In *The Degrees of Knowledge*, he undertakes to demonstrate the precise matter in which the principle of identity is the very first evidence of the intellect's direct contact with the real. Although he says that the apprehension of the principle is discovered in the intellectual apprehension of being or the real, Maritain makes clear that the reality in question "does not necessarily belong to the actual (existential) order." The principle of identity is first grasped as incarnate in some sensible existent, for all human knowledge starts with the sensible, the concrete particular. Nevertheless, "of itself that principle bears upon the whole range of being and especially on the order of essences, or the possible real" (DK 77).

If the principle of identity is purported to be the mind's living link with the real, it might well be asked why Maritain says that it pertains especially to the "possible real"? If that is the case, how would the principle be ontologically rather than logically grounded?

Maritain's reason for emphasizing the "possible real" at this point is that the object of intellectual apprehension is the essence or intelligible structure of things; even being is apprehended as an essence. And there is nothing in essence that tells us about actual existence. The essence may be abstracted from an actually existing individual, but there is no way of determining that simply on the basis of the apprehended essence—a *whatness*. Possible being is all that the intellect can grasp in a concept.

But possible being has an important feature in common with actual or extramental being that it does not have in common with beings of reason, which is to say, mental constructions. The intellect derives its ideas from intelligible natures already realized in the world of existence. It also draws from these natures, or essences, ideas of other natures that do not actually exist but that can exist, that is, possible beings. Finally, it can also form, on the basis of these natures—of both possible and actual beings—objects of thought that are incapable of extramental existence, for example, genus and species such as *animal* and *man*, subject and predicate. These are beings of reason.

Although they are objects of thought, beings of reason cannot be called essences because "essence" denotes the capacity for existing insofar as essence possesses a coherent structure. In themselves beings of reason are no more than negations or privations when they are not mere constructs. Chimeras, for example, are nonbeings conceived after the likeness of animals. They are, however, bound to real being in two ways: first, they are conceived in the image of the subjects of the ideas of real beings; second, they are constructed with elements taken from the real. That is to say, it is possible to make judgments about them because we treat them as though they were real beings, that is, beings at least capable of existing. But if, for example, we were to eliminate the nature of the circle and square, we would no longer be able to suggest a square-circle, since it would be impossible to conceive of the components (*DK* 133).

That, then, is the rationale behind Maritain's claim that it is in the principle of identity that we find the very first living connection between intellect and things: it is applied to conceptions of beings that actually exist or that can possibly exist but not to beings of reason, that is, not to beings that cannot possibly exist. What Maritain is getting at here can be illustrated as follows. Consider the logical formulation of the principle of identity, the principle of noncontradiction. Not only is it inconceivable but really *impossible* for a thing at once to be and not be in the same respect. So that, as shown above, to affirm the principle of noncontradiction is to affirm its ontological as well as its logical value, for to say a thing is inconceivable does not mean that it simply escapes the understanding of a given person or of the human mind. What it means is that no mind—not even God's—can conceive of, say, a square-circle, for the simple reason that the expression purports to refer to something that is at once a circle and not a circle, square and not square; it refers to what cannot exist. Thus a being is said to be inconceivable only if it is really impossible. In other words, the principle of identity puts the intellect in communication with objective being, being that is governed by the eternal necessities of the intelligible order (*DK* 92).

And when Maritain consequently writes that this intelligible being that is the first object of our intellect is also "extramental being" (*DK* 94), he is not making an illegitimate transition from thought to thing but is on the contrary proceeding from thing to thought: "If the real existent is first given to us by the senses—whence our intellect draws its ideas—then we are assured that our first intellectual apprehensions do not bear upon beings of reason. *Ab acta ad posse valet consecutio:* since there are ants, the ant is possible" (*DK* 134). Even a being of reason, it has been shown, derives what intelligibility it possesses from our experience of real being. Thus Maritain argues that the primacy of real being is not confined to intellectual knowledge but has its beginning in the order of sensitive knowledge.

But the centerpiece of Maritain's epistemology is his theory of judgment, wherein he undertakes to reconcile intuition and concept. Although his defense of the concept lacks the originality of his theory of judgment, it is nevertheless crucial to an understanding of that theory. And since the defense of the concept is inextricably tied to the distinctions between intentional being and natural being, and between object and thing, his theory of judgment must be led into by the explication of these topics—all the more so as modern philosophy seems content to remain in a state of innocence with regard to them.

Intentional Being and Natural Being. Following Thomas Aquinas Maritain holds that all our knowledge begins with the perception of sensible being. But since our intellect possesses truth as the *thing known*, an intelligible similitude—or concept—of the thing, along with a judgment about it, is required. Thus sense perception alone is not sufficient to account for our knowledge, for intellectual knowledge (as opposed to sense knowledge) requires that we know what the thing is, that we apprehend its essence. This involves a process whereby the intellect abstracts what is intelligible in the thing—and thereby de-individualizes it—to form a concept, the intelligible similitude of it. Were we to apprehend a lamp, say, simply by our senses and imagination, we would possess it materially, we would see the lamp, but we would be unable to name it; we would not know *what* it is. Moreover, we would not know that there is an *I* perceiving it, for the senses are not reflective; they do not turn back upon themselves. From this Maritain concludes that in order to know what the object is, to perceive its nature and its being *as such*, "our knowledge of the object must absolutely be purely immaterial" (*BPT* 156).

Thus if human knowledge is a knowledge of the universal, that is because we must know *what* the thing is. The senses apprehend the object to produce a concrete, particular image from which the intellect abstracts the intelligible species or essence of the thing to form a concept of it. And by immaterializing the sensible object in this way, the intellect becomes the object—forms a vital identification with it—according to its own mode of being (*BPT* 158).

Maritain's methodology so far may be summarized as follows. As an epistemological realist, he begins with the position that we do know *things* and that in knowing them we know *what* they are. He proceeds next to the position that the mere apprehension of the sensible properties of the individual thing does not tell us what it is: to know the lamp *as lamp* it is necessary to define it (though not in the explicit and formal sense of "definition"), and this requires a knowledge of the universal, *lampness*. Thus a process of abstraction must occur in which the lamp is de-individualized, that is, grasped as a universal concept. Since it is not the apprehension of the sensible image of the lamp—the lamp in its materiality—that permits a knowledge of it but rather the apprehension of its abstracted essence, Maritain concludes that to universalize a thing is to immaterialize it (*BPT* 156-57).

This account of the process of knowing underlies Maritain's view of the immateriality of the intellect. The specification of the senses to one or two properties of a thing—for example, sight to color and shape, hearing to sound—results from the fact that the senses are immersed in, and hence specified by, matter; they are material organs. The intellect, on the other hand, is not so specified but knows the thing in its essential nature. Because matter inevitably specifies according to material structures, the intellect must be an immaterial substance (*BPT* 157). It is, then, by forming a vital identification with the thing known according to the intellect's own mode of being, that is, immaterial being, that the *whatness* of the thing can be known.

The immaterial identification of knower and known depends on the distinction between intentional being (*esse intentionale*) and natural being (*esse naturale*). The distinction arises out of the absoluteness of the principle of identity, for if knowing consists in the knower becoming the known, there must be *two* ways of having existence or else this conception of knowing is absurd. Thus besides "the being a thing possesses when it exists in its own nature [natural being], . . . we have to conceive an *esse* that is not the proper act of existing of the subject as such or its accidents [intentional being]" (*DK* 114). The knower cannot be the thing known in virtue of that thing's own natural being; clearly the tree does not exist in the intellect according to its natural being. Yet the fact remains that we do know things. The conclusion cannot be escaped, therefore, that knowing is a becoming of the thing known. If the object of the intellect were the concept or a representation of the thing, then what we would know would not be the thing but a representation of it. Accordingly an account of knowing that remains faithful to the fact, thrust upon us by experience, that we know *things* must conclude that we become the thing, though in its intentional rather than natural being.

But this raises the question of how knower and known are united, how the knower becomes intentionally the thing known. The means by which this is possible are the likenesses or species. The word "species" is difficult to define, for modern language has no equivalent for it. Maritain uses "presentative or objectifying form" to render it. He would prefer "presentative form" provided that "presentative" indicates the notion of "*making present*" rather than "*presenting*" (*DK* 115n). The distinction may seem subtle to the point of suggesting a distinction without a difference, but Maritain is struggling here in the name of epistemological realism: the species is not what is known; it is the *thing* itself that is known; the species presents the thing. Thus he writes:

> Some determination must, of necessity, actually supervene upon the knower, thanks to which a thing that is not the knower will exist in him *secundum esse intentionale* . . . and by which the thing will be able to exist with the very same active superexistence which is the existence of the knower that has become the thing known. The species is nothing but that internal determination. (*DK* 116)

This means that the intellect knows things, first, by abstracting from the material image or phantasm delivered to it by the senses, the presentative form, or *species impressa*. Receiving this form, the intellect is in initial or first act. Having thereby actualized its potency to be the thing known, by means of the *species impressa*, the intellect is then in a position to produce within itself a *species expressa*, a more intelligibly elaborated presentative form, carrying the object of knowledge. The intellect then becomes the object in final act (*DK* 114). The distinction between first and final act is only the noetic equivalent of the distinction between nature and the actualization of that nature. On the level of formal causality, nature is prior to existence: one acts in a human manner because one first has a human nature; because the intellect has assumed the presentative form, it can then actualize its "nature," that is, form, which nature is to be actually identical with the form.

Because we know things and we know that we know things, knowledge is objective; because knowledge is objective, it follows that these species or presentative forms have no characteristics other than the objects of knowledge that they present to the intellect: they

> are purely and formally vicars of the object, pure likenesses of the object (i.e., in the soul, they are the object itself divested of its proper existence and made present in an immaterial and intellectual state). By this title they do not determine the faculty as a form determines a matter or subject. They determine it according to a wholly immaterial and supersubjective union in virtue of which one becomes the other intentionality, first in initial act and then in second act through its vital operation. (*DK* 117)

As opposed to the prevailing view in modern philosophy, whereby knowing consists in "taking a look" or in the assimilation and manipulation of data, Maritain submits that knowing is a becoming, a way of being.

It follows, moreover, that neither is knowing "a making," for this too would destroy the objectivity of knowledge. In knowing, the existence that the intellect enjoys, thanks to its assumption of the presentative form, is superior to the existence that is "made"; for unlike the latter the knower becomes the identical other, that is, without distortion or modification: "to know is to be in a certain way something other than what one is: it is *to become a thing other than the self . . . to be or become the other as other*" (*DK* 112). This is possible because of the immateriality of the intellect. When, on the contrary, matter receives a form, what takes place is a "making" in that the resulting product is a third thing—on the one side a modification of matter and, on the other side, a material embodiment of the form. A material thing can become *other,* that is, it can change or be altered, but it cannot become *the other.* But the knower becomes the known *as other* and all the while retains its own nature intact (*DK* 112). The intellect cannot be of the same stuff as that which it knows, for then there would be no knowledge, at least no objective knowledge. The intellect must possess the thing under the conditions of its own nature, which is to say that the thing must be changed in order to meet the conditions of becoming an intelligible object. It must be expressed in an intelligible similitude, the concept.

Maritain defines the concept within the context of the sign. Thomists differentiate two essentially different kinds of signs: *instrumental* and *formal*. An instrumental sign is anything that, when itself is first known, makes known some other thing: smoke rising in the sky tells us there is a fire; a portrait of someone painted on canvas tells us of the person of whom it is an image-sign. Now a formal sign is one whose entire essence is to signify. It is not a thing possessing its own distinctive characteristic that also points to some other thing. Instead, a formal sign is

> anything that *makes known* before being itself a known object. More exactly let us say it is something that, before being known as object by a reflective act, is known only by the very knowledge that brings the mind to the object through its mediation. In other words, it is not known by "appearing" as object but by "disappearing" in the face of the object, for its very essence is to bear the mind to something other than itself. (*DK* 119-20)

The concept is such a formal sign.

Thus the *species expressae*, or the "elaborated presentative forms," are formal, not instrumental, signs. This is to say that the concept is not *that which* is known by our intellect but rather *that by which we know*. What we know by means of the concept is "the very nature or intelligible determination of an actually or possibly existing thing" (*DK* 120). It turns out that concepts, or elaborated presentative forms, are the only examples of formal signs, an exclusiveness that testifies to the radical originality and uniqueness of knowing. Here again, lest one suppose Maritain to be arbitrary or guilty of begging the question by saying that the concept is the only example of a formal sign, one must bear in mind that this view of the concept follows from his epistemological realism: it is immediately and certainly evident that we know the other *as other;* this means that the concept must be *that by which* the thing is known, not *that which* is known.

If the concept is treated as the object of knowledge itself, then idealism, subjectivism, and relativism are inevitable. Concepts become the objects of knowledge only reflexively, and this requires the production of a new concept *by which* the former concept is known. If the concept were the object of our knowledge, then what we would know would be our representations, and consequently all sciences would be absorbed by one science, psychology. Moreover, contradictory judgments would be true simultaneously: someone judging that two plus two equals four and another judging that two plus two does not equal four would both be correct, since both would be basing their judgment on the object of their knowledge, that is, their representation of the object (*DK* 120-21).

Object and thing. If the concept is not the thing known but instead *that by which* the thing is known, the question arises as to the relation between the object (of knowledge) and the thing (known). Maritain emphasizes the crucial importance of this question and calls attention to the serious errors that modern philosophers, starting with Descartes, have made regarding it. The thing is what, in its natural existence (either possibly or actually), exists outside the mind. The object is what is knowable in the thing. When known, as expressed by the concept in the mind, it exists in a state of abstraction and universality, but as it exists in the thing, it is in a state of individuality and concreteness. Yet despite their differentiation, the *object* and the *thing* constitute only one known term, not two. It is one and the same term of knowledge that *exists* as a thing and is *grasped by the mind* as object. Suppose, for example, the thing is this particular man, Peter. Besides being man, he is animal, substance, philosopher or musician, healthy or sickly. This thing, Peter, can thus be any one of a number of objects of knowledge, such as "man." In Peter, which is to say outside the mind, the object "man" has a natural existence, whereas in the concept, in the mind, it has an intentional one. As an extramental being, the thing called Peter is singular and concrete; but as object, existing in the concept with an intentional existence, it is abstract and universal. The object is indifferent to one state or the other; nothing in the essence man, or in any other essence for that matter, determines it to be either concrete or abstract, singular or universal. Rather these latter are determined by whichever of the two states the object exists in (*DK* 121-22).

From the standpoint of being, concept and thing are two beings: the one intentional being, the other natural being. But from the standpoint of pure knowing, they are not two. As formal sign, the concept's existence is the act of intellection itself, and its intelligible content is the object itself. Thus in terms of its intelligible constitution, the concept is identical with the object. Here again, however, Maritain insists that this identity does not mean that the concept is *that which* is known but rather that "it is identical insofar as it is the inner sign and term *by which* the intellect becomes, in ultimate act, what it knows" (*DK* 124). The entire specificity of the concept comes from the object.

It is now possible to unfold Maritain's theory of judgment. If, as we have seen, his epistemological realism leads him, on the one hand, to maintain that the object of knowing is the direct knowledge of reality and, on the other, that such knowledge is possible only by means of conceptual knowledge, he cannot escape the conclusion, embraced by the Thomistic tradition, that we have a direct knowledge only of the general natures that we abstract from individual things and thus that "we have no direct knowledge of individual things *as such*" (*BPT* 161). This is not, however, to contradict his realism; it is not to say that our knowledge is therefore severed from the varied individuals or the extramental world; for by reflecting the concept of the essence back onto the individual sensible image—a spontaneous operation—the intellect returns from the universal to the singular and in that fashion obtains knowledge of it (*BPT* 161). This reflexive operation is necessitated by the intellect's need to elevate the thing known to its own immaterial level of existence, thereby freeing it from its enmattered state and actualizing its potency for intelligibility. But since what we know are individual things, the abstracted essence must refer to the latter.

The fact that sense knowledge implies the existence of *some thing*, the fact that existence is buried or implied in sensation (since by itself sense is blind and hence incapable of knowing existence), is the evidence that Maritain needs to carry knowing beyond the concept to existence: "If, then, the existence in act of an actually existing thing is implied by sensation, the possible existence, at least of a possible thing . . . is equally implied by intellectual knowledge" (*DK* 96). That is to say, every predicate, besides signifying a specific intelligible structure, also signifies the thing—that which has that intelligible structure. When the philosopher apprehends, say, "triangular," "musician," or "philosopher," he apprehends something that becomes its object under the formal aspect of its intelligible structure or *whatness*. But the mere apprehension of a concept, for example, "man," does not constitute knowledge. It is in *judgment* that knowledge is completed.

Judgment is the act by which the intellect asserts that a subject and a predicate, although conceptually differing in their existence in the intellect, are identical in the thing, that is, outside the mind. In every true judgment, the two terms that are identified are formally different, that is, differ conceptually. For example, the concept "whole" differs formally from the concept "greater than the part"; and the concept "moon" differs formally from that of "earth's satellite." But in a judgment like "The moon is the earth's satellite," or "The whole is greater than the part," the *actual* existence is asserted of a thing in which the object of thought "earth's satellite" is identified; while the object of thought "whole" and the object of thought "greater than the part" is identified.

> Thus, the proper function of judgment consists in making the mind pass from the level of simple essence or simple *object* signified to the mind, to the level of *thing* or subject possessing existence (actually or possibly), a *thing* which the object of thought (predicate) and the subject of thought (subject) are intelligible aspects. (*DK* 97)

Intuition and Judgment. The emphasis on judgment as the vehicle that carries the mind to the existent reveals knowing to be primarily an ontological rather than a logical question. This, to be sure, is part and parcel of the Thomistic epistemology. But Maritain develops that epistemology by going beyond establishing the intellect's capacity to know extramental being; he establishes also its capacity to know being as multiple, diverse, and dynamic. Here we see the precise meeting place of his epistemology and metaphysics, for the primary epistemological task that Maritain sets for himself is to explain how the existent, or subject—that unique source of dynamic activity—is known by us. Again, this is the challenge bequeathed him by Bergson: if the concept is necessary to our knowledge of things, how is it that what is abstract, universal, and univocal can convey what is concrete, unique, dynamic, and diverse? Accordingly, the focus of Maritain's mature epistemological writings is on the integration of intuition with the conceptual functions of judgment: our knowledge of the existent is impossible without an intuitive apprehension of it.

Consider the difference between the concept of essence and the concept of being. The unity that belongs to the concept of being is an abstraction in a way that the unity that belongs to the concept of a being's essence is not an abstraction. Although abstracted from the individual thing that is known, the essence is not thereby deformed or truncated in itself. To know that Socrates and Plato are both men is to entertain an idea that, although embodied in each, has the same signification. It is an abstraction in the sense that the intellect focuses its attention on what is knowable in the thing—on its intelligible structure to the exclusion of all other considerations.

By contrast, however, the concept of being represents an incomplete abstraction in the sense that the intellect does not focus on the being of this or that individual thing insofar as its being is individually and uniquely its own, but only insofar as it is being. That is to say, the generic or specific concepts of essence are univocal, but the concept of being is analogous: all things have in common that they exist, either actually or possibly, but each thing exists in a specific way, a way determined by its essence; a's being is to a as b's being is to b. Everything that divides beings from each other, such as this man from this stone, Socrates from Plato, is a difference of being. Being would be one if that which differentiates this being from that being were not a difference originating within each being itself, that is, within the essence-individuated, specified being. Being would be purely and simply multiple, on the other hand, if it did not have a common meaning; namely, that all these diverse beings actually or possibly exist rather than not. But if multiple, the idea of being would be equivocal, destroying all intelligibility and making thought impossible. It would be impossible to think "This pencil is yellow" or "Socrates is is a man." For the truth and signification of these judgments depends on their affirming an ontological identity between their subjects and predicates. That is to say, in judgment, the copula "is" asserts more than a logical identity; it also asserts the existence (either possible or actual) of the being in which the formal objects expressed by subject and predicate are identical.

This emphasis on the ontological character of judgment brings us face to face with the existent as subject and the injunction that if we have a faithful and accurate knowledge of it—as Maritain insists we do—then the role of intuition in judgment must be affirmed. Thus he argues that being is incapable of adequate representation by a concept, for it is a "super-intelligible":

> [E]xistence is not an essence. It belongs to another order which is other than the whole order of essence. It is therefore not an intelligible nor an object of thought . . . which is synonymous with essence. What are we to conclude if not that existence goes beyond the intelligible strictly so-called, because it is an act exercised by a subject whose eminent intelligibility, we may say super-intelligibility, objectizes itself in the very act of judgment? In this sense we could call it a transobjective act. It is in a higher and analogical sense that it is intelligible. The intelligibility with which judgment deals is more mysterious than that which notions or ideas convey to us; it is not expressed in a concept but in the very act of affirming or denying. It is the super-intelligibility, if I may put it so, of the act of existing itself, either possible or actually given. (*EE* 28)

The reason given in this passage for saying that the concept is incapable of representing being adequately is that, whereas the concept represents things as objects, existence is an act exercised by a subject. As opposed to his notion of subject, which denotes a source of activity, Maritain defines an "object" as that which is acted upon. Concepts represent things as objects in the sense that they present the thing in the mind as *that which is known.* An object, in this case that which is represented by a concept, is passive, for it is something that is acted upon by the mind. Here is the significance of Maritain's expression "transobjectivity of the subject." Things as known by the mind are represented under many different aspects, but just because a thing is a subject, its knowability as an object is inexhaustible; because it is a subject, that is, a unique source of activity, we can never know it fully as a subject; there is always more to learn about it even when the subject in question is the tiniest blade of grass.

The following passage expresses the intense focus that Maritain places upon the intellect's stretching out to grasp the subject and its unique act of existing.

> In forming . . . the judgment the intellect, on the one hand, knows the subject as singular (indirectly and by "reflection on phantasms"), and, on the other hand, affirms that this singular subject exercises the act of existing. In other words, the intellect itself exercises upon the notion of this subject an act (the act of affirming) by which it lives intentionally the existence of the thing. This affirmation has the same content as the "judgment" of the aestimative and the external sense (but in this case that content is no longer "blind" but openly revealed since it is raised to the state of intelligibility in act); and it is not by reflection upon phantasms that the intellect proffers the affirmation, but by and in this "judgment" itself, and in this intuition of sense by which it grasps by immaterializing it, in

order to express it to itself. It thus reaches the *actus essendi*, the act of existing (in judging)—as it reaches essence (in conceiving)—*by the mediation of sensorial perception*. (*EE* 27n)

This passage shows that Maritain is not content to remain within the expressed boundaries of the Thomistic tradition that maintains that the intellect has a direct knowledge only of the de-individualized essence and only an indirect knowledge of the concrete individual that embodies it. He accepts the view as pertaining to conceptual knowledge but goes beyond it to argue that the intellect, through its judgmental operations, apprehends the subject's act of existing. Although the judgment or affirmation has the same content as the external sense, nevertheless, "it is not by reflection upon phantasms that the intellect proffers the affirmation, but by and in this 'judgment' itself, and in this intuition of sense which it grasps by immaterializing it."

Thus, thanks to the Bergsonian influence, Maritain's contribution to the Thomistic epistemology is to have achieved a more explicit integration between the aestimative judgment of the senses, which apprehends the concrete being of the subject immediately but blindly, and the intellect's apprehension—not simply of the subject's essence or its being as an abstract concept—but of its act of existing. The judgment composes the object of thought "not with the *notion* of existence but with the *act* of existing" (*EE* 2n). The intellect duplicates, on the level of intentionality, the act of existing that the thing known exercises on the existential level.

But what precisely is the mechanism by which the conceptual functions of judgment are integrated with the intuition of the subject's act of existing? The importance of this question originates in Maritain's claim that without the concept our intuitions would lack intelligibility.

For the answer, it is necessary to return to Maritain's position tht the intuition of existence does not take place through a concept. To reiterate his rationale for this position, he argues that while the intelligible apprehended by the concept is an essence, existence is not an essence. It is not through or in the concept but rather through the judgment, whereby the two concepts are affirmed as identical in the existent, that the intuition occurs. Yet in order to make this judgment, it is necessary to isolate the subject and predicate. Hence Maritain is compelled to assert that the judgment that things exist requires the intellect to form a concept of existence as one of the terms of the judgment. Simple apprehension must, in other words, make existence an object, make what is not an essence to be represented by a concept. Accordingly, intellect apprehends and judges at the same instant: "It forms its first idea (that of being) while uttering its first judgment (of existence) and utters its first judgment while forming its first idea" (*EE* 32-33).

Thus Maritain finds it necessary to distinguish between the concept of existence, which is to say, the concept to-exist (*esse*), and the concept of being (*ens*), that which is or can be. What he wishes to designate by these terms is the difference between the being that exists or that exercises the act of existing (ens) and the act that the being exercises (esse). But, although distinct, the concept of existence cannot be cut off from the absolutely primary concept of being. The reason is that the affirmation of existence furnishes the content for the concept of being; one cannot perceive that "this is a being" without at the same time perceiving that it exercises the act of existence. It is this act, this dynamism and energy, that is grasped by intuition but not by the concept. Equally, the concept of being, in the order of "ideative perception," corresponds to the affirmation of existence in the order of being. And one cannot perceive the act of existing apart from the being that exercises the act. A reciprocity thus obtains between the concept and the judgment: each precedes the other in its respective order. One cannot judge that "this thing exists" without already having the idea of being; yet one cannot have the idea of being without already having affirmed the act of existence in a judgment. All of which is to say that judgment and apprehension occur simultaneously.

Here then is Maritain's reconciliation of intuition and concept—his definitive response to Bergson and the irrationalists: the concept of existence cannot be detached from the concept of essence. For if one cannot grasp existence apart from grasping that it is, this being (ens), a specific kind of being, whose existence it is, it follows that to know that this being exists is also to know how it exists, that is, to know its what-it-is. A thing exists because its intelligible structure or essence has been actualized. The significance of this consequence is that the dynamism and diversity of reality are preserved without any loss of intelligibility.

The anatomy of his epistemological achievement may be outlined by the following points: (1) the intellect grasps the uniqueness of things, and this grasp, while coming through, or by means of, phantasms, is based on the act of existing, the *esse*, that is unique to things; (2) but this grasp necessarily depends on the concept. Despite the emphasis that Maritain places on the intuitive grasp of the subject's unique act of existing, he nevertheless stresses that there can be no existence without essence. "For if you abolish essence, or that which *esse* posits, by the very act you abolish existence, or *esse*. These two notions are correlative and inseparable" (*EE* 13). The essence and the existent are seized upon and abstracted to form a concept. This process is needed to make possible an identification of the knowing subject and the object known, according to the being of the subject or existent.

Conclusion

In the introduction to this chapter, I observed that Maritain's characterization of Thomistic philosophy as an "intellectual existentialism" encapsulates his distinctive contributions to metaphysics and epistemology, contributions that produce a philosophical interpretation of human experience that accommodates the dynamism, diversity, and uniqueness of reality, along with the autonomy and selfhood of the person, while at the same time affirming its intelligibility and the mind's capacity to know it. His treatment of the intuition of being, the primacy of the act of existing, the subject, and his integration of intuition with the conceptual operations of judgment have demonstrated that philosophy is a wisdom—in that its aim is a knowledge of the ultimate principles of reality—and also that these principles, rather than being held captive in the realm of Platonic ideas, have their ground in our common, daily experiences of the world.

Thus Maritain's Thomism has furnished him with the tools for addressing the fundamental problems of the modern world—to a degree that few thinkers have—while answering Bergson's challenge (and Sartre's too) to harmonize the intelligible with the real and the attempt of Cartesian rationalism to exalt intelligibility at the expense of the existent. Maritain is best known for his social, political, educational, and aesthetic writings. Yet he is first and foremost a metaphysician for whom the intuition of being and the elucidation of its principles are the paramount concerns of philosophy. Considering how thoroughly immersed the other branches of his philosophizing are in these concerns, it becomes clear that it is impossible to understand properly the former apart from his metaphysical and epistemological doctrines.

DEAL W. HUDSON

"The Ecstasy Which Is Creation": The Shape of Maritain's Aesthetics

JACQUES MARITAIN made many friends through his writings about art. He was first introduced to English-speaking audiences in 1923 by the translation of *Art et scolastique* (1920).[1] Since then, both *Art and Scholasticism* and Maritain's other major work in aesthetics, *Creative Intuition in Art and Poetry* (1953),[2] have continued to attract a reading public, even though the Thomism that he advocated with Etienne Gilson, Yves R. Simon, and Mortimer J. Adler has ceased to be a major force in American intellectual life.[3] During the height of his popularity, the 1940s and 1950s, Maritain was also known as a major social and political philosopher who had influenced the framing of the United Nations Universal Declaration of Human Rights (1948). Yet, by the end of the sixties, Maritain's

---

[1] *The Philosophy of Art*, trans. John O'Connor (Ditchling, England: St. Dominic's Press, 1923), limited edition handprinted on the press of Eric Gill. Since 1923 *Art et scolastique* has been translated two more times: *Art and Scholasticism*, trans. J. F. Scanlan (London: Sheed and Ward, 1930); *Art and Scholasticism* and *The Frontiers of Poetry*, trans. Joseph W. Evans (New York: Scribner's, 1962) hereafter cited as *AS;* all references are to the Evans translation.

[2] *Creative Intuition in Art and Poetry* (Princeton: Princeton University Press, 1977); hereafter cited as *CI.*

[3] An example of this continued interest is the volume of *Renascence* devoted to "The Aesthetic Theory of Jacques Maritain," 34:4 (Summer 1982). Interest has also been stimulated by the publication of Flannery O'Connor's letters, *The Habit of Being*, ed. Sally Fitzgerald (New York: Farrar, Straus and Giroux, 1979), and Robert Fitzgerald's *Enlarging the Change: The Princeton Seminars in Literary Criticism, 1949-1951* (Boston: Northeastern University Press, 1985), which contains a chapter entitled "A Man Writes with His Whole Body: Jacques Maritain on Poetry and Reason."

reputation had suffered badly because of the controversy over *The Peasant of the Garonne* (1966). In a period in which almost all Catholic intellectuals celebrated the *aggiornamento* of Vatican II, Maritain's criticism of changes in Catholic thought and practice was bound to be unpopular. Many who had been drawn to Maritain because of his aesthetic sensibility and progressive social ideas felt betrayed. This situation was ironic, since Pope Paul VI had chosen Maritain to receive the council's "Message to Intellectuals" from his own hands.

More than twenty years have passed since the Council and the *Peasant* episode. The continuing interest in Maritain's aesthetics is intriguing, since the same Christian and Thomistic principles that undergird *The Peasant of the Garonne* also inform the aesthetic writings. One may reasonably inquire what it is that makes Maritain's Christian, even medieval, assumptions about the nature of reality more palatable to the reader of these works. Are they less intrusive and, thus, easier to ignore? I think not. Although it is possible to appreciate many of Maritain's specific insights without acknowledging his religious frame of reference, the overall "shape" of his aesthetics cannot be fully perceived without recognizing its vital connections with the content of Maritain's faith. The same point can be maintained with respect to the entire spectrum of Maritain's philosophy. Consequently, as I survey the spiritual background of his aesthetics some portion of Maritain's larger vision will, I hope, emerge.

I

Maritain was reluctant to use the term *aesthetics*. He wanted to disassociate himself from the modern aesthetics, which restricted the consideration of art to the fine arts, and beauty to the spectator's perception of it. Maritain's revival of two ideas—art as a virtue and beauty as a transcendental—from the classical tradition, upon which to erect the foundation of *Art and Scholasticism,* attest to his early antimodernist posture. With few exceptions, most of Maritain's comments on beauty were limited to establishing its objective and transcendental qualities. But his primary concern was always to explore the inner dynamics of the artistic *habitus.* His most important concepts—poetry, poetic knowledge, the spiritual preconscious, creative intuition—emerge out of this preoccupation with the virtue of art.

Maritain's work appears different at different times, depending on whether you are reading *Art and Scholasticism*, from the 1920s, *The Situation of Poetry*,[4] from the 1930s, or *Creative Intuition*, from the 1950s. As his understanding of the virtue of art deepened, Maritain's emphasis shifted from the philosophy of art to

---

[4]*The Situation of Poetry*, trans. Marshall Suther (New York: Philosophical Library, 1955), coauthored with Raïssa Maritain; hereafter cited as *TSP.*

the philosophy of poetry, and finally, to the philosophy of creativity. Yet, it is possible, I think, to speak of the development of an "aesthetic" over these forty years without being implicated in the modernist connotations Maritain wished to avoid. Francis J. Kovach, himself a Thomist, provides a definition that is applicable to Maritain: "aesthetics is a generic field of many specific sciences, all dealing in some manner with beautiful things."[5] In using this definition, we must keep in mind that the artisan, who shares the habitus of art with the artist, creates useful things that may or may not be beautiful. As Eric Gill has shown, Maritain's theory of art contains a message to artisans, encouraging the marriage of beauty and usefulness in their work.[6]

Maritain was always a friend to artists. The painters Georges Rouault and Marc Chagall, the writers Jean Cocteau and Julien Green, and the composer Arthur Lourie were among his closest. Raïssa herself was a poet.[7] But his constant attention to artistic creativity cannot be explained by the mere fact of these close friendships. Maritain sought their help in aesthetic matters and they his, as one can see in his *Réponse à Jean Cocteau* (1926).[8] The slant of Maritain's mind was certainly influenced by these associations—by Rouault in particular—but even more significant was his determination to apply the principles of Christian philosophy, learned mainly from Aquinas, to the situation of modern art.

Art and Scholasticism reflects clearly the religious character of his project. Here Maritain traces the meaning of art and beauty back to an original source and supreme analogate—God.

> [The medieval Doctors] knew that the virtue of Art is predicated pre-eminently of God, as are Goodness and Justice, and that the Son, in plying His poor man's trade, was still the image of the Father and of His never-ceasing action. (AS 21)
> God is beautiful. He is the most beautiful of beings, because as Denis the Areopagite and Saint Thomas explain, His beauty is without alteration or vicissi-

---

[5]Francis J. Kovach, *Philosophy of Beauty* (Norman: University of Oklahoma Press, 1974) 23.

[6]Eric Gill, *Beauty Looks after Herself* (New York: Sheed and Ward, 1933).

[7]Raïssa's influence on the whole of her husband's thought can hardly be underestimated. In the arena of aesthetics she had a particular affinity for poetry and painting that is reflected in more than a few published articles. Jacques remarked at one point that *Art and Scholasticism* was written with Raïssa, and at the beginning of *Creative Intuition* he pays her tribute: "Raïssa, my wife, assisted me all through my work—I do not believe that a philosopher would dare to speak of poetry if he could not rely on the direct experience of a poet" (*CI* xxx).

[8]Translated and published together with Cocteau's "Letter to Jacques Maritain" in *Art and Faith: Letters between Jacques Maritain and Jean Cocteau*, trans. John Coleman (New York: Philosophical Library, 1948); hereafter cited as *AF*.

tude, without increase or diminution. . . . He is beautiful through Himself and in Himself, beautiful absolutely. (AS 30-31)

Similar instances in which Maritain's basic concepts are rooted in theology exist throughout his writings, as in his treatment of epistemological realism and his justification of human rights. In both cases the basis of Maritain's argument is an account of *being* whose intelligibility and purposiveness are guaranteed by the perfect intelligence and finality of its Creator. His aesthetics are no different: without the instrument of analogical reasoning derived from his Thomistic realism, Maritain could never have become a philosopher in the first place. It is no accident that he was baptized before he began his philosophical writing.

By reasoning analogically Maritain is able to draw a likeness between the human virtue of art and the creativity of God. Both minds are creative, but human intelligence must acquire its art through the struggle of habituation. Once a person has become "firmly disposed" toward making he or she can claim the habitus of art. God, by contrast, creates out of his own essence without a need for formation in virtue. As we will see, Maritain's lifelong meditation on this comparison between human and divine intelligence provided the source of his most provocative insights into the creative act.

However, the swelling self-consciousness of modern artists has effaced the difference between these two orders of intelligence and creativity. As a result their art has also become inflated beyond its boundaries by being confused with the other virtues. Neither a form of knowledge nor of wisdom, art belongs rather to the practical intellect, because it does not seek knowledge for its own sake but in order *to make* something. Hence, artists betray their art when they begin to teach or preach: beauty should be their sole aim. Works of art should not be employed as mouthpieces for a philosophy or an ideology. Artists must resist even the demands of prudence, the reigning moral virtue, because art serves the good of the work alone, not the good of human life (AS 15). This rather blunt statement indicates how strenuously Maritain sought to distinguish art from the other virtues in order to protect both its freedom and the source of its fecundity. Maritain's rule seems to be that in trying to become more—whether it be God, metaphysics, or politics—art invariably becomes less.

The sole task of artists is to create beauty in their work. Maritain describes beauty as an effect of art moving outward from the mind of the maker informing the thing made, as Aquinas in the *Summa theologica* moves from God to creation. Even more reminiscent of the method in the *Summa* is the way Maritain's meditation on effects turns his mind toward their cause. Phenomenal beauty invariably reminds him of transcendental beauty and hence the source of all beauty, God himself. Beauty is analogous and belongs to all being (CI 162), making it impossible to experience sensual beauty in isolation from the beauty of God. The artist who creates beauty for the senses draws upon this deeper beauty, while the spectator who experiences it is left with a residue of longing for a more perfect beauty. Beauty "is lacking a lack. . . . A totally perfect finite thing is untrue to the transcendental nature of beauty. And nothing is more precious than a certain sacred weakness, and *that kind* of imperfection through which infinity wounds the finite" (*CI* 167).

Although Plato and Plotinus can be heard speaking clearly in this account of transcendental beauty, it is from Thomas Aquinas that Maritain takes his general definition: beauty is "that which upon being seen pleases" (*id quod visum placet*) and its basic characteristics are order, proportion, and clarity (*AS* 23-24). His use of Thomas's language is not exact, as Umberto Eco has pointed out,[9] and his elaboration of these definitions goes far beyond Thomas himself. But it should be said that Maritain never intended to become a twentieth-century replica of the Angelic Doctor. In revitalizing the tradition of spiritual wisdom, Maritain found that being a Thomist required originality as well as fidelity.

For example, Maritain surpassed Thomas in explaining the intellectual matrix of aesthetic experience. Our delight in beauty overflows from the act of knowing—the "being seen" of a beautiful object (*CI* 161). The three characteristics of beauty are derived from the way each gives pleasure to the intellect. A beautiful thing has *integrity* insofar as it pleases the mind with the "fullness of Being," *proportion* because it pleases the mind with order and unity, and *radiance* since the mind delights in its light and intelligibility (*AS* 25; *CI* 161). Beauty does not startle the mind like a stranger knocking but awakens it with a familiar touch.

> The intelligence delights in the beautiful because in the beautiful it finds itself again and recognizes itself, and makes contact with its own light. This is so true that those—such as Saint Francis of Assisi—perceive and savor more the beauty of things, who know that things come forth from an intelligence, and who relate them to their author. (*AS* 25)

Every experience of beauty is made possible by a dynamic exchange between the eye, the thing, and God. Maritain believed that making this relation explicit

---

[9]Umberto Eco, *Art and Beauty in the Middle Ages*, trans. Hugh Bredin (New Haven: Yale University Press, 1986) 128. Eco correctly points out that Maritain's definition is not found in Aquinas. Aquinas uses a somewhat different formulation in the *Summa* at the place that Maritain cites (I.5.4.1): *pulchra enim dicuntur quae visa placent*. Eco probably stretches the point by calling this definition "sociological," but he is right in drawing attention to Maritain's attempt to emphasize the ontological character of beauty. For an overview of Aquinas's aesthetics and a list of pertinent texts see Wladyslaw Tatarkiewicz, *Medieval Aesthetics*, vol. 2 of *History of Aesthetics*, ed. C. Barrett (The Hague: Mouton, 1970) 245-63.

would heighten our delight rather than subvert it. The reference to Saint Francis typifies the *engaged* quality of Maritain's spiritualized aesthetic. Such allusions, admittedly, often blur the edges between his philosophy and theology. So does his analogical use of the divine nature to describe art and beauty. But Maritain's method was intentional, even if its effect may not be as clear as he wished. He always insisted that philosophy could make various uses of theology and still remain a sound philosophy.

In *An Essay On Christian Philosophy* (1933)[10] Maritain outlines the various advantages that a philosopher who is also a Christian may rightfully draw from the resources of his faith. Here he elaborates further the project of "liberating the intelligence," which he had proposed at the time of *Art and Scholasticism.*[11] His conversion to Catholicism and his discovery of Aquinas had freed Maritain from the artificial constraints placed upon the intellect by the Cartesian idea of mathematical certitude. The "Christian" philosopher need not blind himself to the "objective data" that informs his faith. The only condition placed upon the use of these data is that philosophy "scrutinizes them according to its own order" (*ECP* 19). This method of cross-fertilization is not only theoretically legitimate but also, to Maritain's mind, a historical fact of philosophical development established by the work of Etienne Gilson (*ECP* 18). Maritain's aesthetics takes its place within this tradition and represents one of his most successful attempts at treating a range of philosophical problems as a Christian philosopher.[12]

This relationship between Maritain's faith and his philosophy is easily misunderstood. For example, William Bush asserts in this volume that the Maritains found in the work of Saint Thomas "quasi-official spiritual justification" for their intense aesthetic pursuits.[13] There is little doubt that during the period

---

[10]*An Essay on Christian Philosophy*, trans. Edward H. Flannery (New York: Philosophical Library, 1955); hereafter cited as *ECP*.

[11]One of Maritain's earliest articles, published in the same year as *Art and Scholasticism*, is entitled "La liberté de l'intelligence," *La Revue Universelle* 1 (1 April 1920): 102-107. Near the end of his life Maritain returns to this theme explicitly in *The Peasant of the Garonne: An Old Layman Questions Himself about the Present Time*, trans. Michael Cuddihy and Elizabeth Hughes (New York: Holt, Rinehart and Winston, 1968) 84-126.

[12]Maritain later came to reject the label "Christian Philosophy" but not the integral approach.

[13]Professor Bush has very kindly responded to my remarks as follows:

It was not my intention to imply any limit on the role played by Thomism in the Maritains' very rich, full lives, but only to point to what I feel must have been one of the more attractive possibilities for exploiting it as they nurtured their close ties with such controversial artistic intimates as Jean Cocteau. Cocteau's own evaluation of the Maritains, mentioned in my paper, was, after all, based on

that produced *Art and Scholasticism* and its subsequent revisions Jacques and Raïssa were at the center of considerable artistic activity. But Bush's comment, although provocative, is unduly harsh. One thinks, for example, of the establishment of the Thomistic study circles at Meudon in 1921 and the promise made by all participants to read the *Summa* and to pray for at least a half an hour each day—hardly the concern of people rushing to opening nights.[14] The Maritains were much more interested in their spiritual and philosophical development at this time than in art (which the record of their study circle demonstrates). They were so serious in their commitment that their godfather, Léon Bloy, who could never be accused of aestheticism, was alarmed that they were becoming too ascetical in their contemplative discipline. Bloy reprimanded Jacques and Raïssa after they returned from Heidelberg in 1908 for their "absurd scruples" and "fear of the seduction of art."[15] If anything, their discovery of Thomas Aquinas enabled the newly converted couple to resist a puritanical resolution to the conflict they felt between art and God. Nothing was more natural than for Jacques and Raïssa to seek the spiritual connections, if they could be found, between their love for art and their love for God. In her memoirs Raïssa speaks of her early devotion to the piano, while Jacques, it seems, might just as easily have become a painter.[16] But it is easy to imagine that if no such relationship had been established the Maritains would have reluctantly withdrawn from the world of artists altogether. Their well-known choice of a *mariage blanc* is itself proof of their willingness to sacrifice anything for the sake of sanctity.

---

his association with them as a "principal collaborator," according to Raïssa, on the important series, *Le Roseau d'or.* Cocteau, I feel, as an artist, sensed that there was indeed a basic error being made by the Maritains in trying to reconcile the artist and the saint on what they called "the frontiers of poetry," forgetting that the only final art of the saint is the presence of God in his life, his artistic talent being of no matter. True, one might speak, as did Bernanos, of the artist's total commitment of his entire life to God, but it is doubtful that the Maritains of the 1920s would have settled for this simile, being bent as they were on nothing less than articulating a link between the artist and the saint—a matter they would still be pursuing much later in *Creative Intuition in Art and Poetry.* That Jacques Maritain came to a more solid view of what sanctity was about at the end of his life I have tried to show in my paper. (From his letter: London, Canada; 12 March 1986.)

[14]Jacques Maritain, *Notebooks*, trans. Joseph Evans (Albany: Magi Books, 1984) 138.
[15]Ibid., 48.
[16]Raïssa Maritain, *We Have Been Friends Together* and *Adventures in Grace: The Memoirs of Raïssa Maritain,* trans. Julie Kernan (Garden City NY: Image Books, 1961) 34; Julie Kernan, *Our Friend, Jacques Maritain: A Personal Memoir* (Garden City NY: Doubleday, 1975) 16-17.

The impact of Aquinas upon Jacques and Raïssa Maritain is seriously trivial-ized by an assumption of an intractable aestheticism on their part. Rather, I would argue that for them the idea of "liberating the intelligence" did justify a prior disposition, though not the one Bush suggests. In the face of the atmosphere of positivism at the Sorbonne, the young couple was determined to find the mean-ing in all things, not just physical objects in motion. Their joy in discovering Aquinas (Raïssa was first) came from their recognition of the aid he could offer in creating a new order of Christian intelligence that would no longer be severed from whole domains of experience—moral, political, and educational, as well as aesthetic. The unity of culture, Aquinas taught them, could be retrieved only by referring all human activity to God.[17] Maritain was well aware that the delec-tations of beauty by themselves provide an illusory unity. After all, his reading of Aquinas had been reinforced by Baudelaire, who had warned him against the construction of "artificial paradises."

Maritain's impatience with romanticizing the role of the artist underlies his hope "of finding once more the spiritual conditions of *honest* work" (*AS* 4). The author emphasizes the key word. Due to his extreme self-consciousness, the modern artist needs to be forcefully reminded of his kinship with the artisan. His pretensions have become harmful to himself and his art. Maritain, as is so often the case, finds the medicinal paradigm in the culture of the Middle Ages: "Man created more beautiful things in those days, and he adored himself less. The blessed humility in which the artist was placed exalted his strength and his free-dom." During the Middle Ages the artist's self-consciousness was held in check by his service to court and church. "The Renaissance was to drive the artist mad . . . by revealing to him his own peculiar grandeur, and by letting loose on him the wild beast of Beauty which Faith had kept enchanted and led after it, docile" (*AS* 22).

This gradual deterioration in the "order of savor" (*AS* 22) is explored further in *Creative Intuition* thirty years later. The essential points of emphasis are un-changed: (1) art is a virtue of the practical intellect that aims at making (*AS* 13; *CI* 49); (2) the artist practices his art in making beautiful things (*AS* 33; *CI* 54); (3) beauty is that "which upon being seen delights" (*AS* 23; *CI* 160). Only with the fourth emphasis, the disorder of modern art, can we note a change: Maritain's tone becomes less polemical and more appreciative than in his earlier writing. The spiritual experience of modern poetry is now termed "ambivalent" (*CI* 178). Amidst the spiritual problems of modern art Maritain discovers a unique reve-lation of the source of creativity itself—poetry. In the period between the ro-mantics and the surrealists, poetry became conscious of itself (*CI* 28). The same

[17]Jacques Maritain, *St. Thomas Aquinas: Angel of the Schools*, trans. J. F. Scanlan (Lon-don: Sheed and Ward, 1946) 37-55.

elevation of the self to which Maritain once objected so loudly becomes the subject of a loving, though still critical, scrutiny for what it can tell us about the spiritual roots of art.

II

The topic of poetry dominates Maritain's aesthetic writings after *Art and Scholasticism*. Poetry is the basis of the human urge to create, "the intercommunication between the inner being of things and the inner being of the human self" (*CI* 3). Maritain's development of this idea, as well as the softening of his attitude toward modern art, can be traced from *The Frontiers of Poetry*[18] and the letter to Cocteau through several articles written in the 1930s[19] to its culmination in *Creative Intuition*. This shift of focus, from art and beauty to poetry and creativity, represents a deepening of his original emphasis on the virtue of art. It would be a mistake to overlook the basic continuity in the development of Maritain's aesthetics from 1920 to 1953, even though his increasing preoccupation with the creating self (or subject) appears to be at odds with both his repudiation of modernism and his promotion of Thomism. Neither conflict is substantial, but both reveal a significant tension in Maritain's aesthetics. As he turns toward the "subject," Maritain's guide is still Saint Thomas, but he is joined by the same modern artists and poets whose pride instigated Maritain's search to recover "the conditions of honest work."

Although Maritain delves into the creative self in search of poetry, he does not alter his original approach of working from God as the prime analogue of all aesthetic concepts. He writes to Jean Cocteau that poetry is "the highest natural resemblance to God's activity. . . . [B]ut in order to have some idea of its nobility one must call to mind the mystery of the procession of the Word" (*AF* 89). Poetic knowledge is fecund; it wants to overflow into a work. "Just as God makes created participations of His essence to exist outside Himself, so the artist puts himself—not what he sees, but what he is—into what he makes" (*FP* 126). Poetry exists first of all in God, as do art and beauty. Maritain writes, "One is always severely punished for forgetting the metaphysical transcendance of poetry, and for forgetting that if in the work of Creation the Word was art, the Spirit was poetry," adding a favorite quote from Baudelaire, " 'Because Poetry, my God, it's you' " (*FP* 134). God knows the world, and thus his poetry, totally

---

[18]Published in accordance with Maritain's desire together with *Art and Scholasticism* as *Art and Scholasticism* and *The Frontiers of Poetry*, in order to give it equal prominence; hereafter cited as *FP* from the Evans translation.

[19]"Concerning Poetic Knowledge" and "The Experience of the Poet" are published in *The Situation of Poetry*.

within himself, while human poetry expresses an inner and spiritual connection between a creative subject, his world, and the thing to be made.

Poetry bestows upon art something analogous to the effect of grace upon the moral life; it is the principle of spirituality for the artist (*FP* 129). The laying bare of this principle was not without its heroes—Cézanne, "so obdurately and desperately intent on that bound, buried significance of visible things" (*CI* 30); its dangers—Picasso, "each moment he brushes against the sin of angelism" (*FP* 131); and its fatalities—Rimbaud "is silent" (*FP* 130) and Duchamp "is now playing chess in New York" (*CI* 215). Maritain did not remain above the particulars, safely wrapped up in a *theory* of modern art; he knew the individual artists and their works and attempted to discern the individual spirits behind the labels. He recognized very early that in the spiritual recesses of modern poetry a "battle is being waged between the good and bad angels, and the bad angels are disguised as messengers of light" (*FP* 130).

The modern artist was being crushed under the burden created by the self-consciousness of his poetry. The ability of Rouault to resist compromising his artistic conscience, that is, to work honestly, was part of what prompted the writing of *Art and Scholasticism* (*WHB* 127). Rouault, one might say, did not look around but painted entirely for himself, even when his friend Léon Bloy pronounced his work too bourgeois. Maritain did not agree, thinking instead that Rouault was one of the few modern artists who could "reconcile freedom with the beauty of forms" (*WHB* 129). Maritain takes his example from Rouault, who drew artistic freedom from his spirituality. In *The Frontiers of Poetry* Maritain writes,

> Religion alone can help the art of our epoch to keep the best of its promises . . . by putting it in a position to respect its own nature and true place. For it is only in the light of theology that art today can achieve self-knowledge and cure itself of the false systems of metaphysics which plague it. By showing us where moral truth and the genuine supernatural are situate, religion saves poetry from the absurdity of believing itself destined to transform ethics and life, saves it from overweening arrogance. But in teaching man the discernment of immaterial realities and the savor of the spirit, *in linking poetry and art itself to God*, it protects them against cowardice and self-abandonment, enables them to attain a higher and more rigorous idea of their essential spirituality. (*FP* 139; emphasis mine)

Maritain's evangelical intent could not be stated more clearly. Notice that he does not suggest that religion provide the subject matter for art but the self-understanding of the artist. For those who might recoil at such a prospect, it should be said that the freedom of the artist is Maritain's paramount concern. Maritain sees art, the artist, and all aesthetic matters in an analogical relation to God that preserves their freedom. This does not deprive the aesthetic of its "essential spirituality," but rather allows it to be expressed regardless of a work's subject. Maritain had very little to say about the "religious" art (containing a religious content) of his day, and most of his comments were negative.

Yet, artists use their freedom to sin. A special affinity with the spiritual provides them the occasion for assuming the place of absolute creator. For Maritain, to accept the role of creature, with its attendant limitations, is the heart of realism. Medieval artists knew themselves well, while modern artists have created a false identity. "Get to know yourself so well that you will be able to look at yourself without flinching. Then there will be room for hope" (FP 143). In order to work honestly once again, artists must give up their pretensions about doing the work of the philosopher or the priest and be content once again with making beautiful things.

Honest work will also preserve the integrity of artists by protecting their freedom from the incessant demands of human life. Artists must learn to forget themselves for the sake of beauty. In chapter 1 of *Art and Scholasticism,* Maritain writes,

> Hence the tyrannical and absorbing power of Art, and also its astonishing power of soothing; *it delivers one from the human;* it establishes the *artifex*—artist or artisan—in a world apart, closed, limited, absolute, in which he puts the energy and intelligence of his manhood at the service of the thing he makes. This is true of all art; the ennui of living and willing ceases at the door of every workshop. (*AS* 9; first emphasis mine)

The artist's detachment from the demands of the human world is a theme that Maritain strikes repeatedly in his aesthetic writings. Is "angelism," a repudiation of an embodied, human life, being recommended here? No, for while artists must work beyond themselves, forgetting the human, they do so *for the sake of the human.* It will be "the human," finally, that is served by the beauty that the artist creates. Artists step out of themselves to create the work; viewers step out of themselves to delight in its finite beauty, which, in turn, creates a longing for perfect beauty. It appears that Maritain has imbued his notion of Christian spirituality, specifically the "going forth" of divine love, into his view of the artist's work. And, in doing so, he succeeds in placing *a circle of ecstasy* at the heart of his aesthetics, whether in art or beauty or the correspondence that each bears to God. It is ironic that the idea of artistic ecstasy was suggested to him by two sources, each dear to him but so far apart, the medieval Schoolmen and modern poets and painters.

This exclusive devotion to the work distinguishes art from prudence. Both virtues belong to the practical intellect, but prudence serves the human good, while art serves the good of its work. Maritain insists on the freedom of the artist from the restraints of moral considerations. Raïssa and Jacques experienced their "first violent difference" over this same question. Raïssa thought the subject of

Rembrandt's "Butcher's Shop"—a flayed steer—too vulgar to enjoy. Jacques thought the painting no less great than Rembrandt's other works. "This disagreement was intolerable to us. . . . Thus began our reflections on art" (*WHB* 45). His battle for the freedom of the artist from the demands of prudence began with no less formidable an opponent than his future wife. One imagines that Raïssa, given her self-confessed stubbornness, was difficult to dissuade.

How remarkable that a young man with such earnestness for social reform and Catholic truth would simultaneously protect the artist from moral and religious judgments of his art! Yet, this assertion of artistic freedom is consistent with the analogy Maritain makes between the artist and the freedom of God as Creator. The artist should not be bound in his making by the moral expectations of his audience; he should not be found morally culpable *as an artist*: "If he [the artist] is angry or jealous, he sins as a man, he does not sin as an artist" (*AS* 15). To be burdened by moral considerations would be an abdication of freedom, a giving up of the transcendent perch over the human, which the artist enjoys, and a rejection of his spiritual privilege.

Maritain insists on a distinction between "the artist qua artist" and "the artist qua man." Although this way of speaking sounds clumsy, it protects the artist from the prudent man in his audience as well as from his own conscience, which may take aim at his work. As the same time, he never forgets the artist is also human and must, for the sake of happiness, cultivate moral virtue. The moral dilemma of the artist is paradoxical: to set aside personal and social considerations, no matter how noble, for the sake of art. The possibility of conflict, however, is perennial: think of Plato's *Republic*, Calvin's Geneva, and the trials of Gustave Flaubert, D. H. Lawrence, and James Joyce.

"The ethics of art," the rubric by which Maritain eventually designated this issue, was always important, though somewhat adjunct, to his developing views of art and creativity. Chapter 9 of *Art and Scholasticism* and a series of lectures given at Princeton in 1951[20] address the same problem: if art and morality are autonomous spheres, how are they to be reconciled, since they must exist within the same human subject (*TRA* 22)? "Unhappy the artist with a divided heart!" (*AS* 70). Artists must subordinate their art to their humanity. If happiness, as the final end of the artist, is not of greater importance to him than his work then he is guilty of idolatry: "there is no good against the good of human life" (*TRA* 39). Even so, this is an "extrinsic and indirect subordination" (*TRA* 22) of art to morality and in no way is intended to shackle the imagination of the artist. In other words, Maritain would oppose any kind of moral judgments imposed on a

---

[20]Published as *The Responsibility of the Artist* (New York: Scribner, 1960); hereafter cited as *TRA*.

work of art by the audience or by the artist in the form of thinly veiled preaching. Yes, an artist's moral character will show through a work; therefore, if an artist wants his art to serve the cause of human happiness, then the best he can do is, in François Mauriac's words, "purify the source." Though they may be applauded by the prudent man, artless gestures such as adopting an ideological posture or choosing religious subjects are a dishonest and easy way to resolve the tension between art and morality without suffering an interior reform.

Beauty stands free of morality and the human good, and it is this very freedom that human life needs from the experience of beauty. The artist defends beauty against the moral judgments of those who count themselves on the side of humanity. Again Maritain views the situation of the artist analogously to that of the saints in their heroic service to the supreme good. Artists must have the virtues of the saint but "*in a certain relation*, and in a line apart, extra-human if not inhuman [good]" (*AS* 78).

The artist as artist stands outside of the human good, which is precisely the angle from which he can make his contribution to the human life. He offers us an opportunity for a "disinterested activity" in the beauty he creates. The enjoyment of beauty frees us—albeit momentarily—from our entrapment in the "system of *nothing but the earth*" (*AS* 37). Through aesthetic delight we gain a portion of the freedom the artist knows in his making, a taste of his ecstasy. An entire aesthetics of contemplation still waits to be construed from Maritain's insights.[21]

The disinterestedness of art shows an affinity with wisdom; both are ordered toward an end that is beyond man, not to be used as a means but sought as an end. "Their whole value is spiritual, and their mode of being is contemplative" (*AS* 34). This resemblance of the artist to the philosopher can be extended to the exertions of the saint. As Maritain writes to Cocteau, "art is un-human, as sainthood is super-human. From this come all the analogies I have spoken of" (*AF* 96-97). The Maritains found in the gesture of ecstatic self-denial the intersection of their love of wisdom with their love of God and love of beauty. But what can meet and mix is not necessarily equal. Jacques and Raïssa willingly sacrificed the "mad love" (*amour fou*) they discovered for each other as students at the Sorbonne and embraced a *mariage blanc* in order to love God above all else. *Amour fou* can only be directed toward one object.[22] Thus, for Maritain, art and wisdom, like human love, are directed to their respective objects *through* God. Whatever the

---

[21] A good start is made by John G. Trapani, Jr. in his "Poetic Contemplation: An Undeveloped Aspect of Maritain's Epistemology," in Jean-Louis Allard, ed., *Jacques Maritain: Philosophe dans la cité/A Philosopher in the World* (Ottawa, Canada: University of Ottawa Press, 1985) 197-206.

[22] Jacques Maritain, *Notebooks*, 228.

resemblance between the philosopher, the artist, and the saint, there is no doubt whose vocation is higher.

Surely the many friendships the Maritains enjoyed with artists bore their theory out in practice. Jacques insists that artists and contemplatives share very similar spiritual trials. Each, in distinctive ways, suffers being stripped of the human.[23] The artist, however, must endure this "Jacob's Night"[24] without the special graces given to the saint. He "must wear himself out among bodies and live with the spirits" (AS 34). Again, this is not to recommend angelism but to recognize the suffering required to preserve the love and freedom of the artist in the service of the beautiful.

The analogy between the artist and the saint extends beyond a common sacrificial devotion to the object of their love. The poet, consciously or not, is "an apprentice of the creator" (AF 87). Just as the saint's life may provide a witness beyond itself, so too the beauty created by the artist becomes, in Baudelaire's terms, a *correspondance* with divine goodness.[25] Thus, the poetry that stimulates the artist to create also "gives us, without knowing it, a foreshadowing, an obscure desire for the supernatural life" (AF 90). The artist, suspended between two worlds, is afflicted with an unavoidable spirit in consciousness. As Maritain writes to Cocteau,

> Poetry, too, imposes the narrow road, it presumes a certain sacred weakness— beauty limps, you say, and Jacob limped after his struggle with the angel, and the contemplative limps in one foot, says Saint Thomas, for having known God's sweetness he remains weak on the side that leans on the world. In one sense poetry is not of this world, it is in its way a sign of a contradiction; its kingdom also is in our midst, within us. (AF 91)

The sanctity of artists consists in their bearing this contradiction without escaping into an illusory aesthetic religiousness or mechanical academicism. The artist exists in the "tragic condition" of imitating the creativity of God by freely (though not in the absolute sense of God) making what does not yet exist but without receiving from his work any spiritual relief. He works toward "an end

---

[23]Compare *TSP* 50, *AS* 78, also Jacques and Raïssa Maritain, *Prayer and Intelligence*, trans. Algar Thorold (New York: Sheed and Ward, 1943) 21, which was first published in French in 1922.

[24]The title of a book by Maritain's godson, Wallace Fowlie, whose chapter on Maritain, though written forty years ago, makes a marvelous introduction to his life and work: *Jacob's Night: The Religious Renascence in France* (New York: Sheed and Ward, 1947) 55-76.

[25]*Baudelaire: Oeuvres complètes*, ed. Y.-G. Dantec and rev. Claude Pinchois (Paris: Pléiade, 1961) 705.

that is not his end" (*AF* 93). "Beauty limps" because the artist can only intimate the life of the spirit and create a beauty that provokes a desire it cannot satisfy alone. To ordain themselves into a kind of pseudopriesthood is the perennial temptation of the poets, to which they must respond with heroic restraint (*AF* 97). Maritain recognized such restraint, for a time at least, in the work of Cocteau.

With his aesthetic theory Maritain seeks to purge art of its "priestly" claims by clarifying basic aesthetic concepts. His undertaking clearly depends upon the analogical relation of these terms to God—the Supreme Artist, the First Poet, the Absolute Creator, Beauty Itself. The trick for the artist is to remain within the analogical tension. No wonder Maritain praised Cocteau for his "tightrope esthetics" (*AF* 76)—Maritain's own are hardly different.

Maritain never changes this posture, although some might argue that *Creative Intuition in Art and Poetry* represents a significant departure from his earlier one. Most obvious is the change in rhetoric. *Creative Intuition* contains fewer of the passionately elaborated analogical illustrations that spice the text of *Art and Scholasticism*. Compare, for example, his treatments of art and beauty and the difference becomes apparent. This does not signal a change in Maritain's mind concerning the roots of his aesthetic theory but, rather, a change in his age and his audience. The change of tone can be easily understood as reflecting the difference between a young convert to Catholicism and Thomism seeking to rally French intellectuals, and an established philosopher addressing an international audience as the first Mellon Lecturer at the National Gallery.

Creative Intuition also contains much that is new. In it Maritain discusses non-Western art and aesthetics. His discussion of the creative intuition in the preconscious intellect, however, marks the decisive and final step in the development of his aesthetics. It has been suggested that these new concerns hinted at a change in Maritain from his "aesthetics-from-above approach" to an "aesthetics-from-below," which never materialized.[26] This is true. Maritain never gave up his theologically based, analogical description of aesthetic terms. Maritain's interest in Oriental and Indian culture was not new for him. His friends Olivier Lacombe and Louis Gardet exposed him and the Meudon study circle to a great deal of Eastern thought and culture.[27] Proof of his familiarity with non-Western traditions had been evidenced in Maritain's books for several decades before *Creative Intuition*. His greatest appreciation is for non-Western forms of mysticism

---

[26]Mary Carman Rose, "The Aesthetics of Jacques Maritain: A Retrospective and Prospective Assessment," in Allard, *Jacques Maritain*, 190-91.

[27]A more critical attitude toward Eastern thought can be found earlier in Maritain's *Introduction générale à la philosophie*, vol. 1 of *Eléments de philosophie* (1921), translated as *An Introduction to Philosophy*, trans. E. I. Watkin (New York: Sheed and Ward, 1930) 19-31.

rather than their art.[28] His treatment of non-Western art in the first chapter of *Creative Intuition* serves primarily as illustrative counterpoint to the revelation of the self, which Maritain finds gradually emerging in the history of Western art.

III

Creative Intuition in Art and Poetry is one of Maritain's greatest written achievements, not for any new direction in his thinking, but for his deepening insights into the question about creativity posed nearly twenty years earlier. In "The Experience of the Poet" (1938) he asked, "Why is the percept [object] of poetic experience non-conceptualizable as such, why is it, as distinguished from the percept of contemplation, not ordered *to knowing* but *to being expressed in a work*, to being cast into being? Why is it rather a source of creative activity than termination in objective union" (*TSP* 72)? Maritain's final answer in *Creative Intuition* directs him toward the deepest recesses of human subjectivity. We should not mistake this for a strictly psychological turn. For Maritain the human subject, whose primary power is intellectual, contains an infinite depth. "A subjectivity is a spiritual subsistence and existence, which are radically active, sources of the superexistence of knowledge and the superexistence of love . . . a universe unto itself, a universe of productive vitality and spiritual emanation" (*TSP* 72-73).

The notion of subjectivity provides the metaphysical backdrop of *Creative Intuition* and ensures that Maritain's use of psychological categories will not be mistaken for an "aesthetics-from-below." *Existence and the Existent*[29] was written almost exactly midway between his essay on the poet's experience and his Mellon Lectures. Here he argues that what makes human subjects unique, different from all others—what makes them *persons*—is freedom. A person "acts by setting itself its own ends" (*EE* 68). It is no coincidence that this echoes what has been said about the freedom of artists toward their art. In defending their freedom Maritain defends all of human freedom from the temptations of moralism, intellectualism, and pragmatism, each demanding an exclusive devotion. The privilege of artists, anchored in the virtue of their art, is that they can step out of themselves and create an *other*, which has its own ontological reality.[30] There-

---

[28]Jacques Maritain, "Natural Mystical Experience and the Void," in *Jacques Maritain: Challenges and Renewals,* ed. Joseph W. Evans and Leo R. Ward (Notre Dame IN: University of Notre Dame Press, 1966) 76-106; this essay written in 1936.

[29]Jacques Maritain, *Existence and the Existent*, trans. Lewis Galantière and Gerald B. Phelan (New York: Pantheon, 1948); hereafter cited as *EE*.

[30]For a thorough study see John W. Hanke, *Maritain's Ontology of the Work of Art* (The Hague: Nijhoff, 1973).

fore, artistic creation, like God's, does not issue from necessity but from love. "Only by love does it [subjectivity] attain to its supreme level of existence— existence as self-giving." The artist reaches into the fullest expression of the human subject: "it is better to give than to receive" (*EE* 83).

By giving us beautiful things, artists are given a privileged knowing of themselves, akin to that belonging to mystics. Poetry grasps both the things of the world and the inner world of the self. Thus, poetic knowledge provides a fragmentary, though real, look into the subject through the created work (*EE* 71). Subjectivity cannot be contained in a concept because it is fully knowable only as a subject and not as an object. Therefore, a subject can be fully known only by God (*EE* 73), but poetry approximates that knowledge, touching the "transcendent subjectivity to which all subjectivities are referred" (*EE* 76). Maritain's exploration of poetry, subjectivity, and creativity leads him to discover a spiritual connection within the self that he earlier found in the world: "The artist, whether he knows it or not, consults God in looking at things" (*AS* 61).

This universe within the self Maritain calls the "spiritual unconscious or preconscious." Maritain's explanations of it have a metaphorical quality that give the impression he is operating beyond the limits of any strict philosophical vocabulary. Perhaps this is appropriate since Maritain thought that subjectivity defied conceptualization. The spiritual preconscious lies so deeply within the human subject that recourse to metaphor is necessary. Plato, who was never averse to coining a philosophical metaphor, uses the name Muse (*mousikè*) to talk about the origins of knowledge. For Maritain, the declared task of *Creative Intuition* is to place the Platonic Muse within the human intellect and imagination. Inspiration "from above the soul becomes inspiration from above conceptual reason, that is, poetic experience" (*CI* 91).

Maritain's interest in inspiration, like Plato's, is not limited to poetic knowledge. The spiritual preconscious is the origin of all knowing. Why, however, does Maritain go to such lengths to investigate this interior space in his aesthetics? The answer goes back to his earliest intentions (1) to define the conditions of "honest work" and (2) to liberate the intelligence. Appreciating the dynamics of the spiritual preconscious is crucial to the interconnection of both Maritain's projects: the "honesty" of an artist's work depends on freeing intelligence outwardly in the direction of the work and inwardly toward the preconscious.

The tendency for modern art to pursue knowing in the place of making typifies, in Maritain's mind, its problematic relation to the intellect. Still, modern art is no different from the rest of modern culture, where the exercise of intelligence has gone awry. *Integral Humanism, Three Reformers*, and *The Dream of Descartes* are among Maritain's books that attempt to address the broader problem of modern reason, but in less forgiving terms. Arthur R. Evans observes,

And so, we have this duality: on the one hand, a tolerance, nay a sovereign permissiveness in all that has to do with artistic creation; in Maritain's best of all possible worlds, unlike Plato's, the *poets* hold court; on the other hand, an intolerable, an overbearing exclusiveness in all that pertains to the life of reason. In the discourse of *philosophia perennis*, Maritain will permit no dialogue. Sympathy: dogmaticism. Why should this be? Is the answer to be found in the differing nature of the two orders of the mind?[31]

Evans's suggestion is surely the right one. Artists are under no compunction to conform their work to any set pattern: their only obligation is to work "honestly" for beauty's sake. Philosophers cannot claim the freedom of the artist to conceive of anything they please. "Truth," according to Saint Thomas, "follows from the being of things." Using this principle of Thomistic realism, Maritain would naturally be more demanding of modern philosophers, many of whom have been guilty of idealism. Indeed, in *The Peasant of the Garonne* modern phenomenology is dismissed as "ideosophy" because of its unrepentant devotion to the Cartesian substitution of ideas for reality.[32] Another reason for Maritain's severity may lie with the preference for clarity and simplicity in expression that Wallace Fowlie mentions.[33] The often ponderous terrain of Husserl, Heidegger, Sartre, and others surely had little appeal for someone with such a strong affinity for the musical textures of Erik Satie and Igor Stravinsky. The question deserves discussion at length. A thorough perusal of Maritain's texts may yield some as yet unnoticed parallels to his view of modern art. Maritain, it should be remembered, was able to meet Henri Bergson "halfway."

It is no exaggeration to say that Maritain sees more hope for the intellect in modern art than in modern philosophy. "Modern art longs to be freed from reason (logical reason)" (*CI* 71)—that is, the stunted and diminished reason left in the wake of Descartes. "Descartes, with his clear ideas, divorced intelligence from mystery" (*CI* 162). Because it has been "bitten by poetry" (*CI* 72), modern art opens the way, once again, to the unconscious recesses of intuitive knowledge, where, as was shown earlier, the human subject verges on the mystery of the divine subject.

Of course, the bite of poetry is not without its dangers. The rejection of reason by the surrealists is Maritain's prime example (*CI* 80). They helped to open the preconscious intellect but turned poetry into a "craving for magical knowledge" (*CI* 184). The failure of their attempt, as in Rimbaud's desire to become

---

[31]"Jacques Maritain: A Point of Interpretation," an address to a meeting of the American Maritain Association at Mercer University Atlanta, 10 April 1984.

[32]*The Peasant of the Garonne*, 99-102.

[33]Fowlie, *Jacob's Night*, 68.

a seer, spills out into irrationalism or simply silence: "He ceased to write" (*CI* 186). Poetry cannot be perverted into a concept without eventually shutting off the imagination from the sources of its images.

Surrealism took the poetic quest for absolute knowledge to its limit, dismissing beauty for the sake of truth. Maritain calls the result "magic" because the knowledge that is gained cannot conform to any of the logical rules, such as the principle of noncontradiction. Magical knowledge obeys its own "law of images" (*CI* 188), which, of course, retains only a private meaning. As a consequence the surrealists had to rely on occult means and, finally, the force of their own personalities to make their "truth" persuasive. Any claim of truth that cannot be rationally discussed in public depends for its power upon the person who utters it. To make their "truth" known, the surrealists further inflated the artistic ego, a strategy instigated by Rousseau, so that the devotion to "knowledge" obliterated the self-forgetting love of the work. For Maritain, the consequences have not been entirely destructive. Modern art is

the spiritual advent, not of the self-centered ego, but of creative subjectivity. . . . The basic significance of modern art lies in this advance, and in the effort to discover and penetrate and set free the active mystery of poetic knowledge and poetic intuition. There would be no more unfortunate error than to mistake the wounds from which modern art is suffering for the substance of the élan that they threaten and mask. (*CI* 195)

IV

The final step in the development of Maritain's aesthetics is his idea of "creative intuition." It is the culmination of Maritain's attempt to liberate artistic intelligence and to preserve artistic freedom. The creative intuition also answers the long-standing question of how knowledge can be oriented entirely toward making and still be considered knowledge. Maritain's original intention to locate the "spiritual conditions for honest work" is now fully realized: the creative intuition frees the artist inwardly toward his intellect and outwardly toward his work. No longer content with a simple distinction between the speculative and practical intellects, Maritain goes on to specify the kind of "intellectual" act underlying the virtue of art. Thus, his two masterworks, *Creative Intuition* and *The Degrees of Knowledge*, share the same aim: to demonstrate the primacy of the intellect in all human action and to reestablish the hierarchy and mystery of knowledge.

The intellect has suffered from being portrayed too simply. Descartes ignored the preconscious depths of the intellect by his definition of "the soul by the very act of self-consciousness" (*CI* 95). Freud commited the opposite error of placing the mind in the grip of dark, irrational forces. Maritain thanks Freud for having brought the unconscious back into discussion, but distinguishes his "spiritual preconscious" from that of Freud. This "automatic or animal" unconscious is, he says, "deaf" to the intellect, a closed determinism based upon the dynamics of instinct and desire (*CI* 91). Human beings, for Maritain, are neither angels nor beasts. He sought a way around their modernist either/or by proposing a view of the unconscious that is both free and rational. He rightfully insists that his idea of creative intuition implies a "whole philosophy of man" (*CI* 91). Does any twentieth-century philosopher go further than Maritain in defending the nature of man as *Homo sapiens?*

> Reason does not only consist of its conscious logical tools and manifestations, nor does the will consist only of its deliberate conscious determinations. Far beneath the sunlit surface thronged with explicit concepts and judgments, words and expressed resolutions or movements of the will, are the sources of knowledge and creativity, of love and supra-sensuous desires, hidden in the primordial translucid night of the intimate vitality of the soul. Thus it is that we must recognize the existence of an unconscious or preconscious which pertains to the spiritual powers of the human soul and to the inner abyss of personal freedom, and of the personal thirst and striving for knowing and seeing, grasping and expressing. (*CI* 94)

For Maritain all human powers proceed from the intelligence that is at the preconscious core of the human soul. Imagination, external senses, concepts and ideas, explicit images, sensation, even the Freudian unconscious: all are empowered by the preconscious, according to the Thomistic dictum that the "more perfect powers are the principles or raison d'être of others" (*CI* 107). Everything human is, as it were, literally drenched with intelligence, though not necessarily in the service of "conceptual" reason.

The creative intuition arises out of what Maritain calls "the free creativity of the spirit" (*CI* 112) bearing a unique freedom from the demands of logic, science, and morality. Once again Maritain argues analogically, connecting creative intuition with the divine ideas. God's ideas are creative: what he thinks and wills is made. The difference between God, "the First Poet," and the artist is that God's poetry is not dependent upon things, since he knows everything entirely through himself. "Well, it is clear that the poet is a poor god. He does not know himself. And his creative insight miserably depends on the external world" (*CI* 113). But what God does absolutely, man can partially accomplish: "In a way similar to that in which divine creation presupposes the knowledge God has of His own essence, poetic creation presupposes, as a primary requirement, a grasping, by the poet, of his own subjectivity, in order to create" (*CI* 113).

Thus, the creative intuition that forms the germ of the work will be imbued and marked by the poet's own character. Who is more like God than the artist who in continuing creation brings things into reality that reveal himself? This aspect of Maritain's aesthetics dances across an unmistakable tightrope. The revelation of the self proves to be the greatest blessing or the greatest curse, at once an initiation into a divine mystery and a goad to egotism. The poetic "I" has the difficult and spiritual task of remaining generous, disinterested, and free, revealing itself only for the sake of the work. "The creative Self," he says, "is both revealing itself and sacrificing itself, because it is *given;* it is drawn out of itself in that sort of *ecstasy which is creation*, it dies in order to live in the work (how humbly and defenselessly)" (*CI* 144-45; second emphasis mine).

The tension of ecstasy constitutes the form of Maritain's aesthetics. It keeps the creative act from feasting on itself and resolves Maritain's dual concern for the "advent of the self" in modern art with the "disinterested" making of the artist. Another kind of Christian sensibility might have instinctively condemned the "advent of the self" but Maritain sees behind the "wounds" of modern art into the human subject and its desire to share life. Maritain's voice is an evangel to the artists, a reminder that their art and its beauty point to God. It is also an evangel to us, an aid in understanding and loving our artists.

Artists, then, cannot escape God. If they turn inwardly, into the subjective dynamics of poetic knowledge, they turn, as in Augustine, toward God. At its deepest level the human subject can imitate God by loving things into existence. If artists look outwardly, at the beauty of their work or of the world, this beauty is itself a glimpse of God. As in Aquinas all created effects speak loudly to the human mind of their Cause.

As much as artists need their interior inspiration, they need contact with the world. Human poetry imitates God in its desire to increase the world of things but remains creaturely in needing more than itself to create. Unlike the angels, human beings require the senses as the stimulant to thought. Poetry needs things. Things are the source of its knowing and the object of its making. Shut poetry off, disallow its connection to sense, corrupt its desire to make, and poetry will whisper to itself it is a god. Poetry, like art, must be consciously linked to God in order to attain its "essential spirituality" (*FP* 139).

The shape of Maritain's aesthetics is consistent throughout the four decades in which he wrote about art, beauty, poetry, and creativity. His aesthetics remain spiritual in *substance*, ecstatic in *form*, and evangelical in *intent*. This inner coherence springs from his early desire to unify culture by referring it to God. Human things may appear diminished by comparison with God, but Maritain believed that such a gesture toward seeming less miraculously opened the door toward becoming more. The meaning of a passage quoted earlier can now be fully understood. In 1927 Maritain wrote that there will be room for hope when you "know yourself so well that you will be able to look at yourself without flinching." He challenged artists to recognize something much harder to see than their sin—their likeness to God. Though Maritain understands the human impulse to look away from the gravity of a calling by which we are "obliged to do the impossible" (*FP* 143), he does not pull his punch:

> If you speak with artists, tell them to make haste while they have the light, and to fear Jesus who passes and does not return. (*FP* 148)

CURTIS L. HANCOCK

Maritain
on Mystical Contemplation

I

As A PHILOSOPHER Jacques Maritain was intensely interested in the various types and degrees of knowledge. As a Christian philosopher he was especially interested in our knowledge of God. Of special importance in this latter connection is his account of mystical contemplation, which is the highest wisdom attainable in this life and is, in its supernatural form, an imperfect anticipation of beatific vision.[1]

Maritain's fascination with mysticism has its beginnings in his earliest philosophical interests. He was dramatically influenced by Léon Bloy, whose life and literature no doubt inspired a belief in the power of affective and aesthetic experience to glimpse God. The young Maritain was also strongly influenced by the natural mysticism of Henri Bergson and, through Bergson, of Plotinus. This curiosity about Plotinus and his school perdured into Maritain's maturest writings, particularly revealing an interest in the Neoplatonic influence on the Chris-

---

[1]See Jacques Maritain, *Distinguish to Unite or The Degrees of Knowledge,* trans. under the supervision of Gerald B. Phelan (New York: Scribner's , 1959) 7 n. 370; hereafter cited as *DK.* Other works by Maritain containing significant passages on mysticism are *Prayer and Intelligence,* trans. Algar Thorold (London: Sheed and Ward, 1929), written with Raïssa Maritain; *Scholasticism and Politics,* translation ed. Mortimer J. Adler (New York: Macmillan, 1940); *Redeeming the Time,* trans. Harry Lorin Binsse (London: Geoffrey Bles, 1943), hereafter cited as *RT; Liturgy and Contemplation,* trans. Joseph W. Evans (New York: P. J. Kennedy and Sons, 1960) also written with Raïssa; *The Situation of Poetry,* trans. Marshall Suther (New York: Philosophical Library, 1968).

tian mystical writers, the most interesting of whom, Maritain believed, is Saint John of the Cross, who escapes Neoplatonic influence more than most.

The early instruction in mysticism convinced Maritain that the philosopher must seriously consider knowledge by "connaturality," a type of which is mystical knowledge. In its broadest signification connaturality is any cognitive agreement between two natures, any union of knower or known. In this sense even the rational science of metaphysics is knowledge by connaturality, achieving an identity of rational intellect and intelligible form. But in its stricter application, which Maritain more commonly prefers, "connaturality" refers to an experimental, nonrational union of knower and known. It is this nonrational kind of connaturality that bears closely on Maritain's account of mysticism.

Examples of knowledge by connaturality occur in both moral and aesthetic experience. Through our affective or practical lives we may acquire a preconceptual knowledge of moral truth (for example, of the virtue fortitude), which, while not formally articulated or philosophically understood, is nonetheless vital and profound, operating regulatively in our moral conduct. Additionally, our aesthetic experience may dispose us habitually to discover beauty in creation; and, unconsciously, through our own creative, artistic production, to know God as the ground and condition of beauty.

These preconceptual kinds of knowledge through morality and poetry are not, Maritain cautions, to be confused with mysticism, the highest knowledge by connaturality. Both moral and poetic experiences "terminate in creatures," not in God. Through morality and poetry we may be connaturalized to virtue and beauty but not to God Himself. These connatural forms of knowledge may glimpse God but only "at a distance."

Mystical experience, when genuinely supernatural, is far different, being an immediate union with God.[2] "Mystical experience" Maritain defines as "a possession-giving experience of the absolute," which is not to be confused, as commonly occurs today, with a "procession of phenomena, ecstasies, and extraordinary gifts belonging, when they are genuine, to what theologians call *charisms* or gratuitous grace."[3] Quite simply, mysticism is belief in the possibility of a living, personal, experimental cognition "of the deep things of God," that is, of God's disclosure of himself as himself. In a word, mystical experience is a connatural

---

[2]For Maritain mystical wisdom is, in the last analysis, of two kinds: supernatural and natural. Only the former is a personal knowledge of the life of God. I will remark below on his interpretation of natural mysticism.

[3]*Scholasticism and Politics*, 188.

knowledge, as profound as can be attained in this life, of the transcendent life of deity.[4]

So understood, mystical experience is purely supernatural, for "the absolute" to which Maritain refers is not the absolute being of the philosophers but the God of Abraham and the Triune Deity of the Christian saints. As a Christian philosopher Maritain denies that a knowledge of the deep things of God can be achieved through our natural human powers. Revealed theology, which Maritain scrupulously observes in his treatment of mysticism, teaches that God, as he exists in himself, is infinitely removed from finite human intelligence. Accordingly, no effort of the human knower can attain to divine disclosure. Mystical experience, when truly a knowledge of God in himself, occurs only as a free act of divine love and grace.

Given such a conception of mysticism, one might conclude that Maritain rejected altogether the possibility of natural mystical experience. In fact, his first position, as outlined in *The Degrees of Knowledge,* was to reject it as illusory, as a state of mind producing at best a cognitive void mistaken as a divine intelligible object, and at worst resulting from the deceptive actions of malevolent spirits. But while it is true that Maritain never abandoned his conviction that our natural powers cannot attain to God as the supreme, personal, supernatural reality, he conceded in certain later writings, such as *Redeeming the Time,* that natural mystical experience is not in every case illusory. Indeed, it may culminate in an experience of a profound and mysterious reality. While natural mysticism may not know *the* absolute, the Triune God, it may yet know *an* absolute.[5]

Only by such an interpretation, Maritain was convinced, could the philosopher do justice to natural mysticism as a genuine kind of knowledge and at the same time preserve the Christian doctrine of God's infinite transcendence over nature and of the infinite superiority of supernatural mystical experience.

My task in this chapter is simply to examine how Maritain develops this interpretation. I shall proceed by outlining the central themes in his exposition, first, of supernatural mystical experience, and afterward, of natural mysticism.

---

[4]Mystical union, however, is not to be identified with beatific vision. In the former the soul unites with the divine will only. In the latter the soul also unites with the divine intellect, so as to know the very essence of God (*DK* 370-71).

[5]For the discussion in *DK,* see 268-77; his amended interpretation appears in *RT* 225-55. Supernatural mystical experience is a personal knowledge of God. I will discuss below what Maritain identifies as the objects of natural mysticism.

II

I have already noted that Maritain describes supernatural mysticism as a personal, immediate, experimental knowledge of God, "a suffering of divine things." This experience is a knowledge by connaturality that is strictly nonrational. As Maritain expresses it, mysticism is purely negative (*apophatic*), in no way achieved through concepts, the formal means of rational cognition. It is a knowledge consisting of a personal union with God and therefore superior to any knowledge attainable by concepts, which can know God only at a distance. Concepts of their nature are limited and inadequate to know in his depths the perfect, infinite, and transcendent object. Consequently, mystical knowledge is the highest wisdom attainable in this life (second in kind only to beatific vision, which is reserved for the next life and which is an intellectual intuition of God's very essence), since the other sciences, such as revealed and natural theology, depend on concepts in their apprehension of God (*DK* 260-65).

At this point Maritain introduces a distinction so as to avoid confusion. Because mystical knowledge occurs nonrationally and without concepts, Maritain names it "negative theology." But in proposing this alternative name for "mysticism," he does not mean to identify it with the kind of negative theology studied by revealed theology, the rational science of revealed truth. As we have just noted, Maritain considers mysticism a higher or more perfect knowledge of God than revealed theology. The latter is a wisdom accessible to human reason illumined by faith. Mystical wisdom is produced by the supernatural infusion of God's grace and is consummated by the elevation of our intelligence beyond its natural limits. The negative theology that is theological science is *propositional,* not mystical. It is merely a system of cautious formulations of what God is not, resulting from an awareness of the inadequacy of limited or analogous concepts to capture an unlimited and supernatural object. But negative theology in this traditional sense is itself only so much rational thinking about God by connaturality. Still, the negative theology that is simply another name for mysticism is *experimental* rather than propositional. It is not a distant knowledge of God imperfectly attained through reflection on what concepts must be denied of him; instead it is an actual connaturality, a nonrational union of soul with deity itself.

These remarks should indicate that while Maritain identifies mysticism as the highest wisdom, he nonetheless accepts the legitimacy of the other wisdoms within their respective, limited spheres. In fact, one could say that his chief study of mysticism, *The Degrees of Knowledge,* is an attempt to justify in principle all science, even though in this life it is mystical wisdom alone that connaturalizes the soul with God as triune and supernatural.

In other words, contemplation for Maritain is a continuum of varying degrees, a unity consisting of different capacities whereby the human mind comprehends being. Mysticism is the highest knowing, a suprarational contemplation of the principle of all beings, God. Far below mystical contemplation in its apprehension of reality, but still above the prescientific cognition of ordinary, prereflective experience, is purely rational or philosophical contemplation. This type of knowledge divides into three degrees, the lowest of which is scientific contemplation, according to which the mind "considers bodies in their mobile and sensible reality, bodies garbed in their empirically ascertainable qualities and properties. Such an object can neither *exist* without matter and the qualities bound up with it, nor can it *be conceived* without matter. It is this great realm that the ancients called *Physica,* knowledge of sensible nature, the first degree of abstraction" (*DK* 35). Knowledge of sensible nature subdivides into two separate kinds of contemplation: empirical science and the philosophy of nature. The former proceeds by observation, experimentation, analysis, and classification so as to formulate hypotheses that in the end may be interpreted as theories or natural laws. This science is limited by empiriological method and is descriptive. Superior to empirical science but within the same degree of abstraction is the philosophy of nature, which is not purely descriptive but is explanatory, examining the ultimate reasons for the conditions and modes of physical nature. The second degree of abstraction is mathematics, in which the mind separates matter from its sensible properties and thinks of it purely as quantity, number, and extension. Beyond these sciences occurs the third degree of abstraction, which considers being altogether independently of its physical modalities, where nothing remains of things except "the very being with which they are saturated, being as such and its laws. These are objects of thought which not only can *be conceived* without matter, but which can even *exist* without it, whether they never exist in matter, as in the case of God and pure spirits, or whether they exist in material as well as in immaterial things, for example, substance, quality, act and potency, beauty, goodness, etc." (*DK* 36). Intermediate between philosophical contemplation and mysticism is revealed theology: a suprarational science in its contents (special truths communicated by God to humankind) but rational in its method and formulation. This outline of the various kinds and degrees of contemplation shows that science, taken as a whole, is a unitary structure formed out of diverse disciplines, each with its special object and concentration. Mysticism defines the pinnacle of this structure, exceeded only by beatific vision.

In adopting this position—that the belief in the superiority of mystical wisdom does not compel the philosopher to reject the legitimacy of all other science—Maritain opposes many proponents of mysticism. For there are those in the mystic tradition, including both students and practitioners, who insist that mysticism is not the highest but the only wisdom. For these thinkers mysticism transcends and contradicts rational science; it alone gives insight into reality, existing as the sole alternative to the bankruptcy of rational intellection.[6]

Maritain unequivocally rejects this conception of mysticism. As the above paragraphs show, mysticism is for him the highest wisdom, not because it disqualifies all other science, but because it is simply more perfect than the other kinds of knowledge. Mystical knowledge does not contradict or render negligible any science. Above all, it respects both revealed and natural theology. These disciplines, too, have their special noetic loci in the hierarchy of sciences. Mysticism differs from these sciences, not because it grasps what the others fail to grasp, but because mystical knowledge penetrates more deeply into ultimate reality. Mysticism attains far more perfectly in this life what theology and metaphysics can attain. But insofar as theology and metaphysics are free of error, they apprehend and formulate the same truth that one experiences mystically. Only the limitations of theology and philosophy prevent that truth from being known as deeply as it is known through the non-rational, superelevated dimensions of mystical experience (DK 277-80, 283-90).

Maritain finds this position on the integrity and harmony of all sciences realized dramatically in the relationship between Saint Thomas Aquinas, whom he regards as the greatest philosopher and theologian in the Catholic tradition, and Saint John of the Cross, whom he considers the greatest mystic writer in the same tradition. These are the two great doctors whose lights (actually the one is "the Doctor of Light," while the other is "the Doctor of Night") guide Maritain in his investigation of mysticism as it relates to other science. He discovers in this harmony between Saint Thomas, "the Doctor of the supreme communicable wisdom," and Saint John, "the Doctor of the supreme incommunicable wisdom," a resounding triumph for the perennial philosophy, resting as it does on the conviction that all truth is a unity, never fragmented into conflicting parts. These two masters agree because the truths of the three wisdoms—mysticism, theology, and metaphysics—are compatible and complementary. Occasionally, Maritain describes their complementary roles in terms of practical science. Saint Thomas is the master of moral theology, a *speculatively* practical science. This discipline is speculative because, while its end is action, it aims first at understanding ultimate moral principles and rules. This differs from the science of which Saint John is the master. His is a *practically* practical science, the whole mode of which is practical, meaning "that there is no question of explaining and resolving a truth, even a practical truth, into its reasons and principles. The question is to prepare for action and to assign its proximate rules" (DK 315). Accordingly, Saint John complements Saint Thomas's pursuit of pure understanding with the

<hr>

[6]For a representative of this view, see S. N. Dasgupta, *Hindu Mysticism* (1927; rpt., New York: Ungar, 1959).

supreme practical prescription for the attainment of the human person's good, even in this life. In the end Saint Thomas and Saint John are the authoritative voices of all Christian science, the former (the Doctor of Light) being the voice of supreme rational science (metaphysics and theology, including moral theology, a *speculatively* practical science), and the latter (the Doctor of Night) being the voice of supreme nonrational science (a supernatural mysticism, a *practically* practical science). Indeed, perhaps the best sign of their brotherhood as thinkers and saints is Aquinas himself being taken up in his last days into a mystical wisdom empowering him to undergo, like Saint John, "a suffering of divine things."

Now we reach the very heart of Maritain's exposition of supernatural mysticism. I refer to his explanation of *mystical union,* which emerges out of his commentary on certain writings of Saint John of the Cross. This is the central theme in "the incommunicable wisdom," the elements of which Maritain analyzes and elaborates in *The Degrees of Knowledge* (DK 326-85).

Maritain's account of mystical union—his explanation of mystical experience as constituting, in a certain sense, a real union of God and soul—primarily aims to harmonize with the teachings of Christian faith. This objective is not easily attained, however, for it demands, Maritain believes, that the philosopher avoid the pantheistic tendencies of Neoplatonism, a school that has powerfully influenced the development of Christian mysticism.[7] But as difficult as this task may be, Maritain insists that the philosopher cannot be excused from it, for no less reason than to preserve a fundamental Christian teaching—namely, that every human soul is real and destined for eternity and that therefore monism or pantheism, which would reduce the soul to the oneness of deity, granting it phenomenal distinctness only, must be rejected as pagan, philosophical error.

To express the problem more precisely, the risk in interpreting mystical union is this: given the debt of Christian mystics to a medieval tradition steeped in Neoplatonism, the philosopher may be tempted to follow (perhaps unknowingly) Plotinus and his followers so closely as to annihilate the individual human soul in mystical union. For if one follows Plotinus's principles consistently, the consequences would seem to be that the soul is lost in mystical experience, ab-

---

[7]The principles of Neoplatonism have been admirably outlined by Leo Sweeney, "Basic Principles in Plotinus' Philosophy," *Gregorianum* 42 (1961): 506-16. According to Sweeney, Neoplatonism is a monism committed to three principles: (1) reality is a unity (i.e., to be real is to be one); (2) unity is perfection (i.e., to be one is to be good, so that the One is also the Good); (3) unity is prior to multiplicity in the universe (i.e., whatever is prior—namely, the One and the other hypostases—has more reality than the posterior, the products of the hypostases). For complementary discussion see R. T. Wallis, *Neoplatonism* (New York: Scribner, 1972) 37-93, and John Rist, *Plotinus: The Road to Reality* (Cambridge: University Press, 1967).

sorbed into the sole Platonian reality, God (the One/Good).[8] This incautious adherence to Plotinus accounts for the pantheistic tendencies in such writers as Pseudo-Dionysius, Erigena, Eckhart, and Nicholas of Cusa, who sincerely embrace Christian teachings but must struggle to align them with the monistic encroachments of the Neoplatonism they also accept.

As it happens Maritain finds a mystic who, perhaps because he dates after any of those just mentioned, provides an account of mystical union escaping from the Plotinian and pantheistic influences that dominate in other interpretations. In the texts of Saint John of the Cross there occurs an elucidation of mystical experience that, if interpreted in harmony with Thomistic principles, preserves the soul as an entity, while allowing for the mystery, transcendence, and *reality* of supernatural mystical union. Hence, in Saint John of the Cross, Maritain discovers a truly Christian, rather than a Neoplatonic, mystic (*DK* 9n, 376n).[9]

His esteem for the work of Saint John inspires Maritain to unfold his analysis of supernatural mystical union through a commentary on the saint's writings. The essential results of his analysis are as follows. Since mystical experience is a suprahuman and supernatural event, it has its basis in faith rather than natural reason. But faith itself is not a sufficient condition for mystical experience, which is an "infused contemplation" of God effected by divine grace and charity. Divine love alone, a gift of santifying grace communicated by the Holy Spirit, connaturalizes the soul with God. In other words, God becomes really present in the soul. The soul is "transformed into God" through an actual interior presence of the Triune Person. When this transformation occurs, the soul is superelevated beyond rational cognition and also beyond the obscurity of faith. What faith knows remotely the soul now knows immediately and connaturally by union. Divine charity achieves a real union of soul and God, initiating a spiritual experience that will culminate in the next life in beatific vision.

---

[8]For a helpful account of the reasons compelling one to interpret Plotinus's mysticism as radically monistic, consult Plato Mamo, "Is Plotinian Mysticism Monistic," in Baine Harris, ed., *The Significance of Neoplatonism* (Norfolk VA: International Society for Neoplatonic Studies, 1976) 199-216. For an opposing interpretation, see Rist, *Plotinus: The Road to Reality.*

[9]Maritain describes the contemplative science of Saint John of the Cross as distinctly Christian and purely practical. This "practically practical science" Maritain studies carefully in the following works of Saint John: *The Ascent of Mount Carmel; The Dark Night of the Soul; Living Flame of Love; Spiritual Canticle; Spiritual Sentence and Maxims; Spiritual Warnings.* These works are contained in *The Complete Works of St. John of the Cross*, trans. E. Allison Peers (Westminster MD: Newman Press, 1953). This collection also serves as Maritain's English source for his quotations of Saint John in *The Degrees of Knowledge.*

While this mystical union is real,[10] it is, revealed theology insists, imperfect by Neoplatonic standards. That is to say, Christian mystical union does not reduce the soul as an entity to God. But we may ask how this reduction is avoided. What principles does Maritain employ to show that Christian mystical union, on the one hand, is real and, on the other, avoids monism? He refers to a distinction developed by Saint Thomas and accepted by Saint John of the Cross to answer this question. This is the distinction between union *secundum esse* (according to existence) and union *secundum intentionem* (according to intention or intentional object). According to this distinction mystical union, while real in one sense, does not dissolve the one entity into the other. A real, but not absolute (or complete), identity is achieved between soul and God. This union, then, is not secundum esse, for the mystic does not lose his existence or become God. Instead the union is secundum intentionem, in which the soul appetitively (but not entitatively or according to esse) is transformed into God.[11] "The mystery of cognitive union and of the true compels the philosopher to conceive a 'being of knowledge' and an *esse intentionale* which is not entitative being or being of nature. The mystery of the union of love and of the good compels him to conceive an *intentional being of love* which is not entitative being either" (*DK* 369). Thus, Maritain admits that mystical union is, in a sense, real and yet maintains, at the same time, that creature and God are eternally separated.

> From the point of view of entity, in the register of the proper being of things, there is always a duality, nay, say an infinite distance between the soul and uncreated love. But there is a another order than that of entity, and it is to that order that St. Paul makes allusion in his words, "one spirit," he says, not "one single being." This is the order of love, considered not in its ontological constituents of essence and existence (for there it is considered as being) but in the absolutely proper reality of the immaterial intussusception [a pulling inward] by which the other within me becomes more than myself. (*DK* 368)

The human will and divine will are entirely different as they exist, but they may unite in the operation of love. "In the spiritual marriage the created will and uncreated love remain entitatively distant to infinity, yet the soul, in its supernatural activity of love, loses or alienates itself in God who, according to the being or actuality of love, becomes her more than she herself, and is the principle and agent of all her operations" (*DK* 369).

The nature of this "spiritual marriage" implies an account of the operations of soul in relation to the activity of God. Since the infusion of God's love is

---

[10]Maritain insists that this union is real, that is, "physical" or ontological, not merely moral or metaphorical (*DK* 255; see also 7, 257, 320-21, 356).

[11]This distinction is elaborated in *DK* 368-75.

achieved by the purely supernatural means of God's charity, the soul remains passive throughout the experience. The soul acquires love and deep knowledge of God but not through its own power. The soul's appetitive and intellectual powers are now actuated by God, by supernatural, not natural, agency. Our appetitive power is actuated *totally,* now having actually become God in its object and its operation. Our intellectual power is actuated *partly,* not having been transformed into God, but having been elevated beyond the limits of rational intellection, so as to know, now, the deep things of God. By the formal means of divine charity, the intellect is elevated to the level of supernatural nonrational insight, so that now what it knows is like "a ray of darkness" to the natural or rational intellect (*DK* 264, 339). Mystical experience, then, is paradoxical: the soul, while remaining passive in divine infusion, enjoys through God's supernatural agency the active exercise of its appetitive and intellectual nature far more profoundly than it could ever achieve naturally.

In sum, with these distinctions—union secundum esse and union secundum intentionem—Maritain explains, following Saint Thomas and Saint John, that mystical experience is not a Neoplatonic but a partial union, a union of wills. God's presence is as an *esse intentionale* for the will.[12] This union elevates our intellect so that we partly know God as He exists supernaturally. Our intellect has an insight into the depths of divinity, an insight that will be surpassed only by beatific vision, in which our intellect also, not only the will, will be connaturalized with God, empowering us to see the Divine Essence itself.

Lastly, since contemplative infusion is achieved as a supernatural event through divine charity, there is no contemplative technique to ensure its occurrence. As the effect of God's love and grace, mystical union is a mystery beyond natural conditions or powers. Maritain notes this as simply a matter of theological doctrine: neither rational science nor technique alone can elevate the soul to divine union. The ignorant are as likely to be blessed by infused contemplation as are the learned. The lowly shepherdess may know God more perfectly than the greatest philosopher. No more clearly than in its mystical teaching does Christianity reveal that wisdom that is so much "foolishness to the Greeks."

III

As Maritain's reflections on mystical experience matured, he came to appreciate the depth and significance of natural mysticism. That which he dismissed as at best "a counterfeit" in *The Degrees of Knowledge,* he declared a "fruitive experience" of something absolute in later writings. His change of mind on this

---

[12]The divine object of love is called "intentional" by analogy with the intentional being, the intentional object, of knowledge (*DK* 369 n. 5, 448).

question emerged in part out of a respect for the sincere claims of great mystics, such as Plotinus and the Eastern masters, who appear to acquire a deep nonrational cognition of reality through contemplation directed and consummated by their natural powers alone. But it would appear that the principal reason Maritain came to admit the possibility of natural mystical experience is that he discovered a way to explain its place among the "degrees of knowledge" that does not threaten the higher value of supernatural mysticism and, of equal importance, accords with Aristotelian-Thomistic principles. The following exposition outlines this discovery.[13]

Maritain speculates that through a refined and powerful technique, contemplation may become unreceptive of and unresponsive to any and all intelligible content. The mind withdraws from every essence, including the very intelligibility of one's own soul. It actually operates "against the grain of nature," for, whereas the mind naturally moves toward intelligible objects, in natural mystical contemplation it withdraws from intelligibility. Contemplation, then, terminates in a *void,* in which no intelligible content is intended or apprehended. The mind is "emptied of being," if by "being" one means intelligibility or essence. And yet in this void a wondrous reality is known. For while the mind now perceives no being as essence, it experiences that without which essence remains unactualized, "the act of existence" (esse). At this point Maritain is careful to identify this pure esse in a way that does not compromise his Thomistic philosophy of God. The act of existence grasped in natural mystical cognition, while profound, mysterious, and real in its own right, is not the perfect Esse (Pure Act) of supernatural mystical experience. No, the mystic who contemplates under his own power perceives only the esse of his own soul, the soul stripped of its essential characteristics and reduced to its purely formless but purely actual dimension.

But this is not to say that the mystic fails to attain a knowledge of reality as a whole. Maritain explains why this is the case. By prescinding from all essence or intelligibility, natural mystical contemplation attains the void, which performs a role similar to the role that love plays in in supernatural mystical knowledge: it becomes the formal means of the knowledge (RT 233, 244).[14] This void leaves the mind with only one object, the formless (nonessential) nature of the soul as it exists in itself. The void puts the mind in touch with the self in its purity, in its very act of existing. Since esse (the act of existing) is the primarily real, *intrinsic* principle of every existent, however, mystical contemplation, by knowing esse, perceives the metaphysical principle of all reality. Accordingly,

---

[13]Maritain presents his interpretation in RT 225-55.

[14]Also see Henry Bars, "Maritain's Contributions to an Understanding of Mystical Experience," in *Jacques Maritain: The Man and His Achievement,* ed. Joseph W. Evans (New York: Sheed and Ward, 1963) 122.

mystical contemplation connaturalizes the mind to an absolute, the principle of existence, which is "immense," because it is unlimited (limited only by essence) and it belongs to everything real.

The mind now apprehends in a single nonrational vision the unity and immensity of all reality, from God to the lowest creature, actualized as they are by the principle intrinsic to each, the act of existence. Moreover, this interpretation enables Maritain to speculate about why the Yogis call "atman," or the self, this absolute they claim to attain. By knowing the esse of their individual souls, Yogis know the principle actuating and belonging to everything. Thus, they perceive all reality in terms of the reality of self. This further explains why natural mysticism gravitates toward monism. Yogis exclude everything from their contemplation except this unitary principle, esse. They reduce the plurality of the universe to this real, actuating principle. Mystics fail to realize that this principle is not everything but is only intrinsic to everything. The universe is pluralistic, but it consists of beings made actual by the act of existence. Hence, while natural mysticism is a genuine kind of knowledge, not mere illusion, its monistic tendencies and formulations must be corrected by Christian faith and metaphysics. [15]

Accordingly, natural mysticism can attain "a possession-giving experience of *an* absolute," since esse is the absolute principle actuating, making real, every existent, but it is not a possession-giving experience of *the* absolute, for God as supernatural and personal is not accessible to natural intelligence. He is revealed only by the love and grace of His free choice. The infinite expanse between the natural and the supernatural can never be bridged by man's finite and fallen powers. Only grace bridges the unbridgeable distance between man and God. It is for this reason that technique, which is indispensable in natural mystical experience, is of limited and only preparatory value in supernatural mysticism.

But in spite of the limitations of natural mystical experience, Maritain insists that forbidding the Yogi any supernatural knowledge of God would result from too austere a theology. This possibility—that a Yogi too can know God—he accepts as being in harmony with what the church teaches about the infinity and mystery of God's grace.

> Everything leads us to think that such cases [practitioners of natural mysticism knowing God as supernatural] are encountered since we know that unbaptized persons, even though they are not stamped with the seal of unity so as to participate through the virtue of the Church in the proper work of the Church (which is the redemption continued), can nevertheless (inasmuch as they receive without knowing it the supernatural life of the self-same divine blood which circulates within the Church and of the same spirit which rests upon it) belong invisibly to

---

[15]Ibid., 122.

Christ's Church. Thus they can have sanctifying grace and, as a result, theological faith and the infused gifts. (*DK* 273)

While it must be true that Yogis cannot know God by natural technique, they nonetheless could unconsciously be the recipients of sanctifying grace and thereby be elevated to a supernatural wisdom. This elevation, of course, occurs in spite of and not on account of natural contemplative technique. Yet it is no conflict with Christian teachings to admit the possibility of divine grace intervening independently and mysteriously in any kind of contemplation so as to raise the soul to a suffering of divine things.

To summarize, then, in his treatment of mysticism, Maritain sets for himself the task of showing how mystical understanding agrees with the perennial philosophy, which he understands broadly as a system of knowledge embracing and harmonizing all truth. If the perennial philosophy is understood in this way, Maritain's account of mysticism satisfies its synthetic demands in two important respects: first, by harmonizing supernatural mystical knowledge with the range of all other science; and, second, by defending the possibility and value of natural mysticism, showing how it, like the other "degrees of knowledge" has its own proper object and range. In a word, supernatural mysticism transcends but does not conflict with rational science, and natural mysticism is not necessarily illusory.

Maritain's achievement has been nothing less than to elucidate the mystical wisdoms, supernatural and natural. It is in his handling of the former type what we witness the consummate affirmation of his Christian faith. That faith is the governing principle in his entire exposition, and it is nowhere more clearly evident than in his conviction that, while mystical wisdom completes the edifice of science, it is achieved by a nonrational surrender to the sovereignty of God's infinite grace and charity.

DONALD A. GALLAGHER

Integral Education for Integral Humanism: Jacques Maritain's Christian Philosophy of Education

Thus the prime goal of education is the conquest of internal and spiritual freedom to be achieved by the individual person, or, in other words, his liberation through knowledge and wisdom, good will, and love.

—*Education at the Crossroads*

Background and Writings

"INTEGRAL EDUCATION FOR INTEGRAL HUMANISM"—this watchword uttered by Jacques Maritain himself is no mere slogan. It expresses his ideal of what should and must be achieved in education even though in practice it is difficult of attainment. His ideas on humanism and education, that is, on society and school, are expressed in terms of a "New Christendom" to be struggled for and of an "ideal educational republic." For Maritain these are not utopias but concrete, realizable ideals. As with every great philosopher, each aspect of his philosophy is related to his educational philosophy. Thus in Jacques Maritain, his metaphysics of knowledge, his anthropology or philosophical psychology, his personalism and integral humanism—each has its contribution to make to his philosophy of education.

Maritain uncovers and explains the humanism of education, which cannot be understood apart from what he called theocentric humanism and the vision of a new social order. Maritain's own educational background helps provide a clue to his educational writings and helps in consideration of the significant themes in these works, such as the humanities and liberal education at various stages of development and formation, knowledge and the human person, natural intelligence and the spiritual preconscious, the conquest of internal freedom as the primary goal of education, the teaching of the democratic charter, the paradoxes of education as illustrated and illuminated by Maritain, and, finally, the prospects "with regard for the world of tomorrow" for his educational goals and programs.

As a teacher Jacques Maritain taught for many years at the Collège Stanislas (Paris) and the Institut Catholique de Paris; in his later years, he lectured regularly at universities throughout Canada and the United States and on occasion in other parts of the world. He served on the faculties of the Pontifical Institute of Medieval Studies (Toronto), Columbia, Princeton, Chicago, and Notre Dame, among others. He was invited to give lectures in distinguished series, notably the Terry Lectures on education at Yale University in 1943. In the last decades of his life (he died at the age of ninety in 1973) he gave "little seminars" to the Little Brothers of Jesus, a congregation he loved and that he joined following the death of his wife, Raïssa.

In his school years in Paris Maritain absorbed at the Lycée Henri IV the classical education prevalent in the late nineteenth century. With the young people of his generation, he derived benefit from the emphasis on the humanities, the classical languages, and Hellenistic culture. Still, as he points out several times in his educational writings, there are limitations inherent in this tradition with its heritage of Epicureanism and Cartesianism. The *end* in view, the "foursquare man" (as it was put in the English schools of the time) was admirable but somewhat narrow. It was, he stresses, weak on *means* and on pedagogy attuned to the various stages of development through which youth progresses. Maritain discovered that contemporary schools of psychology and pedagogy had much of value to contribute in regard to methods or means but were at the same time weak in regard to ends, which these schools tended to think of as relative "goals" or "objectives" rather than as "final causes."

In his early eduation, Maritain was later to note, there were many Christian values retained, but they (and the whole fabric of education) were becoming increasingly secularized. He would also say in later years that bourgeois individualism was doomed and would reflect that in his youth (particularly in the circle in which he was brought up, his grandfather Jules Favre being one of the founders of the Third Republic) it had still been vigorous, paying lip service to high moral standards but in practice being self-seeking.

The generation of Jacques Maritain was destined to face up to "the crisis of civilization." Not only the Oswald Spenglers but Catholic historians such as Hilaire Belloc and Christopher Dawson were writing on this theme. In the 1930s, the age of the Great Depression and of the totalitarian menace, much attention was paid to this topic. Maritain wrote about it in *Integral Humanism* (French ed., 1936; English ed., 1938), *The Twilight of Civilization* (French ed., 1939; English ed., 1943) and other works. In his view, we are witnessing before our very eyes the collapse of "the modern age" (including "bourgeois humanism") and the emergence of a new one. Viewed dramatically on the scale of a clash between principalities and powers, the struggle for predominance is between what Maritain calls "theocentric humanism" and "anthropocentric humanism" (compare the "secular humanism" of our day). It is against this backdrop that Maritain says in the 1940s that education is at a crossroads. As I shall develop more fully below, we are faced with a loss of the sense of being, of love, of knowledge, as Maritain points out, and at the same time with a weakening even among persons of goodwill of the structures supporting religious faith: "verification" tends to supplant knowledge of *things*. Education in consequence has the task of reintegrating as well as integrating both in regard to its programs and in regard to the formation of the person.

Jacques Maritain's writings in the field of education are not as extensive as those in sociopolitical philosophy and other fields, but they do provide a comprehensive Christian philosophy of education, as he himself calls it. His major studies in English in this topic are available in *Education at the Crossroads* (1943) and *The Education of Man* (1962).[1]

---

[1] The principal writings by Jacques Maritain on education are:

Education at the Crossroads (New Haven: Yale University Press, 1943); hereafter cited as *EC*. There are many paperbound reprints of this work, which emerged from the Terry Lectures at Yale. It was translated into French as *L'education à la croisée des chemins* (Paris: Egluff, 1947).

The Education of Man, ed. Idella and Donald Gallagher (New York: Doubleday, 1962; paperbound ed., Notre Dame IN: University of Notre Dame Press, 1967); herafter cited as *EM*. This book supplements *Education at the Crossroads*, and the two works together contain all but one or two of Maritain's major writings on education, including "Thomist Views on Education" and "Some Typical Aspects of Christian Education."

Pour une philosophie de l'education (Paris: Fayard, 1969) includes a translation of *Education at the Crossroads* and other studies, such as some of those in *The Education of Man*; edited by the author himself, this is the definitive edition of his educational works.

It should be noted that *Education at the Crossroads* and *Pour une philosophie de l'education* have been published in several foreign languages; a Japanese edition of *The Education of Man* has been published by the Kyushu University Press (1983). It should be noted also that chapters and excerpts from these books have appeared as articles in periodicals in a number of countries.

Numerous studies on Maritain's philosophy of education have been published in various languages by Jean-Louis Allard, Giancarlo Galeazzi, Pierre Lambert, Piero Viottok

Philosophical Themes
Bearing on Education

A number of ideas emerge from Maritain's writings that are the keys to understanding the core of his philosophy of education. Important as it is, I do not dwell upon the curriculum he presents as suited for the student of the humanities but upon what he means by *integration* and *liberation* and by the primary goal as "the conquest of internal and spiritual freedom." Philosophical "themes" from every phase of his philosophy pertinent to education are so numerous that only the central ones can be considered here.

What Is Man? Maritain himself proposes that if education indeed has for its purpose the formation of human persons, the "guiding of man toward his own human achievement," then it is obliged to answer the question or seek that answer from its basic philosophy, namely, "What is man?" Maritain answers the question in *Education at the Crossroads:*

> Thus the fact remains that the complete and integral idea of man which is the prerequisite of education can only be a philosophical and religious idea of man. I say philosophical, because this idea pertains to the nature or essence of man; I say religious, because of the existential status of this human nature in relation to God and the special gifts and trials and vocation involved. . . .
>
> There are many forms of the philosophical and religious idea of man. When I state the education of man, in order to be completely well grounded, must be based upon the Christian idea of man, it is because I think that this idea of man is the true one, not because I see our civilization actually permeated with this idea. Yet, for all that, the man of our civilization *is* the Christian man, more or less secularized. . . .
>
> In answer to our question, then, "What is man?" we may give the Greek, Jewish, and Christian idea of man: man as an animal endowed with reason, whose supreme dignity is in the intellect: and man as a free individual in personal relation with God, whose supreme righteousness consists in voluntarily obeying the law of God; and man as a sinful and wounded creature called to divine life and to the freedom of grace, whose supreme perfection consists of love. (*EC* 6-7)

Leo R. Ward, and other scholars. On the themes directly concerning us, see especially Jean-Louis Allard, *Education for Freedom,* with a preface by Donald A. Gallagher, published jointly by the University of Ottawa Press and the University of Notre Dame Press in 1983, and the French edition, *L'education à la liberté ou la philosophie de l'education de Jacques Maritain,* published jointly by Les Presses Universitaires de Grenoble and the University of Ottawa in 1978. See also Pierre Lambert, "Universal Liberal Education: The Cultivation of Natural Intelligence," in *Maritain: philosophe dans la cité / A Philosopher in the World,* ed. Jean-Louis Allard (Ottawa: University of Ottawa Press, 1985).

The Person and Knowledge. The "person," his worth and hs existence, stands at the very center of Maritain's philosophy. His social and political philosophy rests on his "personalist-and-communitarian" thesis (*The Person and the Common Good*, English ed., 1947). His exalted concept of personality envisions divine personality as well as human. In his eyes, a person is a center of liberty. In a magnificent passage in the *Degrees of Knowledge* (French ed., 1932; English ed., 1937, and the authoritative ed., 1959), Maritain writes of the person that his "metaphysical root, hidden in the depth of being, is only manifested by a progressive conquest of the self by the self accomplished in time." He continues:

> Man must win his personality as he wins his liberty; he pays dearly for it. He is a person in the order of acting, he is *causa sui* only if rational energies and virtues, and love—and the Spirit of God—gather his soul into their hands—*anima mea in manibus meis semper*—and into the hands of God, and give a face to the turbulent multiplicity that dwells within him, freely seal it with the seal of his radical ontological unity. In this sense, one knows true personality and true liberty; another knows them not. Personality, while metaphysically inalienable, suffers many a check in the psychological and moral register. There it runs the risk of contamination by the miseries of material individuality, by its meannesses, its vanities, its bad habits, its narrowness, its hereditary predispositions, by its natural regime of rivalry and opposition. For that same man who is a person, and subsists in his entirety with the subsistence of his soul, is also an individual in a species and dust before the wind.[2]

In the last sentence of his passage, Maritain expresses his version of the paradox of the greatness and the wretchedness of the human condition, expressed eloquently by poets and philosophers (for example, by Gerard Manley Hopkins in man as "immortal diamond" and "matchwood," by Pascal as "the thinking reed"). Maritain stresses, moreover, that the notion of personality belongs primarily in the ontological order. "It is a metaphysical and substantial perfection in the operative order in psychological and moral values."[3]

For the student pursuing his or her liberal studies, it is essential to acquire, on the level of natural intelligence rather than that of intellectual virtue, some understanding of what philosophy teaches about the grandeur of the person.

Philosophers know they must "explain" or "account for" knowledge. Knowing (cognitive or conscious) beings range from minuscule organisms endowed with at least some modicum of touch or tactile awareness to the higher elevations of intellectual knowing in the natural order. These "elevations" in-

---

[2]*Distinguish to Unite or The Degrees of Knowledge*, trans. under the direction of Gerald B. Phelan (New York: Scribner, 1959) 232.

[3]Ibid., 231.

clude metaphysical knowing or wisdom, poetic knowing, knowing by connaturality, a kind of "mystical experience" in the natural order bordering on
"unknowing." All this is evidently from the classical tradition of the Greeks,
Saint Augustine, and Saint Thomas Aquinas, and on this theme Maritain ex-
patiates in one of his masterpieces, *The Degrees of Knowledge*.[4]

Knowing is qualitative and should not be described in terms of quantity, yet
we may indicate that even the least "amount" of knowing, the slightest stirring
or fluttering of awareness is something stupendous. It cannot be accounted for
by reduction to a complex organization of material factors; it remains a "mystery" in the natural order.

Knowledge, then, is every cognition from the humblest to the most sublime.
In the intellectual order there is a scale of cognitions. "Real" knowledge and
"mere" information are rightly contrasted, but information is also knowledge of
a sort.

The knowledge with which we are primarily concerned I set down as follows:

1. knowledge—anything worthy of the name.
2. Knowledge—the knowledge attainable in Liberal Education.
3. KNOWLEDGE—the knowledge possessed in the state of intellectual
   virtue.
4. NOLEJ—to be explained below in the final section of this chapter.

For those students pursuing their liberal studies, it is essential to acquire,
not on the level of intellectual virtue that culminates in *cognito certa per causa* but
on the level of what Maritain calls "natural intelligence," some grasp of what
knowledge is in all its depth and height and in all its integration and diversity.
In *Science and Wisdom* (French ed., 1935; English ed., 1940) Maritain points out
that Western civilization has given to mankind the gift of "the *pure sense* of speculative truth . . . the absolute value of complete detachment from affective inclination, of the severity and purity of a chaste science where unique function and
end is to discern that which is, to *see*."[5] It is one of the major paradoxes in the
educational sphere pointed out by Maritain that moral education is ultimately
more important than intellectual education, yet the *direct* aim of liberal educa-

---

[4]Ibid., 111-35. See also 136-38 on the main types of knowing, and 236-41 on the
way of knowing and the way of nonknowing. Obviously, I am not providing a formal
exposition and definition of what knowledge is, nor am I trying to "demonstrate" that
minute organisms are in fact aware. I am simply indicating my own philosophical view
of knowledge. It may be that if it can be shown that an organism is definitely an animal,
it has awareness; indeed the way to show or "monstrate" that an organism is animal is
to establish that it is cognitive.

[5]*Science and Wisdom*, trans. Bernard Wall (New York: Scribner, 1940) 70.

tion is intellectual formation and the *indirect* is moral formation. In the total educational environment, which embraces far more than the classroom (although Maritain sometimes says this covers the "extra-educational sphere," properly speaking) the two cannot be or should not be separated. The developing sense of truth, fostered by the teacher as something to be reverenced and to carry one beyond the mere selfish or individualistic or self-preoccupied self, should sustain one in the quest of the good (*EC* 24-25).

Jacques Maritain recognizes much of merit in the pragmatic and instrumentalist theories of education, particularly in the area of techniques, means, methodology. Still, he criticizes these theories for their failure to have "trust in truth."

> Every human idea, to have a meaning, must attain in some measure (be it even in the symbols of a mathematical interpretation of phenomena), what things *are* or consist of unto themselves; it is because human thought is an instrument or rather a vital energy of knowledge or spiritual intuition (I don't mean "knowledge about," I mean "knowledge into"); it is because thinking begins, not only with difficulties but with *insights*, and ends up in insights which are made true by rational proving or experimental verifying, not by pragmatic sanction, that human thought is able to illumine experience, to realize desires which are human because they are rooted in the prime desire for the unlimited good, and to dominate, control, and refashion the world. At the beginning of human action, insofar as it is human, there is truth, grasped and believed to be grasped for the sake of truth. Without trust in truth, there is no human effectiveness. Such is, to my mind, the chief criticism to be made of the pragmatic and instrumentalist theory of knowledge. (*EC* 13)

Since he asserts that "teaching's domain is the domain of truth" (*EC* 26), it follows that Maritain would also insist education should not be denied to anyone. His thesis of *liberal education for all* is best understood by beginning with his distinction between *natural intelligence* and *intellectual virtue*. In the older traditional societies it was a major aim of education to form leaders or an elite group, whether it be clergy (especially in the Middle Ages) or gentlemen being trained "to run the Empire" (in the English schools and universities in the past two centuries). In the democratic societies of our day, it is vital that everybody of normal capability be afforded the opportunity of education that is truly liberal and centered on the humanities. For Maritain, there are three great periods in education.

> I should like to designate them as the rudiments (or elementary education), the humanities (comprising both secondary and college education), and advanced studies (comprising graduate schools and higher specialized learning). And these periods correspond not only to three natural chronological periods in the growth of the youth but also to three natural distinct and qualitatively determinate spheres of psychological development, and, accordingly, of knowledge. (*EC* 58)

At the third level of advanced studies, it is proper to aim at the development of intellectual virtue, in which students or, rather, scholars come to possess a steady and steadfast grasp of the principles, methods, arguments or demonstrations, and causes or ultimate explanatory factors of their discipline, thus possessing what I termed above KNOWLEDGE, or mastery of their field. In the past and perhaps even today, according to Maritain, the second level of the humanities was conceived along the same lines, as though aiming at intellectual virtue itself. This notion is misguided, says Maritain. The studies in the humanities program, which in his general plan comprises a period of seven years, ages thirteen to nineteen (three years of secondary education and four years of college education), should aim at laying "the foundations of wisdom" in adolescents. The program should aim at guiding and forming "the natural intelligence." Otherwise, we risk producing intellectual dwarfs. (Here again Maritain explains that modern psychology helps us to understand the world of children and the world of adolescents; they are not little adults.)

In contrasting natural intelligence and intellectual virtue and what each learns, what one says (even what Maritain says) about natural intelligence may seem vague. "Intellectual virtue" is definite and clear-cut; what exactly does "natural intelligence" arrive at? Yet every good teacher and good student knows the difference between the scholar's knowledge of his or her field and the student's appreciation of it; the difference between an English major's appreciation of physics and the physics major's appreciation of history.

> We act as if the task of education were to infuse into the child or the adolescent, only abridging and concentrating it, the very science or knowledge of the adult— that is to say, of the philologist, the historian, the grammarian, the scientist, etc., the most specialized experts. So we try to cram young people with a chaos of summarized adult notions which have been either condensed, dogmatized, and textbookishly cut up or else made so easy that they are reduced to the vanishing. As a result, we run the risk of producing either an instructed, bewildered intellectual dwarf, or an ignorant intellectual dwarf playing at dolls with our sciences. (EC 59)

At the stage of college education, the objective is

> less the acquisition of science itself or art itself than the grasp of their *meaning* and the comprehension of the truth or beauty they yield. It is less a question of sharing in the very activity of the scientist or the poet than of nourishing oneself intellectually on the results of their achievement. (EC 63)

To appreciate the insight of Jacques Maritain into education, one must recognize the importance of his argument that the liberal arts must be reintegrated so as to include the physical sciences, the human sciences, the literary and historical disciplines and philosophy.[6] As I have written in the introduction to *The Education of Man:*

> The physical sciences, and others patterned upon them, must regain their humanistic character. One of the principal contributions of Catholic education could, in our opinion, be the achievement of this synthesis of the humanities. Physics and mathematics, according to Maritain, are liberal arts of the first rank and integral parts of the humanities. Indeed, physics is akin to poetry, if we look upon it in the light of the creative impulse within it which has led to so many marvelous discoveries. Maritain likes to imagine a curriculum in which all the humanities would be animated by the creative spirit. "In such a perspective," he says, "science and poetry are at one; humanity appears as a single being growing from generation to generation thanks to the inner quickening spirit it has received from God." (*EM* 18)

For Maritain, the primary goal of education is the attainment of internal freedom. What this means in the life of persons is explained more fully below. For our philosopher of education an essential though secondary goal is preparing citizens for participation in the social and political order to which they belong. (It is true, of course, that every society, even the most "primitive," has some "training" or "formation" for preparing the young to be useful members therein.) Maritain writes: "In a social order fitted to the common dignity of man, college education should be given to all, so as to complete the preparation of the youth before he enters that state of manhood. To introduce specialization in this sphere is to do violence to the world of youth" (*EC* 64).

He also speaks of "the highest aim of liberal education." Here one may raise a question: Wisdom as enjoyed as intellectual virtue is one thing; it is KNOWLEDGE. What is the 'wisdom' or 'foundation of wisdom' or knowledge enjoyed by natural intelligence? Does 'wisdom' count as 'wisdom' if it is qualified in this way? Maritain shows, in my judgment, that liberal education is not merely a stepping-stone to advanced study. It does attain something "terminal," that is, what he calls terminal freedom or freedom of autonomy. It should not be compared perhaps with the depth and certitude of one possessing KNOWLEDGE, but the liberally educated person does have Knowledge with a broad view and a richness all its own. "Nobody," Maritain asserts,

> can do without philosophy, and . . . the only way of avoiding damage wrought by an unconscious belief in a formless and prejudiced philosophy is to develop a philosophy consciously. Furthermore metaphysics is the only human knowledge which actually claims to be wisdom, and to have such penetration and universality that it can actually bring the realm of the sciences into unity, cooperation,

---

[6]On the reinterpretation of the humanities, see *EM* ch. 3, and pp. 17-18.

and accord. . . . Education deals ultimately with the great achievements of the human mind; and without knowing philosophy and the achievements of the great thinkers it is utterly impossible for us to understand anything of the development of mankind, civilization, culture, and science. (*EC* 71)

When Maritain uses the term "natural intelligence" he does not simply mean "intelligence in the bare state." Rather, he refers to an intelligence ready to embark on the study of humanities, fresh from the first period of studies filled with "rudimentary" learning and awakened to the depths of the spiritual preconscious (in its childlike state) to the beauty of things. Speaking of the child's "mysterious expectant gravity," he says,

> beauty is the mental atmosphere and the inspiring power fitted to a child's education, and should be, so to speak, the continuous quickening and spiritualizing contrapuntal base of that education. Beauty makes intelligibility pass unawares through sense-awareness. It is by virtue of the allure of beautiful things and deeds and ideas that the child is to be led and awakened to intellectual and moral life. (*EC* 61)

Maritain's conception of natural intelligence, of liberal education, of knowledge and awareness, all in relation to what he calls "the dynamics of education," is rooted in his idea of the "spiritual preconscious."

Education, says Maritain, should be concerned with the irrational and subconscious domains of the child's psyche. Within the depths of the human person there dwells, according to Jacques Maritain, the "spiritual unconscious or preconscious," specifically distinct from Freud's "automatic unconscious," though in vital intercommunication with it. Drawing from Aquinas and Aristotle, as well as modern psychologists and psychoanalysts, Maritain developed this conception into one of his original and profound contributions to philosophical anthropology and to philosophy of education. He sets it forth at length in his masterwork, *Creative Intuition in Art and Poetry* (English ed., 1953; French ed., 1966), and the idea permeates his writings on apparently disparate topics.[7] He stresses in his educational works that important changes would take place in teaching and learning if the school accorded priority to awakening and liberating the spiritual aspirations of the person. "In reality that to which we are called by our genuinely human aspirations is to free and purify the spiritual preconscious

---

[7]*Creative Intuition in Art and Poetry* (New York: Pantheon Books, 1953), particularly chaps. 3 and 4. In a work concerned with art and poetry, Maritain points out that "it is in this translucid spiritual night that poetry and poetic inspiration have their primal source" (106). What Maritain says here of the "spiritual preconscious" and poetry may be applied to other "knowings," and it is this "free life of the intellect" to which the master teacher guides the student.

from the irrational one, and to find our sources of life and liberty and peace in this purified preconsciousness of the spirit" (*EC* 42).

According to Maritain, what matters most in the life of reason is intellectual insight or intuition.

> With regard to the development of the human mind, neither the richest material facilities nor the richest equipment in methods, information, and erudition are the main point. The great thing is the awakening of the inner resources and creativity. The cult of technical means considered as improving the mind and producing science by their own virtue must give way to respect for the spirit and dawning intellect of man! Education that calls for an intellectual sympathy and intuition on the part of the teacher, concern for the questions and difficulties with which the mind of the youth may be entangled without being able to give expression to them, a readiness to be at hand with the lessons of logic and reasoning that invite to action the unexercised reason of the youth. . . . What matters most in the life of reason is intellectual insight or intuition. There is no training or learning for that. Yet if the teacher keeps in view above all the inner center of vitality at work in the preconscious depths of the life of intelligence, he may center the acquisition of knowledge and solid formation of the mind on the freeing of the child's and the youth's intuitive power. (*EC* 43)

Here as throughout the work on education, Maritain stresses that the task of the teacher is liberation.

Ranking in importance with his teaching on the preconscious of the spirit is Maritain's insight into what he calls "the conquest of freedom." His major study on this topic (first published in 1940) has important implications for education, even though it is more concerned with internal freedom in itself and with true and false emancipation in the sociopolitical order.[8] Along with other dominant

---

[8]*EM* 159-79. I present here texts from "The Conquest of Freedom" indispensable for an understanding of its relevance to education.

If the proper sign of personality consists, as I have just said, in the fact of being independent, of being a whole, it is clear that personality and freedom of independence are related and inseparable. In the scale of being they increase together; at the summit of being God is person in pure act. . . . In each of us personality and freedom of independence increase together. For man is a being in movement. If he does not augment, he has nothing, and he loses what he had; he must fight for his being. The entire history of his fortunes and misfortunes is the history of his effort to win, together with his own personality, freedom of independence. He is called to the conquest of freedom.

Two basic truths must be noted here. The first is that the human being, though a person and therefore independent because he is a spirit, is, however, by nature at the lowest degree of perfection and independence because he is a spirit

themes of his philosophy of the person and philosophy of eduation, it is developed out of and in accordance with the Aristotelian and Thomistic tradition (not overlooking his recourse to Saint Paul), and at the same time it stands out as yet another profound and original contribution to educational thought.

Jacques Maritain tells us in the first chapter of *Education at the Crossroads* that the primary goal of education is "the conquest of individual and spiritual freedom to be achieved by the individual person, or, in other words, his liberation through knowledge and wisdom, good will and love" (*EC* 11).

The freedom he speaks of here is called *terminal* freedom as distinct from *initial* freedom or freedom of choice. It is also called freedom of autonomy, freedom of fulfillment or exultation. In liberal education such freedom is the terminus of one's pursuit of humanistic studies and even though it is true that education is lifelong, it is also true that there are moments in one's school education when Knowledge is possessed and one finds oneself at or with a fulfilling end of term. In other words, humanistic education is not a means to an end, it is not merely

---

united substantially with matter and implacably subject to a bodily condition. Secondly, no matter how miserable, how poor, how enslaved and humiliated he may be, the aspirations of personality in him remain unconquerable; and they tend as such, in the life of each of us as in the life of the human race, toward the conquest of freedom.

The aspirations of personality are of two kinds. On the one hand, they come from the human person *as human* or as constituted in such a species; let us call them "connatural" to man and specifically human *insofar as he is a person* or participating in that transcendental perfection that is personality and which is realized in God infinitely better than in us. Let us call them then "transnatural" and metaphysical aspirations.

The connatural aspirations tend to a relative freedom compatible with conditions here below, and the burden of material nature inflicts upon them from the very beginning a serious defeat because no animal is born more naked and less free than man. The struggle to win freedom in the order of social life aims to make up for his defeat.

The transnatural aspirations of the person in us seek superhuman freedom, pure and simple freedom. And to whom belongs such freedom if not to Him alone who is freedom of independence itself, subsistent by itself? Man has no right to the freedom proper to God. When he aspires by a transnatural desire to this freedom, he seeks it in an "inefficacious" manner and without even knowing what it is. Thus divine transcendence imposes immediately the admission of a profound defeat on the part of these metaphysical aspirations of the person in us. However, such a defeat is not irreparable, at least if the victor descends to the aid of the vanquished. The movement to win freedom in the order of the spiritual life aims precisely to make up for this defeat. (*EM* 165-66)

a preparation for intellectual virtue in the strict sense, for advanced studies, or for specialization. It is an end or culminates in an end (though it is what Maritain calls an "infravalent end," not the ultimate end), one in which liberal education liberates and leads to the winning of an autonomous liberty.

Besides the primary aim, there is a secondary essential aim: "Man's education must be concerned with the social group and prepare him to play his part in it." Of this he says,

> Shaping man to lead a normal, useful and cooperative life in the community, or guiding the development of the human person in the social sphere, awakening and strengthening both his sense of obligation and responsibility, is an essential aim. But . . . the ultimate end of education concerns the human person in his personal life and spiritual progress, not in relationship to his social environment. (*EC* 14-15)

He goes on to show that there is a sort of "intermingling" of these freedoms, another prime instance of this integration in liberation to life to be fostered: "Man finds himself by subordinating himself to the group, and the group attains its goal only by serving man and by realizing that man has secrets which escape the group and a vocation which is not included in the group" (*EC* 14-15).

One of the dominant themes of Maritain's philosophy and education is "liberal education for all." Each person (at least of normal capability) should have the opportunity to attain education's primary aim of internal freedom in the intellectual order (though it could be and is in a different but analogous sense in the moral order) and its secondary aim of participating fully and autonomously in the social-political order. Corresponding to this secondary aim is the duty of free society *to teach the democratic charter* so that the freedom is effectively safeguarded and available to all.

For Jacques Maritain, one of the most vital tasks of a democratic society is to teach the charter by which it lives, its table of rights and duties based upon natural law and codified in positive law. There have been neo-skeptics, particularly in the tumultuous thirties haunted by the specter of totalitarianism, who claimed that teachers in a democratic society should be "impartial" or "neutral" and merely expose all sides of a question. Maritain argued that we should not imitate or ape the venal propagandizing of the Fascists and Communists and above all we should reject their shrewd use of psychic coercion. As is well known, they propagandize their views in state-controlled schools and ruthlessly suppress divergent views and at the same time claim and demand freedom to expound theirs in free societies. Maritain is keenly aware of the menace in this situation (as he brings out in "The Gospel and the Pagan Empire" in his *The Twilight of Civilization*, 1943). His own position is simply put. On the one hand, teaching the democratic charter is not mere propagandizing; on the other hand, the teacher in a democratic society should not be "neutral." He should profess his convictions, teach democratic values, yet discuss all aspects of a question and respect the student's mind.

The question of teaching the charter by which a political society lives could not arise in totalitarian and most other societies. Such regimes simply inculcate the ethos every societal member accepts or is constrained to accept. In a democratic society the notion arose that every side of a question should be heard and that the teacher should be neutral even regarding those questions involving its own survival.

In his "Some Typical Aspects of Christian Education," Maritain provides a more complete account of the role of Christianity (and even of the Church) in education.[9] What we have touched upon so far is mainly from the perspective of his Christian philosophy of education. Here we have the perspective of theology, religion, and spirituality presented not in a formal way but with a view of showing their valuable and indispensable practical role in the total education of the human person. According to Maritain, Christian education has a twofold task, to incorporate or assimilate into itself whatever is valuable in human thought and to foster and impart the appreciating of religious values and the living of the supernatural life.

With regard to the first task, the mission of the Christian school is to survey and impart the ensemble of human culture. Our watchword should be "enlargement," a Christian-inspired enlargement and no narrowing, even Christian-centered narrowing, of the humanities (*EM* 136).

The deep explanation of this view of Maritain, which goes back to Saint Basil and Saint Augustine and other Christian humanists, is to be found in another paradox in his philosophy: the secular and the sacred in creation and in the human order. The secular, the political and social order, has its distinctive place, and in recent times its proper autonomy has been recognized (this is a dominant theme in *Integral Humanism*); there is nothing that is not sacred in God's creation (this he says in *The Degrees of Knowledge*).[10] In the field of education, nothing is alien or remote from Christian scholars and students; all things are part of creation and those that have a role in the secular, with its distinctive character, merit study. This extends to the study of pagan classics in which ancient Christian writers detected an evangelical preparation.

The distinctive features of Christian education emphasized by Maritain are those of a more practical nature rather than those of formal structure and the formal program or curriculum. He stresses the need for small groups or teams of

---

[9]*EM* 129-53.

[10]*DK*, ch. 1, "The Majesty and Poverty of Metaphysics."

students to take the lead in religious life and practice, and to study sacred scripture in small circles and not only in class; he stresses the supremacy of sacred theology in the scale of sciences or knowledges, but insists that imperialism should be avoided. He emphasizes the benefits of studying theology, at least under certain conditions, not as a compulsory subject but as a free choice. Much more might be said about this important topic; it should be recalled, however, that Maritain's Christian philosophy of education embraces ideas available to what we call "natural reason" but which were attained by properly philosophical reasoning under the influence of the Gospel.[11]

---

[11]*EM*, ch. 6, esp. 133-42. In regard to liberal education for all as a *"late* fructification of a Christian principle,"* he says in the same essay,

The notion of liberal education for all is, in my opinion, one of those concepts which are in themselves close to the requirements of natural law, and appear obviously valid once we think them over, but which were long repressed, so to speak, or prevented from being uttered in consciousness, because social conditions and social prejudice, condemning the greater number of men to a kind of enslaved life, made such concepts impracticable, which is as much as to say unthinkable. This concept of liberal education for all is a late fructification of a Christian principle, it is intimately related to the Christian ideal of the spiritual dignity of man and the basic equality of all men before God.

I present the following text from *Education at the Crossroads*, one of the most characteristic on education in Maritain's works:

Speaking therefore from the Catholic point of view, I should like to say that what seems to me to be especially required by our time is the creation of centers of spiritual enlightenment, or schools of wisdom, in which those interested in spiritual life would be able to lead a common life during some weeks, to be trained in the ways of spiritual life and contemplation, and to learn that science of evangelical perfection which is the highest part of theology. The immense treasure of the writings and doctrines of the great spiritual authors and the saints, which compose the mystical tradition of Christendom, from the Desert Fathers to St. John of the Cross and the mystics of modern times, would thus be made available to them. They would become acquainted both with the theological knowledge concerned and with the history, personality, and teachings of those heroes of faith and love whose call, according to Henri Bergson, passes through mankind as a powerful "aspiration" toward God. I conceive of these schools as houses of hospitality and enlightenment for human souls, which would be grounded on the integrity of a given religious faith and way of life, but which would be open not only to those sharing in this faith but also to all who desire to spend some days of spiritual refreshment there and to learn what they are ignorant of. People who assure the continuity of life and teaching in these schools of wisdom would stay there permanently. (85)

The Prospects for Implementing
Maritain's Christian Philosophy of Education

In this study I have not treated explicitly Maritain's program for each educational level (elementary schooling, humanities or liberal education, advanced or university study) but have concentrated principally upon the middle ground of liberal education. It should be noted that the idea of this kind of education permeates all levels, that is, there is a sort of preliberal education in the elementary stage. In the advanced stage (to which in the European manner Maritain limits the term "university"), the scholars became proficient in their own disciplines (their specialties, if you will) and acquire a deeper appreciation of other fields (if only by way of play or in their free time). Thus, this level is in turn pervaded by a spirit of universality and humanism. Throughout every phase of education *integration* or *reintegration* is called for. This unification, the teacher's chief task, should be accomplished not only by basic structures and formal programs but also by special institutes (Maritain even outlines the orders or levels on which these would operate), by small organized teams of students, and by other groupings inspired by kindred educational ideals.

The fulfillment of these educational aims is threatened in our time by a degrading of knowledge from the qualitative to the quantitative order. In my view, there is a subtle *materialization* of knowledge and knowing, a materialization that is winning the minds not only of savants but of ordinary mortals. Stanley Jaki pointed out in the 1960s the danger in "quantizing" knowledge, in reducing it to what can be measured. [12] Obviously, we have faced this danger since the days of the early Greek philosophers, but in our time science has worked so many wonders that wisdom seems like a wraith. Obviously too, as Maritain points out in his *Science and Wisdom*, the two knowledges are harmonizable, but in practice it is becoming difficult to accomplish this end. [13]

This can be illustrated by placing knowledge (knowledge, Knowledge, KNOWLEDGE) on the computer screen. It must be "shrunk" to one dimension; it must become unidimensional. For simplification and avoidance of ambiguity the word "knowledge" should be replaced (as I imagine) by the term "NOLEJ." With this simplification ambiguity may be avoided, but the rich diversity of meaning (compare the evocativeness of poetic language) evanesces and there is naught but NOLEJ.

---

[12]Stanley L. Jaki, *Brain, Mind, and Computers* (South Bend IN: Gateway Editions, 1969) esp. 252-61.

[13]In *The Degrees of Knowledge* Maritain says, "It is only too clear that the march of humanity under the sway of money and mechanics marks a progressive materializing of intellect and of the world" (15).

All this is of course only a dream, or perhaps a nightmare.

This exposition of Jacques Maritain's educational ideas and ideals leads us to the threshold of the question we are bound to ask: What are the prospects of these ideals? What likelihood is there that they will be implemented in the free societies of the world?

Maritain has told us that he envisages immense tasks ahead in the following areas:

1. the building of a new social order (the "New Christendom");
2. the building of a fully constituted Christian philosophy—autonomous yet with evangelical inspiration;
3. the building of a new "educational commonwealth."

As for the ideal liberal education and the ideal university that he has portrayed in his educational writings, they are described in lofty terms comparable to those used to characterize the new social order itself. Maritain emphasizes that these are not pure utopias but concrete realizable ideals. It is clear that he does not anticipate the imminence of such a realization. Rather we should face up to the reality that generations will be laboring at these tasks. Such endeavors would involve scores of dedicated, knowledgeable women and men banded together by leaders of colossal stature. In the case of ardent Catholics, there would be the inspirational guidance of the social teachings of such popes as Pius XI, John XXIII, Paul VI, and John Paul II.

Against such a movement, if movement it did become, there stand arrayed the powerful forces of secularism and scientism (not science itself but an excessive addiction to it). There are the following obstacles: (1) the *loss* of the sense of being (Maritain frequently returns to this and related themes, the lack of a sense of love, truth, and so forth); (2) the *weakening* of appreciation for knowledge and fidelity (Maritain in his inspiring study *Ways of Faith* points out the insidiousness of the spreading substitution of verification for truth, methods of verifying replacing insight into truth and reality), which undermines the support system for those who believe; (3) the slough of indifference, the lack of discernment prevalent today (on a scale even greater than when Maritain was writing in the 1940s) in which the "immoral" becomes "amoral" and in which the line between the moral and the immoral is obliterated or blurred.

Jacques Maritain speaks of the "superadded burdens" (I call them obstacles) faced by the "education for the world of tomorrow." One of the worst dangers is not the active hostility to what Christian philosophy propounds but the indifference to it. (There is a parallel in what John Paul II excoriates as the mentality of consumerism.)

In the 1930s and 1940s Jacques Maritain wrote about the modern world's dying away and a new one emerging. Forty years later the modern world is still very much with us. One understands, then, that Maritain does not imagine that great changes are going to occur overnight. There is, however, another side to the situation. He asks us not to overlook the inestimable significance of little groups acting on a small scale but striving for a great goal. This is an idea to which he returns again and again, the importance of little teams and little flocks striving for the aims outlined in this essay on his educational thought. He is wont to hold up Little Brothers and Little Sisters of Jesus as inspirational and apposite examples. A grand educational commonwealth may not come for a long time, but the teams of teachers, scholars, and students can build little "educational republics." These in turn not only pave the way for the grand one (the "concrete realizable idea") but have a value all their own.

We have here another of the paradoxes (sometimes merely apparent, sometimes indicating a mystery in the natural order) brought out by Maritain in every "area" and "aspect" of his philosophic thought. On the one hand, the task is so immense that generations are needed for its realization; on the other hand, even little flocks of dedicated persons are able to accomplish great things albeit on a small scale and bring themselves and others to freedom and fulfillment. Even a "little" act like awakening a mind to a simple truth has, like the proverbial drop of water in God's name, consequences far reaching and beyond measure. This is the ultimate message of Jacques Maritain on education; this is why it is neither pessimistic nor optimistic but, rather, realistic, as befits his Christian philosophy.

JOSEPH PAPPIN III

Maritain's Ethics for an Age in Crisis

Our Age in Crisis

MARITAIN LEAVES NO DOUBT that ours is an age in crisis. He declares,

> For the moment we are at the lowest point; human history today is in love with fear and absurdity, human reason with despair. The powers of illusion are spreading all over the world, throwing all compasses off direction . . . men are simply losing the sense of truth . . . they will believe nothing they are told, but will rely only upon savage experience and elementary instincts.[1]

In this chapter I wish to offer some reflections on Maritain's ethics, not in an exhaustive way but rather with an effort to understand some of the moral problems of our times.[2] In doing so I hope not to invite the reader to share some sense

---

[1]Jacques Maritain, *The Range of Reason* (New York: Scribner's, 1952) 116-17; hereafter cited as *RR*.

[2]Maritain develops his ethical philosophy in a great many books and essays. In addition to the major texts, which are cited throughout the present chapter, see *Neuf leçons sur les notions premières de la philosophie morale* (Paris: Pierre Tequi, 1951); *The Rights of Man and Natural Law,* trans. Doris C. Anson (New York: Scribner's, 1943); *Freedom in the Modern World,* trans. Richard O'Sullivan (New York: Scribner's, 1936); *An Essay on Christian Philosophy,* trans. Edward Flannery (New York: Philosophical Library, 1955); *The Responsibility of the Artist* (New York: Scribner's, 1960); and *Education at the Crossroads* (New Haven: Yale University Press, 1943). Another work pertinent to an attempt to approach the ethical implications of our age's crises is *Integral Humanism,* trans. Joseph W. Evans (New York: Scribner's, 1968).

of superiority to our times through focusing upon obvious signs of our moral dilemma but to see how timely are the reflections and analyses of the human condition by a philosopher in the realist tradition of Thomas Aquinas. In some respects I will explore precisely Maritain's own ethical formulations; but throughout I will seek to draw Maritain's thought into a constructive confrontation with the ethical existential condition of our times. My purpose, therefore, is to highlight the human condition as expressed in our present age from the moral standpoint and to consider how that condition can find a guide in the Thomistic realism of Jacques Maritain.

In an essay called "Integral Humanism and the Crisis of Modern Times," Maritain condemns the "anthropocentric conception of man" in these words: "Having given up God as to be self-sufficient, man has lost track of his soul. He looks in vain for himself; he turns the universe upside down trying to find himself; he finds masks, and behind the masks, death."[3] We have here the end result of the secularizing process, a process in part begun with the Enlightenment's turn to pure reason and away from all authority or dogma, save the authority of individual reason. But even here mankind risks self-defeat. Instead of the autonomy of reason securing, through this process of secularization, an unassailable foundation of truth upon which to firmly ground all action, we witness, as Maritain proclaims,

> the progressive loss, in modern ideology, of all the certitudes coming either from metaphysical insight or from religious faith, which had given foundation and granted reality to the image of Man in the Christian system. The historic misfortune has been the failure of philosophic Reason. . . . Human Reason lost its grasp of Being, and became available only for the mathematical reading of sensory phenomena (*RR* 186).

But is this not all rather extreme? Is it not compounding bleakness upon bleakness? Is this depiction of modern man not myopic and severe? Does it not result from a false generalization of certain moral trends that come and go, rise and fall with the moral pulse of the times? Is there not a corrective mechanism lodged within the heart of at least Western civilization, which mechanism, once regulated to current conditions, will restore sufficiently our moral balance in order that, as a minimum, civilization will prevail, muddle forward, and, if not achieve lofty heights, secure safe passage adequate to forestall the fate of previous civilizations? Granted, each of us possesses a certain inclination to evil, yet is not the historical impact of Western civilization on the common consciousness such

---

[3]Jacques Maritain, *Scholasticism and Politics*, translation ed. Mortimer J. Adler (Garden City NY: Doubleday, Image Books, 1960) 13; cited hereafter as *SP*.

as to ensure an adequate quotient of common goodness, if not occasional saintliness?

Two immediate responses come to mind here. First, Maritain's prophetic voice does not go without a contemporary echo. We are all familiar with the prophetic zeal of Aleksandr Solzhenitsyn, Malcolm Muggeridge, and Mother Teresa of Calcutta. But very recently, and from a philosophical quarter, comes a startlingly similar assessment of the moral crisis of our times from Alasdair MacIntyre in a book that has captured, as few recent books in philosophy have done, the attention of the broad spectrum of the philosophical and intellectual world: *After Virtue*. At the beginning of this work MacIntyre declares that "we have—very largely, if not entirely—lost our comprehension, both theoretical and practical, of morality."[4] It is true, we still utilize fragments, bits and pieces of our inherited moral language, rooted as it is in the classical tradition, especially through Aristotelianism. But the consistency of rational support has been withered and corroded by a plethora of moral valuations that really reduce to the triumph of emotivism as the ground of morality. Thus, there is no rational foundation; there is no objective morality buttressed by an adequate appeal to rational, coherent standards. The ground of moral valuations lies in personal preference, or an appeal to the human emotions. And what is emotivism? It is, MacIntyre states, "the doctrine that all evaluative judgments and more specifically all moral judgments are *nothing but* expressions of preference, expressions of attitude or feeling, insofar as they are moral or evaluative in character" (*AV* 11). But what is this other than the triumph of liberal individualism, the glorification of the autonomy of the individual human will, or, as Maritain conceives it, "the false deification of man"? This is the triumph of radical individualism rooted in a metaphysical nihilism. But these are not MacIntyre's words, so I shall return to his further assessment.

MacIntyre, in surveying the moral theories of modern philosophy and our present age, concludes "that the language—and therefore to some large degree the practice—of morality is in a state of grave disorder" (*AV* 238). He speaks of having to survive "in these hard times," and further maintains that "the integral substance of morality has to a large degree been fragmented and then in part destroyed" (*AV* 5). MacIntyre believes this destruction of the substance of morality "marks a degeneration, a grave cultural loss" (*AV* 21). So grave is the loss that on the final page of his book MacIntyre can only point to "the new dark ages which are already upon us." This time, however, MacIntyre makes clear, "the barbarians are not waiting beyond the frontiers; they have already been governing for some time. And it is our lack of consciousness of this that constitutes part of our predicament" (*AV* 245).

---

[4]Alasdair MacIntyre, *After Virtue* (Notre Dame IN: University of Notre Dame Press, 1981) 2; cited hereafter as *AV*.

This is bold stuff, sobering talk from a much-respected member of the philosophical community, not just another Catholic philosopher baying in the wilderness. In short, man appears to have lost his way, and his thinking on moral matters seems to be incoherent, lacking in any sense, unjustifiable, without reason. If this is so, either our moral universe simply operates irrationally or there are reasons for what we do or should do that are being ignored or suppressed on a large scale.

Maritain's assessment of the human condition is thus confirmed almost exactly by at least another major contemporary philosopher. But why is this assessment of our times so important in an essay on Maritain's ethics? It is important because Maritain has refused to concede the existential dimension of philosophy exclusively to existentialists. The human condition is of vital importance to what Maritain regards in *Existence and the Existent* as "the fundamentally existential character of Thomist ethics."[5] Of course Maritain qualifies this "existential character" by reminding us that "Thomism is an existentialist intellectualism" (*EE* 47). I take this to mean that Saint Thomas's existentialism does not entail a foreclosure of reason or an embracing of irrationalism or radical subjectivism. Yet this existential character I believe as qualifying Thomist ethics requires that we place man accurately in his existing human condition in order to concretize our ethical considerations. And this human condition as Maritain views it hinges upon the false deification of man, a secularized worldview, an exaltation of the autonomy of the individual will, a narrowing of reason to the quantifiable and the rise of a nominalistic perspective, a reversion to primitive instincts and experience as a realm of authentic human experience—this does not exhaust the list, yet it helps specify components of our condition.

Both Maritain and MacIntyre warn that we are on the brink of a new age of barbarism—and by barbarism I take these authors to mean the destructive and chaotic character of so much human action that is a consequence of the moral relativism that has come to dominate the collective consciousness. We should also consider another almost paradoxical component of our situation. Amazingly, given the background of our situation I have depicted, Maritain can yet further characterize in this manner Western civilization: "It is dominated, no matter what it may do, and even when it denies it, by Christianity" (*SP* 225). After such a bleak depiction of the human condition how could this be the case? We should think on this point. In this same passage Maritain in effect goes on to say that so prominent has Christianity been, especially in certain areas of Europe, that it is almost unspoken of, so assumed that it bears no mention. Christianity is the horizon that envelops all discourse and action, and within which

---

[5]Jacques Maritain, *Existence and the Existent*, trans. Lewis Galantière and Gerald B. Phelan (New York: Vintage Books, 1966) 49; cited hereafter as *EE*.

all understanding proceeds. So enveloping, so encompassing has it become that it is taken for granted (*SP* 225). Human beings assume it when they set out to "free" themselves from it, prizing certain of its advances, such as its emphases upon liberty, love, and justice, yet wishing to secure these values independently of their proper context.

People may wish for the civility and humaneness that have their source in Christianity's impact upon civilization and yet disavow the context of faith, obedience, reverence, and yes, dogma that provides their support. The attempt at a Humean natural religion bears witness to this, as does a Rousseauian sense of community. In effect we can see in our times that civilization can forget the reasons for its actions—and in doing so rob human beings of any reasons for doing good and avoiding evil, of the knowledge of good and evil, of their purpose for acting in a virtuous manner. The context for ethical action within Western civilization has been provided for by Christianity. Christianity extolled certain virtues as reflecting God's glory, as proper to man's nature, as perfecting that nature and aiding in the perfection of the other, and as requiring the grace of Christ in order to be most fully realized in man. To separate love and justice from the Christian context is to attempt a disjointed, ruptured form of existing.

If Christianity has provided the ground of action then where do the moral virtues stand, virtues that aim to perfect our human nature? If, for example, honesty is a virtue, and if we urge others to govern their actions by this virtue and, at the same time, deny that there is any objective morality and claim that the basis of moral evaluation lies with personal preference, how can we justify honesty? At best honesty comes to play a utilitarian function—it is good business, or it secures the regime in power or the prevailing social structure. Conversely, honesty can come to be seen as an antivirtue within a certain political context in which violence and disruption and the grand lie are prized for political gain. Here honesty would have no intrinsic value—only an extrinsic value, requiring a certain sociopolitical context.

Maritain is vitally concerned with the moral condition of human existence. We must seek to understand as accurately as possible that condition in its total context, which requires that moral philosophy not become purely a speculative enterprise; it must include the results of anthropology, psychology, sociology, and every other discipline that can inform us of the existential ethical condition of man.[6] It is this concrete, existential motive that forces Maritain to place moral philosophy within the broader setting of moral theology.

We have noted the existential character of Thomist ethics, which Maritain represents. We have traced the outline of the crisis of our times as it affects the human moral condition. Eventually, we must turn to some of the specific ele-

---

[6]Ibid.

ments of Maritain's moral philosophy to see if it provides some direction out of the moral predicament of our times. But first, in order adequately to consider these elements, a brief synopsis of Maritain's metaphysics is necessary.

Preliminary Metaphysical Remarks

One of the dilemmas haunting modern man is human reason's loss of the grasp of being. There is no element or aspect of Maritain's philosophy that fails to rest ultimately upon his metaphysics. For Maritain, being is real, it is knowable, it reveals itself according to a hierarchy known in proportion to the human intellect, revealed according to the principle of philosophic analogy.[7] Metaphysical knowledge of being has its foundation in an intuition of the act of existing and is developed as a causal knowledge, originating in the senses, separated through abstraction, and revealed by an intellectual act of judgment. Each thing that *is* bears within itself a real distinction between its essence and existence, save the pure, infinite being who is God. It receives its act of existing according to its essence, which, in relationship to its *esse,* or act of existing, is a limiting principle. Its essence defines its nature, and its act of existing is the source of all its being, in its various modes and aspects, and the realization of its being through its acts is in terms of its nature. The nature of the thing is its defining, stabilizing principle, structuring its range of possible becoming, but ensuring its constancy throughout its duration. The intelligibility of the thing is therefore grounded in the twin metaphysical principles of existence and essence, and the essence of the thing provides the terra firma for the intellect in the act of knowing to comprehend the thing as it truly is.

In contrast, the moral ignorance and irrationalism permeating our age and witnessed by the rise of emotivism has, insofar as it makes a metaphysical statement at all, reduced all being to becoming. Gone is the Aristotelian-Thomistic universe of a hierarchical order of being. Remaining is being reduced entirely to becoming and parading under the guise of pure phenomena. Empiricism, in reducing knowledge to knowledge of phenomena, was actually, in trying to be scientific, denouncing all metaphysics and thus removing the support for all science.

The process commenced with rationalism; in despair of knowing with any certainty reality as it first comes to the knower by way of the senses, rationalism recoiled within the mind to discover knowledge deduced from the rules of thought, giving rise to a bifurcated world of thought over against matter. Thus

---

[7]Maritain's metaphysics is developed especially in *Distinguish to Unite or The Degrees of Knowledge,* trans. Gerald B. Phelan (New York: Scribner's, 1959), *A Preface to Metaphysics: Seven Lectures on Being* (New York: Sheed and Ward, 1948), and *Existence and the Existent.* This summary of his position reflects my own understanding.

severed, the material world lost its intelligibility, things were denuded of their essences, and the lawfulness and constancy governing the material world were stripped bare, leaving the ordering of the universe to calculative reason and the imaginative projections of the mind. What emerged was a pure world of becoming, which Hegel tried to salvage by postulating an absolute mind and idea that all becoming tries to realize.

Nietzsche saw the bankruptcy of modern philosophy's project of achieving an adequate knowledge of reality based on pure reason and declared the foundation of all reality to be, not a substrate of forms or a world of ideas or a phenomenal realm categorized by pure reason, but rather the will—the will as the will to power. In this he believed that he overcame the pretended virtues of classical philosophy and Christianity and supplanted them with the virtues of the Overman, who through the sheer strength of his will alone triumphs over the pretense of reason, acknowledging that all thought is fiction. Becoming had completely devoured being and in the process, all intelligibility. And as the nature of the thing according to classical philosophy signified what a thing is and thus established the law of its own actions, for a thing's actions were just and good as they served to perfect its nature, then any law of nature was simply a relic of a bygone age of fiction-thought for Nietzsche. The radical affirmation of being as becoming dismantled all semblance of order and intelligibility and opened morality to the claims of power. This conception of being therefore conditioned likewise the conception of morality. Here, right resides in the person or movement or ideology whose will can most forcefully establish itself as a law for all others.

Here enters an important qualification for Maritain. When we turn the eyes of philosophy to human nature what we see there is not pure nature but human nature in its existential state, a graced nature, a nature that has been elevated by the unmerited grace of God. As such, human nature, possessing an end beyond natural happiness, aims for a supernatural beatitude.[8] Philosophy, unaided by revelation, cannot know this, but a Christian philosophy, which in itself does not so much identify an organic knowledge, but is a complexus that receives insights from revelation and moral theology, can receive this knowledge; it cannot confirm it by pure reason, but it can acknowledge it by faith and use this knowledge as a secure guide for an otherwise truncated moral philosophy.

Pulling these strands together, Maritain's metaphysics affirms the intelligibility of being and avoids the slide into pure becoming. It affirms the reality of things in possession of natures, and of persons in possession of a human nature, which nature the Christian philosopher, in his concrete existential state of exist-

---

[8] Jacques Maritain, *Science and Wisdom*, trans. Bernard Wall (London: Geoffrey Bles, 1954) 109; cited hereafter as *SW*.

ing, recognizes both as fallen and elevated by grace. This being so, the destiny of an actually graced nature bears upon the actual moral conduct of the human person. And it is a fundamental tenet of Maritain's ethics that philosophy is subalternated to moral theology. We cannot do less in the area of Maritain's ethics than to reflect briefly upon his understanding of a Christian philosophy.

Christian Philosophy

How does Maritain seek to interpret the meaning of "Christian philosophy?" He finds the basis for a solution to lie in what he terms the "order of specification" and the "order of exercise," or, phrased differently, "nature" and "state." First, the "order of specification," or the nature of philosophy. Considered in its barest essence philosophy refers to a domain whose object is being both in its essence and act of existing and which object is knowable by the natural light of reason, whether this be the knowledge of a pagan or a Christian. In this sense, philosophy is in no way dependent upon Christian faith. Now consider the existential state in which many actually philosophize.

Man is not an abstracted essence; he is incarnational, spirit enfleshed, temporalized by the flux of history, and yet eternal by the nature of his spirit as received from his Creator. A contemporary philosopher in the actual content of his philosophizing, this content being twenty centuries of civilization permeated by Christianity, is aware of a minimum of basic tenets of the Christian faith as they have permeated the common consciousness. Such tenets as the creation of the universe and the immortality of the individual soul have helped shape the questions considered by all philosophers. Thus, when Maritain speaks of the "Christian state of philosophy,"[9] he means that Christian revelation has brought to the philosopher's consciousness questions to consider and even notions that in theory were possible to obtain but never were prior to God's revealed Word, such as "the notion of God as *Ipsum Esse per se subsistens.*"[10] In particular, modern moral philosophy since the Renaissance represents the "progressive secularization or 'naturizing' of the traditional Christian heritage."[11] With reference to Kant's moral philosophy Maritain goes further, stating that Kant's "accomplishment was dependent on fundamental religious ideas and a religious inspiration he had received in advance" (*EE* 49).

---

[9]Jacques Maritain, "About Christian Philosophy," in *Challenges and Renewals,* ed. Joseph W. Evans and Leo R. Ward (Cleveland: Meridian, 1986) 112.

[10]Ibid.

[11]Jacques Maritain, *Moral Philosophy: An Historical and Critical Survey of the Great Systems* (New York: Scribner's, 1964) 92; hereafter cited as *MP.*

Maritain construes the expression "Christian philosophy" not to refer to a bare essence but to an essence found in a certain state, hence a "complexus." He goes on to define Christian philosophy as "philosophy itself, insofar as it is placed in the typical conditions of existence and of exercise into which certain objects are *seen*, certain assertions are *validly established* by reason—which, under other conditions, more or less escape reason."[12]

Moral Philosophy
Subalternated to Moral Theology

The speculative concern with the possibility of a Christian philosophy has a specific application in the area of moral philosophy, and further emphasizes the existential character of Maritain's ethics.

No philosopher succeeded more fully in the natural order of ethics than did Aristotle. And yet his ethics necessarily failed. It failed not in the sense that it lacked a metaphysical foundation; not in the sense that it failed to recognize an ultimate end governing human acts, an end that culminates in "the primacy of the Supreme Good, or the happy life" (*MP* 35); not in the sense that it failed to note the relation of the virtues to the attainment of happiness; not in the sense that it failed to recognize a measure of our acts, that measure being right reason, which "was to become the keystone of moral philosophy in the Christian tradition" (*MP* 36): what Aristotle lacked was the recognition of the supernatural order as providing the actual completion of man's natural desire for happiness, being the vision of God in his essence—in short, beatitude. But, even in the natural order he failed to carry through to the natural conclusions of his principles. For Aristotle the common good attained in the polis comes to be the supreme good for individuals. Even his emphasis upon contemplation does not offer a transtemporal, transpolitical good; rather it serves to attain the common good in the city. Maritain replies to Aristotle: "For even in the purely natural order (where there is no question of beatific vision) it is not the earthly city but God Who is the absolute final end of man as of the whole universe" (*MP* 46).

More to the point, Aristotle's ethics failed to escape a fundamental egoism, an egoism grounded in the basic flaw of Greek ethics, the fusion of the good with happiness. Maritain protests this fusion and speaks of happiness as the "subjective side of the Good" (*MP* 48). The failure to separate the two makes the desire for happiness for the sake of the subject who desires it, not for the love of the good for its own sake. All of this serves to underscore what Maritain terms the "practical, existential weakness of Aristotle's ethics" (*MP* 49). Perhaps Aristotle

---

[12]Maritain, "About Christian Philosophy," 114.

went as far as philosophical reason could take him, requiring a supernatural wisdom to see that the good in itself is to be loved for itself, and that the good desires our own happiness and therefore, for the love of the good "our Happiness itself is loved." Maritain continues his critique of Aristotle: "the true principles of Aristotle's moral philosophy do not penetrate the concrete existential reality of the human being. . . . In a word, what is infinite in man has been forgotten" (*MP* 50).

What *is* the existential problem here for a correct moral philosophy? It is the ultimate inability of philosophical reason to provide an adequate guide for human conduct. Human reason *must* be supplemented in ethics or it runs the twofold and related risk of slipping into despair and egoism. Without the recognition that mortal man is destined to achieve his supreme end through an eternal life with God and the resultant perfect happiness this will bring, despair may seize the soul. And without the recognition that it is the good, which is not an idea but an existent being that is the full perfection of being, which man wills to see and love and attain friendship with, then man risks the snare of an egoism that desires above all else its own subjective happiness. It is the existential state of man, of actual man, that impels him beyond the paucity of a natural moral philosophy if the actual end of human conduct is to be realized and the perfection of the human person attained. In this light Maritain concludes:

> When moral philosophy wants to have an effective hold on the human being, and wants to deal not only with an abstract and simply possible man but with the real man, and with human conduct considered in its real condition of existence, it cannot remain pure moral philosophy and must enter into communication with a world of human data and aspirations more existential than that of philosophy isolated within itself. (*MP* 70)

Maritain develops the relationship of moral philosophy to moral theology, especially in his work *Science and Wisdom.* Of course, practical philosophy is concerned with the entire range of human action, and it must concern itself with those objects perfective of action. For Maritain, the notion of a pure moral philosophy that is sufficient to guide human action could have existed in the manner in which pure nature could have existed. And yet it never has so existed (*SW* 109). Moral philosophy is "subalternated" to moral theology. The former requires the latter in order to have its knowledge perfected, the principles of which are earthbound, commencing with the data of sensation. Otherwise, it is not adequate to guide human action.

Although subalternated to moral theology, moral philosophy is not absorbed into theology. The principles of theology are divinely given and shape a distinctive order of knowledge different from that of philosophy, which has its own principles.

On the principle that "grace completes nature and does not destroy it" (*SW* 112), Maritain justifies both the separation of moral theology from moral philosophy and the dependence of the latter on the former. The perspectives and approaches they bring are different and appropriate in their own sphere. Maritain illustrates by showing that both disciplines can be concerned with the same object, such as the supernatural last end of man, but consider the object under different aspects, moral theology being concerned with the intimate life of the soul with God and moral philosophy with the perfection of human nature (*SW* 117). Their separation and operation, in one sense, must be maintained; and yet the completion and perfection brought to moral philosophy by moral theology are required by the former if it is to function *as* moral philosophy. Therefore, Maritain can conclude:

> Moral philosophy adequately considered considers human conduct with its eternal and supernatural end, and its natural and temporal end primarily according as the life of man, without being in a state of pure nature, is ordered to a natural end and to temporal work, which are elevated but not abolished by their reference to the ultimate supernatural end. And this distinction is imposed on us because nature and grace are two worlds of different kinds which come together in man, one perfecting the other but not destroying it. (*SW* 119).

If one argues against Maritain that all of this is well and good, but that, nonetheless, a moral philosophy can and should function on its own, prescinding entirely from all admixture of faith and theology, Maritain replies that, in man's present existential state, it simply cannot be done. "It is not possible," Maritain declares, "to escape from the results of the irruption of faith into the structures of our knowledge" (*SW* 109). Having stated it in this manner, Maritain refuses to give ground on the distinction of moral theology from moral philosophy. The former is developed from "revealed truths" and focuses on the "mysteries of man and the drama of his life as a creature of flesh and spirit" (*SW* 120). The existential state in which Maritain finds man fuels his bold conclusions and leads him to deny any such thing as a pure philosophy, because philosophy cannot act in complete autonomy without going awry; rather, "it must be subalternated to theology because its object is not only human but—in the measure in which it is existentially human—also divine and supernatural" (*SW* 126).

Maritain's ethics centers on man's existential condition. To fail to see the dependency of ethics on theology, he holds, is to risk falling prey to an anthropocentric humanism; and so he is unswerving in his demand that ethics be properly related to theology in order to avoid just such a fate.

The Natural Knowledge of Moral Values

The sublaternation of moral philosophy to moral theology must not lead one to conclude that there is no natural knowledge of moral values, for in fact there is. By "natural" knowledge Maritain means a "prephilosophical" knowledge and means to distinguish this from a "philosophical" knowledge.

Moral philosophy presupposes moral experience. It is a "reflexive knowledge," a reflecting upon moral experience in order to understand it through concepts and judgments. This is not, however, what Maritain refers to as natural knowledge. He has in mind a knowledge through, as he phrases it, "inclination." There are two orders of inclination. The first is that of instincts: these are biologically rooted, shaped by childhood, not completely predetermined, capable of perversion but necessary to human life.

The second order of inclinations presupposes the first but have been swept into the "dynamism of the intellect's apprehensions."[13] The roots of these inclinations lie in reason and are the subject of an insight that is preconceptual, residing in a preconscious realm. We know by inclination that it is wrong to injure an innocent human being. When reason reflects upon this it feels at ease, "at home." These inclinations, which are known and yet may not ever be reflectively articulated by the one who bears them, may be at odds with inclinations that irrupt from our animal instincts, which may agitate us to murder another person. While the correct articulation of this second order of inclinations may be on the level of the moral injunction to "do unto others as you would have others do unto you," it remains an inclination, an inchoate yet "concrete notion," enveloped in the actual situation one encounters. Two insights are borne along in this order of inclinations, insights that are known preconceptually, felt, but, as it were, bathed in reason.[14] These insights are, "in lived act" (1) to treat "others as men" and (2) that in so doing to act in conformity "with something true that we carry within us (the philosopher will say, with reason)."[15]

Maritain is providing an integrated view of important recent psychological explorations, such as those provided by Freudian investigations, without plunging the human person into a cauldron of animal instincts as if the latter constituted the true humanity. Yes, there are strong affective and tendential dynamisms that are rooted and possibly perverted in our animal instincts and they *are* us, although not entirely us, constituting a certain material of our ethical substance that must be controlled, directed, given form to, but not extirpated. And concrete notions are already radiating in an ordering way through the affective animal inclinations by way of the second order of inclinations, which latter order

---

[13]Maritain, "The 'Natural' Knowledge of Moral Values," in Evans and Ward, *Challenges and Renewals,* 231.

[14]Maritain reminds us in *Creative Intuition in Art and Poetry* that "reason indeed does not only articulate, connect, and infer, it also sees" (New York: Meridian Books, 1958) 55.

[15]Maritain, "The 'Natural' Knowledge," 233.

is in basic conformity with the principle "what is in tune with reason, pleases the rational animal; what is out of tune with reason, displeases him."

Maritain goes further. Our common judgments of value, such as to give sustenance to the beggar at our door, come by the "mode of inclination," not by the "mode of cognition." Such judgments of value become embedded in the ethical conscience of mankind; they are values that, insofar as we permit them to do so, govern our actions. Maritain argues, "In reality, we are in the presence of judgments determined by inclinations which are themselves rooted in reason operating in a preconscious manner."[16]

Maritain is not claiming that such knowledge is sufficient. The explicit, conceptual knowledge obtained by the moral philosopher can help perfect the knowledge by inclination as moral theology helps perfect and complete moral philosophy. And yet such knowledge is not irrational or simply the product of social causes. To rise above our animal instincts and to recognize by a concrete, preconceptual insight that doing harm to an innocent person is not a justifiable act—such a concrete insight is pleasing to reason. But the moral philosopher wants to know in a reflexive manner why the concrete insights governing our actions are in fact authentic.

Freedom and the Moral Law

To this point, our discussion has attempted to situate ethics in the existential parameters within which man lives. In the remainder of this chapter I wish to turn to the substance of ethics as it crystallizes itself in two crucial concerns to the human condition, that of freedom and freedom's relationship to the moral law. To provide a guide for the human person an ethics can do no less than to develop an adequate response to these concerns.

Important and powerful currents in modern thought have served to attack our belief that our actions are in any way free. Determinism gained momentum with the favor obtained by Charles Darwin, Karl Marx, and Sigmund Freud. Our free actions appear to give way in determinism to the various iron laws of necessity unveiled by these thinkers. In popular form, Darwinism reduces human actions to a struggle for survival, making survival an end in itself, tied in with the improvement of the species. Marx reduces activity to a function of one's historical epoch and socioeconomic class. What we are is identifiable with our class interests, while the superstructure of ideas is determined by the material substructure of economic conditions. For Freud, our actions are governed by a subterranean undercurrent of desire, especially of sexual fulfillment, and dominated by an incestual component that places patricide at the heart of our motivations.

---

[16]Ibid., 234-35.

In order to "make it" within society we must repress our most fundamental dispositions, and thus civilization is constructed on the stooped shoulders of neurotic tendencies. The existential condition described here is one of deceit, of appearances. What appears to be the case is *not* the case. Manners, upon which so much of civilization is built, may become, to a Marxian, a veil upon which apparently gentlemanly comportment is really a function of tacit class warfare. Laws become a form of systematic class oppression, not a fabric of justice whereby order is achieved. Things are not what they appear to be. They cloak a realm of being that impedes the achievement of authentic human existence.

A different view of the human condition emerges with Jean-Paul Sartre. Sartre holds, against the determinists, that human beings must be free.[17] They cannot escape their freedom, try as they may. As we know, a Sartrean ontology divides the realm of being into being-in-itself and being-for-itself. The former realm contains all order of being that lacks consciousness. Such beings are identical with themselves. They are complete; they lack nothing; there is no process of becoming. But it is different with human reality.

Existence is becoming for Sartre. Essences are fixed. And as such they necessitate; they are static and prevent becoming. So, freedom is coterminous with existence as becoming. This process of becoming reveals a lack, a nothingness at the center of human reality. Man is not yet. But this condition of incompleteness ensures his freedom, for as a being whose very center possesses a lack of being, his future is open—he is not made or reduced to a thing.

Man's nothingness, the lack at the center of his being, is due to consciousness. Consciousness is beyond itself in the direction of the other. And yet man is a self-presence in the prereflective mode of consciousness. He is aware of himself in the process of becoming. He is not captured by the other, due to the nihilating action of consciousness. Nothing assures freedom more than the capacity of denial. I am not the other; I am not what you take me to be; I will not do what the tyrant demands—denial assures freedom.

Nevertheless I desire to become a freedom-thing, which is what God would be if he existed, *per impossible*. God would be a being-in-itself and for-itself. But this is a contradiction. Being-for-itself is a lack of being, which is the condition of its freedom. The former is completed, in no wise becoming. A freedom-thing is impossible. Therefore God does not exist. And yet it is the human project to become God. As this cannot be, life is reduced to a useless passion, a passion of striving-to-be, where striving remains and being is beyond us.

---

[17]The following discussion of Sartre's ontology of human reality reflects my own understanding of the same, especially as detailed throughout his main existential work, *Being and Nothingness* (New York: Washington Square Press, 1968).

Further, one's freedom is not subject to any nature or any law. As I am essenceless, lacking a nature, there is nothing to govern my acts. But this is liberating. There is no law of nature to condemn me. There is no God to compel me; all things are permitted—but here a hesitation arises; a moral "ought" begins to break through. My freedom can be fully achieved only when all others are free. Therefore to reduce others to servitude makes me dependent upon the acquiescence of the servant in order to be the master. Hegel has detailed this process. No one is free until all are free. Freedom, however, has no law to which to bow. Freedom is not a law but the ultimate value. Strictly, though, one is free to wrap one's self within a contradiction and suffocate one's being through the snare of enslavement, or bad faith. One *is* free to do what one will with one's freedom, save actually to deny it. We *are* condemned to be free. As Sartre declares, "In fact we are a freedom which chooses, but we do not choose to be free. We are condemned to freedom . . . or, as Heidegger says, 'abandoned.' "[18] It *is* the one necessity, by a strange twist of language.

The Sartrean view as developed in *Being and Nothingness* is so radical as to appear to be disconnected from any rootedness to community, tradition, or past. Though he speaks of being-in-a-situation, he gives the notion a distinctively Sartrean meaning. For some, our place or community would be determining features of our identity. For Sartre, yes, we are in a situation, and yes, "there is freedom only in a *situation*." But our situation has meaning for us only through our freedom, through our choices.[19] Again, freedom is so radical as to make of my world something arbitrary, forced, without reason—absurd.

What is the trait that characterizes modernity? As stated at the outset, for Maritain it is that our age has succumbed to an anthropocentric humanism. Everything revolves around human beings. We embrace a radical humanism in which one's own designs and self-interest undermine the basic thrust of a Christian ethics—love of one's neighbor as oneself. Our age is in danger of becoming a narcissistic, egocentric age that breaks down the former bonds of community, of tradition, and thus of the restraining and shaping fabric of civilization. But a freedom without a purpose that is more than the result of choice and is, instead, given in the order of things, leads Sartrean man to slide grievously into nausea and probably accounts as much as anything for Sartre's subsequent embrace of an existentialized Marxism.

In Maritain we discover an ethics in which freedom is given structure and order through the moral law. And hence the fullness of being is restored, for freedom requires law. An essenceless universe will not ground an adequate morality.

---

[18]Ibid., 623.
[19]Ibid.

And the nominalism of a sociologist will not suffice, either, in which appropriate action is considered to be that which mirrors prevailing mores or accepted custom. Sartre's answer to an essenceless, lawless freedom was to supplant essences with projects. Here my choices reflect self-chosen ends—ends without reason. Pushed far enough, a freedom without any check by law is an irrationalism. Hobbes precedes Sartre, as does Descartes. Will must precede reason in a Sartrean world, for all ends are a projection of an infinite will. Modern radical individualism harbors an irrationalism at its core; to Sartre, being is without reason or cause, since reasons and causes would restrict freedom.

For Maritain, there is a natural law that ought to govern human actions. The natural law is not meant to obstruct freedom but rather to ensure the complete realization of the human person through action. "Natural Law is the normality of functioning of the human being," Maritain reasons. He continues:

> Every kind of being existing in nature, a plant, a dog, a horse, has its own "natural law" that is, the proper way in which, by reason of its specific structure and ends, it "should" achieve fullness of being in its growth or in its behavior. . . . Natural Law—strictly speaking, Natural Law for man—is moral law, because man obeys or disobeys it freely.[20]

Maritain thus holds that freedom requires law, and in this conclusion he finds agreement from the father of existentialism, Søren Kierkegaard, who writes in the *Works of Love:* "without law freedom simply does not exist. . . . It is the law which gives freedom."[21]

Certainly Sartre saw at least two threats to acknowledging a natural law. First, laws restrict freedom, and second, law dissolves individuality, for it absorbs the particular into the universal. For Maritain it is the provision of universal moral laws in ethics that secures the authenticity of personal existence. Rather than restricting freedom, the natural law directs the authentic realization of myself through actions that are not random or arbitrary but that comport in a distinctively unique fashion—for they are mine—with the natural law. Thus Maritain concludes that "by suppressing generality and universal law, you suppress liberty; and what you have left is nothing but that amorphous impulse surging out of the night which is but a false image of liberty. Because when you suppress generality and universal law, you suppress reason, in which liberty, whole and entire, has its root" (*EE* 60-61).

---

[20]Jacques Maritain, "Natural Law and Moral Law," in Evans and Ward, *Challenges and Renewals*, 213-14.

[21]Søren Kierkegaard, *Works of Love*, trans. David Swenson (Princeton: Princeton University Press, 1946) 32-33.

What of the second threat, that law absorbs particularity into universality? Sartre fears that a universal law in ethics eliminates the uniqueness of our personal choices, reducing all of us to programmed, preordained behavior, insofar as we are law abiding. Again, Maritain rejects this position:

> When a man obeys the law in the manner of one faithful to the law . . . it is his own desire, deeper and stronger than that alluring attraction, his own appetite for the ends he desires beyond all else and desires for himself—it is this which harmonizes his will with the law (since it remains a will to good) and makes him identify his *self* with the *everyman* who is subject to the universal precept. (*EE* 58)

To order one's action to the universal law of ethics is not to check a vast book of predetermined responses in order to know what to do. Law *is* radically existentialized in the particularity of individual choices. The illuminating light provided by the law should penetrate the darkened recesses of our unique human acts and provide a guide sufficient for our prudential acts of moral judgment to expand the realm of being through the love of God and neighbor that should motivate our acts. Enter prudence and personal conscience; enter the incalculable aspects of the circumstances within which we act, which we must grasp and order in our moral judgments. There is almost too great a room, even when illumined by the natural law, within which individual choices and acts must move. For Maritain, "in every authentically moral act, man, in order to apply and in applying the law, must embody and grasp the universal in his own singular existence, where he is alone face to face with God" (*EE* 59).

The element of transcendence through love of being is missing in atheistic existentialism and in much of modern ethics. Self-interest expressed ethically through emotivism replaces this transcendence. Gabriel Marcel has characterized modern philosophy as a refusal of being. Instead, love of being, charity, must be the pulsating center of ethics. Maritain makes this clear as he cites the first doctrine in Thomist existentialism to be "the perfection of human life." Maritain holds that this consists in charity. . . . All morality thus hangs upon that which is most existential in the world. For love . . . does not deal with possibles or pure essences, it deals with existents" (*EE* 49-50).

Concluding Remarks

Jacques Maritain provides more than a corrective for what he takes to be the moral crisis of our times. A corrective simply adjusts the present course of action. Maritain requires that we go to the roots of our crisis and recover a mode of thought that it is in danger of annihilation, one that does not situate humanity at the ontological center of being, but, rather, restores us to our place in the hierarchy of being. Human beings are not the originators of thought and being, not the lawgivers for human actions. Instead, for Maritain, human beings discover an order in the realms of being and note a lawfulness that governs their thought and actions. We are free to refuse, but as we have seen, the price of refusal is our personal loss of freedom. Maritain's ethics hinges upon the acknowledgment of an infinite Being who freely creates and gives to us both the necessity of our own being and the freedom to actualize our nature through our moral acts. But more than that, the Christian moral philosophy Maritain espouses requires that we acknowledge the authentic existential destiny of man, a destiny revealed to us through Christian revelation, a destiny where the human person is called to spend eternity in the felicitous state of friendship with God and neighbor as the highest fulfillment of the moral law and the simultaneous realization of genuine freedom.

The modern age, on the other hand, reveals a tendency, one that is attempting to do the impossible: to build itself upon the refusal to be. It denies any authentic human nature save that which is self-legislated. It denies any law save that which absolutizes freedom independent of law. It obeys no objective standards, for it flounders in the subjectivity of a radicalized, insulated individualism. The refusal to be is a refusal of transcendence; it is the refusal, as Maritain noted, of the infinite in each of us, an infinite that marks our spirit and seals it as received from another, and, so, not our own. Our being is received—we are not thrown into being, or abandoned, we are the result of God's creative and sustaining existential act. Our response should be gratitude, love, and obedience to our Creator, and love for one another. To do less, or attempt less, is to constitute ourselves and our age as in rebellion. Maritain's ethics assists us in recovering the authentic truth of our own destiny and provides a standard by which to evaluate, criticize, and correct the crisis of our age. He requires that freedom, happiness, and goodness, the ethical end of man, be achieved in what Karol Cardinal Wojtyla terms the "surrender to the truth"—a surrender in thought and action.[22]

---

[22]Karol Cardinal Wojtyla, *The Acting Person,* trans. Andrzej Potocki (Boston: D. Reidel, 1979) 155.

THOMAS FLYNN

Time Redeemed:
Maritain's Christian Philosophy of History

LIKE HIS ERSTWHILE MENTOR, Henri Bergson, Jacques Maritain had a long-standing interest in the philosohy of culture and society. Given his Aristotelian-Thomistic philosophical convictions, it is not surprising that he pursued this topic under the aspect of *practical philosophy*, specifically as a subdivision of ethics, thereby giving primacy to the question of the good for the human agent as a social being. Yet, despite his unwavering Thomistic loyalties, Maritain shared Bergson's interest in the temporal as such. Hence, it comes as no surprise that his approach to culture and society is more *diachronic* than those of Aristotle and Saint Thomas. Indeed, neither of these giants bequeathed us a philosophy of history.[1]

Maritain's concern with the meaning-direction (*sens*) of history finds expression in a number of works penned in the 1930s and 1940s, but especially in his classic, *Integral Humanism* (1936). Still, it was not until 1957 that he published his ex professo treatment of that topic, as if he had waited for the oncoming clash between fascism, communism, and democracy to occur before spreading his wings in definitive theoretical flight.[2] By then he had already announced and developed the leading components of his theory.

---

[1] Neither did Bergson, for that matter, although his *Creative Evolution* and especially *The Two Sources of Morality and Religion* come much closer to the undertaking. Aquinas certainly provides a theology of history, reflecting on the divine plan of Redemption as revealed in scripture. He even sketches a kind of ontology of history, taking as the model of the *Summa theologica* the Plotinian "exitus a Deo/reditus in Deum."

[2] *On the Philosophy of History*, ed. Joseph W. Evans (New York: Scribner's, 1957), hereafter cited as *PH*. Like so many other of his works, this is a series of lectures. For a

I

Among professional philosophers, the philosophy of history has been under a cloud for some time due in large part to what are taken to be the excessive claims of Hegel, Comte, Marx, Spengler, and Toynbee in this field. Their distrust of the discipline is shared by many historians, who view it as an unwarranted encroachment on their own territory. Some rare philosopher-historians (or historian-philosophers) like Collingwood in England, Weber in Germany, and Aron and Marrou in France have helped raise the reputation of the enterprise. But the main source of relief, in the English-speaking world at least, has been the gradual adoption of a distinction between analytical and speculative philosophy of history. By neglecting the latter—history with a capital *H*—philosophers could concentrate on a critique of historical knowledge and explanation, thereby assimilating the philosophy of history to the philosophy of the social sciences.[3] Analytic or, as it is called on the Continent, "critical" philosophy of history addresses such issues as the knowability of the past, the nature of historical explanation, and the meaning of historical "causality."

Valuable though it is, the analytic approach leaves unasked many "perennial" questions in this realm, such as What is the meaning of it all? and How does one make sense of the proliferation of global wars and the technological domination in our times? People do ask such questions just as they raise normative and not merely metaethical issues. One of the few groups of philosophers in our day who have taken seriously both the speculative philosophy of history and normative ethical questions has been the Marxists. Another has been the Christians. Both have been accused of dogmatism.

To the extent that Maritain deals with matters of analytical concern, he does so chiefly in his masterwork, *The Degrees of Knowledge*.[4] But in fact he did not occupy himself nearly so much with questions in the epistemology of history as with issues in the rather discredited speculative philosophy of history. (Doubtless, this is why he saw his leading opponents as Hegel and Marx.) It is Maritain's speculative philosophy of history that I wish to reconstruct and examine.

---

valuable summary of Maritain's theory of history, see Charles Journet, "D'une philosophie chretienne de l'histoire et de la culture," *Revue Thomiste* 48 (1948): 33-61. Maritain praised Journet's essay as "an indispensable complement to the present volume" (*PH* x).

[3]Raymond Aron made popular a similar distinction in France, echoing in many ways what Max Weber had done in Germany. See his *Introduction to the Philosophy of History*, trans. George J. Irwin (Boston: Beacon Press, 1961).

[4]*Distinguish to Unite or The Degrees of Knowledge*, trans. under the direction of Gerald B. Phelan (New York: Scribner's, 1959). The first chapter of *PH* also treats epistemological issues.

William Dray has noted three large, interrelated questions that almost any speculative philosophy of history would try to answer, namely, (a) What is the *pattern* to that jumble of events that constitutes human history? (b) What is the productive *"mechanism"* of these events? and (c) What is the *meaning-significance* of human history as a whole?[5] In effect, Dray is addressing to history as a whole the Aristotelian questions of formal, efficient, and final causality. Let us consider four responses to Dray's queries.

Maritain's bête noire in this domain, Hegel, would answer these questions respectively: (a) forms of dialectical relationships, (b) the "cunning" of Reason, and (c) the ultimate triumph of Spirit in the historical process. Marx, as we know, inverted Hegel's dialectic (a), claimed primacy for class struggle and economic "Reason" (b), and preached the advent of a classless society, free from the contradictions that afflicted "prehistory," as he termed it (c). Spengler saw a prime symbol, such as "infinite extension" in the case of Western culture, as the intelligible key to each historical culture (a); his historical mechanism was a quasi-biological one of childhood, adolescence, maturity, and senescence (b); while his answer to the last question was in the negative: cultures simply succeed one another without meaning or purpose aside from the ongoing needs of life itself (c). Finally, Toynbee, whose position is closest to Maritain's in that he gives pride of place to the role of religion in the evolution and demise of "civilizations," finds the distinguishing pattern in each civilization's attempt to rise above primitive history toward some higher kind of spiritual life and birth and death of each in the process (a); the mechanism is his famous "challenge-response" dyad (b); and the purpose of it all is a hypothetical plea for democracy and a world federation of nation-states, though not a world government (c). These theorists of history in the grand style all seek an intelligible contour to historical phenomena that differs from statistical generalization or physical law.

II

Because Maritain has taken the speculative turn in the philosohy of history, one can learn much from his responses to the foregoing questions. But to do so in detail presumes a prior grasp of the essential components of his theory of history. So let us discuss five theses constitutive of that theory as a prelude to reviewing his answers to Dray's queries.

The Centrality of Analogical Reasoning in Historical Understanding. Maritain has always insisted on the Thomistic thesis that "being" is a concept predicated not univocally or equivocally but analogously of the hierarchy of created and un-

---

[5]William Dray, *Perspectives on History* (London: Routledge and Kegan Paul, 1980) 101.

created beings. Thus, inanimate, human, created suprahuman, and uncreated "beings" would each exist in a manner proportionate to their proper "essences." Traditionally, analogous predication has enabled Thomists to avoid pantheism (univocity) as well as agnosticism (equivocity) when discoursing about subsistent Being (God).[6] But Aquinas uses analogy in political philosophy as well, where he specifies different ends (common goods) for diverse polities.[7]

Maritain employs the analogy of proper proportionality, as it is technically called, to give suppleness to otherwise rigid, "Platonic" concepts—whether in moral reasoning or in legal, political, or cultural predication. So the concept of a "Christian civilization," for example, can be realized in analogous fashion across different epochs of the world's history.[8] Maritain's call for a "new Christendom" is neither a historical anachronism (univocity) nor a play on words (equivocation). Rather, it presumes that the "moral physiognomy" of the modern world is "far more profoundly different [from that of the medieval or classical worlds] than is ordinarily believed" (*IH* 140). And yet he will not sink into historical relativism. The *principles* of culture, he assures us, as supreme rules of human action, are always the same. "But they are applied in ways essentially diverse, ways answering to the same concept only according to a similitude of proportion" (*IH* 138-39).

Like the great theorists cited earlier, Maritain is searching for intelligibility in history, not a mere concatenation of factual statements ("one damn thing after another"). More recently, philosophers have sought this understanding in theories of narrative where the "glue" of history is a likely story and its basis is our fundamental ability to follow and repeat stories;[9] or in a native power to comprehend the purposes of other intelligent agents (*Verstehen*);[10] or in forms of the hypothetico-deductive model of explanation borrowed from the natural sciences.[11] (Oddly enough, Maritain seems to favor a form of this last model, as we shall see.) The challenge in each case is to keep the historical linkages sufficiently tight to make sense of the welter of events, institutions, and states of affairs that

---

[6]See Jacques Maritain, *Existence and the Existent*, trans. Lewis Galantière and Gerald B. Phelan (Garden City NY: Doubleday, Image Books, 1956) 38-42; hereafter cited as *EE*.

[7]Thomas Aquinas, *In libros politicorum Aristotelis expositio* VII.6.

[8]Jacques Maritain, *Integral Humanism*, trans. Joseph W. Evans (Notre Dame IN: University of Notre Dame Press, 1973), hereafter cited as *IH*.

[9]Paul Ricoeur, *Time and Narrative*, vol. 1, trans. Kathleen McLaughlin and David Pellauer (Chicago: University of Chicago Press, 1984).

[10]See Aron, *Introduction*, 45-155.

[11]See Carl G. Hempel, "The Function of General Laws in History," reprinted in *Theories of History*, ed. Patrick Gardiner (New York: Free Press, 1959) 344-56.

constitute the matter of history, while allowing enough *Spielraum* to preserve that human freedom without which history is an illusion. Maritain's analogical reasoning is intended to achieve this delicate balance between historical "laws" and diverse empirical conditions.

The Primacy of Philosophical Anthropology. In a remark echoed by a historian of a far different philosophical persuasion,[12] Maritain insists that any philosophy of history must be based on "a sound philosophy of man" (*PH* 7). This has both methodological and substantive implications for his theory. Methodologically, Maritain's understanding of human nature affords him a deductive "governor" on inductive reasoning. Given that the human is a rational animal, and allowing full implication to each component of that complex term, one can exclude a priori both idealistic, in the sense of "angelistic," and materialistic hypotheses in working out the meaning of history.

From the substantive viewpoint, the fact that the human is an agent of two dimensions—animal and spirit, individual and social, temporal and eternal—introduces a *tension* as well as a fundamental *ambiguity* into human history, giving it a "nocturnal" character such that those who would play the historical agent must dirty their hands in the arena of consequences they can neither fully foresee nor control.

The individual-social tension provides the focus for Maritain's political philosophy. He regards eighteenth-century theories of natural rights as a permanent acquisition in political history and as a bulwark against totalitarian philosophies, chiefly of Hegelian inspiration, which grant a spurious sovereignty to the state as a person.[13] But it is the fact of these theories, not their philosophical foundations, that Maritain respects. The latter are often individualistic in nature and fail sufficiently to respect the other pole of the relationship, the body politic of persons realizing their human potential under just laws. Maritain's appreciation of the evolution of theories of human rights and their incorporation in a new understanding of civic friendship and "pluralism" in a rejuvenated body politic offers a glimpse of his understanding of historical *progress*, for he was truly convinced of its reality.[14] If most contemporary philosophers of history find such confidence problematic, it is doubtless because they wish to separate themselves from a discredited social Darwinism or from the naive hopes of scientific humanism now recognized as such in our nuclear age. But here as elsewhere, Maritain's opti-

---

[12]Paul Veyne, *Writing History*, trans. Mina Moore-Rinvolucri (Middletown CT: Wesleyan University Press, 1984) 156.

[13]See Jacques Maritain, *Man and the State* (Chicago: University of Chicago Press, 1951) 195; hereafter cited as *MS*.

[14]"Pluralism" is Maritain's term for the principle of subsidiarity as it came to be known in Catholic social thought after *Quadragesimo anno* of Pius XI.

mism is grounded in a sturdy Christian faith. We are operating in the milieu of a Christian philosophy whose nature and import we shall discuss later on.

The second source of tension Maritain notes stems from human nature as embodied and besouled. Although accepting the Aristotelian doctrine of potency-act to account for the fundamental unity of the human agent (two in act cannot be one in act; soul is the first act of the body), he is not blind to the moral dilemmas that arise from the conflict of appetites, rational and nonrational, especially when the former is "clouded" and the latter "wounded," as theologians insist, by "original sin" ("sin" being taken in an analogous sense). Like the human lives whose stories it recounts, history is an intelligible operating of contingencies. Our inability to "legislate" history reflects the give-and-take of the interaction of human freedoms. But the theological concept of nature as somehow de facto "flawed" tempers the optimism mentioned previously. In fact, it leads Maritain to speak of a "law" of twofold contrasting progress (of good and evil) at work in history (*PH* 43-52). Although we shall discuss historical "laws" in due time, it is illustrative of the role played by Maritain's anthropology in his philosophy of history to note at this juncture his grounding of historical ambiguity in human nature itself.

Perhaps the chief tension that Maritain observes in history arises from the human spirit itself, namely, from its unbounded desire to know, expanded by Aquinas in light of biblical teaching and Augustinian thought into the "natural desire to see God."[15] This thesis, basic to a properly Thomistic theology that avoids a two-tiered understanding of nature and supernature, affects Maritain's philosophy of history both by accounting for the individual's "extraterritoriality" with regard to the terrestrial order (a guard against economism and other reductionisms) and by indicating why, collectively, the end-terminus of history is not itself a point in time. "Even in the natural order," he insists, "the common good of the body politic has a transcendent orientation" (*MS* 149). And yet the "natural" end of the world is a *real* end and no mere means; the various cultural goods that history catalogs are not to be dismissed as insignificant or despised as spiritually noxious. The tension arises from that very respect for these "infravalent" ends, as he terms them. It surfaces especially in Maritain's political philosophy and in the question of church-state relations in particular. But it also implies that no purely economic or technical advance, industrial capitalism, for example, can be assessed positively without weighing in the balance its eth-

---

[15]See, e.g., Thomas Aquinas, *Summa contra gentiles* 3.25, 50, 57, 59-62, and Henri De Lubac, *The Mystery of the Supernatural*, trans. Rosemary Sheed (New York: Herder and Herder, 1967), as well as Pierre Rousselot, *The Intellectualism of Saint Thomas*, trans. James E. O'Mahony (London: Sheed and Ward, 1935), for further texts and discussion.

ical and religious significance. Again, we issue in the domain of Christian philosophy.

The ambiguity of human history, its "nocturnal" character we noted, reflects our existential condition as "wounded" by sin (*vulnerati in naturalibus*). Accordingly, neither our actions nor the world itself is neutral with respect to the kingdom of God (*PH* 136). Although we can judge the moral value of the former rather quickly, the "objective significance" of the latter, that is, of large-scale historical events, must be assessed more slowly and will always entail elements of good and evil, which points to his third basic thesis.

An Understanding of History as Theodicy. "No philosophy of history can be genuine," Maritain points out, "if the general philosophy it presupposes . . . does not recognize the existence of human free will . . . and the existence of God" (*PH* 34). This implies that human history is permeated by two contingencies, namely, created and uncreated freedom. In face of the gross injustices of history, the theorist must come to terms with the mystery of evil and of the "fair play of God," as Maritain writes, "[W]ho gives those who have freely chosen injustice the time to exhaust the benefits of it and the fullness of its energies?" (*PH* 60). Like the humanism that supports it, the concept of history must be "integrally taken" (*PH* 166); in other words, it must be seen in its concrete relation to existential reality, including "the ontological perspective of Christian wisdom."[16] Created and uncreated freedom enter into Maritain's account of the mystery of evil in human history.

He accepts the Thomistic doctrine of human finitude, nuanced by his own understanding of the term. The *possibility* of moral evil, he argues, stems from the creature's very existence as limited, from the nothingness (to speak in existentialist terms) that pervades it; its actuality, indeed, its practical inevitability, follows from the fact of "original sin," itself a function of finitude and freedom. He remarks in *Existence and the Existent* that moral evil has no efficient cause; as a privative reality (the absence of a due order), it points to the creature as its "de-efficient" cause.[17] Maritain sees this as following from the fact that, while God is subsistent Being (*ens a se*), the creature by definition is being by participation (*ens ab alio*). Unlike certain rationalistic systems that see evil as the natural consequence of human finitude, Maritain's approach carefully distinguishes the possibility from the actuality, metaphysical from moral evil, the ontological from the ontic (historical). These distinctions are motivated by his acceptance of the "Christian wisdom" just mentioned, with its doctrine of sin and redemption. That he addresses the issue of moral evil at its ontological and ontic sources is a

---

[16]Jacques Maritain, *Redeeming the Time*, trans. Harry Lorin Binsse (London: Geoffrey Bles, 1943) v; hereafter cited as *RT*.

[17]See *EE*, esp. 98.

sign of the comprehensiveness of his theory of history; that the answer moves him beyond common (secular) philosophical categories is symptomatic of a philosophy "Christian" to its core.

Having restated the traditional defense of divine omnipotence and goodness in the face of moral evil by appeal to finitude and freedom, Maritain goes on to add a particularly Christian dimension to the question by setting the scandal of historical evil against the mystery of the cross. This is the root of his recommendation that the triumph of moral good, for which he fervently hopes, be the work of saints who teach as much by their poverty and suffering as by their exalted doctrine (RT 156).

The Philosophy of History as a Branch of Moral Philosophy. The reason why Hegel is Maritain's chief philosophical adversary in this realm lies in the master dialectician's substitution of history for metaphysics, which absolutizes and necessitates what Maritain considers relative and contingent. As we have just seen, Maritain regards history as the field of created freedom and responsibility, subject to the inconstancies of the human heart and liable to judgments of moral success and failure. Besides immanentizing the ultimately transcendent end of human history and idolatrizing the state in the process, Hegelian (and in its own way Marxist) metaphysics of history dissolves human contingencies—the very stuff of history—in a dialectical rationalism impervious to moral assessment.[18]

Although Maritain has always admitted that philosophy is ultimately grounded in metaphysics or first philosophy, he supports the traditional distinction between metaphysics and practical or moral philosophy. Situating the philosophy of history in the latter domain has two major consequences for his theory: it justifies his *normative* approach to historical events and movements, and it tempers the degree of certitude that he can claim for his generalizations in this realm in accord with Aristotle's famous caveat not to seek greater certainty in an area of inquiry than the field allows.

His normative conception of the theory of history warrants his particular approach to the question of *progress* in history. For Maritain, such progress will be moral or it will not be at all. Not that he ignores technological advance. He simply considers it a relative criterion, itself subject to moral assessment as the advent of the atomic age made clear. History is an account of human freedoms in collective interaction and, as a kind of moral philosophy, the philosophy of history must ultimately assess its events and institutions in terms of their *long-range moral significance:* Do they ease or impede the growth of freedom and charity?

Accordingly, the issue of a hierarchy of means and the means-end question cannot be avoided. It is at first blush ironic that Maritain resembles the Marxist

---

[18]Marx's amoralism is more readily admitted than that of Hegel. See, for example, Allen Wood, *Karl Marx* (London: Routledge & Kegan Paul, 1981) 141-56.

existentialist Jean-Paul Sartre in this respect. Both think we live in a period of social "sinfulness." But whereas Sartre ascribes this to socioeconomic conditions (with due respect for existential "freedom"), Maritain grounds it in fundamental selfishness and our "wounded" nature (while reserving space for created freedom's response to the promptings of grace). Correspondingly, each thinker projects a "redemptive" vision in our historical morass. In a famous interview shortly before his death, Sartre spoke of a new *fraternity* that would realize the egalitarian, anarchistic ideals he had propounded over the previous two decades. Tellingly, he allows that the role of "violence" in this regard remains an unresolved problem for him.[19] Maritain envisions a "pluralistic" *world political society*, where civic friendship will render the coercive function of government minimal (*MS* 202-16). So the relation between the political and the ethical faces both Sartre and Maritain with similar problems in their philosophies of history, notwithstanding their distinctively different "solutions" (in large part a function of diverse theories of human nature). Their being mentioned together in this context should not surprise anyone who realizes they both belong to the French tradition of moralists that reaches back to La Rouchefoucauld and Montaigne. They are both what Charles Journet said of Maritain, "moralists de grand style."

The Nature of Historical Laws. Maritain's conception of historical laws is a consequence of his philosophical anthropology and his notion of the "certitudes" proper to the realm of practical philosophy. In *The Degrees of Knowledge* he defends our scientific knowledge of nature. Subsequently he argues that history can be a science in the broad, Aristotelian sense of "intellectually cogent or demonstratively established knowledge" (*PH* 3n), since we can grasp both the "quiddities" or raisons d'être of human nature itself and the intelligible contour or "constellation," as he calls it, of a particular historical period. These "constellations" resemble Durkheim's "social facts" and constitute the proper métier of the philosophy of history. Maritain describes them as "significant general facts and factual relations" (*PH* 6). He will treat such constellations in light of his fundamental theory of human nature.

In his lectures entitled *On the Philosophy of History*, he states as his "first principle" the thesis that "history can be neither rationally explained nor reconstructed according to necessitating laws." But he assures us, "History can be *characterized, interpreted* or *deciphered in a certain measure and as to certain general aspects*—to the extent to which we succeed in disclosing in its meanings or intelligible directions, and laws which enlighten events, without necessitating them" (*PH* 32). The "necessary" knowledge that enters Maritain's theory of history originates in his metaphysics of human nature, which, as we said, serves as a guide

---

[19]Jean-Paul Sartre, "The Last Words of Jean-Paul Sartre," *Dissent* (Fall 1980): esp. 407-15.

and limit to historical induction. But because we are dealing primarily with a branch of moral philosophy, the "laws" that render human events intelligible do not necessitate them. Other philosophers of the social sciences have spoken of "tendencies" or "probabilities" in this context. Maritain shares their regard for accounts of history that are neither merely empathetic nor narrativist but "scientific." But, in addition to the use of analogical predication, Maritain insists that historical "laws" "neither explain [history] nor subject the course of historical events to *necessity;* these events are necessary with respect only to general features and patterns within which it is up to human freedom to determine the particular orientation which gives them typically human significance" (*PH* 165).

We noted that Maritain's historical reasoning is in large part analogical. The source of this analogy lies in the twofold contingency of history as the concomitant opus of created and uncreated freedom. Because humans are free, because they are capable of deliberation and choice, history assumes a direction attributable in a decisive manner to the acts and intentions of individuals. But the meaning-direction of the historical process as a whole, Maritain argues, is guided by the transcendent cause who is a "maker of natures" and not a deistic clock maker. Correspondingly, the world is "a republic of natures; and the infallible divine causality, by the very fact that it is transcendent, causes events to occur according to their own conditions, necessary events necessarily, contingent events contingently, chance events fortuitously."[20] The transcendent or universal cause is such only analogously to created causes. The resolution of the freedom-determinism antinomy here as elsewhere lies not with some kind of incompatibilism but with the distinction of orders, both causal and temporal. Like Aquinas, Maritain insists that the created cause is a real cause and not a mere occasion; its temporality is linear and irreversible. So history is date-progressive and real. The uncreated, universal cause is a creative "cause," bringing about that each creature exercise created causality according to its proper existential condition. Uncreated "causality" is no more temporal than creation itself; it stands at right angles to the horizontal temporal sequence of created causes and effects. This traditional Thomist response to the antinomy of time-eternity, in Maritain's view, preserves the mutual integrity of human actions and eternal design—a basic question of theodicy.

Five theses fundamental to Maritain's theory of history, then, are the centrality of analogical reasoning, the primacy of philosophical anthropology, an understanding of history as theodicy, the location of theory of history in moral philosophy, and a concept of historical laws as enlightening but not necessitat-

---

[20]Jacques Maritain, "Réflexions sur la Nécessité et la Contingence," *Raison et Raisons* (Paris: L.U.F., 1947) 62n; hereafter cited as *RR*.

ing. The closest he ever came to uniting them into a comprehensive theory was his lectures *On the Philosophy of History*, where, in the implicit context of these theses, he distinguished and discussed two types of historical laws, the functional and the vectorial. Let us conclude this reconstruction of Maritain's comprehensive theory with a discussion of each.

Functional laws, or axiomatic formulas, are the basic laws of history, denoting functional relations that obtain between certain universal objects of thought. Thus the "law" of twofold contrasting progress of history (toward good and evil) mentioned previously counters Enlightenment myths of unalloyed progress with the claim that, despite periods of ascendency for good or for evil, both coexist at any moment of history and will continue to do so. This implies a correlative "law" of the *ambivalence* of history, which we also spoke of earlier. A third law, "the historical fructifications of good and evil," is an ethicopolitical generalization to the effect that "justice and rectitude . . . *tend in themselves* to the preservation of human societies and to a real success in the long run; and that injustice and evil *tend in themselves* . . . to the destruction of societies and to a real failure in the long run" (*PH* 61).

Leszek Kolakowski cites a beautiful passage from Romain Rolland in which the "revolutionary" argues with the "intellectual" that the end justifies the means, that one must be willing to sacrifice the present for the sake of the future. The intellectual responds that to sacrifice truth, respect for oneself, and all human values for the future—means to sacrifice the future.[21] Maritain's law of fructification is an attempt to codify that insight.

One more functional "law" bears mention, since it typifies what we may call Maritain's *ascetics* of history. This is the twofold "law of the hierarchy of means." The one notes "the superiority of humble temporal means over rich temporal means with respect to spiritual ends." In effect, this is the wisdom of Francis of Assisi resisting the native Pelagianism of Western thought. The other law underscores "the *superiority of spiritual means* of temporal activity and welfare over carnal means of temporal activity and welfare" (*PH* 71; emphasis mine). This is the wisdom of Gandhi in the political realm. Though Maritain's attitude toward universal nonviolence is quite nuanced, he holds in the highest respect a theory of political involvement that avoids inflicting harm for the sake of goodness even to the point of martyrdom. At this juncture his philosophy of history converges with a theory of political struggle and moral asceticism that calls for the heroic.

Typological formulas, or vectorial laws, are diachronic rather than synchronic. They denote certain directions in historical development reached by inductive generalization. Maritain uncovers four such laws. The first deals with the

---

[21]See Leszek Kolakowski, "The Escape Conspiracy," *Toward a Marxist Humanism*, trans. Jane Zielonko Peel (New York: Grove Press, 1969) 94.

passage from the "magical" to the "rational" state of human culture, whose primary appeal is made to the intellect rather than to imagination in psychic and cultural life as a whole. Although he agrees with Bronislaw Malinowski that the intellects of primitive peoples are of the same kind as ours (*PH* 99), he argues that their existential conditions are such that in fact imagination, not intellect, has the final word in their accounts of their world.

His second law concerns our connatural knowledge of the natural law. In a bold statement he affirms: "I think that this progress of moral conscience as to the explicit knowledge of natural law is one of the least questionable examples of progress in mankind" (*PH* 105). He quickly points out that this progress is solely in knowledge, not in moral behavior. As example, he cites the issues of slavery; the treatment of prisoners of war; human, especially child, labor; and his favorite example, our gradual evolution of a scheme of human rights (*PH* 110). He sees these as permanent acquisitions of the human spirit.

The passage from "sacred" to "secular" civilizations is the topic of his third vectorial law. This shows a certain similarity to the Spenglerian schema in that Maritain focuses on the "dynamic idea" that predominates in a civilization at a particular historical period. (Characteristically, Spengler's unifying theme was less conceptual and more symbolic.) The medieval social body, for example, shared the dynamic idea of "fortitude at the service of justice," whereas the dominant dynamic idea of modern civilization, for Maritain, is that of "the conquest of freedom and of social conditions conformable to human dignity" (*PH* 111-12). He sees a similar distinction at work in the history of Indian civilization and asks whether a sacral civilization like the Moslem can in fact become secular—a disturbingly relevant question in our day.

Maritain's final vectorial law refers to the political and social *coming of age* of a people. His criterion is the development of a "democratic cast of mind" within a population. He believes that the spread of such a mentality in the second half of our century is "an obvious sign of its basically natural character" (*PH* 117). Where early apologetes spoke of the human soul as "naturally Christian," Maritain seems to believe that it is "naturally democratic" as well. The crucial difference, one that indicates the inductive and hypothetical cast of these vectorial laws, is that the latter claim refers to the humans in their existential, historical condition at a certain stage of development. But Maritain holds that the democratic spirit answers to "deep-seated demands of the order of nature" (*PH* 116), which he links with the natural law.

III

It is on the basis of the foregoing collection of theses and historical "laws" that we can construct Maritain's answer to Dray's three "large, inter-related questions" that "almost any" speculative philosophy of history will try to answer, namely, questions of pattern, of mechanism, and/or meaning or significance.

(a) The Patterns of History

Human history is made up of periods each of which is possessed of a particular intelligible structure, and therefore of basic particular requirements. These periods are what I have proposed calling the various historical climates or historical constellations in human history. They express given intelligible structures, both as concerns the social, political and juridical dominant characteristics, and as concerns the moral and ideological dominant characteristics, in the temporal life of the human community. (PH 36)

More than Spengler or Toynbee in our day, Maritain addresses the epistemological issue of our ability to graph the patterns that he uncovers in various historical eras. His Aristotelian-Thomistic theory of knowledge, buttressed by a Bergsonian respect for intuitive (i.e., direct, unmediated) awareness, provides the context in which he can assert that the philosophy of history treats "universal objects of thought" that are grasped *inductively*, not imposed in an a priori manner. Such objects comprise "typical features of a given historical age" (the "constellations" just mentioned, subject to the vectorial laws discussed above) and "essential aspects of human history in general," captured in functional laws. Appealing to the primacy of philosophical anthropology, he insists that such universal objects of thought "must be philosophically verified, i.e., checked with some philosophical truths previously acquired." In other words, they must be stabilized by philosophical reflection "founded in the nature of things" (PH 8). Maritain admits that the role of conjecture and hypothesis in the philosophy of history is all the greater "as the part of mere induction is greater in it" (PH 18). Still, respecting the degree of certitude the subject matter allows and given the stabilizing role of deductive reasoning, there is nothing to prevent this discipline from being "scientific" in the broad, Aristotelian sense noted at the outset.

The pattern of history in the Occident that emerges from Maritain's inductions tempered by deductive reasoning from a "sound philosophy of man" is that of the "secularization" of Western culture along a continuous track of ambiguous moral progress. The moral advance, as we noted earlier, occurs primarily in terms of consciousness-raising (*prise de conscience*).

Periodization is a thorny problem for historians. Depending on one's choice of criteria, the Renaissance, for example, could be seen as lasting a few decades or centuries.[22] Maritain is rather sanguine about his appeal to "historical constellations" in marking the historical changes that have occurred in the West

---

[22]See Paul Oskar Kristeller, *Renaissance Thought and Its Sources*, ed. Michael Mooney (New York: Columbia University Press, 1979) 17 and 261 n. 1.

over the last millennium. He does acknowledge the tentative nature of his claims (*PH* xi) and insists that any systematic philosophy of history should be thoroughly versed in the recent findings of anthropologists (*PH* 96n). But his "moderate realism" in epistemology affords him the means to articulate patterns without which a speculative philosophy of history would be impossible.

(*b*) *Historical mechanisms.* Here, too, the incomplete character of Maritain's reflections on history come to the fore. Admittedly, he allows a universal, creative, and providential "cause," and he has paid more attention than most philosophers of history to the paradoxes of freedom and necessity as individual created causes exercise real influence on events in time.[23] But he has not given much attention to the issue of collective action—one of the main concerns of much historiography—and what he says about the influence of prior events, institutions, and states of affairs is often vague and metaphorical. Thus in *On the Philosophy of History*, he speaks of the "energy" of history (*PH* 46) without analyzing the type of causality, for example, psychological or social, operative here. It must be said that Maritain employs a form of what Max Weber calls "objective possibility" (and which Marx valued in his criticism of Hegel) when he insists that, "given the structure and circumstances of human history, certain things become impossible." He elaborates this by appeal to certain historical changes "which are necessary in themselves or with respect to the cumulative needs they answer" (*PH* 25). Later, when speaking of the "slow advance of consciousness, conscience, and experience in mankind," he adds that this means "not only an advance in rational knowledge but primarily an advance in our lived awareness of our basic inclinations—an advance that may be conditioned by social changes" (*PH* 110). As we noted, his favorite example of such an advance is the progressive awareness that led from natural law obligations to theories of the rights of man in the eighteenth century. Such progress does recommend that the mechanism of "need" be examined in detail. Again, it is the metaphysics of human nature that Maritain has in mind, not properly sociocultural causation, when addressing the question of the formation of patterns in history.

Again, Maritain notes "a certain internal necessity" in the historic transition from the magical to the rational state of human society (*PH* 78). But he never elaborates on its nature. We can assume that ultimately it is grounded in our nature as rational animals and on its consequent tendencies toward growth (reason) and decline (animality). Indeed, Maritain formulated this as an axiom or functional law of history.[24] No doubt, one could respond that "historical" causes are the province of professional historians, that philosophy treats in deductive

---

[23]This is the philosophic version of the old theological controversy over grace and freedom (*de auxiliis*).

[24]See his "law of twofold contrasting progress," *PH* 43.

fashion of essences and the intersection of natures. But the challenge of the field of the philosophy of history is precisely to focus on this "middle distance" between metaphysics and chronology, between abstract and concrete "causes" and reasons. This aspect of the problem of historical mechanics is not dealt with to any extent by Maritain, though he is clearly aware of the hypothetical and probabilistic nature of the "moral" realm (*PH* 19).

(c) Meaning or Significance. Although Dray sees this as a topic addressed by "almost any speculative philosophy of history," Spengler is notable for having denied any meaning to the whole of history. If history for him is not "a tale told by an idiot, full of sound and fury, signifying nothing," it is at most a series of episodes each with its biological pattern of growth and decline, succeeding one another monotonously and for no reason at all.

Understandably, Maritain will have none of this. For him, history has a *sens*, a meaning and a direction. In fact, its meaning *is* its direction. The vectorial and cumulative nature of time assures us that the past is neither simply repeated in eternal return nor shed like a worn garment. He agrees with Mircea Eliade that it is difficult for humankind to bear the burden of its past actions (*PH* 36). It is the Judeo-Christian concepts of creation, redemption, and apocalypse that he sees at the root of our acceptance of time and history in the Occident (*PH* 37). In fact, without the presence of some *transhistorical* meaning to this directional progress, he argues, we could be easily driven to despair.

It is at this point that he throws down the gauntlet: "Here we have either to accept or to reject the data of Judeo-Christian revelation" (*PH* 37). He immediately assures us that, having opted for the "facts of faith," as they have been called, one is not *eo ipso* propelled into the stratosphere of theology. It is a feature of Maritain's thought throughout his career to distinguish philosophy from theology and, in this case, a philosophy from a theology of history. Though both disciplines treat of the kingdom of God and of the world, he argues that theology adopts the viewpoint of the former, philosophy that of the latter. "Christian moral philosophy," he explains, "is more disposed than theology to feel the proper importance of time and the temporal order. It is more disposed to see that they have their own finalities and their own created values, even though they are means in relation to eternity" (*PH* 39-40). This "relative autonomy" of the temporal order, to borrow a Marxian term, enables Maritain to respect "humanistic" insights and values even as he places them in the larger context of a transtemporal *telos*. Again, this restatement of the traditional natural-supernatural dyad respects the "formal" distinction between philosophy and theology, while exploiting the metaphysical consequences of "created causality" as real, though analogous, efficacy. Maritain is too Christian to dismiss the human drama as mere appearance or illusion; but he is equally too Christian to accept the atheistic humanist dichotomy: either God or humanity, not both. His philosophy of history is resolutely *incarnational* in the full sense of that word.

If the relative autonomy of the created order and appeal to "reason" support the discursive field common to believer and nonbeliever in philosophical dialogue, Maritain is sufficiently "existentialist" to realize that we do not philosophize *in vacuo*, that the "situation" out of which we seek to understand our collective nature and destiny is inevitably colored by our religious beliefs or secular convictions. What makes this awareness more poignant in Maritain's case is the robust *nonrelativism* of his Christian faith in general and of the Thomistic philosophy that explains it in particular. So he finds himself thrust into the arena of a Christian or "integral" philosophy. The easy resolution of the apparent conflict between noun and adjective in this complex term would be some kind of subjectivism or relativism, or perhaps a form of "double truth" theory. Maritain was no more willing to employ these easy exits than was Aquinas before him. "The integrity of the concrete perspective in which some disciplines perceive human things," he argues, "depends on the truth-value of the religious tradition with which they are connected" (*PH* 39). Courageous words in the second half of the twentieth century, but then, Maritain was noted for his courage to be consistent. Clearly, if one is to understand Maritain's philosophy of history at its core, one must appreciate his comprehension of the *relation* between faith and reason in approaching the issues of the discipline.

IV

At every turn we have encountered aspects of Maritain's Christian belief. It is as if the theological adage, *omnia exeunt in mysterium* (everything ends up in a mystery) applied to philosophy as well. Indeed, Maritain does contrast a philosophy with a theology of history in terms of primary concern with the "mysteries" of the world and the church, respectively (see *PH* 38). His search for understanding in history is no rationalistic passion to dissolve everything in some critical liquor. We have noted his sensitivity to the basic *contingencies* of history. His faith sensitizes him likewise to the hope that guides the historian through the great spiritual and physical tragedies of humankind. The "mystery" of the world and of our history is underscored by the great metaphysical question Why is there something rather than nothing? by the theodicean query Why is there suffering and moral evil in the world? and by their concomitant What may I hope for? Maritain's Christian philosophy wrestles with each but respects the limitations of its response in each instance.

His justification for referring to religious teaching at these "ground" or "terminal" points is twofold. First, he notes the poverty of "pure philosophy" in dealing with ultimate questions. "Where," he asks, "would the pure philosopher find authentic prophetic data" of the kind required to make ultimate sense of history (*PH* 40)? It is doubtless their distaste for the "prophetic" that lies behind the neglect by philosophers of speculative philosophy of history, which we noted at the outset. Typically, Maritain faces this objection squarely and turns it upside down: as long as we ignore the "facts of faith," we shall offer truncated answers to "ultimate" questions, if indeed we ask them at all.

Second, his desire to be concrete and "integral" in his philosophic treatment of human reality renders abstraction from theological data unconvincing. Ironically, here Maritain is anticipating a thesis of many current philosophers regarding the impossibility of "disinterested" knowledge. What he shares with such neopragmatist thinkers is a distrust of rationalism and a common sense of the "existential" aspect of our reasoning process. But whereas these thinkers emphasize the social, indeed the "conventionalist" dimension of sense making, Maritain preserves the foundationalist belief in first principles and ultimate truths: each religious tradition is subject to assessments of its truth value that are not merely internal to that tradition itself. How Christianity handles this difficulty is a matter for apologetics that need not concern us here, but it must be faced.

What does concern us is Maritain's claim that one can appeal to the facts of faith without thereby ceasing to do philosophy. This has always been the challenge of a Christian philosophy. Let me conclude this reconstruction of Maritain's theory of history by contrasting his solution with that of another Christian philosopher, Josef Pieper, as both face the issue of propounding a wisdom that is at once Christian and philosophical.

Two models for a Christian philosophy capture the distinction between these thinkers. Maritain's is that of the *guidepost*, Pieper's that of the *agon*, or combat. The point of Maritain's metaphor is that theology indicates to philosophy paths to follow or dead ends to avoid but that philosophy must proceed under its own power; that is, it must judge its conclusions on the quality of their rational arguments, not on theological warrants. Thus, the need to distinguish person from nature or the unidirectional thrust of history are theological data, but the arguments in their favor must be purely rational. Likewise, theology directs philosophic speculation away from materialism as a fruitless hypothesis, but it is philosophy's task to construct its own arguments.[25]

Josef Pieper, whom Maritain has criticized for making "the whole *opus philosophicum* too dependent on theology" (*HP* 41), claims that no philosophy of history is possible without the illumination of theology. His model of the relationship

---

[25]By introducing the concept of moral philosophy "adequately considered" as a science "subaltern" to theology, Maritain has pushed to the limits, and perhaps exceeded, his distinction between philosophy and theology. For such moral philosophy accepts as premises the conclusions of theological reflection on Christian revelation. Faith is now exercising more than an extrinsic or a negative influence on reason. See Valentine Rice, "Jacques Maritain and the Problem of Christian Philosophy," *Hermathena* 134 (Summer 1983): 7-34.

between theology and philosophy, faith and reason, is the struggle, or agon. As each contestant challenges the other, the strain elicits the utmost creativity in the other's response. Left unchallenged, each side could slip into complacent mediocrity, hoeing and rehoeing the same old rows. Faced with apparent or real contradictions, each must generate from its own resources the means to combat the threat. In fact, this resembles Toynbee's challenge-response motif. The history of the "proofs" for the existence of God as well as recent discussions in the philosophy of mind suggest that the agonistic model has in fact been operative among believing philosophers for some time. The Christian mystery of the Trinity, for example, has forced philosophers to temper and nuance their understanding of "relation" and of the person-nature distinction. But the philosophical concept of process in its turn has challenged believers to reflect on the meaning of "creation" and divine immutability.

The guidepost model has the advantage of respecting the formal distinction between theological and philosophical reasoning, while allowing a positive, if extrinsic, role for faith in the philosophic enterprise. In fact, the ease of the resultant relationship between faith and philosophy will strike some philosophers who are also believers as too good to be true. They will prefer something like Pieper's agon as a more adequate image of what they are living: faith keeping reason modest; reason keeping faith honest.

Although Maritain criticizes Pieper for not giving philosophy its due, could it be that, despite avowals of "existential" situating, Maritain emerges the more "formalist" of the two Christian philosophers? Could it be that Pieper's *agonistic* is a more accurate account of how the believing philosopher actually works? that the wisdom of the world often breaks and foams on the rocks of faith?

However this may be, it is to Maritain's credit that he has not sacrificed clarity or rigor for what today is called "edification" as he undertakes to apply Christian wisdom to our quest for historical meaning and truth.

Contributors

HENRY BARS, author of *Maritain en notre temps* and *La politique selon Jacques Maritain*, was a close friend of Jacques and Raïssa Maritain. He lives in Plouha, Brittany.

WILLIAM BUSH, professor of English, University of Western Ontario, is perhaps North America's leading authority on the work of Maritain's friend the novelist Georges Bernanos, a definitive translation of whose *Monsieur Ouine* he has recently completed.

RAYMOND DENNEHY, professor of philosophy at the University of San Francisco, has written widely on ethics and metaphysics. The author of *Reason and Dignity,* he is president of the American Maritain Association.

BERNARD DOERING is professor of French at the University of Notre Dame and author of *Jacques Maritain and the French Catholic Intellectuals.* He will soon publish his translation of the correspondence between Maritain and Julien Green.

RICHARD FAFARA, a program analyst with the U.S. Army Community and Family Support Center, has published articles in *The Modern Schoolman, Dialectics and Humanism*, and the Polish Journal *Studia Filozoficzne.* He is a cotranslator from the Polish of Mieczyslaw Krapiec's *I-Man.*

THOMAS FLYNN recently authored *Sartre and Marxist Existentialism.* He is professor of philosophy at Emory University.

DONALD GALLAGHER is the president emeritus of the American Maritain Association and one of the earliest American scholars of the work of Jacques and Raïssa Maritain, whom he knew well for many years. He is coauthor, with his wife Idella, of the definitive Maritain bibliography, *The Achievement of Jacques and Raïssa Maritain.*

CURTIS HANCOCK is assistant professor of philosophy at Rockhurst College, Kansas City. He has published in *The Modern Schoolman* and *The Journal of the History of Philosophy*, and is also the author of a forthcoming essay and book on Neo-Platonism.

JOHN HELLMAN, professor of history at McGill University, Montreal, is the author of books and articles on Emmanuel Mounier, Simone Weil, and French-Catholic culture in the interwar years.

DEAL W. HUDSON is associate professor of philosophy and religion at Mercer University Atlanta and vice-president of the American Maritain Association. His articles and reviews have appeared in *Cross Currents, Notes et Documents*, and *International Journal for Philosophy of Religion*. He is completing a book on happiness.

STANLEY L. JAKI, a Hungarian-born Catholic priest of the Benedictine Order, is Distinguished Professor at Seton Hall University, South Orange, New Jersey. With doctorates in theology and physics, he has for the past twenty-five years specialized in the history and philosophy of science. The author of twenty books and over seventy articles, he has served as Gifford Lecturer at the University of Edinburgh and as Fremantle Lecturer at Balliol College, Oxford. *Membre correspondant* of the Académie Nationale des Sciences, Belles-Lettres et Arts of Bordeaux, he is the recipient of the Lecomte du Nuöy Prize for 1970 and of the Templeton Prize for 1987.

ERASMO LEIVA-MERIKAKIS is associate professor of comparative literature at Saint Ignatius Institute of the University of San Francisco. He is the translator of several works by Hans Urs von Balthasar and the author of *The Blossoming Thorn: Georg Trakl's Poetry of Atonement*.

MATTHEW J. MANCINI, associate professor of history and philosophy at Mercer University Atlanta, has published articles and reviews in *The Journal of Negro History, Notes et Documents*, and *The Journal of Southern History*. He is presently engaged in a study of Tocqueville.

MARTIN E. MARTY is Fairfax Cone Distinguished Professor, Divinity School, the University of Chicago. The most recent of his nearly two dozen books is *The Irony of It All*, the first of a four-volume history of twentieth-century American religion.

JOSEPH PAPPIN III is assistant dean of Emory College, Emory University, and the author of the forthcoming *The Metaphysics of Edmund Burke*.

PETER REDPATH, associate professor of philosophy at St. John's University, Staten Island, New York, has written extensively on Aquinas, including *A Simplified Introduction to the Wisdom of St. Thomas*. Professor Redpath is writing a book on the history of modern philosophy as a form of "psycho-theology."

PAUL SIGMUND is the author of numerous works on politics, political theory, and Latin America. He has recently edited the Norton Critical Edition of Locke's "Second Treatise" and "Letter on Toleration." He is professor of politics and director of Latin American Studies at Princeton University.

ANTHONY O. SIMON, as secretary-treasurer of the American Maritain Association for many years, has been instrumental in the propagation of Maritain studies in North America. The son of Maritain's student and intimate friend, the distinguished philosopher Yves R. Simon, and the godson of Véra Oumançoff, Mr. Simon has worked extensively as a translator and editor.

Index